Art as Performance, Story as Criticism

Art as Performance, Story as Criticism

REFLECTIONS ON NATIVE LITERARY AESTHETICS

Craig Womack

University of Oklahoma Press : Norman

Also by Craig S. Womack

Red on Red: Native American Literary Separatism (Minneapolis, 1999)

Drowning in Fire (Tucson, 2001)

American Indian Literary Nationalism (Albuquerque, 2006) (with Jace Weaver and Robert Warrior)

Reasoning Together: The Native Critics Collective (Norman, Okla., 2008) (with Janice Acoose, Lisa Brooks, Tol Foster, LeAnne Howe, Daniel Heath Justice, Phillip Carroll Morgan, Kimberly Roppolo, Cheryl Suzack, Christopher B. Teuton, Sean Teuton, and Robert Warrior)

Text quoted in chapter 8 is drawn from Edward L. Wheeler, *Deadwood Dick, the Prince of the Road; or, The Black Rider of the Black Hills,* Beadle's Half Dime Library, vol. 1, no. 1. (New York: Beadle and Adams, 1877).

Library of Congress Cataloging-in-Publication Data
Womack, Craig S.
    Art as performance, story as criticism : reflections on Native literary aesthetics / Craig Womack.
        p. cm.
    Includes bibliographical references and index.
    ISBN 978-0-8061-4064-3 (hardcover : alk. paper) — ISBN 978-0-8061-4065-0 (pbk. : alk. paper) 1. American literature—Indian authors—History and criticism. 2. Indians of North America—Intellectual life. 3. Indians in literature. 4. Indian authors—Aesthetics. I. Title.
    PS153.I52W65 2009
    810.9'897—dc22

                                                    2009006876

The paper in this book meets the guidelines for permanence and durability of the Committee on Production Guidelines for Book Longevity of the Council on Library Resources, Inc. ∞

1   2   3   4   5   6   7   8   9   10

An' Tookpafka Micco he smoke 'is ol' hatchet-pipe slow an' say, "Well, so in olden times, seven cities want to be Homer's birthplace; an' same way, all the politicians claim the credit for statehood an' dispute with one 'nother."

Alexander Posey, The Fus Fixico Letters, 247

Contents

Acknowledgments

Daniel Justice, whose cover art does much to capture the spirit of
the book
Lisa Brooks and James Cox, for their instructive readings of the
manuscript
Ted Isham and Rosemary McCombs Maxey, for their patience with
me as coteachers of Creek Language and Literature, spring
semester 2009, Atlanta, Georgia, and Okmulgee, Oklahoma
Alessandra Jacobi and Steven Baker at OU Press, for putting up with
all my mess
Gerardo Tristan—partner, reader, animal rights advocate
Geary Hobson, mentor all these years

Art as Performance, Story as Criticism

The Song of Roe Náld

Who could have guessed that my dance partner would die the night before I filmed him in my greatest scene? But it started before that, really, when that very same dancer, the pesky little actor I was trying to shoot—with a camera at the time, though later I'd have been happier if it were a gun.

That was the summer of Oklahoma weirdness when each and every citizen of the state, from the panhandle to Sallisaw, should have fastened their seatbelts for a bumpy ride—what with white frat boys getting drunk and naked and pissing on a ceremonial tipi set up for Native American Awareness Week at the University of Oklahoma; trailer trash in Yukon seeing the bloody brow of Jesus in the peeling paint of their bathroom walls and charging $3.00 admission to their neighbors, aided by unlimited publicity from the Oklahoma City newspaper; a state legislator proposing a bill in the senate to publish a list by county that would "expose" all those with HIV and suggesting hanging these notices in post offices like FBI wanted bulletins; and, finally, me, an untoward artist whose only love is the camera, showing up at none other than the dancer's own doorstep, my nose dripping and water running down my face in a humid summer downpour, asking him to chop off all my hair, to shear me down to the stubble, the director kneeling before his actor, actor's porch transformed to a cutting room floor, *my* two long braids falling between the snip-snip of steel blades, each lying across the concrete steps like edited film, my body, to quote the apostle Paul, a living sacrifice. Or, as Hitchcock said about the perfect murder—you do it with scissors.

In other words, a typical Oklahoma summer.

I wish I could report some kind of miracle after standing in the rain and pleading for him to shear me, an unearthly change like Garbo as Ninotchka, the faithful commie servant, stripped of her femininity by her undying loyalty to Marxism, but transformed into something human and womanly by the end of the film because of the touch of a man.

I only have a story, no miracles, and none of it translatable to celluloid. Perhaps, film or no film, my storyline is too busy. The old ladies in my family, all my aunties and great-aunties over 'Darko way, when they commence to talking they go so far back in the past that they never get to the part they actually wanted to tell you about in the first place. Working their way up to present-day concerns is put perpetually on pause for as long as they live and speak. I'm going to take you back even farther than that.

In the beginning was Justin. Or, as a certain writer might say, in Justin was the beginning. Was he or wasn't he, goddammit? That was the question. I had hired Justin for my version of a commedia dell' arte–type farce that I was casting called *Transvestite Witches Take Revenge on a Redneck Farmer for Gay Bashing*. A title that was difficult for potential financial backers to imagine appearing on marquees in Oklahoma. My choice certainly didn't make it easy to try to convince my tribe they needed to spend a little money on the arts, as if such a request were ever easy under any circumstances. Justin suggested shortening it to *Chicks with Dicks Beat Up Pricks*, which, though pithy, seemed to me to diminish the seriousness of the film somewhat; not to mention confuse the difference between transsexuals, transvestites, and transgendered folks as well as promote retro and sexist word choices such as "chicks," but bless his heart anyway for trying. Justin's title suggestion, like his own ambiguous sexuality which drove me crazy from the moment I laid eyes on him, revealed some savvy about things gay, some misinformation, some curiosity, and even some willingness to play around with the idea, if not to dance around it—dancing was, after all, his truest calling.

I first saw Justin in ballet tights, and did that ever send me over the edge. If *you* were walking along the carefully manicured lawns of the University of Oklahoma, past the Allan Hauser sculpture of an Apache drummer, and you saw a man in black tights in a *pas de deux*, in front of this very granite singer whose drumstick is raised in midair and the words on his lips are not quite frozen in stone, always on the verge of escaping rock and becoming sound, and if you saw this musical duo, Song and Dance, one granite, the other living flesh, one as still as Kawliga the wooden Indian, the other inspired to dance before his stone-faced muse, and if this man in tights, glistening with sweat, the sun dripping golden light over his naked and pale upper torso, grinned at you and shrugged his shoulders as you walked past the Fred Jones Museum of Art, wouldn't you stop and look? Men in tights, generally speaking, are a little light in their moccasins, and my hopes shot up higher than the humidity index for that day, but, as always, I was nothing less than controlled *discretion*. PROCEED WITH CAUTION, the sign in my head seemed to read.

Oh, hell, it's not what you think. I wanted him for my *film*. I turned on my heels and walked back toward the two of them, the statue and the human. I've never fought any siren's call, why resist? I always run toward trouble as fast as my feet can carry me, and this was no less the case as I approached Dance, the living one, by now fully locked in his gaze.

Neither have I ever lacked for opening lines equal to the moment. Once inside the magic circle, I brought myself up to their powers. I introduced myself to the two of them thus:

"My name is Ronald, but at age thirteen I changed my name to the French pronunciation. You must call me Roe Náld, throaty 'r,' nasalized long 'o,' and the accent on the second syllable. My name is most definitely not *Rah*-nuld," I said, dismissively sounding out the best down-home Carnegie twang I could muster. "It is Roe *Náld*, and you must address me accordingly. Nobody in Oklahoma can say my name, but I expect better of you." I then explained that the Rah-nuld misnomer was merely a false pronunciation forced on me by my parents, and recounted for my two listeners, in as much detail as I could, the mental, spiritual, and physical courage I had to summon up in early adolescence in order to launch the French version of my name in Carnegie, Oklahoma.

First impressions are always important, and you leave them with something they'll never forget. So I turned on my heels before they could reply to my breathless speech and continued on my way toward Boyd Avenue, not looking back lest I be turned into a pillar of salt, and I don't go in for boring biblical epics, so fuck that. I felt that I had definitely given them a thing or two to ponder. "Let them put that in their pipe and smoke it," I said to myself.

I had to hatch a plan to get this young Ganymede in my film; he was just too perfect to let slip away, but how? I changed directions and hurried over toward the Health Science Center and entered the doors of the university pool. Swimming laps not only got me out of the heat radiating in nearly visible waves off the sidewalk and pavement, it would help me think, give me uninterrupted time to have an important talk with myself. I changed before slipping into the swimming lane, and, of course, I never enter these waters without my sequined bathing cap, nor my matching black Speedos. I imagined myself as an underwater Joan Crawford, dolphin dearest. I pulled the goggles over my eyes and pushed off with great aplomb and a greater splash that sent waves over the side of the pool. Unlike a certain famous southern plains writer, I am not given to composing epigrams to offset the boredom of lap swimming. I have bigger fish to fry. But we have ALREADY alluded to him, haven't we?

What can I tell you about *Transvestite Witches*? It was the greatest departure yet from my earlier works, which were collages of rapidly moving images, the idea that they would pass by you on the screen before you could figure out what they meant. Before you can get a handle on one image, the camera moves quickly on to something else, never allowing anything to develop even into the length of a scene. On the other hand *Witches,* my most accessible work to date, actually followed a story line. The film has to do with a peace-loving Mennonite farmer who becomes a white version of Billy Jack (Remember the half-breed Indian Bruce Lee of the early seventies who defended white ladies from redneck rapists?). My gentle Mennonite has a boyfriend, another Mennonite in the colony with whom he's having a secret affair, who is killed in a tractor accident because the John Deere implement dealer in Perkins, Oklahoma, sold him a bad steering column. The surviving boyfriend wreaks revenge on the parts salesman, as well as the greater Perkins area, and even the Mennonite colony that fails to recognize his grief over the death. I had composed this musical farce as a dance-drama, a light opera cum Oprah.

Why would Dance, the subject of my recent encounter with the sculpture, be perfect for the role of Danny, the wronged Mennonite, other than the slight similarity you may have noted in the sound of their names, Dance and Danny?

First of all, he seemed like the right physical type. I had imagined a brooding, artistic Tom, the one whose father, employed by the telephone company, fell in love with long distance. Except this Tom would be a Danny and he would be more like a Mennonite Freddy Krueger—he's back and he's pissed and he's singing about it. I had no luck whatsoever casting this role. I'd come closest with a snuff-dipping cowboy, a student in the Animal Science program at the rival university, Oklahoma State. He drove down from Stillwater for an audition, confidently detailing his theatrical experiences in the small recital room before he read his part. Like a true budding starlet, he named all the community theater musicals he'd sung in, then went on to tell about his family's cow-calf and winter wheat operation which gave him time to act during the fall after they got the seed in the ground, he said.

Unlike most of the lost causes who star in musicals, however, this guy was an unbelievable strapping hulk of a six-foot-and-then-some man; broad chested and dropped down snug into a pair of Wrangler cowboy-cut jeans. He was so fair-skinned his cheeks were always red, as if he'd just come in from the cold, even though it was summer, and he had the associated fair features—straw colored hair, blue eyes. As white as he could be without looking like an albino or a corpse—just off ivory, a real piece of china. A more pedestrian feature was the ring in the back pocket of his Wranglers, where his snuff can had worn a circle like an off-centered asshole. And speaking of rings, I noticed the gold one on his finger right away, and found my gorge rising to see one so tragically fallen in the prime of his youthful beauty before he'd experienced the world, or at least me. The kind of white boy I might dream having on top of me after he set down his hay hooks and lifted me up on top of an alfalfa bale. You get the picture. Wholesome.

In the audition scene I'd asked him to read, the Mennonite character, Danny, runs toward the tractor wreck and raises his dying boyfriend's lolling head. That's what's supposed to happen, anyway. The boyfriend, uttering his last words, says, "My daddy always told me to drive an International Harvester," and he bitterly tosses his John Deere seed cap into the furrow, his arm falling back to earth after his hand releases the hat. Last shot on the unfisted hand, the crumpled cap in the dirt. Of course I had to play the dying lover, but when the ag student was supposed to take me up in his arms, he bent over at the waist with his ass pointed in the air toward the audition audience and grabbed a hold of me more like one of his dad's feedlot steers fixing to paw the ground and back up before butting heads with a shit-caked opponent. Not a bit how I'd conceptualized Danny, the heartbroken Mennonite. My sensitive Tom turned out to be a bombshell farm-boy Marilyn, stripped of all of Marilyn's vulnerability.

After the audition, I had finally decided that the role called for more character than any one actor could give, at least any Oklahoma actor. I was a visionary in a feedlot state. Given I was aiming at farce, I was almost ready to accept a feedlot Marilyn, no other possibilities seeming to present themselves.

That was before I saw Dance in front of the sculpture, and my vision had been restored. I pulled myself out of the pool and shook the water from my ears, then went and stretched out on the empty sideline bleachers. But how to recruit this vision? How, even, to find out his name? Well, how hard could it be to identify a man who went about in ballet tights in Norman, Oklahoma?

There is a clarity that only comes to me beneath the surface, with the rest of the world blocked out, and my focus turned inside myself. Armed with this new sense of purpose after my underwater gambol, I rose from my bench and strode to the lockers. My inquiries must begin immediately, I thought, so I threw my bathing cap and goggles in, spun the numbers, and rapidly changed out of my Speedo. Did I already mention it was black?—in case you're the type who fancies underwater codpieces.

I hurried over to the drama department. Such a busy day! I strategized as I strode. No, not briskly. Make that meandered. One must not appear overeager. Playing dumb had always worked well for me; having grown up in a state where it came so naturally to so many, no one ever guessed I was acting. In Oklahoma, the white polyester trash come by their stupidity naturally, having descended from a bunch of lowlifes, bootleggers, and convicts that (yes, that, not who) illegally entered Indian Territory or rushed in later on the heels of the land run at the end of the century. Dumb had been passed down through the generations; by now it was the basic stuff of Oklahoma DNA.

Oh, puh-leaze, don't give me that look. How smart can you be if you send money to Oral Roberts and Kenneth Copeland?

These very rednecks thought the same about us, that we were a bunch of stupid Indians. Dumb was one of the most convincing subterfuges you could mount around Okies because you most always fit right in with them, and they expected the same from you.

In the department office, I said to the secretary, "Professor Walker is giving us extra credit for going to the dance recital, but I lost the announcement." I could have simply asked, "Did you see a man in ballet tights go by?" but I have found that the kind of ruse that raises slight suspicion actually elevates your adversaries' interest level and increases the likelihood that they might string you along for curiosity's sake until they unintentionally give you the information you seek.

It was working; the secretary spent a good while hunched over a bunch of forms before looking up and glaring at me. "Justin Crossman," she muttered. "Room 383, tomorrow at 4:30. Your whole class has been in here," she said, returning to her forms. Then she grumbled under her breath, "The damn thing's posted all over campus."

It seemed too easy, but I had a good feeling that I'd hit pay dirt. It was early in the summer recess so there was no onslaught of senior recitals, projects, and the like, and Dance, who now had emerged into the light with the name Justin, must have been rehearsing for a performance when I'd seen him in front of the museum—unless he was the kind of drama queen who just liked to stand around on street corners stopping traffic. Please, god, I thought, not one of those bitches.

The next day I left my apartment and made my way over to the recital hall: a gothic structure, gray, ancient, and carved out of rock, one of the original buildings constructed at the turn of the century just before statehood. The secretary was right—how had I ever missed the poster? It hung on every board and pole in Norman. Once inside the hall I could see dust floating down on beams of light stretching from the high stone-cut windows to the floor. I'd come in late, naturally, and onstage a single cellist had begun to play an imitation of a hoedown, like a fiddle tune with double stops a-blazing, if you could do double stops on a cello—and in Oklahoma, you can. An old-fashioned claw-footed bathtub on a flat dolly was being pushed to center stage by a bearded man dressed in hospital whites and a stethoscope hanging from his neck. Lying languidly in the tub was none other than my boy, Justin, and water sloshed over the sides as the intern pushed it like a hospital gurney. Justin, his upper body as naked as the first time I saw him, had the lower torso of a fish—that is to say, a black neoprene plastic fish suit with a giant tail that lopped over the side of the white porcelain. Justin started flapping around inside to the rhythm of the cellist's hoedown until the stage was covered with a damn inch of water. I thought, "What is this, Darryl Hannah in fucking *Splash*?"

With the help of the intern, Justin emerged from the tub, water dripping off his chest, and he had his arm thrown around the doctor, who was supporting him like a wounded soldier, his fish tail stretched out in front of him as the bearded man helped him stand in that ridiculous getup. At that moment what I would later identify as Justin's poisonous vulnerability infected me once more, the first time occurring when he locked me in his gaze in front of the statue. There he stood—his chest heaving from his raucous flailing about in the tub, his arm reaching for a man to lean on, each ripple and convexity of his upper torso glistening from the effects of water and light. He was making me thirsty.

But I thought, "This is too strange, even for modern dance." I got up as the Caravaggio-like intern began singing to his young objet d'art. I was not interested in wasting energy trying to understand these strange happenings. Outside a couple other people had left, and they stood around laughing their asses off, evidently having seen enough to grind out the written summary for their prof. Of course it was the usual, "Did you see when . . ." followed by "or that part where he . . . ," but I heard one of them say, "At least there's a party afterwards," and he gave the address.

Sometimes luck is like drowning, so beautiful once you quit struggling.

At the apartment I had no trouble gaining entrance to the party and didn't even get to test my prefabricated fabrication. When the host opened the door, Justin, seated on a raggedy couch in the cramped living room of a student apartment, saw me right away and exclaimed, "Roe Náld! You made it!" I strode immediately over, pushed a gushing young actress I vaguely recognized out of my way—since there was plenty of room for *her* at the end of the sofa, put my hand on Justin's knee, and intoned, "*That* was a wonderful performance," completely obscuring whether I meant his dance piece or his ecstatic greeting as I entered the door.

To this Justin had no response whatsoever, nor was he taken aback, leaving me to wonder—as I oft would in days to come—what he was thinking. And instead of squirming when I sat so close to him, or moving away, he put his arm around me, a seeming reenactment of his leaning on the intern during the dance piece I'd just witnessed, except here it was in that buddy-buddy hetero way, his arm on the back of the couch, resting just behind my head, so that I could imagine, if not feel, the beginning of my two braids touching the inside of his arm. Out of costume, Justin had dressed in a carefully purchased alternative artsy look, a black, gauzy knit shirt and baggy black synthetic dress pants with a thin white stripe that ran down the leg, cuffed just over an Italian half-boot, which was, naturally, also black. Not anything like my own art nouveau wardrobe purchased at the Salvation Army and dictated by the exigencies of surviving as an artist and an Indian in my beloved state, that is to say the state of Oklahoma, not the state of my mind. There was something most un-Oklahoma looking about Justin, an ethnic look of a Mediterranean sort, curly black hair and brown eyes, olive-colored skin. But could he act?

The party had started raging as the theater and art crowd arrived, and I found it not only festive but *most* gay. It was very cruisy in that theater-world way where everybody is bi and curious in their disgustingly liberal open-minded fashion, as if sex is like taking a vacation to Morocco just to see it for the first time. They were tourists in the land of libido: a short visit to a foreign country, oohs and aahs at all the sights, followed by a hasty retreat back to the safety of home and its capital city, Hetero. I preferred rednecks to their stupid theater bullshit because the trailer trash captured my imagination, whereas this bunch bored me to tears, what with their talk of all the "shows" they'd acted in and their undying puppy love of all things oppressed which made little ole Wichita and Caddo Indian me the object of their affection in their neverending search for their own authenticity. It was part of what made me want to leave for New York where I could be just a damn filmmaker, not a damn Indian filmmaker. But pour me some bourbon over ice, honey, and I'll get over it—which, actually, is the next thing Justin did, rising from the sofa and offering to get me a drink, heading for the kitchen before I could even tell him what I wanted, which, actually, was mineral water with a lime twist. I don't drink.

When Justin returned, as if he'd been psychically tuned into my bitchy interior monologues, he handed me a tinkling glass and muttered, "Chivas Regal." Making his way back to the sofa from the kitchen had been like wading through spawning beds, since the apartment had gotten crowded and the cruising had intensified. All the while I was wondering how to land this particular fish in my film. Thus far, I hadn't figured out Justin's own spawning habits, and I didn't know if the pretty young actress scrunched up against him when I came in was his idea or hers.

I didn't touch my glass once I sat it on the table.

The way to a performer's heart is through his ego, and there were always the old standbys—a little praise for his artistry, some intrigue about my interest, an offer of something he needed. The problem was I didn't know what he needed, other than the one thing no exhibitionist can do without, an audience. While I was thinking, he had returned to conversing with the young actress, leaning forward, his elbows on his knees, and laughing with her, while I sat in the middle, my grand entrance forgotten in the party chatter. Without any warning, I snatched his drink from his hand, set it on the coffee table in front of us with a clunk, and said with the utmost seriousness, "Justin, I would love to film the performance I saw tonight."

"You make films?" he asked, startled for a moment, then turning back toward me while eyeballing the drink I'd just spirited away. Before his eyes caught mine, I gave the young actress, once again abandoned at the end of the sofa, a bitchy smirk.

Am I the only one who imagines that dolphins are always grinning? By the time Justin picked up his drink again, that was what he looked like—Flipper just before his trainer throws him a fish, and willing to tread water backwards to get it.

"Everyone knows, the king of the sea," I started to hum, smiling to myself at the memory. "Yes, I'm an independent filmmaker," I said. "I'm beginning my third film now. I'm presently casting the lead," I said suggestively.

"What are your films like?" Justin asked.

"What are they like for me to make them?"

"No, I mean what are the films about?"

I fell back, our original pose restored, Justin's arm on the back of the sofa, me leaning into it. "Well, your use of the word 'about' throws me," I reacted. "It's so reductive to come up with some sound bite about their meaning. I'm as interested in images as ideas."

Justin gave me a playful look, a self-conscious one along the lines of "I'm not as dumb as you think I am, even though I'm a dancer." With that mere glance, I had a premonition of what I was up against, though I could have never guessed at the time just how slippery things would become.

"But, I mean, can you describe them?" Justin asked. He seemed to be losing interest, and I'd made a mistake lecturing him.

"Enough about my work, what about yours?" Maybe I could pull him back in.

He took a breath, then leaned over again, his elbows on his knees and his chin cupped in his hand, as if considering his response. One of his stock poses, evidently, and *très* Rodin. There was something of a tease in his posture, though, and I could see down his billowy shirt. Cheap thrills are free thrills, I've always maintained, but I worried: Just who was working whom? So I kept up the illusion that I was anxiously awaiting his answer while my eyes took in as much of him as he seemed to offer. All this physical scrutiny for casting purposes, of course. The perfect Danny was sitting right here inches away from me.

"It's funny you mention film," he said, all quiet and serious. "I've been hoping to go beyond dancing or at least take the dancing somewhere else beside the usual venues. You do the classical stuff for the elderly who sleep while you're twisting your groin on stage, and the modern stuff for kids doing extra credit assignments who volunteer their interpretations backstage, then ask, 'Am I right?' They never understand," he sighed.

Maybe that's because you dress up in a fucking fish suit, I thought to myself, but didn't say anything. Instead I sympathized. "I know what you mean," I said. "In Oklahoma the art crowd, apart from university students, is the rich oil money crowd and the beef cattle crowd and the wheat farmer crowd and the car dealership crowd. A refinery doth not lead to refinement.

"When oil's high and wheat prices are good, the arts are a hot commodity for well-to-do hillbillies who want to rise above their roots. We're one of the few art communities whose health can be gauged by following the commodities page of livestock journals. Who wants to be tied in with all that shit? That's why I make independent films. By the way, what's the story with your dance number in front of the drummer?" I said, shifting the subject quickly, remembering what happened just moments before when the topic of conversation drifted away from him.

I could tell you the story of Justin and the Apache drummer, but I'm not going to, because, as I always say to friends and loved ones, "Enough about you, let's talk about me." Some call this vanity; I call it narration. That night at the party I promised to shoot some dance footage for Justin. I didn't want to suffer through the drowning mermaid number again; I'd just as soon see her go under. So I came up with the idea of making a kind of collage of Justin's work, something that could serve as a working video résumé that he could actually use for auditions. Not a bad idea, when you think about it—some high-quality videotape of your best performance excerpts, ready to go. We'd discussed some upcoming pieces he was performing at recitals and campus events that we could film live and other things we could stage in spaces on campus. I asked him if he wanted to see the location I was working on for my film, and he said, sure, and I think he was especially agreeable since he was still pumped from all the attention he got at the party and the seductive idea of having a camera pointed solely at him, perhaps even feeling a little in my debt for the generous offer.

I felt a little nervous, putting off the actual moment when I revealed to Justin the subject matter of the film, and my desire for his part in it—no, my growing religious conviction that a Higher Power had chosen him to play Danny, the wronged Mennonite.

Days later, on the way out to location, Justin may have doubted the seriousness of my filmmaking or the artistic nature of my intentions, since I drove him to an isolated cow pasture, a graveyard for broken down farm implements and their parts near Lexington. Justin showed no sign of losing his nerve, however, and he took charge as soon as we stepped out of the car. He walked over to the fence line and held apart two strands of barbed wire, so I could squeeze through, then nimbly hopped over and cleared the top wire of the fence as easily and as gracefully as a whitetail deer, showing up my more sissified, less dramatic entrance.

The only thing I had in common with the bounding buck was that my tail was probably twitching.

Well, that certainly wasn't in my plans. Justin strode over to a broken-down tractor and climbed astride it, and I had to conceal my surprise, because driving by this rusty machine and seeing it so many times out in the field marked the very genesis of my idea for the fatal crash that would take the life of Danny's boyfriend. It was like Justin was already a part of the story, as if the film had started rolling the moment we first saw each other.

The gray, overcast sky had, at least, brought the temperature down. I kicked over an empty oil drum and straddled it, talking a little bit, in vague terms, about the spirit of the film and explaining some ideas I had about the location.

I wondered how I could keep Justin here, the two of us alone in a cow pasture. People in Oklahoma sneak off to such places to drink, to have sex, or to drink and have sex. The cows are a subterfuge. But as I watched Justin it seemed like he required no explanations. He just waited. It felt more like adolescent boys hanging out in junkyards or tree forts or other hidden shared places, understood secrets between you that need not be articulated. *Stand by Me*, Chris and Gordie, tears on the train tracks.

So I just launched right into it. "It's like this spot embodies a certain feeling I want to capture in this film, you know?"

Justin was listening from atop the tractor, still silently urging me to go on, to come out with it.

"I mean look around—the disrepair, discs and harrows falling apart under the sun and rain, an oil well clanking in the background. Look at it," I said, pointing to the giant black arm that rose and fell like a huge crow pecking the earth. A gathering cloud above the oil well cast a field-length shadow over the misplaced red hill that had been moved to dig a pit. "Christ, I wish I had my camera right now," I said wistfully.

"So everything seems to be falling apart here," I went on, "but there's always this incredible integrity that shines through. That's Oklahoma. I know that sounds stupid, but I mean how can you describe an Oklahoma evening next to a farm pond like this?" A meadowlark sang up a storm from a fence post, and the bluebells were in full bloom in all of their breathtaking purples, so I didn't need to go into any details about what I meant. Just sitting there as bass started to rise and feed on the insects landing on the water, and the quality of the dusky early evening, put the junkyard in sharp relief, even under the overcast sky.

Justin interrupted me. "Roe Náld," he said, seeming to have decided just how long to let me blather on. "What do I have to do in this film of yours?" He had been cleaning his fingernails with a rusty piece of baling wire that hung from the steering wheel of the tractor. That he was to be in my film seemed to be a natural assumption that he'd made and taken in as casually as the fact that the two of us were sitting out here in the middle of some stranger's cow pasture.

Did the grinding hum of the cicadas in my ears shake something loose in my brain? Was it the magic of Justin's body, his comic pose as he slumped over the steering wheel and playfully rapped a hollow thudding drumbeat on the tractor body as I had been talking? Maybe the raccoon, who'd come down to the shore of the pond to snatch up crayfish in the weedy shallows, had reached inside my head and pulled out my most ridiculous thought?

I blurted out foolishly, "You have to kiss a man!" as if that summarized the sum total of my film aesthetically, conceptually, and technically.

I'd had no intention of describing the film in such terms and was taken aback at my own outburst. I had no plans for kissing.

"Cool," Justin said, laughing, and he returned to softly thudding out his drumbeat on the top of the tractor.

——

In the days to come, I found myself thinking of Justin every waking moment. Trying to second guess him, figure him out, and wondering what he was thinking. I lived for the film, for those times we would work together, because keeping busy and actually directing him provided me the only respite from this constant curiosity. And yet the more we rehearsed, the more inscrutable he became, and the more I wanted to know. Oh, I learned all the details of his life, all the facts, his history, from him and from what I carefully pried out of those who knew him. That was the easy part. His ethnicity—his grandparents were Italians who had come to Oklahoma and found work in the coal industry around Krebs and McAlester. During World War II and all the war hysteria against the Japanese and Italians, his relatives had gone through a living hell, and his family hadn't forgotten, fifty years after the war. His high school years and his dance beginnings in local Teen Oklahoma competitions, where contestant after contestant would stand up to perform their own unique version of "New York, New York," and he would come out and do modern dance interpretations. I told him I had dreamed of being in one of those competitions myself as the first Indian to sing Ado Annie's line, "I'm just a girl who cain't say no," my idea of a tribute to our wonderful state, the musical that created it in the public's image, and the queer Cherokee from Claremore, Lynn Riggs, who wrote the play that Rodgers and Hammerstein turned into the Broadway smash *Oklahoma!* Instead I'd been typecast in my early theater beginnings. Just how many times can one person play the giant Indian in *One Flew Over the Cuckoo's Nest*? Especially if you're a short, skinny artist, whatever might be said about Will Sampson being a fellow Oklahoman. Like Will I was dark; unlike Will I was dwarfed. It never worked since all the patients looked like they could beat me up—even apart from Nurse Ratched, who could beat anyone up.

Justin himself would answer any question put to him, and we became regular sisters, except I never quite knew if Justin was actually a sister. He had a girlfriend, that much was certain, but theirs was the most casual relationship I knew of, even for college kids. They were company for each other, whenever either needed it, but they would go long stretches without going out or even calling. Justin had seen little of her in the last few days since we'd started our work on the film. I imagined Justin and me as more of an item than Justin and his girlfriend, and we had become regulars at the campus corner coffee shop, La Baguette—which I'd christened La Faguette from the first day it opened its doors—where we spent hours telling stories about the peculiarities of growing up in eastern and south-central Oklahoma, his sense of difference as an Italian guy with an Okie accent, and my dramas about being Indian and gay in a state we used to own but was now overrun by Baptists and Methodists and Pentecostals—a good number of them among our own people—and how Oklahoma had practically killed me.

One day Justin arrived an hour and a half late at the coffee shop. I said, "Just in time, Justin," only a little bitchily since I'd grown overly forgiving of his lack of punctuality. He always arrived in a rush, as if he'd just flown in from a summit meeting with world leaders, a sense of drama as highly refined as my own. He sat down and grinned, a seductive and somewhat effective way he had of garnering pardon, flashing his pearly whites and a sexy smile and brushing off a wisp of curly black lock that had fallen over his forehead.

"Oh, I was talking on the phone to Jill," he said, as he sat down at our table on the outside front patio facing the campus.

I felt that little stab, one I had tried to rationalize lately. Why should I care that he was talking to his girlfriend? Why did I want to know what they said to each other? Why did I get angry whenever he mentioned her name? Perhaps it was the mystery with which he surrounded their relationship, my feeling that this ambiguity was purposeful, intended to piss me off, the implied "it's none of your business" regarding whatever it was they meant to each other.

"How long have you and Jill been dating?"

"Oh, not very long."

"What does Jill think about you doing the movie?"

"We never talk about it."

"What is Jill doing this summer?"

"I think she's taking a class."

This was a typical conversation where Jill was concerned. One didn't get the sense she'd be there for Jack if he fell down and broke his crown. Rather than let Justin jerk me around any more I changed the subject.

Justin was wearing a tank top that day, and I said casually, "You never told me what happened to your arm." I'd seen him shirtless on two other occasions, once in front of the statue, and the other time in the fish suit, and I have a mind for physical details. Justin had a nasty gash that ran off-center on his chest, toward his shoulder—a mangling of flesh that looked a little like a burn but not exactly.

Justin's large brown eyes narrowed to slits as he eyed me suspiciously, and he said, "I wondered when you'd finally ask." He was practically spitting venom when he hissed, "Everybody loves a freak show."

Well, this broadsided me. The scar tissue, if anything, contributed to Justin's overall attractiveness—here you had this tall, lean, aesthete dancer, whose grace was offset by a perfectly placed imperfection that drew attention to his natural musculature. This well-built, sometimes effeminate, more often really masculine, man was one interesting combination, anyone could see and feel that, and, unlike his weird dance numbers, none of it came off as a performance. His body reeked of authenticity. Like I said; he was the perfect Danny; that's why I'd chosen him.

"Christ, Justin," I said. "Don't make it such a cross to bear. It's hardly noticeable."

"That's easy for you to say," he shot back. "You don't have to live with it." He was looking straight at me, not backing down any, and, clearly, this was a subject Justin was going to insist that I take seriously. So I sat and listened while he laid bare his story.

"I got a job in tenth grade working for a Coke bottling plant in McAlester. Not everybody was happy I got the job; it was the kind of work that grown-ups around there aspire to as a career since it pays a little better than minimum wage, and there's not much else to do. It was a step up from the kind of work their parents had cut their eyeteeth on, working in the coal mines. So for me, as a high school kid, to get this work, well, let's just say there were people around who thought they should have got that job, not me. It was a simple matter, really, of my grandpa knowing the foreman, one of the few locals who'd been friendly down through the years. There's not that much to tell. One day I was loading these molded plastic cartons that held Coke bottles onto a conveyor belt that sent them into a cleaning machine. I was wearing a damn copper bracelet that my tenth-grade girlfriend had given me as an anniversary present for going out with her for a year. It caught on one of the wheels of the conveyor belt and jerked my arm into the machine, where one of the lifters came down hard on my shoulder and dislocated it. It was my shoulder that shut down the machine, rather than a safety switch that is supposed to automatically detect any obstructions. There's a lawsuit that's still going on. They've tried to settle out of court once. I'll probably get some money out of it," he said bitterly.

Now I had to force myself to keep from staring at his scar. I wanted to touch it. I started playing with my braids whenever my eyes would drift toward his shoulder. How seriously was I supposed to take this mock-epic tragedy? "When you get the settlement, do you want to help finance the film?" I joked.

He didn't laugh. We sat in silence, drank our coffee, and read our papers. I'm not sure if I could have loved him any more than during that hour. I don't mean I was *in love* with him, but my feeling for him was strong. I only have eyes for the camera. I've been with enough men, mostly just sex, some great sex, but no great meaning in any of it. Men were too much trouble; I'd rather make a movie about them. After about an hour I said, "Let's go do some work," and he agreed.

At rehearsal that day I decided to depart from the usual part readings we'd begun, to try something more improvisatory. I wanted him to go through that process, not unlike my own in creating the characters, where I started to have conversations with them, imagine their thoughts, wonder how they would respond to certain situations. This took place at my apartment since he would never invite me over to his, another facet of the secrecy between us. He'd remained silent since I'd brought up his injury. I cleared books and papers and grant applications off the kitchen table, and made a place for Justin to sit.

Hung on the wall around my table were various pieces of bad "Indian art" I had collected, the kind where the figures look like brown versions of Farrah Fawcett or Cheryl Tiegs, layered hair and all, except black and with a feather in it, and always a wolf or an owl in the background. *Charlie's Indians*. The men look like Jon Bon Jovis mounted on horseback posing as warriors, with a lance or a war shield. Under each of these "paintings" I had written a caption that captured the spirit of the piece, and invited guests and Indian friends and relatives to provide their own cartoon lines beneath a favorite princess or warrior. This ever-changing living collection always got a laugh from anyone who visited my kitchen, but Justin said nothing. Maybe he didn't get it, even though his people had always played us in the movies, and one might therefore expect some insight from him. Was he still pouting? The hell with it; we had work to do. I sat down at the table and gave him a scenario.

"Imagine Danny at the coffee shop where he hangs out in Perkins, Oklahoma. He goes there, like many of the local farmers, and talks and drinks coffee from around seven in the morning until eight or eight-thirty, every week day. Danny's lover comes with him most of the time, and for the five years they've been together, they have pretended that the boyfriend is the hired hand who lives out in the guest house on the farm. Danny and his boyfriend are Mennonites; the rest of the farmers at the coffee shop are Baptists and Methodists; one or two are Holy Roller crazies. They're sitting at a table with two other farmers. I'll be the boyfriend. Let's talk."

"Oh, Danny Boy, the pipes, the pipes are calling . . ."

"Why, Danny, you're singing. You're sure in a silly mood this morning," I said, looking at the other farmers, a little embarrassed.

Danny just slumped over his plate of hotcakes and went to town eating them. "Hey, big spender," he said, pausing to take a drink of his coffee. "What shall we call you; how can we give you a name?"

"What do you think I should be called?" I asked.

"I don't know," Danny said. "I'm more worried about whether you got those high school boys to help us pick rocks next week. Been bustin' hell on those cultivator blades with all those stony stones in the corn field."

Danny's fork would freeze in midair as he addressed me between bites; then he'd jab it in my direction every time he mentioned the rocks. He set it down on his napkin and wiped it off, then went on. "I heard Randall and some of his buddies need a little extry summer money, and we could pry get some of 'em to help."

"Who is Randall?" I asked.

"Who is Randall?" Danny said, irritated that I'd forgotten. "Who is Randall? Why none other than your very own nephew, your kin, your shadow, rock picker, a rock picker just like you. Why I'm right proud of that boy myself, rock-picker or not, seeing's how he just lettered in varsity baseball. He needs some money to buy his school jacket. Let's help the boy out, give him a little work, why don't we? We could get him and his buddies out in that corn field and show 'em what rock pickin's really about!"

"How much are we going to pay them?" I asked.

"I'm talking about saving farm machinery, goddammit," Danny exploded, slamming his fist on the table.

"Danny, we're Mennonites. Don't cuss."

"Now, I'll tell you what, you cocksucker. You get Randall and his little buddies out here and we're gonna really show 'em how to pick rocks. And if they won't pick rocks, we'll make them pitch silage!"

I was beginning to wonder—was this acting? The anger seemed real enough, a weird aggression that felt connected to our earlier exchange, possibly some homophobia intended to intimidate me, and yet imbued with innuendo and familiarity. A more practical problem was that it was hard to physically stake Justin down and get him to say lines without having to move all over whatever space we were using. Here you could really see his dance background, his need to incorporate movement, and I'd spent a lot of time getting him to simply sit or stand still when the situation called for it. I'd been promising him we'd work on the dance numbers next, as soon as we got the right feeling and delivery for the dialogue.

So when Justin got up from the table and grabbed a hold of a poker next to the brick fireplace mantle and started dancing in place, it felt like an implied "Fuck you and your direction, Roe Náld. I'm dancing now, like it or not!" Justin started prancing like a boxer before a match and jabbing the poker in my direction. Without any words, with just the movement, it came off like Muhammad Ali jumping around and baiting George Foreman at the press conference, weeks before the actual fight. The dance also felt like some kind of demonstration of a primitive savage, and I felt offended, like when I was in grade school and all these little white kids would run around in a circle clapping their hands over their mouths, imitating the Indians of their imaginations. I sensed revenge, Justin getting back at me.

And then he started chanting, just off the top of his head:

> hands, farm hands the hands
> of farm hands. Rocks, pick rocks, the
> rocks of rock pickers, the rocks of farm
> hands picking rocks, picking the rock pricks of farm
> hands' big beautiful stone sacs.
>
> Randall, the baseball player, lettered
> in varsity baseball, letter jacket, leather
> jacket, inside Randall's leather jacket the letter,
> Randall's rocks, getting Randall's rocks off.
>
> Silage, dark green silage, the sweet-sick smell
> of silage, pitching silage, Randall the pitcher,
> the sweet-sick smell of Randall's rocks.
>
> Come ye back, when summer's in
> the meadow, Come to the meadow,
> Randall, come pick rocks with Danny boy,
> his pipe is calling you.

Justin collapsed on my sofa after that, didn't bother to even move all the books and papers and clutter, just fell back, breathing hard from all the exertion of dancing and speaking. Something had transpired in this incredible exchange, a bridge had been crossed. It came off as a mean revenge for my questions about Justin's scar, but I had a realization that was much more serious. These rehearsals, the script, the film I was making, were no longer mine. Justin had wrenched them away from me. He knew exactly what kind of weird edge I wanted to bring to the film, and now I could see how indispensable he was to the project: I couldn't make the film without him. This gave him tremendous power, and I was beginning to suspect that he knew it. As disconcerting as his improvisation had been in terms of the way it felt like he was talking about me and him rather than just Danny and his lover, no one else would be able to create this character the way Justin could. The tensions between us were becoming part of the role, and they matched the spirit of the film to a T. I didn't like sharing my project with Justin one bit. I was the one, after all, who'd first conceived of it.

We were definitely ready for the dance numbers. In the next few days I tried to get the main dance piece really well scripted as well as talking it over with Justin. Although the script had a number of songs and dances in it, they were all minor preludes to the main piece called "Rabbit Dance." The smaller numbers could be worked out later with Justin's help. "Rabbit Dance" starts as a loving operatic tribute to the farm and the two men's lives there, yet foreshadows the fatal tractor wreck and turns into a mad, frenzied expression of grief after Danny's boyfriend dies. Justin himself wasn't a singer; one man can only have so many talents, but I knew a number of ambitious opera queens who'd do anything to get a few steps further down the road to divadom, and Justin was going to lip-sync along with a soundtrack in order to amplify the overall campiness of the film. Some of the singers had already helped me write the songs after hearing the film scenario, and they'd had a great time with it. I'd written the lyrics; they'd provided melodies. We were going to do all the numbers really minimally with just some piano accompaniment because there's no way I could ever get all this stuff orchestrated. I'm an Indian filmmaker, not Andrew Lloyd Webber.

"Rabbit Dance" begins with Danny walking alongside a harrow being pulled behind the tractor his boyfriend is driving. Danny whistles and half ambles, half dances along at a jolly gait, not unlike the Scarecrow following the yellow brick road, arm and arm with Dorothy, except Dorothy is up on the tractor. The mood of the piece changes when the harrow unearths a nest of baby rabbits, and Danny discovers the small pink creatures exposed and shivering in the bright sunshine. He gently scoops them up and sings the first full song of the piece, "Emergence, the Blinding Light," which laments the sudden disturbance of the rabbits and foreshadows cataclysmic events in the two men's hitherto idyllic existence. The song ends tenderly with Danny placing the rabbits in a depression next to a fallen tree at the edge of the woods alongside the field and singing to their mother to come and find them.

While Danny is thus occupied, his boyfriend has come to the end of the field where he has to make a sharp turn but finds his steering wheel locked. The north end of the plowed earth is against a steep wooded bank that leads down to a small creek, and as Danny lovingly looks up from the baby rabbits, he catches a glimpse of the tractor going over the embankment. He runs along the field edge to where the John Deere has plunged through the barbed-wire fence and sees smoke coming up from the creek bed. He slides down the bank, finding, to his horror, that the tractor has rolled.

His boyfriend is pinned under the harrow blades, a slight trickle of blood coming out of the corner of his mouth. Danny, pumped with adrenaline, removes a pin and detaches the harrow, lifting it off his boyfriend enough to pull him out from under it. The boyfriend struggles to speak but is unable to say anything before drawing his last breath. Danny's "No!" echoes along the creek banks, and he begins the last dance piece of the film, an expression of grief and fury, before he will set out to take revenge on the town. Grief at never knowing his boyfriend's last words. Fury at himself, at both of them, for living in secrecy all these years. Hatred of the town for making them ashamed and afraid. Desperate speculation regarding what his boyfriend wanted to tell him before he died. This is mostly danced; the lines are spewed out in a frenzy, not sung. I'd written them recently, inspired by Justin's bizarre rock picking improvisation.

Putting this piece together would take a lot of work. There was some technical stuff where complicated effects would have to be accomplished using really simple techniques, given the small budget of the film. Out on location, we'd have to simply hook up one of the implements to the tractor, and tip it and the tractor over, then I'd crawl under the wreck and die for Danny. I'd have to splice this into the creek footage. I happened to know that the owners of the pasture were retired and elderly, living in town in Smyrna, so with any luck at all we wouldn't get arrested for trespassing and destruction of private property. It's not like I could just go and ask this retired white farm couple if they minded having an Indian out in their pasture tipping over their tractor and making a queer dance-drama. I might as well ask for the hand of one of their grandsons in marriage.

Some of it would have to be shot in the country at my uncle's tribal allotment outside of Lawton. He had a tractor that actually ran, and we could use it for the field scenes. Back at the original location, there were all the problems of choreography over a rough landscape and following it with a camera. In this area Justin would be indispensable with his physical strength and agility, but I hadn't figured out how to overcome the challenges of getting a steady shot while working with hand-held equipment and moving.

We started off slow and filmed the easiest parts first. We got some friends out at the site and lined up against the tractor and tipped it over. Unbelievably, it still had gas in it, which leaked out the sides of the rusty tank, so all the smokers had to put out their cigs lest we turn our final dance into a conflagration that would fill the pasture with black smoke and announce our trespass to everyone in the county, or, worse yet, bomb us with exploding tractor shrapnel. We dragged the harrow behind it, lifted it up, and braced it with a concrete block so the weight of it wouldn't be on me, and I crawled under and died for the camera. That was the easy part; it went over without a hitch. We were even considerate enough to set the old rust bucket upright again so it wouldn't suffer the indignity of decomposing on its side for the next century or so. Well, actually, so we wouldn't get caught because we still had film to shoot there later.

When I watched some of this footage, I found myself wincing. There I was, long braids and all, dying for Danny the Mennonite. At first I saw this as pointed sarcasm. If you could have decades of Italians playing Indians in Gary Cooper and John Wayne movies, why couldn't an Indian play a Mennonite? We weren't exactly going for realism or naturalism, after all. Something was still bothering me though. A disturbance like this becomes a total obsession with me, and I can't let it rest until I've played out every possible scenario in my mind. I've stayed up through many a night until dawn wrestling with a script or editing film until I got it right or just lying in bed fucking worrying.

Lately, if it wasn't the middle of the night, I would walk over to Justin's when I was all worked up over some production detail, and wait on his front porch (he never let me inside), until he'd come out and we'd stroll over to the coffee shop and hash out the problem. So I headed for Justin's. It was early evening, nine-ish, not unusual for one of our get-togethers.

I wasn't capturing the spirit of the film in the wreck scene with the in-your-face artifice of the dying Mennonite who is an obvious Indian. In terms of appearance and dress, I wanted to avoid campiness. Where the character would become overblown, where the film should fail to be taken seriously, needed to be on the level of performance. Danny and his boyfriend should look like Mennonites, dressed according to the mores of their colony. The absurdity comes through because they are Mennonites who dance and sing their way in and out of tragedy, not because of the incongruities of their appearance, that is, the boyfriend being played by an Indian. I had as my inspiration Hitchcock's *The Trouble with Harry*, with its exacting focus on realistic detail—down to the different hues of red in the changing colors of autumn trees in New England—yet in this abundance of concrete naturalness is a story that is completely wack.

As I walked along, it had clouded up and started to rain; some of those really big Oklahoma thunderclaps were booming, the kind that make you jump out of your pants, the ones that sent your grandparents diving down into their storm cellars back when everybody had one to dive into. There came a downpour, but I soon forgot that I was dripping wet. Danny and his boyfriend had to look like Mennonites. I wasn't about to go to the trouble of finding someone other than me to play Danny's lover; that would set us back eons. I grew more and more agitated as I approached Justin's house, thinking about my two long braids. It's not like I'm some kind of AIMster, the bone-choker walking pow wow poster kind of guy out to prove something with all the beads and feathers. It was just hair to me, yet it was long, beautiful hair: two braids that dangled down to my butt, six years in the making. It was what made me not look like all the obnoxious white gay clones that congregated at the pretty-boy cha-cha palaces on Saturday nights for their meaningless promenades up and down the stairs to the various floors of the dance clubs. To this extent, my hair constituted an identity.

I stood on Justin's front porch, cold and shivering, wiping my dripping nose on my shirt sleeve, an Oklahoma lightning storm touching down on the horizon. This time I didn't ask to be invited in; I just pushed my way through the door, as I should have done long before, stood in the middle of his living room and picked up a red bandanna off of his very messy floor and blew my nose. I seemed to have become mute; perhaps because I'd realized that I'd forced myself into Justin's apartment—something I'd wanted to do since I first met him—and now that I was here, I didn't know what to say.

Justin seemed to be responding in kind, he'd sat down on the floor, arms folded defensively. He didn't have a stitch of furniture in the place—it was spare as a monk's cell, except messier for all the clothes lying about. I started pacing the length of the apartment and gesticulating like Woody Allen when he plays himself in all his movies except, most unlike Woody, I still hadn't been able to grunt out even a syllable.

Justin got up and started stacking books into piles, evidently having decided to pretend I wasn't there. Finally he looked up from his stacking and said skeptically, "What's up with you?"

I don't know; perhaps, Justin was thinking that the evening smacked a little of a performance along the lines of act 4, *Hamlet,* enter the mad Ophelia. Whatever he thought, he seemed to have decided to continue to ignore me and went about his business. He started arranging his books on some make-shift shelves constructed of boards and concrete blocks. I snapped out of my speechlessness just as Justin had nearly finished. I was pissed at my sudden recovery which, given the timing, probably didn't seem very convincing. I was about to say something when Justin threw down the last book in his hand, and hissed, "What the fuck do you want from me?"

This seemed exactly the right cue for me to enter the scene, and I said to Justin, "You've just brought me back from the edge of insanity!" I felt myself coming around further and continued, "You are the only one who can possibly understand why I need to do this. Do you have any scissors?"

Justin looked at me as if to say, "Whatever is fixing to transpire—suicide, murder, making paper dollies—I'll be goddamned if I'm the one handing you the scissors." He shook his head no, a little afraid I think, and I went into his kitchen and started rummaging through drawers. As I threw things out on the countertop, I told Justin that I was chopping my braids off in order to play the boyfriend of Danny the Mennonite. I think it took Justin a while to take all this in, and, after it registered, I sensed that he was searching for arguments to keep me from lopping off my locks. Why he should care, I don't know, but he was probably trying to make sense of my sudden return to the land of the living from the deaf-mute state in which I'd entered his apartment.

Finally, he said, "Since you're turning the film on its head, why not play the part with long hair?"

"That's what I thought at first," I answered. I didn't offer a further explanation, but kept pulling things out of drawers and looking for the scissors.

"Don't you think it's a little unfair," he said sarcastically, "to ask me to take responsibility for this? I mean you're acting just a bit erratically, Roe *Náld*," he sneered, overemphasizing the French pronunciation of my name. "What if five minutes from now you're pissed at me for chopping your hair off? If you want your hair cut, why don't you do it yourself?" he asked.

"I will. I'm going to do it anyway, with or without your help," I said desperately, but I knew I would die if Justin wasn't the one to put the blade to my braids. I needed him to touch my hair, to be the one to do it. But what I said to Justin was, "Don't worry, I'll go to the salon and get it evened out tomorrow."

"I don't know what you think you are doing, Roe Náld, but I'm going to bed," Justin said, then went in his room and slammed the door behind him.

My braids had been saved but not the film. So I pulled a steak knife out of the kitchen drawer and doubled one braid over it and sawed until I felt it come loose. I did the same with the other, ignoring the pain of pulled hair. I held them in my hands, for the first time, feeling their weight unanchored. The heft of them impressed me for something that weighed nothing. Should I bury them in the ground like a newborn's umbilical cord? I looked at Justin's door. Should I join him in his bed? How could he turn me down after what I'd just done for him, for the film? Behind the door lay Justin sleeping, and I imagined it locked, no entry possible, Justin as hidden away from me now as since the first day I met him. Was he crouched, shivering in a corner, traumatized by my request? Was he shedding his clothes and slipping under the covers? Was he already slumbering peacefully or tossing and turning, agitated at his failure to do the one thing I had ever asked of him? I would go forward with the film, but nothing could be the same. Our friendship was over, the trust betrayed; this was Judas off to collect his silver, Peter's denials before the final cockcrow. The film would only serve as a bitter reminder of all that I'd lost with Justin, and no matter how well it might be received, it would torture me, and I would know that my artistic successes could never make up for my personal losses.

Nothing remained but to finish the dance scenes before and after the tractor wreck and to cut my losses with Justin and the film. I walked out of the apartment and placed the braids on his concrete steps, where he would find them in the morning, then strode bitterly into the night.

I walked over to the duck pond, hurrying through the park as mallards complained noisily at having to clear a path for me as I made my way furiously past benches and picnic tables. The horde of mosquitoes buzzing around my head helped me make my mind up in a hurry. I would leave the park and go back to Justin's. I would burst in his door, since I'd forgotten to lock it behind me and it would still be open. I would enter his bedroom. I would throw back his bed covers. I would run my finger down the line of his scar, then lay my braids across it.

When I got to Justin's place; however, I just left a note in his mailbox for him to meet me the next day on location to begin shooting some practice footage of "Rabbit Dance." Better this way; I didn't have to speak to him, I'd keep it professional.

On location the next day I was nervous and embarrassed having to see him after begging him to cut my hair. What would be the nature of our relationship now, my having offered him this intimacy, his having turned it down? I sat parked on the gravel road side where we usually met and talked before entering the field. We never crossed over without these rituals together first, little strategy sessions where we put our heads together about what we were going to do and how we'd go about doing it. I had parked under some scrubby post oaks struggling to survive in a sandstone bank. Sitting with my car door open in the little bit of inconsistent shade they offered, I surveyed the ground where I would shoot the dance scene, by far the most complicated bit of film work that I had planned to date given the layers of dance, narrative, and song; the problems of shooting over a field, off by the tree line, and down at the creek; and the technical difficulties of putting all this footage together with the soundtrack so that it flowed as one seamless piece. If I pulled it off, nothing I had ever done before could match it.

I waited a long time. No Justin. Bored, I hopped the fence, but I immediately regretted it, feeling disrespectful to the sanctity of the location without Justin there to make the proper preparations before entering. Like I was just storming the place without the talking and planning that had always come before and our shared camaraderie in these formulations. The pasture even looked different. It had been dry the last few weeks, and weedy yellow dandelions had replaced the variously colored bluebells and firewheels. I decided to take advantage of the wait by cleaning up; I'd need the site cleared for more camera work anyway. People in Oklahoma often use abandoned pastures for dumps. White trash is a literal term, not a metaphorical one, that conflates racial identity with the Okie's most salient characteristic: disregard for everything, even dirt, which he litters over in his own image. I finally finished by dragging an old laundry dryer off toward the woods, cursing the local gods of refuse who see every tree line as a potential landfill. Of course, if you've ever seen the morning after a pow wow, you know our own people drop trash on the ground without a moment's hesitation. What does that make us?

I crossed another fence and walked to the creek where the tractor was supposed to crash after careening down the embankment, making my way through green briar and nettles and finally down to the water, which swirled around a sandbar where a heron stood goggle-eyed at my intrusion. Have you ever seen a water moccasin swim right at you, making many s-s-s-s-ses as he moves on top of the water? Some of them are aggressive, and they'll come right up to your feet, which is what this one did, stopping just before the bank and swimming in place as if he was looking up at me. The snake seemed on the verge of speech; I felt like I was in one of those bad pet movies for kids, like my line should be, "What are you trying to tell me, little feller?" He swam away before he could answer.

I studied the water where he had been swimming just above a submerged trunk, looking into the shadows for crappie hovering in the pool, but I didn't see any. I started back up the path and my eye caught a silvery reflection in a tree. It looked like a lure snagged on a small branch, probably a bad backward cast. I went over and grabbed a leafy shoot and pulled the branch earthward. When I had the spinner down to eye level and looked at it, I could see some words etched in the concave spoon. I popped the rusty treble hook out of the bark and held the lure closer and read, "Cast Master: Spin Your Way to the Bottom." I left the field and waited back in my car, studying my lure, turning it over in my hand, rubbing the rusty spoon with my thumb.

When the other car pulled up in front me, the man who slowly stepped out had on a black patch, like he only had one good eye. His customized license plate read "Sweetheart." A cream-colored beautiful old Ford Fairlane—that car was destined to become a classic. He ambled over slow and friendly and smiling—and holding a ticket pad. He showed his badge, which revealed he was a state game warden. Evidently off duty, given the lack of uniform and state vehicle. "I noticed you come from over the pond," he said, friendly like. I hadn't, but maybe he'd seen me there other days. I was still holding my fishing lure in my hand which didn't look good in terms of my innocence. Hiding it would have hardly been convincing, not to mention the problem of the rusty treble hooks, which would make sticking it in a pocket a permanent act. The officer never let on that he was upset, and he put his right front boot on the bumper of my car, and looked out into the pasture. "Now, son," he continued. "I don't have a thing in the world against you being here."

I hate it when they try to be nice to Indians; it makes them even more patronizing. So I cut him off. "Of course you don't; it's our state."

Don't use sarcasm on the irony impaired. I should have remembered my fundamentals from Don Birchfield's *Oklahoma Basic Intelligence Test.* The officer kept grinning; you'd think a redneck would at least be offended when you question the legal title to his property. But not officer Sandy Dennison, the name I'd read on his badge.

"I just been observing for a couple weeks now you been pulled off to the side of the road. The bass sure have been hitting good lately on those top water lures." He looked down at the rusty culprit in my open palm. "Of course, you gotta get down below the schoolers to get to the really big ones."

Hell, he wanted to see my fishing license, didn't know I had no interest in the pond, only the creek for filming a wreck.

"You wouldn't mind showing me your license would you? If you happen to have it handy," he added, making his request sound optional—except, we both knew it wasn't.

I decided I could play this game of good-ole-boy indirection as well as he could. He had a really strong Oklahoma accent, but not like the white people in the southern part of the state with their copycat Texas and Panhandle drawls. He was from Eastern Oklahoma, all those nuances of thick hillbilly and their Appalachian Scotch-Irish forebears. "Where you from?" I queried.

He didn't act put off at my evasion, just continued to stand there with his foot on the fender, gazing dreamily off at the cows. He seemed like he had all the time in the world. He knew that I wasn't going anywhere, and that he'd eventually write the citation in due time. I had hoped to get a little rise out of him, an Indian assuming the right to speak casually to an officer of the law, pulling the same good-ole-boy act as his.

"Oh, I'm from over McAlester way," he said. "Yeah, if you happen to have that fishing license . . . ," he added whimsically.

I didn't bother to explain or produce a license. I was having too much fun. No chance of a fine; no poles, no tackle, no fish. And here the guy was from McAlester, hometown of my no-show actor. "Do you know Justin Crossman?" I asked. "Student over at OU."

For the first time the fish cop broke out of his grin and frowned. "Yeah, that was terrible what happened to Justin, wasn't it? I hate to see a thing like that. No matter what they say about him. His parents is good people. And him so young."

What? I was confused, the sudden serious transition out of the cat-and-mouse game we'd been playing. And the warden had this bizarre habit of adjusting the strap at the back of his head that held his eye patch in place, as if the damn thing was going to slip down over his mouth, out of which had come this story about Justin. Unlike the Kubrick film, however, all his other limbs were his own—no involuntary Nazi salutes.

"Yeah, they say that other boy didn't even have a driver's license. He could barely see over the windshield. They let these farm kids start driving too damn young. Two cars in a head-on like that, neither one of them had a chance."

Jesus Christ. When could this have possibly happened? It had to have been yesterday. Did Justin drive home because he was upset with me? Had I killed him off with my dramatic intrusion into his apartment and my demand that he cut off my braids?

"Yeah, terrible," I mumbled. I was feeling dizzy. I hoped to god the guy didn't ask me to stand up.

"You wouldn't mind if I had a look-see, then?" It was a rhetorical question; he'd already started walking around the car and peering in the windows. He asked me to open the trunk, and I wobbled over, hoping he didn't think I was drunk. There were no beer cans anywhere in sight, as he must have suspected there would be, as well as no fish. "Well, now, if I was to go over to that pond, I wouldn't find any fishing poles, would I?" he laughed.

"No, you wouldn't."

"I won't even bother crossing the fence, then," he said, patting me on the shoulder so I knew that he'd let me off easy.

"Thanks," I said, without thinking, then hated myself immediately.

"No problem. My mistake." He ambled back over to the Ford, and as he shut the door and started the car up, I tried to review what he had just told me. Instead of thinking, "Justin's dead," my mind wouldn't let go of the part of the conversation where I'd been told that Justin was a good kid, no matter what people said about him. What did they say about him? Was this a reference to his parents' ethnicity or something about Justin himself, an unspoken secret that made him the target of collective backwoods hatred? Now Justin was dead, and maybe I would never know.

The red light flashing on my answering machine back at the house must have served as a beacon that had guided me home since I drove back in a thick fog and not because of the weather. After walking in the door I couldn't even remember how I got there. I had messages from every Indian queen I had ever known. We ran into each other at clubs like Angles. We hung out at after-hours parties at houses and apartments. We became aunties to the new babies running off from rural Indian communities to Okie City and Tulsa to dip into the life. We gave them advice, a couch to sleep on when they needed it; as gay "elders" we passed on wisdom about staying healthy and out of trouble in this racist state where being Indian was hard and being gay and Indian was impossible. We somehow made it not impossible for each other. Our little support system had no formal meetings, no creeds, no name and it ranged from hookers and drug addicts and unemployed disco divas to state employees and tribal politicians and auto mechanics. Oh, you want me to name names, do you? Let me just say it was amazing how we kept up with each other, the contact we had through giving someone a place to crash, helping a person who'd just run away to the city, conversing in the bars and cruising holes on 39th Street, crossing paths at pow wows and other doings, gossiping about the members of our little tribe, and the inevitable fact that everyone had slept with each other at some point—even the ones who didn't want to or were too drunk to fuck each other. That didn't mean we'd ever do it again; twice is not always the charm. I had fallen once or twice for these guys, though I try to uphold my ideal of chivalrous, unrequited love—two star-crossed lovers whose lives are intertwined from birth to death, fate refusing to allow these soul mates to be together. Their love consists of constant yearning, an eternal state of melancholy, a lifetime of the blues.

I sat down at my desk and pushed play.

The first message was from William. "Sorry to hear the news, honey, but to quote the immortal ex-Cherokee-now-disco-queen Cher, 'Do you believe in love after life?' Meaning life goes on and your film will get made, no romantic interpretation intended. Call me if you need to talk." That bitch never did get the lyrics to anything right, but, then again neither could the chanteuse who couldn't make up her mind whether she was from Armenia or Tahlequah, if she even knows where Tahlequah is. I couldn't remember her ever doing a concert there. BLEEP (audibly intoned).

The second message was from Giles. "I'm down in Dallas. The gig sucked, but we get to come home tomorrow; they canceled the last night. Trumpet player is threatening to quit. Fine by me; he can't even follow the chord changes. God, how did I get hooked up in this combo? OK, Roe Náld, don't answer that. I can hear you now. William left a message that I need to give you a call. Ciao, babe." I never got tired of hearing that man's voice, on the machine or in person. Yum, yum.

The third message was from Josh. "Roe Náld, you better read the paper. Check out the guy in the car wreck at McAlester. I hope not, but isn't he in your film? I'm going to call Jimmy." Sure, Josh, I'll buy every Gaylord newspaper in Oklahoma; I hear the Straightlords desperately need the money or maybe another building named after them at Gaylord University in Norman.

The fourth message was from Jimmy himself. "Josh just called me at work. He said he thought that Justin was killed. Sorry. Call us." Yikes, couples! Even their phone messages start to sound the same. Please shoot me should I ever be foolish enough to run off and get married.

Early the next week, I called my mom, Delia, and asked her to accompany me to the funeral. I couldn't help it; with the demise of the film and all, I felt like a widowed Jackie Kennedy, mourning yet trying to be brave for the cameras. I could use some support, and I knew I wouldn't let myself go all creepy and maudlin if someone went with me. Mom had driven up the morning of the service, and we sat visiting for an hour or so in the coffee shop, where I had spent so many hours with Justin, before me and mom took off on the long drive over to McAlester.

My mom was a good choice. I enjoyed catching up with her on the drive over. After I had graduated from film school at UCLA, tried to make some independent films in New York, got a little critical attention and won a couple of competitions but had gone belly up financially, I had finally moved back to Oklahoma, settling for Norman as the least redneck city in the state, an atypical oasis with some sort of intellectual and arts community because of the university. My mom and I had grown closer since I'd come back home, much closer than we had ever been when I was growing up. As an Indian woman in rural Oklahoma in the 1960s, my mom hadn't had too many opportunities for education and work, other than raising me and my brother and doing some part-time house cleaning to help make ends meet. She married young and never graduated from high school, though she would have liked to, and she had really emphasized education to us kids. My older brother had disappointed her a little by dropping out himself when, unlike her, he had the choice of staying in and graduating.

When I moved back home a curious thing happened. My mom began her education—not a formal one by enrolling in classes, but, vicariously, through me at first until she took off on her own. She would ask me what books to read, and the subject matter made no difference; she devoured them all, seemingly starved for intellectual nurturance. She read political essays, novels, interviews with artists, books of poetry, anything I gave her. At first she depended on me, and I had to pull a book off the shelf of a library or store and physically place it in her hands. I would take her to see films, ones that she would never see with my dad, the few foreign or art house movies that we could watch in Oklahoma City. She'd drive up all the way from Carnegie and meet me, then stay in my apartment and go back home the next morning. I became her entry point into the art and intellectual world. In the last couple years she had "graduated," though. She no longer needed me to recommend anything, and she had developed the feelings and knowledge to make her own choices. Now she called me up and asked me to go see films and told me what she'd heard about them or which other movies by the same director that she liked or disliked. Mostly she had just needed me to point her in the right direction and say, "Start here," or "See if you like this."

Early on in my mom's education, one of the most puzzling problems was how to respond to her own son's films. Although proud of the whole educational process I'd gone through in order to learn filmmaking and the fact that I'd graduated from UCLA and that some of the stuff was starting to get some regional attention so that relatives and people in her tribe knew me as a filmmaker, the stuff that she had seen didn't really tell a story in the manner that she was used to. But this had brought us even closer together as I tried to explain to her what I was doing, and she had asked a lot of questions. For the first time in our lives, we had a mutual interest, something to talk about.

When asked to speak at a local showing of my work at a gallery or some other small venue, I never backed down from the gay aspects of the films. What was the point? They could see the subject matter with their own eyes, and some damn Indian artist somewhere needed to be out. I was sick and tired of all the ridiculous closet cases. Who were they fooling other than themselves? Why should they pretend not to be gay? This was as ridiculous as if they were to somehow try to disguise the fact that they were Indian. During these discussions after showings of my work, which sometimes occurred in front of a few members of our tribe or other Native people we knew, my mother would sit with such a sense of refined dignity that it was imposing to the point of intimidating any of the homophobes from our community who might have been present. Her bearing suggested a challenge, as in "I dare you to question the subject matter of my son's films." Nobody was brave enough to tangle publicly with my proud Indian mother, though god only knows what they said on their way home. What worried me more recently regarding my mom was, given her highly developed taste and all, what did she think of this low-budget stuff I was filming out in the pastures of rural Oklahoma? I sensed that maybe she wished that I would go back to New York and try to make another go of it.

Justin's funeral wasn't exactly an art opening or a film preview, the kind of event I usually attended with my mom—it was more like a closing. We'd brought the newspaper obituary along with us, and we found the church easily enough when we got to McAlester. The funeral service was a Catholic Mass, and I was nervous at having dragged my Baptist mother along, but, as usual, her curiosity about how other people did things kept her interested enough that she didn't lose patience with all the standing and sitting and kneeling. I was glad though when it finally came time to come forward and receive communion so me and my mom could sit down in our pews while the faithful received the body and blood of Christ within a few feet of the body and blood of the car wreck. As the family began their sad procession, I tried to identify some revealing sign of kinship, a facial or physical similarity, a movement that I could connect to Justin, something that might explain him to me.

The first communicant was an old man who held out his hands to receive the host, his tired face never even looking up at the priest. Young kids came forward and returned to their seats, uninterested and fidgety as they waited for the funeral to end. No sign of Jill, the girlfriend—very strange. No recognizable sibling or parent, though any number of people passed by who could have been either. As relatives rose up and filed back to their seats, nothing further was revealed to me. Justin was still an impenetrable mystery. After the Mass, some of the family went up to the coffin to pay their last respects. My mom said to me, "Let's get out of here. I hear this is when these people really start to make a scene."

I couldn't leave just yet. I'd poured body and soul into this film. It was as if Danny the Mennonite and his boyfriend were calling from beyond the grave, "Roe Náld, don't let them forget us." Funerals gross me out with all their sentimental morbidity, but I had to look at Justin one last time, and I felt myself rising, moving toward the coffin, pulled by some invisible force and unable to retreat. Surprisingly, there was my mother, moving by my side, though I thought she'd be disgusted with me and go wait out in the car. Maybe it was the heat; anyone would melt outside sitting in an automobile.

People were chatting as the line moved forward, none of it about Justin. The kind of small talk people make in a movie theater queue, except this line was moving faster. Just in front of us, an old lady in a fake ermine stole and glitzy costume earrings was talking about compost, her husband's failure at proper soil tillage, and the blighted cucumbers they'd have to live with all summer. She would touch her husband's arm every time she said "blighted," a guilty reminder of his lack of responsibility. My mother nodded toward the cucumber lady and said, "I hope they have the ground ready for this one." Mom had a terrible habit of making us laugh in solemn places, and we'd grown up suppressing hilarity at church, tribal meetings, and family reunions, sometimes to the point of nearly injuring ourselves from swallowed laughter. I tried to keep from breaking into a grin or laughing out loud as we careened toward Justin. The viewing line felt like we were hiking down hill toward the coffin; our footsteps heavy thuds, an imaginary incline almost pulling us into a jog if we'd let it.

I had a sudden thought that terrified me. Somehow, when I got to Justin's coffin, I wouldn't be able to restrain myself from touching him in front of all these people. I'd want to stop, but the more I'd touch him, the more I'd want to continue until I'd be groping him in a frenzy that would freak everybody way out. I was creeping myself out, as a matter of fact, and I saw myself as Frankenstein's creation, tottering toward the casket, arms extended, waiting for my chance to embrace Justin while the crowd looked on in horror. Maybe I'd rip off his shirt and kiss his scar.

Now we were close enough to see Justin's shoes: Doc Martens, a terrible choice considering the more formal gray double-breasted suit they'd dressed him in. The cucumber lady kept pushing her husband forward as if he were a balking steer freezing up before being prodded into a cattle chute. She had just about moved him in position for viewing when one of Justin's arms jerked so hard that it landed over his handkerchiefed pocket, as though he might remove the delicately folded monogrammed linen and wave it over the side of the coffin.

Everyone in the line turned and looked at my mother, waiting for an explanation. She shrugged and said, "Oh, they do that sometimes. Just nerves or something."

The cuke lady sighed, "Well, then," and her husband moved past the body, this time without urging.

"We should have brought a gift or something," my mother said, as we stood there looking at Justin. "Do you have anything to give them, Ronald?"

"Who?" I asked.

"The family," my mother said, looking at me in exasperation. "This one's dead. Maybe we can find something out in the car."

We never got a chance. When we returned to our pew and sat down, Justin already had one leg over the coffin. He was sitting up and looking around, a little disoriented at first, as if he'd woken up in an unfamiliar room, but quickly regaining his composure. He looked out over the congregation and smiled, then stepped elegantly from the coffin in a gold lamé evening dress and clutching a little white designer purse to his side—Dolce and Gabbana, designer Italian. He strode right up to the front pew without missing a beat and shook hands with each person sitting there, fingertips presented regally, body posed perfectly in the tight-fitting dress, head cocked a little to the side as he bent at the knees and whispered in a sad yet seductively throaty voice, "Thank you for coming." He never even looked at me, which I thought was pretty rude, considering. He was evasive in his resurrection as in life. Now that he was back from the dead, we could start shooting again, which was probably exactly the reason he was avoiding me.

At first the congregation just sat in stunned silence, mouths agape, but now people were starting to talk as Justin moved down his self-styled receiving line. A sea of faces, hidden behind hands, started whispering, and by the time he'd moved to the front pew on the other side of the church, they were growing more and more vocal.

"Not only did he rise from the dead," said the cucumber lady's husband, "but he's a little queer acting."

The priest, who was removing his vestments, turned and said to the altar boy, "His family's all like that. Every time I baptize or bury one of them, somebody's got to get out of line. You know what they say about them."

Back in the pew, the cucumber lady herself said, "Maybe he's coming out?" more puzzled than sure of her statement.

"At his funeral?" I asked sarcastically. I was no longer impressed with this overblown performance. I was trying not to be mad at Justin, given all he'd put me through lately, but, dammit, just a minute ago he'd been as still as the statue I'd first seen him in front of, and now he was up and about, getting all this attention. I never trusted that sculpture, the way its drumstick was raised in midair and words formed on its lips; its lack of movement raised my suspicions. The carved singer wasn't an artist's sculpture, fixing to defy the rules of stone, step out of his rock form, and begin to greet visitors coming up the sidewalk to the museum. No, there was a living person hiding inside the white rock, refusing to step out, and making me want to dance whenever I walked by, and now I had to walk around the other side of the building just to avoid losing control whenever I passed the Fred Jones Museum of Art. My customary path had been diverted.

My mom seemed to have grown tired of the whole business and stood up to leave. Everybody ceased talking and stared at her. "Quit acting like Indians," she scolded, then walked out of the church, head held high, the novel *Vanity Fair* tucked under her arm.

I became aware that we were being watched. I turned, and at the back of the vestry was a man with a video camera on a tripod. Engaged couples, knowing I made movies, had frequently insulted me by asking me to videotape their weddings. When times were hard, nonetheless, I'd obliged them in order to scrape up some quick cash. But a funeral? This defies all credibility.

We were being filmed.

Art, Death, Desire

This work of novelistic criticism focuses on the relationship between visual, narrative, and performance art, as well as the way it shapes those who create it.

What could possibly motivate the artist or intellectual who makes the obscure historical figure the subject of his or her investigation? In my own case I think of my fascination with Lynn Riggs, a writer I take up in the fourth chapter, and often wonder why I keep publishing on a person who might only make my potential audience grow smaller. The tenure process, and the trivia it engenders, became a moot point for me in 2001. So why do I do it? Why does an artist give up free time, neglect friends, family, recreation—a life?

Because he falls, hard, for the subject of his art. Sometimes even physically attracted to those we depict (And who wouldn't be, since in our own heads we make them over into whatever we want them to be?), we get off on the person, not just the act of depicting. We probably should be getting off on something or someone else. Often we feel as if we are cheating on one or all the parties in the affair—real loved ones, fictional characters, ourselves, and the biggest cuckold of all, death—whether or not we consciously consider these quagmires. Those who research historical fiction enter the special collection like a crypt, an image taken up in countless literary renditions of the archive, and the affair is a little like falling for a stiff. And it's hardly metaphorical, since often the subject of the study has spent years underground. Perhaps we hope people will keep coming around visiting us after we, too, are long gone, even if they disturb papers, documents, and the sacred materials we were interred with. We hope they'll sing the right songs to open and close our bundles yet one more time. I'm reminded of tenor saxophone player Jim Pepper's rendition of the old 49: "Do not forget me when I'm long gone, for I love you so, sugar honey."

My own necrophilia in relation to Lynn Riggs has always had something to do with his inscrutability. The more I have delved into the archive—and it has been a deep probing, if you will, into letters, journals, criticism, and the plays themselves—the less certain I am I really understand Riggs. A man who received letters from friends, by the hundreds, if not thousands, many of whom claimed that the time they spent with him during a play production, on a movie set, in the city of Santa Fe, and so on, was the most meaningful in their entire life, is matched only by a man who can never bring the same level of joy to himself. While I have posited a good number of theories as to why this is, the truth is, I'm stumped. And the more Lynn Riggs resists my intellectual advances, the greater the ardor of my pursuit.

In the curiously titled "The Song of Roe Náld," Justin, the subject of Roe Náld's artistic gaze, and the gaze of his camera, is such a figure. Take for instance, Justin's mysterious sensitivity about his scarred shoulder, his off-limits apartment, his girlfriend, Jill, whose very existence seems suspect, Roe Náld's susceptibility to rumors reflected in the game warden's report: "I hate to see a thing like that. No matter what they say about him."

Indeed, what do they say about him, and what is Justin's relationship to some larger community other than the scrutiny of Roe Náld and the machine he carries with him, his intrusive soul catcher, his own film archive? Because Justin does not fall prey to Roe Náld's seduction, by camera or otherwise, Roe Náld cannot let him go. Unfulfilled desire drives the artistic impulse in the story, and a camera in hand, whether pointing it (Roe Náld) or leading it on (Justin), whether the one "shooting" or the one being jizzed on, becomes the central chaos necessary for artistic risk and unpredictability. Justin's terminal ending, the car crash, does not suffice if the story is to maintain the integrity of its chaos, its open-endedness. Anyone knows however many times the Road Runner might run over Coyote with an Acme truck, the Coyote will be resurrected for additional rounds of pianos falling off cliffs and smashing him to smithereens, and an eternity of other delicious tortures—no matter how much some might want to roast that chipper bird on a spit, as one novel would have it.

Death's nemesis, its enabler in a co-dependent relationship, is eternity, and the artist's obsession with his subject involves a keen attraction to both: loving one, hating the other—and neither emotion is stable—a topic explored at some great length in Oscar Wilde's *The Picture of Dorian Gray.* There are many deaths in "The Song of Roe Náld," and even, one might note, the occasional resurrection. Here I am suggesting that we leave the erection in resurrections. Roe Náld dies for the camera when he plays Danny's fated lover, for the film when he sacrifices his braid to realism, and for performance when he swaps his improvisational voice that opens the story to a more scripted, analytical one—essentially the voice of a critic—that characterizes his storytelling after the visit to the cow pasture–cum–film site outside Lexington. Art captures an image forever; or, so we think until we find out art also must square its account with finitude: moths eat canvas, film cans rust, and university presses let our books go out of print. In Wilde's exploration of these matters immortality has its price, a certain ironic ugliness, even repulsion. Those who write vampire bestsellers also seem to know this.

Desire's firstborn might be a slightly disturbing obsession with the artistic subject, but the second born could be out and out hatred. I do not know how true it is, but rumor has it that by the time Leslie Marmon Silko finished *Almanac of the Dead* she despised the book. If the story is more than apocryphal, she certainly wouldn't be the first artist whose creation found himself cradled in the arms of a less-than-enthusiastic parent, more of an ugly stepchild than beloved heir. See *Frankenstein,* dear reader. One could easily imagine, after staring so long at the witchery that is America, Silko may have been marked by the deadlier side effects of artistic desire. This is what happens when you write about something real instead of Indian grandmothers, mixed-bloods, and tricksters.

In Roe Náld's case, his growing ambivalence with his artistic subject, which started out as a repressed physical attraction to the flesh and blood Justin, has to do with Justin's usurpation of Roe Náld's movie; Justin is the trusted loyal subject who betrays his King. Those who do not like Roe Náld may wonder what ever made him think he could be King in the first place. Those who make films, however, might simply argue they call you the director for a reason, and those who dare create art of any stripe might recognize the frustration involved when artistic projects burgeon out of control. They can take on a life of their own, and this is both their power and danger.

Justin's increasing control of the film, and Roe Náld's deeply troubling realization that the movie cannot go on without Justin, says something about the artist's vexed relationship with his muse. Secretly, the artist wants to believe he created the muse and not the other way around. At the heart of this particular love affair, rooted in a singular insecurity, is this question: Are my ideas really my own? Or am I simply a pipeline through which flows all that came before me? In this case one's lover not only seeks independence from his creator (one of the themes of the aforementioned *Frankenstein,* surely), but credit for his very creation! How much recognition does one give to his "individual talent," to borrow T. S. Eliot's phrase, rather than the tradition that precedes him and the contemporary persons that inspire him? Can't I at least get credit for the fictional characters I make up, since, after all, they did not exist before I gave them life? Or did they? Who could have ever predicted they would be such ingrates? If I can shift art forms for a second, there are only twelve notes in the Western musical scale, and when I play a guitar solo the chances of improvising something entirely original are simply illusory.

It is best not to think about these matters too much, and most divas don't.

In Roe Náld's case, simply put, how much of the credit should go to Justin: his muse, his inspiration, and the subject of his study? After the high-blown drama of the braid snipping—one is reminded, I hope, just a little, of Alexander Pope's *The Rape of the Lock*—the deterioration of Roe Náld's relationship to Justin is marked. One wonders to what degree the downward spiral occurs in Roe Náld's head, and if Justin feels similarly, but Justin is not the viewpoint character, and his motivations remain obscured.

One's hair, like other parts of one's body, is a highly personal possession—part of one's corporeal sovereignty, I would say. One might wonder not only about Roe Náld's personal sovereignty, but whatever happened to tribal sovereignty in this story? We will return to this question later.

Asking Justin to take Roe Náld's braids in hand, wield the blade, and lop off the locks, shows how far Roe Náld has transgressed any kind of professional artistic detachment, in which one sacrifices personal involvement for the good of the finished project by staying aloof rather than getting involved with the actors.

In the latter regard, one of the factors that defies credibility is the fact there is only one actor. Where in the world is the rest of the cast?

Playing Danny's lover Roe Náld, pinned under the harrow blade, calls into question whether this is about making a film or making Justin, whatever Roe Náld's comments may be about being in love with no one but the camera. Can he really separate the camera that way from those he points it at? Such have always been the dangers of the medium. Wrapped up in these layers of desire is a competition between the rational and irrational, underscored by Roe Náld's thoughts of charging into Justin's bedroom and laying his sawed-off braids against Justin's scarred shoulder. Ironically, rationality wins out in Roe Náld's case, at least to whatever extent it is measured by the switch to a more detached analytical voice, the voice of criticism that lays out a significant portion of the rest of the story, and Roe Náld's decision, however precarious, of keeping his distance from Justin and finishing the film. Of course, keeping things under control only lasts for a short period of time, the loss of it reaching its peak at the funeral, where even Justin's corpse refuses to follow the rules.

Rationality, the friend of the critic to some degree, is a more dubious companion to the artist, and this has created a great deal of tension between those who make art and those who discuss it. The same personal involvement that gets Roe Náld in trouble in the first place also comprises the energy that inspires the very content of the film. Here Apache artist Allen Houser's sculpture in front of the music building on the Norman campus, an artistic subject that both opens and closes the story, plays an important role. The first depiction of the statue emphasizes two kinds of performers, a dancer and a singer; two kinds of artistic cultures, European ballet and tribal music; two kinds of bodies, stone and flesh; two kinds of motion, frozen and fluid; two kinds of vision, a stone exterior and the life inside; and two kinds of sexuality, a glistening homoeroticism and a stony heterosexuality.

The final image of the beautiful Houser sculpture, which is depicted in relation to Justin's resurrection, bridges all these oppositions. The dangerous aspect of the statue has always been the way its very posture, drumstick raised in midair, threatens to break out of stone just as Justin does in increments— the jerk of an arm, the leg that lifts rakishly over the side of the casket, and finally the diva who steps out of the coffin fully coiffed and dressed to, well, not so much to kill since that would be redundant. Similarly the very stillness of the Houser statue, contrasted with its suggestions of movement, foreshadows its invigoration. It's rather like watching a mime pretending to be a statue.

My parents were taken in by a mime imitating a Will Rogers monument the other day in downtown Oklahoma City, and my partner could do nothing to persuade them they were looking at a human, something the mime must have enjoyed immensely; this has to be the greatest compliment a mime can receive. And the compliment, of course, can only be finally bestowed by the mime's own movement that reveals the great artistry in the deception. The mime reveals his art by breaking free of it, moving, and giving away the ending. If, unlike my parents, you're standing close enough to the statue to recognize a person, you want to stay there until you catch him breaking his pose, a different game than being taken in and walking by.

On November 19, 2006, Western Cherokee principal chief Chad Smith published a column on the editorial page of the Muskogee Phoenix about the upcoming Oklahoma state centennial and attempts to claim Will Rogers as native son. Smith's point was simple and profound: Rogers was born in the Cherokee Nation, Indian Territory, not Oklahoma, and he left the nation and the territory before it became a state and resided elsewhere, eventually California, for the rest of his life. Rogers, therefore, can be claimed as a native son of the Cherokee Nation, and Indian Territory, but not of the state of Oklahoma, where he never lived. The gist of Smith's observations is that

Oklahoma has created a statue, a monument, that they cannot claim as their own; in fact the statue has been stolen from its rightful owners. Further implied by the Smith article is the problem of depictions that lock living people inside stone, the way monolithic totality may conflict with lived realities. The living being inside the stone might come back to life when someone like Smith decides to talk back to the statue and those Oklahomans who too easily claim it as their own.

Is Justin real, or has he ever been anything more than Roe Náld's shifting perceptions of the Houser statue? And if that's "all" that Justin is, might this be enough, given the beauty of the statue and its ability to evoke such wildly creative imaginings? A question we will explore later in the chapter is this: how much does the artist owe to social realism? To what degree must Justin be a person rather than a stone carving?

The statue and Justin—Song and Dance, Roe Náld dubs them—are two of many instances of doubles in the story. In the Socratic dialogues dramatized in Plato's writings, Aristophanes, the great comic playwright, gives a speech that recalls the origin story of humans as perfect doubles, joined at the navel, with duplicate faces, ears, genitals, and all other body parts. Zeus found such powerful creatures a threat, cut them in half, and had Apollo repair the mess, so the resulting beings could get around after their 50-percent reduction, a bit like Siamese twins separated at birth. The problem was that taking the scalpel perfectly down the central dividing line also had a spiritual effect, and their "very essence," to borrow Aristophanes' phrase, also got split in two. Humans to this day are searching for their missing half, and this is also the origin story for sexual orientation: former half-males, half-females became hetero; half-males and half-males became gay men; half-females and half-females became lesbians. Reuniting with the lost half is the driving force behind the human impulse to search for the love of his or her life. The perfect match with an intimate companion restores the seeker to his lost self. In this sense all sexual acts are masturbatory ones.

Roe Nald, like all artists before him, is not only trying to capture the essence of Justin on film; he is trying to present images of himself through Justin, to heal the parts of himself that remain other, unknowable, elusive, shrouded in mystery—even to his own understanding of himself as subject. Some aspect of this knowledge will always be encased in stone, and the degree to which it reveals itself may be beyond the artist's control.

The Houser statue is so lovely in all its suggestiveness that I am going to make an artistic decision here to shut up and leave it to readers to create their own story about the statue and its relationship to Roe Náld, Justin, and their own artistic lives. If you come to OU, I hope you get here before they take it down and replace it with something far less interesting. If you make it in time, spend some time with the drummer, and see if you can stand still.

No doubt readers will notice that "The Song of Roe Náld" is a very different work than *Drowning in Fire,* and that this musing proceeds along different lines than *Red on Red.* First, I do not have any intention to keep writing the same book over and over again, but let me also say something about this seeming departure from Muskogee Creek concerns.

I made my protagonist Wichita and Caddo for a reason. The Indian art world is, and has always been, very much a plains (northern and southern), and a southwestern, phenomenon. There are exceptions we can all name, of course, but the truth remains no Indian artist is unaffected by the influence of these regions, even if her intentions are to deviate from them. I wanted a Southern Plains artist because I wanted the story to have to suggest the un-wieldy prominence of the plains in Indian art, even if this isn't its major theme. I also wanted Roe Náld to have a braid, an unlikely adornment on a Creek man. I didn't want to figure out how to make him both Creek and braided. Wichita and Caddo origins also straddle geographies between the southern plains and Southeast—another factor in my choice.

My story is not a reflection of how Wichita and Caddo concerns might inform interpretations, a subject I would be ill equipped to address. Rather it is a compendium of pop culture references from movies, television, drama, Greek myth, the Oklahoma legislative season, and local state school rivalries. There are also direct and indirect references to Indian art; the centrality of the Allen Houser statue is important, but did anyone catch the subtle references to a particular Joy Harjo poem, and to one of Simon Ortiz's as well? I've hidden lots of secrets throughout my books, and most go unremarked upon by readers. Most prominently, Roe Nald's is very much a story about European and Euro-American popular film, an art medium that has a tremendous impact on my own thinking. (In *Red on Red* I have a letter that is about Alfred Hitchcock's *Strangers on a Train,* a foreshadowing of things to come).

The story, obviously, moves in and out of many worlds, tribal and non-tribal. I have long maintained that arguments to the effect that artistic quality is diminished by tribally specific subject matter, or even limited by being identified simply as Indian, are absurd. Roe Náld may seem less certain about these matters, but Roe Náld is not Craig Womack.

Roe Náld says, "It [obnoxious posturing at a party] was part of what made me want to leave for New York where I could be just a damn filmmaker, not a damn Indian filmmaker." I wanted to imagine the other guy, the Indian artist who sees the world this way, all the people I've shared writing panels with who claim they don't write for Indians, but they write for "everybody" (many of them have positions on this much more nuanced than Roe Náld's).

While making my concerns tribally specific over the years, I have also argued for opening up tribally specific subject matter as broadly as possible—that is, erring on the side of inclusivity rather than exclusivity. If one takes this stance, admittedly an imperfect one, the troubling question remains: what is the bottom line, the minimal criteria of what makes something tribal? Creeks, for example, faced this dilemma several years ago when citizens first started debating whether the Creek National Holiday should include a pow wow, a foreign tradition, as part of their celebration (the pow wow supporters eventually prevailed). Answering these questions is difficult, and I wanted to create a story that straddles the bottom line, the minimal criteria.

Is "The Song of Roe Náld" liberatory because of its refusal to trot out the usual beads and feathers both non-Indian—and often even Indian—readers demand, or does it fail to maintain a minimal tribal integrity? How do you tell the difference? Can we bring readers up to a level where they might understand the reasons some Creeks might have concerns about a pow wow at a Creek holiday? Will our audience ever be that smart? Will very many people be troubled enough to wonder about the integrity of "The Song of Roe Náld?" What does Roe Náld himself want from Justin, the film, himself, his tribe? Given the subject of his films, why mention belonging to a tribe at all? These are essential questions.

At this point in my life I cannot answer all of these, and maybe I never will. In defense of Roe Náld I will assert two tribally specific criteria that I believe he meets successfully. Stories take place, as they say, and this story engages a very specific geography, as does Roe Náld's film which names a particular environ, Perkins, Oklahoma. I remain enough of an essentialist to argue that a landless Indian literature is no Indian literature at all, and by this I mean a literature that refuses to locate itself on a map in relation to a particular community (and no, I don't buy the argument that maps are a European construct).

While Lexington, and Lawton, two of the film locations, are not within Wichita or Caddo jurisdiction per se, my opinion is that the tribal artist will narrate specific landscapes wherever he or she might "land" (see Joy Harjo's poem "The Place the Musician Became a Bear," for example, about Creek concerns in Brooklyn). To me, this is what it means to be an Indian artist. It also so happens that this is what it means to be an artist, period. (I realize that in visual art in which towns, and various geographies, are depicted by visual images rather than narrative ones, the task of creating land works differently than for writers who I'm more qualified to analyze). At any rate, such endeavors intensify for Native artists because of the inevitable reality of claiming and maintaining land given the constant threat of its loss to tribes.

"The Song of Roe Náld," then, takes land out of its usual jurisdictions in relation to a Wichita-Caddo filmmaker, yet Roe Náld is still focused on describing particular places, reflecting on their meaning, and considering the aesthetic options available to him in depicting them:

> So everything seems to be falling apart here," I went on, "but there's always this incredible integrity that shines through. That's Oklahoma. I know that sounds stupid, but I mean how can you describe an Oklahoma evening next to a farm pond like this?" A meadowlark sang up a storm from a fence post, and the bluebells were in full bloom in all of their breathtaking purples, so I didn't need to go into any details about what I meant. Just sitting there as bass started to rise and feed on the insects landing on the water, and the quality of the dusky early evening, put the junkyard in sharp relief, even under the overcast sky.

These natural images are more than pastoral; by placing them near Lexington we can ascertain, if we are willing to do our homework, that they are within the Chickasaw Nation, for example. This constitutes a different act, I hope, than writing romances about "the people" in some vague geography that the author never quite names concretely. Roe Náld, as does Harjo in the tribute to Jim Pepper, not only reflects on a landscape away from Wichita and Caddo country but also relates it to the meaning of present-day Oklahoma which, of course, is part of the Wichita and Caddo homescape, too. There is an Indian culture that is definitively Oklahoman and shared between the thirty-nine tribes there. If you grew up Indian in the state, then you might know the words to "Heleluyvn," even if you're not a Creek Christian; you won't scratch your head if someone starts talking about 49s, even if you're not Kiowa; and there's a good chance you'll be aware there are some damn good stomp dance leaders around Miami, Oklahoma, who excel at an art form that is not part of their tradition, and they even have competitions—a bizarre notion to those of us in the stomp dance religion. If you grew up Indian in Albuquerque you could articulate a similar body of shared knowledge, things that Navajos know about Hopi practices, for example, that formulate a regional consciousness that comes from living in a particular place. Whatever "The Song of Roe Náld" lacks in tribal specificity, it nonetheless has some of this territorial sensibility, as in Indian Territory sensibility, a term that itself illustrates a shared Oklahoma knowledge since we know this means the political status of tribes before statehood, not some vague "territory" or frontier. I would argue that "The Song of Roe Náld" captures in some small way an Oklahoma sensibility (even if through Oscar Wilde), and its Okieness is part of its tribal integrity. Even Roe Nald's expressions of hatred for the place amplify the story's relationship to Oklahoma.

The second sign of Roe Náld's tribally specific integrity is his refusal to leave the territory. He is the exceedingly rare Oklahoma artist who has not fled Oklahoma (this would be truer of artists with national reputations, almost none of whom ever stay). Some might criticize Roe Náld's seeming lack of references to Oklahoma tribal subject matter, but would any of these critics have the balls to actually try surviving in the state where Roe Náld lives day in and day out? There will always be a good many people with much to say about Oklahoma who don't live there. And, don't get me wrong, we need them.

But there's something to be said for both depicting Oklahoma and living in the actual place. Carter Revard's sarcastic response to those who have much to say about the state and little to show for actually living here (ironic, perhaps, given that Revard lives outside the territory yet had a rich upbringing here) is apropos. His poem, "In Oklahoma," the word "in," the first word of the title, being the most important preposition, if not the most important word in the poem, addresses the geographically estranged Oklahoma experts: "Shall I tell you a secret, Gert? You have to be there before it's there. Daddy, would you pass them a plate of fish? See friends, it's not a flyover here. Come down from your planes and you'll understand. Here" (3).

As for Roe Náld, does he stay in Oklahoma because he is particularly brave, or has he simply acquiesced to mediocrity, something that happens to many of us who remain in the state—like those who stay in a bad marriage out of fear of risk and change? Roe Náld's mother seems to believe the greater valor would be in Roe Náld striking out, not for the territory but New York again, where he could further mature as an artist.

I'm not Roe Náld's mother, exactly, so I'm going to give him credit for staying here because at the end of the day I want to cut myself some slack for the same thing even if it's less brave than I would like to believe. If you lived in a state, and some of you do, where art councils are made up of white Southern Baptist Sunday school teachers, you'd know what I mean. If you add to this tribes trying to pass hate legislation against gay marriage or attempting to disenfranchise African American citizens as if the civil rights laws of the 1950s and 1960s never occurred (often both), you might give Roe Náld a break. Roe Náld doesn't have a chance in hell here, yet he perseveres. Most people would, and have, run. I make no promises; I may be soon on their heels. Yet, like countless numbers of my relatives, I might run back.

In addition to these concerns about our state, "The Song of Roe Náld" is a vehicle for discussing some of the more universal aspects of the role of the artist. In this regard, the story carries forward that very Wildean notion of art that can turn into loathing, or fear and loathing according to one gun-toting psychedelic. Multiple images of water, fish, mermen, drowning, and even fishing lures that promise to sink to the bottom, suggest what Creeks would consider an essential Lower World characteristic: unpredictability. As Roe Náld's project spins out of control, and his fear and loathing of Justin amplifies as he associates him with the source of the chaos, a curious thing, perhaps, happens to readers who may start to find Roe Náld more than a little obnoxious.

This projection of a reader's, or viewer's, hatred onto a character or the artistic medium that portrays him is not unusual. When we view experimental films, for example, sometimes they are just too damn weird, so much so they are simply boring, and we make fun of the French or the filmmaker or the characters. We like thinking, we tell ourselves, and we like challenges and even claim we appreciate the disruptions that make us approach narrative skeptically by drawing attention to its own artifice, or so we say, but there is also a very human need for cohesive, entertaining storytelling. People buy genre fiction for a reason; its rhythms and pacing constitute a real attraction. Scholars like Walter Ong have described how certain rhythms of repetition actually have a physiological appeal and serve as mnemonic devices in the oral tradition (which I'm not equating with genre fiction). When patterns of cohesiveness are shattered in experimental art a somewhat natural attraction is abandoned, and we only have so much patience for weirdness for weirdness's sake before boredom overtakes our generosity toward learning from narrative subversion.

In this way a narrator like Roe Náld becomes suspect. He is in a borderlands position of breaking our trust when we hear how weird his actual films are, but he also finds ways to keep us on board by stringing us along with a fairly cohesive and entertaining story about how one of those films is getting made—or not getting made. We might think, OK, as long as I don't have to watch the damn thing.

Somewhere along the route of this bumpy but entertaining ride (fasten your seatbelts, La Bette would remind us), readers might ask this question: can I believe anything Roe Náld has to say?

Clues abound that the answer may well be no. We might wonder, for example, about the opening statement that seems to give away the farm, to reveal the story's ending at the beginning. Students in our classes always say, "Don't tell me the ending"—a difficult demand in a teaching situation where you need to analyze the story and endings most frequently are relevant to that analysis. In the context of fiction itself, however, the narrator usually keeps the ending for the end. Since the narrator gives away Justin's death at the outset, the reader is put on guard about issues of reliability even though the story later reveals that Justin's death is not the ending at all—the ending is his resurrection.

Careful readers might also note the story begins with some information that will later be contradicted. There were no scissor-blade snips of Roe Náld's braids; he sawed them off himself with a steak knife, at least according to a later version of the story. It seems the more poetic snip is claimed in the second paragraph as a means of heightening Roe Náld's performance by creating the metaphor of editing film and quoting the famous Hitchcock statement to effect in regards to the perfect murder. This is a means of dramatically "artsifying" Roe Náld's own experience which we may suspect could be a good deal more mundane than the way he tells it. There are many other contradictions I'll leave to readers to discover.

Some sentences suggest an ongoing process of revision of Roe Náld's story: "I hurried over to the drama department. Such a busy day! I strategized as I strode. No, not briskly. Make that meandered." The last two phrases, which directly address the reader, indicate that not only might Roe Náld change the facts of his story, but that he expects his listener to understand this to be the case.

A stylistic shift occurs from the breathless oral performances, replete with artistic flourishes, that characterize the complex sentences in the first part of the story to the shorter, more emphatic, declarative sentences that characterize the analytical voice after the visit to the cow pasture outside of Lexington, the film's major location. The single sentence that is the second paragraph is one of the longest I've ever written, and the sentence about first spying Justin in front of the Houser statue (the one that starts "If *you* were walking . . .) is a real whopper, too, pun intended in relation to both length and issues of verisimilitude.

All of this relates to Roe Náld's credibility. Is Roe Náld the critic—a role indicated by his more analytical diction in later parts of the story, criticism usually being associated with non-fiction and rationality—telling the truth? Or is Roe Nald the performer who we "pay" to lie to us, speaking with a great level of ornamentation and dramatic flourish that we might more often associate with fiction? What happens when you so thoroughly mix up the two roles, a question, obviously, of a great deal of concern to me personally given the way I write both as critic and storyteller, often in the same work.

Since "Roe Náld" embeds so many stories inside other stories, a real question is this: when do any of these actually touch the earth? What is the relationship between the narration and mimesis, social reality? We have, for example, the surreal cyclops of a game warden who steps out of a 49 song, compounded by the absurd ending and the last line, which reveals the possibility that every aspect of Roe Náld's narration might occur only in his imagination. Specifically, it may be a mere matter of brainstorming one of his plans for another weird film, but there is no real way to be certain.

A key issue here, actually examined at great length in N. Scott Momaday's essay "The Man Made of Words," is the meaning of the word "only" that I just used myself in one of the previous sentences. I have quoted Momaday on these matters so many times before that I will just briefly paraphrase here, but when he engages one of his characters, the old Kiowa woman Ko-sahn, in a conversation, and protests that all his imagining of her is "only" in his head, she rebuffs him by instructing that imagination is the most important reality of all, that it, in fact, is a form of reality, and that without imagination the author himself cannot even exist much less his characters. Ko-sahn, evidently, would replace "only in one's head" with "powerfully in one's head," and she is an important ally for artists and intellectuals, much of whose labor takes place inside their own minds. She is the kind of person you might want around when you debate whether the goal of a university degree is a job.

The fact that Roe Náld's record of narrative inconsistencies, and the very narrative itself, stretch the limits of our belief, the events possibly occurring nowhere other than his own mind, does not mean that Roe Náld has nothing to say about art or that flights of fancy, by default, are necessarily irrelevant to social realities. Yet one wonders about the meaning of Roe Nald's work in general and a film like *Transvestite Witches Taking Revenge on a Redneck Farmer for Gay Bashing* in particular. A central question is how does one write or paint or film things that matter? What is the difference between honest and dishonest art, between depicting the verities of the human heart and wasting a reader's time?

"The Song of Roe Náld" lapses into certain mysteries I am unable to explain. What is the nature of the magic kiss that seems to re-animate the sleeper; or, less folklorically, why does Justin come back to life?

I don't know, really. I hesitate to mention this because you start talking about dreams and people think you are implying something about visions, weighted as all that is in religious notions. I like what Ray Young Bear has said about dreams in an interview: they're free, why not use them in creative writing? Every now and again I have dreams I remember and, believe me, it's not a Black Elk kind of experience. I'm not looking for recruits for a shaman workshop in Santa Fe, and I take it neither was Black Elk. I dream; I'm not a visionary, only a literary critic, maybe a fiction writer. Rarely, once every five years maybe, I'll have a dream that unfolds like a film in scenes and is always comic when it is structured this way. I will remember most all of it which also makes it unusual.

Some years ago at the University of Lethbridge I was supervising a student who is now a friend of many years, Geraldine Manossa, an exceptional modern, and tribal, dancer. Geraldine was writing a thesis on Cree drama. The path had been difficult for both of us, and the task put Geraldine in a different kind of performative role since she was writing an analysis rather than creating a dance piece. She had a dance performance coming up which also coincided with getting some of her work done which I think worried me. I had a dream, much more detailed than what I am relating here, in which she approached me and asked for an extension because her dance partner had died, and this had created all kinds of difficulties for her. In the dream I said something callous, like, "Oh, you can still get it turned in, and you can still do the dance piece, too." The statement was comic because in the dream I had the sense of watching this as a film and recognizing some of the worst tendencies of my own pedantry.

More happened in the dream when Geraldine and I attended the funeral, and her dance partner came back to life, aspects of which make their way into the story "The Song of Roe Náld." This means of writing is the exception, not the rule in my case, and the dream took a much different shape in the fiction. Yet it contains many of the themes I have discussed in my mus(e)ing in regards to the tensions between being a performer and a critic, a central dilemma in Geraldine's thesis project, and a major struggle for me, too, over the years.

The theme is especially crucial to Indian art because artistic performance has been the major means of breaking away from the ethnographic gaze, and the former has been associated with creativity, deviance, and defying anthropological expectations; whereas the supposed rationality of criticism has been associated with the act of ethnography itself, as if criticism were a synonym for anthropology. Some critics have even suggested terms like "ethnopoetics" or "ethnocriticism," which conflate both fields.

I have tried to deviate from ethnography in criticism, yet I have not completely succeeded at avoiding its voyeuristic gaze which seems somewhat unavoidable, and this is no less true of art. One of the reasons we love movies so much is because we get to peep inside other people's keyholes, people's bedrooms, and private places we are incapable of seeing inside without the magic of the camera (there it is, poking around again) and of fiction. No one explores this idea any better than Alfred Hitchcock in *Rear Window*. (Maybe we'd better not continue our prodding camera metaphor here given the title of the film—or maybe we should.) At any rate, characters in fiction, as well as people in real life, sometimes resist the subject position, and this is the case with Justin who ends up a difficult subject of Roe Náld's film. In a later chapter, on Charles Red Corn's novel *A Pipe for February*, I will talk about the ways the Osage sitters for John Joseph Matthews's portrait painter "talked back" to the painter and even the paintings, thus defying the conventional role of "subject."

Since neither art nor criticism escapes the voyeuristic gaze (like queuing up in a funeral line for a chance to peek at the corpse, or spying on the neighbors, even photographing them, in *Rear Window*), I have always been interested in exploring both in forums that under more conventional treatments have assumed that one involves a different kind of performance and language than the other. I like to follow a guy like Roe Náld around to see what happens when everything gets mixed up, in genre terms—when performance gets its chocolate inside criticism's peanut butter.

In the remainder of this book you can expect a fictional and critical mess, more committed to conveying ideas in an interesting way through integration, rather than segregation, of genres.

I include fiction in a critical study because I believe the former is as direct a pipeline to Indian experience as nonfiction (both are subject, obviously, to discursive mediation). What is important is the quality of the experience and its articulation in either genre. Indian fiction, at its best, can be an Indian performance, thus a form of Indian experience, both in its expression and in terms of the Indian experiences it represents. Readers also bring a set of experiences to textual encounters, and the act of reading itself is an experience. I do not believe nonfiction is necessarily closer to experience than fiction is. This, obviously, is not the same thing as saying nonfiction is unworthy of our attention, and a whole set of historical factors make it a rich area of investigation without granting it some kind of essence of authenticity in relation to experience where the literal becomes more directly related to the actual.

Some of my detractors have claimed my criticism is fiction anyway. They probably did not realize I would take it as a compliment. The point is, I have my reasons: I want authors, and the subjects of their creations, to emerge as characters, the way fully rounded subjects of fiction do. In earlier works I have avoided the survey approach—a handful of pages about scores of writers—instead devoting entire chapters to authors who interest me. Even in my more obviously nonfiction work I was trying to tell stories, thus giving each author considerable attention in order to have the time to unfold something about him or her. Hoping that readers will feel like they come to know the people I have chosen to love, occasionally hate, I continue that tradition here by refracting characters through as many different fiction and nonfiction angles of vision as possible. I hope to apply principles of character development to criticism.

Fiction depends on suspending disbelief, which is a performative act. I have sought similar possibilities in criticism. In *Red on Red* I did not want to write about Creek literature; I wanted to write a Creek book. "The Song of Roe Náld," I hope, is as much an artistic performance as an analysis of art. This process of enacting, becoming, and performing (rather than talking *about* something) is essential to storytelling. Performance interests me in terms of the way analysis might intersect with actualization. Something happens in good stories, a moment when you are no longer talking about events but reliving them. What transpires when you bring the powers of invocation into criticism? Do the gods come down? Can the muse be invoked? What does it mean to dramatize criticism? Early Greek philosophers presented ideas as dialogues between characters, drawing on the popularity of Greek theater, as well as the culture's roots in an oral tradition, as a means of enhancing philosophy.

I have decided to quit resisting the siren's call of my fictional muse, even in criticism, and I hope I don't crash on the rocks. If I do, at least I have tried something new, and I feel the impulse is not entirely unlike the way in which recently I have begun refusing to separate musical performance from readings and even academic presentations. If you go back far enough, a poet's most important tool was not only the pen but also a lyre he used to accompany himself.

I'll continue bringing out the lyre, in my case a 1954 Gibson ES 175 archtop guitar, and the liar, the storyteller, as long as you all continue to let me get away with it.

Early Greek philosophy and theater also shared mutual influences with evolving democratic forums, their open-air discussions, the terraced hillsides and specially designed gathering places whose very structures facilitated voiced opinion, buildings that could accommodate large gatherings of citizenry for either political debate or artistic enlightenment. The politics inherent in my discussion of art, I hope, are born of that spirit, a gathering place for discussion, an invitation for those who wish to act like citizens with civic responsibilities, rather than anything I say being taken as the last word on the matter.

Works Cited

Revard, Carter. "In Oklahoma." In *An Eagle Nation,* 3. Tucson: University of Arizona Press, 1993.

Womack, Craig. *Red on Red: Native American Literary Separatism.* Minneapolis: University of Minnesota Press, 1999.

Christine among the Winonas

Some Thoughts on E. Pauline Johnson's Prose Writing

We have reflected together on visual art with regard to Roe Náld's unruly camera, his unruly subjects, and his unruly self. Now I would like to turn my attention to the potential for turning literary essays into art by considering prose style. In the next two chapters I want to focus on E. Pauline Johnson's 1893 short story "A Red Girl's Reasoning" and her less well known 1892 essay "A Strong Race Opinion," which is seldom given much attention in Native literary studies or anywhere else. My purpose here is to discuss the relationship between content choices and stylistic ones in the creation of art, beginning with the rhetorical style Johnson used when presenting the subject of marriage, and continuing in the next chapter with a discussion of the satirical style Johnson employs to represent gendered individuality, arguing that the artfulness of her essay is an important component of what makes "Race Opinion" so effective—as compared to some of Johnson's other work, which seems so much more dated.

The lack of attention to the Johnson essay, compared to the interest in her poetry and fiction, is surprising for several reasons: "Race Opinion" might be the strongest single piece Johnson ever wrote, a fine achievement in irony and satire, as well as a mature statement about balancing authenticity and originality in the work of fiction. In relation to Native literary history, "Race Opinion" is the first example of Native-authored criticism, a milestone, strangely, no one has ever claimed given that it may also precede any non–Indian authored criticism of Native literature. If earlier examples exist, I don't know of them. Finally, the essay is, as blurbers are wont to say, laugh-out-loud funny. I wonder how this particular work has remained almost entirely off the radar of Native literary studies, and I don't have the answer.

In her essay Johnson reminds us that real Indians act like human beings, not like essays about Indians, and fictional characters should capture something of this capacity to surprise and delight rather than conform to textual expectations. Criticizing the generic term "Indian," Johnson complains that writers often lack the understanding to depict tribally specific communities and individuals. This problem relates to the fact that some authors have no experience themselves in lived communities, outside of textual representations. Johnson mentions a number of stock themes, but the three she lampoons most are the failure to name, the failure to survive, and the failure to love. In relation to the first failure, Johnson writes, "[H]er name is 'Winona.' Once or twice she has borne another appellation, but it always has a 'Winona' sound about it" (Johnson, "A Strong Race Opinion" 178–179), and Johnson then lays bare the various Winonas, Ramonas, Wacoustas, Ienas, and Wandas who typify stock depictions of her time. These floating Winonas, not so infinite in their signification, always lack surnames and "are possessed with a suicidal mania" (179).

As goes the second failure, then, Johnson actually celebrates the heroine's death wish: "[S]he always does die, and one feels relieved that it is so, for she is too unhealthy and too unnatural to live" (178). Johnson goes on to say that such fictional characters are "all fawn eyed, unnatural, unmaidenly idiots and . . . merely imaginary make-shifts to help out romances, that would be immeasurably improved by their absence" (182).

By the time of the third failure, a hapless love life, readers themselves, according to Johnson, are ready for the Indian woman to drown herself. Johnson queries, "Will some critic who understands human nature, and particularly the nature of authors, please tell the reading public why marriage with the Indian girl is so despised in books and so general in real life?" (179). No Native American satirist would emerge with a cutting voice as funny as Johnson's in this essay until Vine Deloria, Jr., a very different writer in a markedly different era. Johnson, unlike Deloria, does not achieve a consistently effective level of satire throughout the rest of her work, although much sarcasm is evident elsewhere.

Johnson briefly alludes to some other matters that are just as important but treated more sketchily than the three failures. Johnson points out the lack of stories depicting educated Native women, the treachery of the Indian woman who betrays her own people in deference to her non-Indian boyfriend, who dumps her in the end for the non-Indian heroine, and the way Indian women "lend a dash of vivid colouring to an otherwise tame and somber picture of colonial life" (183).

Johnson's musing is certainly haunting when she wonders just before the end of the essay, "Do authors who write Indian romances love the nation they endeavour successfully or unsuccessfully to describe?" (183).

My discussion of Johnson is organized according to the good news–bad news model. The good news is that the short story "A Red Girl's Reasoning," exemplifies the fine celebration of individuality Johnson insists upon in "A Strong Race Opinion." The bad news is outside this story, and even sometimes in it, Johnson fails to take her own advice, in fact very consciously drawing attention to the uniformity of Native women in meta-discursive asides that summarize the universality, rather than individuality, of their personalities.

Believe it or not, this is one of the reasons I admire Johnson a great deal. I know from personal experience that authors only suffer when they follow their own advice, not to mention the suffering of any others unfortunate enough to have to listen to them and take them seriously. Having written some books, I've come to appreciate the fact that an author's recommendations should by no means pertain to himself.

I want to examine the artfulness of both pieces of writing and consider the way style drives their content and creates such very different art forms.

If instead of style, I were dealing solely with content, and if I were writing a book about this story instead of a chapter, I would more exhaustively cover the many themes of "Red Girl": the way in which a father-in-law's advice to his newly married son-in-law is weighed down in all kinds of essentialisms about the so-called Indian mind, which the story sometimes endorses and other times subverts; the way Charlie, the new son-in law, is othered by the end of the story and faces a theological crisis when he realizes his non-Indian world is not the normative measuring stick for the entire universe; the way Ottawa, as the nation's capital, contributes a set of symbols that have to do with codified law as opposed to natural reason; the way in which genre fiction is subverted somewhat since Christie doesn't marry her brother-in-law, Joe, after Charlie's moral failure—which would be a typical ending in romance; the way the theme of mothering men, dominant throughout Johnson's fiction, applies to Charlie's immaturity; the way the story might be informed by the 1867 landmark Canadian court case *Connolly v. Woolrich*, which recognizes Cree oral law regarding marriage and inheritance in Canadian courts; the way the economic authority of the Hudson's Bay Company facilitates the moral authority of religious institutions and vice-versa; or I might hold forth on the wonderful ironies of a boy's best friend, his dog, that create the hilarious parody of Charlie's rescue by Hudson the Saint Bernard.

And so on and so forth. There's a lot in the story.

Further, readers might naturally expect me to write about Mohawk literary history and how E. Pauline Johnson's work fits in relation to it, as well as connect this to my penultimate chapter, on Beth Brant. I already wrote a book like that about my own tribe. I know little, if anything, about Iroquoian history, culture, and literature. Other people need to write such a book, and I will be grateful. Lisa Brooks, in *American Indian Literary Nationalism,* makes the point that national literatures help those of us rooted in the histories of our own tribes learn about ones we do not know as much about, given the impossibility of in-depth knowledge of each of the peoples of the Americas. *Art as Performance, Story as Criticism,* however, is about art and deviance, and even readers' expectations about the contour of earlier tribally specific writings I have authored have great potential for subversion. Deviance is one of the forces that drives the universe.

The critical framework that is part of the introduction to the 1998 University of Oklahoma reprint of Johnson's short story "A Red Girl's Reasoning" in the collection *The Moccasin Maker* is inadequate—perhaps because of the nature of short introductions and the fact that the editor of the volume, A. LaVonne Brown Ruoff, has to say something about Johnson's background and each of the stories in a very limited space rather than delve into their contents in close readings. Ruoff, an important contributor to Native bibliographic studies, writes, " 'A Red Girl's Reasoning' combines the theme of the mixed-blood woman's love for a weak white man with a forceful attack on white religious hypocrisy. The central issue in the story is white refusal to accept the sanctity of Indian marriages conducted in tribal ceremonies" (26). After some plot analysis, Ruoff continues, "This highly melodramatic story emphasizes that in order for a mixed-blood and a white to achieve a happy marriage, each must respect the other's culture. It also stresses the arrogance of the dominant white society which assumes that only its laws and customs are valid" (26).

I want to assert that these are not, to borrow Ruoff's phrase, the central issue—although I think all of them are, in fact, issues. Apart from the theoretical conundrums of locating the story inside a central issue, I want to attempt to draw attention to Christie's actual arguments, a subject seldom taken up in published responses to "Red Girl." Beginning with the title, I hope to examine an idea that I find every bit as provocative as those claimed in relation to a central issue—Christie's claims regarding marriage and how they are mediated by the artistic medium they are presented in.

Veronica Strong-Boag and Carole Gerson's treatment of Johnson's writing in *Paddling Her Own Canoe* almost fails to mention the short story "A Red Girl's Reasoning" at all—a strange lapse considering their chapters have such titles as "Finding Her Way as a New Woman," not to mention the title of the book itself. This is largely because of a structural necessity as indicated by the subtitle of the book, *The Times and Texts of E. Pauline Johnson Tekahionwake,* which means their survey has to cover a lot of bases in terms of both historical biography and literary analysis and cannot delve into individual stories at great length.

It should be noted that Strong-Boag herself had a much more developed earlier essay, in the anthology *Painting the Maple: Essays on Race, Gender, and the Construction of Canada,* and the name of it is "A Red Girl's Reasoning: E. Pauline Johnson Constructs the New Nation." As the title would indicate, however, the essay has to do with the idea of nation more than the challenges of stylistic expression involved in the process of making rhetorical arguments, which I want to examine here. In the later work, *Paddling Her Own Canoe,* devoted exclusively to Johnson, an exceedingly rare sentence on the subject is too abstract to conclude much about their take on the story. They write, "[T]he outspoken Johnson captured the *Dominion Illustrated*'s prize for fiction with her short story 'A Red Girl's Reasoning.' Its strong-minded heroine is no man's pawn and, like her author, speaks to the condition of women and Natives" (Strong-Boag and Gerson 188).

The very reason we know Christie is strong minded, however, is because she makes strong arguments, so here goes: Womack's take on "A Red Girl's Reasoning," with some thoughts on Christine's rhetorical choices in making an argumentative claim about marriage (and, I hope, at this point, people won't respond with silly crap about argumentative claims being European, not Indian).

Authors give their stories titles for a reason, and there is a reason the words "red," and "girl," and "reasoning" are juxtaposed against one another and draw our attention, or should draw our attention, before we even read the first words of the story. "Reason" has its reasons and it has to do with reasoning. Some critics have described the story's most prominent feature as Christie's assertion of opinions, rather than submission, to her husband, a defiance they claim is atypical in Victorian fiction. I find this claim to be somewhat dubious both in relation to Victorian literature in general and this story in particular. Christie does, in fact, talk back, but it is what she says—and how she says it— rather than the fact that she simply says something that matters. The words of the title suggest that what follows in the story is a process analysis of an individual Indian woman's ability to present a very particular argument about marriage, a thesis Christie begins with uncertainty but revises more powerfully as she scrutinizes her rhetorical choices. In short this story is an analysis of a certain woman's ability to present an argument, about a woman's ability to reason, and about the argument itself.

In order to make these points about marriage the story is presented in two styles that weave in and out and sometimes even appear at the same time: that of the essayist, analyst, commentator; and that of the performer, the more familiar narrator of fiction who unfolds a story as if it is happening while it is being told. In more conventional terms the first voice is associated with critics, and the second, with artists. This book, and this story, however, are about what happens when those two roles collide, even collude.

An example of the essayist's voice occurs at the beginning of the story, when Jimmy Robinson lectures his new son-in-law, Charlie McDonald, about the nature of Indians—what various shysters down through the years have claimed as "the Indian mind." (Not everyone who uses the phrase is a shyster but it is highly problematic, of course, to think of Indian, African, Asian, Caucasian, or other racial minds.) Critics have debated whether or not Johnson endorses the "Indian mind," and other matters of essentialism, or subverts such matters, almost always defending her and siding with subversion. Instead of prophesying about Johnson's true nature, however, I want to think about how the language works in this particular story.

The opening discussion of the Indian mind is voiced through the character Jimmy Robinson, and another example of the voice of the essayist occurs in the narrator's many asides about traits shared by all Native women, and these often as not, are not about their minds but their complexions and love of fabric (always velvet), for example. "Red Girl" engenders the Indian mind so that it becomes the Native woman's mind, which, of course, is equally problematic. In terms of the two rhetorical styles in the story, in the essayist mode, the narrator reveals character by telling, not showing.

The narrator paints her world in the broadest of strokes. Settings are so minimally revealed that we know little more than the fact that we are somewhere at a party in Ottawa or at Christie and Charlie's home. Physical features of streets and houses are nonexistent. We know Christie is not at the party anymore when Joe McDonald puts her in a cab and sends her home. Forget the streets they pass through to get there or what it looks like walking up the steps and unlocking the front door. The story in this regard, and many others, is closer kin to sentimental than to realist fiction. Character descriptions involve a proliferation of adverbs and adjectives as much as more concrete nouns (toward the end of the story, for example, Christie is "magnetized" by Charlie's "passionately wistful face" [123], not exactly enough if you needed a police sketch).

In the essayist mode, some characters are not individuated but placed in undifferentiated group scenes: "She [Christie] was 'all the rage' that winter at the provincial capital. The men called her a 'deuced fine little woman.' The ladies said she was 'just the sweetest little wildflower'" (105). Later, when switching to the performative mode, the narrator reveals two of these men and women, Mrs. Stuart and Captain Logan, and gives them lines to speak.

If exteriors are presented in a summary fashion in the essayist mode, human interiors receive almost equally scant attention, and this may strike us as strange in a story whose main point is about the process of thinking. The reader will not find any of the normal tags that indicate character viewpoints in modern fiction such as "Christine thought" or "Christine felt" or more immediate forms like stream of consciousness, and, of course, Johnson writes at the very beginning of movements in fiction that would shift from focusing on exteriors to revealing human consciousness. The narrator looms large, and if there is anything we need to know about the characters, she'll tell us, thank you very much: "'Why, no,' said the girl in amazement at that gentleman's ignorance" (111). Obviously, Christie is not thinking to herself, "I am sure in amazement at that gentleman's ignorance"; this is narrator commentary.

In the analytical mode, the narrator sounds a little like a small-town social columnist trying to impress her local readers with her sophistication. Diction is stilted. The narrator is arch: "There was a dance at the Lieutenant-Governor's, and the world and his wife were there" (108). Locals are pilloried—a party-goer is quoted, then the narrator refers to her as "the wife of a local M.P. who brushed up her etiquette and English once a year at Ottawa" (106).

The narrator moves away from the role of commenting analyst, however, in some crucial scenes. In one, Christie gets "outed" (as a "bastard child") at the snobby Ottawa party hosted by the lieutenant governor. The men and women, who formerly were cast in the vaguest terms as the collective social milieu of Ottawa, now become Captain Logan and Mrs. Stuart, a couple of mean bluebloods.

When the story moves into performance it does so through dialogue more than any other fictional technique. In modern fiction, dialogue is supplemented by setting, plot, pacing, and other features in order to reveal character. In "A Red Girl's Reasoning," dialogue is virtually the sole technique used to move into the realm, normally a regular occurrence in fiction, of the story's unfolding rather than being summarized. Yet in spite of the clunky storytelling that results from dialogue being the story's sole performative feature, we feel more like we've arrived at a particular place and something is happening there at the party than during the narrator's analysis of Christine's character, the traits of Indian women, and so on, that leads up to it. People speak to each other, don't like what they hear, and get pissed off. If we don't exactly see Captain Logan's hands shake as he rages against immorality, stubbing out his cigar so hard he knocks the cuspidor over, we take his threat regarding Charlie, "If he had [failed to marry Christie legally] I'd have blown his brains out tomorrow" (111), to indicate he is angry. This comes from Logan rather than the narrator discoursing on the nature of army captains and their quick tempers, the kind of role she has in many other parts of the story.

In terms of dialogue, then, in the performative mode, a conversation reveals that Christine's parents were married under the authority of tribal law at a time when no missionaries were in their part of the world. (Here Johnson is not specific about the geography, nor the tribe [one of the instances alluded to earlier where she refuses to take her own advice about specificity].) As much as anything Christine's husband, Charlie, feels shamed because these facts about Christie's background are brought up in public. Charlie's friends are marked by the intensity of their colonial gaze, exemplified by the way they first clamor for exotic tribal details from Christie, then feign shock when they get them; they discover that one of the quaint customs they begged to hear included a marriage without a priest.

After the party, having returned home, an argument breaks out between Christie and Charlie about the legitimacy of tribal marriage. The story continues mostly in the performative mode, and I think it becomes increasingly apparent during the debate why Johnson has split the story into two different rhetorical styles. At the party, which is depicted more as a story unfolding, Charlie had told the fatuous Mrs. Stuart, "[T]here are not two of Christie; she is the same at home and abroad" (106–107), and the statement reveals Charlie's oft-repeated insistence on his wife's simplicity and unvarying nature.

Clearly the narrator, as commentator, disagrees. At home when Christine begins to defend her position on marriage to Charlie, the narrator comments, "It was the voice of another nature in the girl" (115). It would seem that there are two of Christie, maybe more. The idea that Christine's outward appearance is not a good measure of her "interior landscape" is frequently referenced in the story, and Charlie's fatal flaw is underestimating her argumentative prowess. This is ironic because Charlie had been warned.

Charlie had not been schooled well, however. Jimmy Robinson, his father-in-law, in his opening discourse on the Indian mind, had cautioned that the Native woman will dole out cruelty for cruelty in equal measure. He had not said anything about them being excellent debaters. None of the men in the story, including Joe McDonald, the most sympathetic character, understands the intellectual power of Native women.

The story is not stable in the sense that it remains consistently in the essay or performance mode. It often weaves in and out of both, as happens here when the debate ensues and the dialogue creates a much livelier story, but some of the commentary slips back in as well. Though somewhat clunky storytelling, when the narrator finally gives voice to Christie it is as if she cannot help occasionally jumping in the fray and interjecting, "I'm on *her* side" (as opposed to Charlie's). More modern fiction would simply let these two characters duke it out with fewer instructions to the readers about how to interpret the fight. The narrator is so active in the story she is almost like another character, someone for Christine to lean on in a world dominated by stupid men.

Even at the party, normal plot movement is refracted through clunky language that keeps the action from unfolding as effectively: "Christine had risen, slowly, ominously—risen, with the dignity and pride of an empress" (111). The word "had" combined with "risen" creates distance between the reader and the action. The commas after "risen" are more about dramatizing the language, more of the voice of the social columnist proving her sophistication, than making the story happen for us as we read it. The choice of the abstract adjectives "dignity" and "pride" rather than concrete statements about physical details create a blurred picture. A more modern rendition might read, "Christine took Charlie's hand and rose from the settee, turning away from Captain Logan without saying goodbye to Mrs. Stuart." The narrator, however, has things she wants to tell us about Christie, and describing Christie's dignity is as important to her as effective story performance.

The style of this story creates a very distinct impression: Christie needs an ally; that ally is the narrator, and once Christie leaves her mother's home she is the only friend Christie will have, and this sucks because Christie will never have her—only we readers will, since narrators in third-person fiction are not dramatized as characters in the story. "I'd like to jump in and help her if she could only see me!" the narrator seems to be saying. We have this combination of performance and commentary to underscore Christie's frustrations and the fact she could use the support of a community of women intellectuals who are notably missing. The narrator's helpless desperation to fill the gap by virtually stepping into the story performance heightens the absence of a group of reasoning women since the only person available for support does not exist—she is a fictional technique. This causes the unique hybrid of performance and commentary in the story, the narrator's desire to be real, to help Christie, in an environment where an actual support network of women thinkers seems nowhere to be found.

In this lonely milieu, with her only friend uselessly omniscient, Christie had better come up with some damned good reasons, thus the story's title, to defend herself because she is on her own even though we readers can hear what Christie cannot—the narrator frantically trying to give her direction:

"We're out there, we're just omniscient and invisible." Richly symbolic, the narrator's stance raises this question: where should Christie look for help? Thinking women, obviously, existed in the Victorian era, and in all other eras, but a central question is how to connect to them.

In her lonely search for such a community, Christie's first line of defense leaves something to be desired. Rebutting Charlie's challenge of her very "legitimacy," she argues, "Why should I be ashamed of the rites of my people any more than you should be ashamed of the customs of yours—of a marriage more sacred and holy than half of your white man's mockeries" (114–15)? The idea that her parents' Indian marriage is not any more screwed up than the sham and pretense of a good number of white marriages may not be the best way to establish the validity of tribal ceremony. One might wonder in what sense her parents' union is sacred and holy if it only bests, so to speak, the worst of white marriages. Quantifying the issue with a fraction that determines which half is better or worse seems to merely further confuse things.

Charlie insists that Christine's parents should have been married once the priest, Father O'Leary, arrived on the scene some years later. In relation to the question of where Christie should turn for help—one suggested by the narrator's limbo between performance and commentary—Christie next considers one of the possibilities that the narrator symbolizes. Though separated from her by vast distances (as she is from the invisible and distant narrator), Christie turns to her mother—that is, to one of her mother's argumentative claims. Christie relates a story recalling the priest showing up at her parents' house intending to marry the two. Christine recalls that her mother rose to the occasion with a passionate refusal, declaring, "Never—never—I have never had but this one husband; he has had none but me for wife, and to have you re-marry us would be to say as much to the whole world as that we had never been married before. You go away; I do not ask that your people be re-married; talk not so to me. I am married, and you or the Church cannot do or undo it" (115–16).

By drawing on an immediate source of women's knowledge, her mother, rather than arguing in abstract terms about Indian marriage being no weaker than white marriage, and thus maintaining Europe as the normative authority in such matters, Christie's argument picks up some steam here. In Bakhtinian terms, her rhetorical strategy in this second go-round underscores the power of internally persuasive discourse as much as external, or authoritative, discourse. For better or worse, so to speak, it still leaves the idea of the validity of marriage intact, at least in relation to the more radical argument that is to come. Christie, here, obviously isn't claiming that marriage itself is a lot of hooey. The phrase "you or the Church cannot do or undo it," however, provides some intellectual groundwork for the moment when, under the influence of her own strategic revisions, and her mother's rhetorical example, Christine invests herself with the authority to annul her own marriage.

This annulment of Christine's is a response to Charlie's phrase "God knows" (117), when asked if he would have still married her if he knew of her parents' tribal marriage. Christine's act of annulment, undertaken without priest or magistrate, is no less of an official ceremony that allows her to move on to her closing argument. If I had time to analyze this story in relation to the Canadian case *Connolly v. Woolrich*, I would draw attention to the way the arguments could be compared to two opposing attorneys squaring off with each other, as well as what the case determined about the legitimacy of Cree law. But that is the subject of another book, probably not mine.

After mentioning reciprocity, the notion of Charlie's responsibility to respect tribal marriage the way Christine has respected Canadian marriage, Christie moves deeper into her argument by undercutting Charlie's assumptions about normativity. Christine points out the instability of marriage itself in relation to its variation across cultures and time periods. She asks, "How do I know when another nation will come and conquer you as you white men conquered us? And they will have another marriage rite to perform, and they will tell us another truth, that you are not my husband, that you are but disgracing and dishonoring me, that you are keeping me here, not as your wife, but as your *squaw*" (117–18). Foucault couldn't have said it any better; although we certainly must give the French credit for saying it more inscrutably. Marriage, in other words, is not historically stable; it varies in different time periods and across cultures.

Notably, Christie crowns her argument with a shocking racial epithet. Christine has been the belle of the ball in Ottawa society, poised in her evening dress, witty in her ballroom banter. Partygoers, however, can just as easily view her as a so-called squaw, given a shift in public perception. Chains of signification, in which one word or phrase can too easily be substituted for another, seem to be working against her. The term "potent charm" (106), used to describe Christie's allure among the hoity-toity, doesn't come with a lifetime guarantee, and she might just as easily end up a "squaw" at any time in the near future. The shock of the term, however, marks a new boldness in Christine's tackling of the dark underbelly of certain ideas, and embracing the term, in a sense, leads to painful realizations that come at a price but also mark intellectual growth.

At this point Christine has reached philosophical bedrock in realizing the problem of mutually exclusive truth claims in which one capital-T kind of

Truth cancels out all others—in this particular case the claim that one kind of marriage invalidates all other forms of marriage. This debate is very contemporary in the United States, where the controversy over gay marriage has raged until recently. I say until recently because while the United States was under George W. Bush's military rule, it seems that no one had constitutional rights, not even heterosexuals (I interrupted reading the copyedited version of this manuscript to attend Ebenezer Baptist Church in Atlanta to watch and pray as Barack Obama was elected forty-fourth president of the United States). E. Pauline Johnson actually has a poem entitled "When George Was King." Its first stanza reads,

> Cards, and swords, and a lady's love,
> That is a tale worth reading,
> An insult veiled, a downcast glove,
> And rapiers leap unheeding.
> And 'tis O! for the brawl,
> The thrust, the fall,
> And the foe at your feet a-bleeding.
> (Johnson, "When George Was King" 150)

Rather than thrust this poem, so to speak, on recent events, I'll save these ironies for another day. Suffice it to say two hundred and some odd years ago Americans rose up and threw off another tyrant named George, and we can only hope history runs in cycles if we get such a nincompoop again. At any rate, at the heart of the gay marriage debate is the issue of whether there is only one kind of marriage. But if someone comes along and says, hey, what if there are two? Or three? Or maybe we don't know how many? Or maybe it just means two people deciding on their own terms? Then everything opens up to multiple possibilities. Who decides these matters, after all? If Cree marriage doesn't count, what is the Methodist going to say to the Catholic who says hers is no good? (There are other issues at stake as well, such as whether or not marriage has been that great for anyone, gay or straight or Cree or Catholic or Methodist, but I'm not sure I can argue the story gets quite that radical.)

Returning to issues of style, at this point in the story the narrator really pulls back, since Christine seems to have found a voice of her own. This foreshadows the story's unusual ending where the narrator seems to almost kill herself off—at least in the sense of assuming a much more minimal role and turning her attention to Charlie, who seems to need increasing levels of support after he literally goes to the dogs, and Christie, increasingly, discovers a life of the mind.

In spite of his dim wit, Charlie seems to intuit the threat of Christine's burgeoning subversive arguments since he reacts violently, and his brother Joe has to intervene, presumably to keep Christie from getting hurt.

Christie leaves home.

Well, maybe the story does get that radical; I don't know. Christie rejects marriage, after all, at least for herself. After months of searching during which he fails to find Christine in any of the places he expected, and after being saved by a starving Saint Bernard who is even more pathetic than Charlie, and whom Charlie ironically enough christens Hudson, Charlie finally locates his former wife, a former wife by virtue of the authority vested in herself.

Charlie begs Christie to come back, and she provides a brilliant reason as to why that is no longer feasible. She says, "I do not like you" (Johnson, "A Red Girl's Reasoning" 123). The phrasing of these few words is important because she does, in fact, love him and is still attracted to him. Love, however, cannot substitute for the free expression of ideas, and she says, "[N]ot even love can make a slave of a red girl" (124). In other words, Christine will not worship at the feet of a philosophical system (I love bad metaphors) that recognizes only Charlie's world, not her own; that bases its legitimacy on technicalities rather than relationship; and that demands a belief system in which only one viewpoint is correct. Most importantly though she will not worship at the feet of a philosophical system that demands she forgo thinking and expressing these thoughts in coherent arguments. Part of the thrill of marriage, in Christine's view, is intellectual development, and one is reminded of Audre Lorde's much more contemporary essay about the way the erotic can be suffused with intellectual excellence.

The story ends hilariously as Hudson the Saint Bernard, "big and clumsy and yellow" (126)—in other words a replica of Charlie, especially the yellow part—licks Charlie's sleeve.

And that's the good news. Not Charlie's salivating friend, that is to say, but the way in which "A Red Girl's Reasoning" celebrates the rhetorical individuality of a Native woman.

The bad news is the fact that in the same story the narrator says of Christine's mother, "Like all her race, observant, intuitive, having a horror of ridicule, consequently quick at acquirement and teachable in mental and social habit, she had developed from absolute pagan indifference into a sweet, elderly Christian woman, whose broken English, quiet manner, and still handsome copper-colored face, were the joy of old Robinson's declining years" (103). The phrase "like all her race" occurs scores of times throughout other Johnson writings, in which we find out that all Indian women, for example, like velvet and have remarkably fine complexions; at least one of these observations occurs in this very story.

This kind of Native universality, presented time and again as explicit truths rather than ironic asides, makes it seem as if Johnson never read her own essay on the matter. One might surmise she is working against dominant culture stereotypes by problematically substituting the negative ones for equally reductive positive statements. Yet this split seems to further emphasize the relationship between Christine and her supportive "friend," the narrator. Initially, Christine needs a helping hand but as she begins to uncover her own capacity for making arguments she can shake off the narrator, given her terminal creeds that threaten deviance. The fact that Christine's individuality is at odds with the narrator's insistence on Native uniformity is a way of emphasizing Christine's evolution as a thinker who grows increasingly independent.

The story, however, is not the only forum in which individuality and uniformity are in tension. Switching to nonfiction, even within the essay "A Strong Race Opinion," readers might wonder if E. Pauline Johnson is paying much attention to her own arguments when she writes, "A wild Indian never kisses; mothers never kiss their children even, nor lovers their sweethearts, husbands their wives. It is something absolutely unknown, unpracticed" (180). Could this be the same author who opens her essay with the sentence "Individual personality is one of the most charming things to be met with, either in a flesh and blood existence, or upon the pages of fiction, and it matters little to what race an author's heroine belongs, if he makes her character distinctly unique and natural" (177)? Although I have no way of knowing, I often wonder if stereotypes like these are the reason the director of the film *Medicine River* has Graham Greene kiss Sheila Tousey with so much gusto. I rather suspect, however, it is simply because anyone of sound mind would want to kiss Sheila Tousey—even me, and that's really saying something.

Yet don't these very inconsistencies of Johnson's, which illustrate the process of revising arguments, remind us of the ways in which our best conclusions were not always so? I love Johnson for all of that, how she, intentionally or not, lays bare her own and her characters' best and worst logical tendencies, sparing us neither. It's as if the essay, published only a year before the fiction, foreshadows the strengths and weaknesses, the high and low points, of Christine's claims, which, overall, progress toward a mature and defensible position in spite of glitches along the way.

Some might wonder about the relevance of all this to larger issues outside the story. My approach to Native studies is not to present authors or their subject matter as noble representatives of the so-called Native perspective, as perfect exemplars of feminism, as the epitome of tribal nationalism, or as any number of idealized icons, but rather as human beings thinking and making decisions in particular sets of circumstances. Native perspectives, feminism, tribal nationalism, and various cultural and social iconographies can, and should, be discussed in relation to these works, but I hope to allow space for the full humanity of the subjects rather than turning them into some kind of object of religious worship where my job is to formulate a kind of apologia for them that defends their sanctity. Native authors, their characters, their ideas, do not come alive when treated like sacred cows. Lack of sanctity, in fact, oftentimes proves more interesting than a catechism.

My aim, then, is simply enriching this story by claiming more than what LaVonne Ruoff calls the "central issue" or, as she writes, "the central issue in the story is white refusal to accept the sanctity of Indian marriages conducted in tribal ceremonies." I want, instead, to convey the particularities of Christie's arguments rather than relegate her to the clichéd abstraction of the powerful woman, atypical for her time period, and so on. Like Johnson, I want to reclaim her individuality.

And that's why, for me, "A Red Girl's Reasoning" will never simply be a story about a woman talking back to her husband.

In its final paragraph and concluding lines, which render Charlie's descent into the abyss, the story seems much more modern in its conception:

> What a bare, hotelish room it was! He tossed off his coat and sat for ten minutes looking blankly at the sputtering gas jet. Then his whole life, desolate as a desert, loomed up before him with appalling distinctness. Throwing himself on the floor beside his bed, with clasped hands and arms outstretched on the white counterpane, he sobbed. "Oh! God, dear God, I thought you loved me; I thought you'd let me have her again, but you must be tired of me, tired of loving me, too. I've nothing left now, nothing! It doesn't seem that I even have you to-night."
>
> He lifted his face, then, for his dog, big and clumsy and yellow, was licking at his sleeve. (125–26)

Charlie's dejection is marked by a much more familiar artistic style for modern readers. The first line about his dismal room is internal discourse, an interior viewpoint. In the next we have physical details, a concrete action—tossing the coat—and the flickering gas jets with all their suggestiveness rather than the abstraction of adjectives and adverbs about emotional states. While clasped hands, and outstretched arms, against a white counterpane certainly have symbolic possibilities in terms of Charlie's theological crisis as he realizes he is not the center of the universe, the implications are largely left to the reader and the overall despair conveys something of the existential crisis so common in modernism. The tragicomedy of the last line, almost as concrete as it can be ("clumsy" and "yellow" are virtually the only deviations from nouns and verbs), and the irony it creates without saying it outright, seem strikingly more contemporary.

These lines are very unlike any that come before them in the story. While a character might get killed off in a short story, a narrator seldom is, and here, the chatty commentator disappears. This certainly isn't the social columnist any longer, peddling gossip in lines of purple prose in a nineteenth century small town newspaper. Why the switch to a much more minimalist narrator? I think the conclusion signals that once Christie is free to think on her own, the narrator can recede, and she doesn't give a shit about Charlie, not like she did Christie, not enough to even wish he could hear her.

Works Cited

Johnson, E. Pauline. "A Red Girl's Reasoning." In *The Moccasin Maker,* edited by A. LaVonne Brown Ruoff, 102–26. Norman: University of Oklahoma Press, 1998.

——. "A Strong Race Opinion: On the Indian Girl in Modern Fiction." In *E. Pauline Johnson, Tekahionwake: Collected Poems and Selected Prose,* edited by Carole Gerson and Veronica Strong-Boag, 177–83. Toronto: University of Toronto Press, 2002.

——. "When George Was King." In *E. Pauline Johnson Tekahionwake Collected Poems and Selected Prose,* 150–51.

Ruoff, A. LaVonne Brown. "Introduction." In *The Moccasin Maker,* 1–37.

Strong-Boag, Veronica, and Carole Gerson. *Paddling Her Own Canoe: The Times and Texts of E. Pauline Johnson (Tekahionwake).* Toronto: University of Toronto Press, 2000.

"In Cold Type"
Style and Criticism

My previous chapter scrutinized the way a narrative style vacillating between performance and commentary underscores the challenges of making connections between "reasoning" women in the Victorian era. Now I want to analyze the way in which a satirical style amplifies the arguments in "A Strong Race Opinion." Johnson opens her satire (in her second sentence, actually) with the statement "Individual personality is one of the most charming things to be met with, either in a flesh and blood existence, or upon the pages of fiction, and it matters little to what race an author's heroine belongs, if he makes her character distinct, unique, and natural" (Johnson, "A Strong Race Opinion," 177). One does not usually meet with personality, as in "Craig Womack, I'd like you to meet my best friend, Personality." The term, then, is personified, and works on us, whether we realize it consciously or not, because of its unusual treatment. The word "charming" is important because Johnson's satire often turns, as we saw in "A Red Girl's Reasoning," around refined exteriors with deeper interiors, Christie's ballroom banter as opposed to her arguments about marriage, for example, typifies social charm that obscures a more profound intellectual commitment.

Throughout "A Strong Race Opinion," within single sentences, or even short phrases, Johnson crosses boundaries between the world of readers, the world of authors, the world of literary depictions, and the world of social realities ("either in a flesh and blood existence, or upon the pages of fiction"). One of the strong features of her satire, the way she takes the reader by the hand and leaps back and forth over these four streams of thought, evokes surprise every time one lands on the other side of the brook with her. Johnson encourages us to consider what is life in relation to authors and depictions and readers; authors in relation to depictions and life and readers; depictions in relation to authors and life and readers; and readers in relation to authors, depictions, and life. One might also note how the first word of the sentence, "individual," is beautifully driven home by the three parallel adjectives "distinct, unique, and natural" that conclude the sentence. Johnson's satire creates a natural rhythm through these parallel forms.

Johnson's satiric comedy, and her famous antipathy toward the United States, is further revealed by her choice of the word "American" when, in fact, much of her essay is about the hackneyed depictions of Canadian writers:

> The American book heroine of today is vari-coloured as to personality and action. The author does not consider it necessary to the development of her character, and the plot of the story to insist upon her having American-coloured eyes, an American carriage, an American voice, American motives, and an American mode of dying. (177)

Satire has a long tradition of pointing out what makes absurdity absurd. Jonathan Swift's "A Modest Proposal" is a case in point, and an American eye color is not as outrageous as eating babies, although it is equally nonsensical. Putting American-colored eyes in a string of ridiculously impossible Americanisms is a classic kind of amplification in satire, similar to caricature, in which an individual foible is blown up to gigantic proportions to make its absurdity that much more glaring.

In addition to "American-coloured eyes," Johnson has other delicious short phrases. "The Indian girl we meet in cold type," we are told, "is rarely distressed by having to belong to any tribe, or to reflect any tribal characteristics" (178). We have another personification "in cold type," which today has evolved other associations because of Truman Capote and recent films, and it is nicely contrasted with an ironic inversion. Type becomes human (albeit cold), and the Indian "girl" is rarely distressed, becoming less human. Next, Johnson examines such inversions by quantifying them, providing some statistical data:

> [Y]et strange to say, that notwithstanding the numerous tribes, with their aggregate numbers reaching more than 122,000 souls in Canada alone, our Canadian authors can cull from this huge revenue of character, but one [stereotypical] Indian girl, and stranger still that this lonely little heroine never had a prototype in breathing flesh and blood existence! (178)

In the earlier passage we have typeface becoming human and a human becoming typeface. Here Johnson wonders about another inversion: How can 122,000 variations turn into one singularity? The data, and words like "aggregate" and "revenue," place us inside the language of a government report that Johnson then reverses at the end of her complex sentence with a particular depiction of the lonely little heroine, and the world outside her book, her very own flesh-and-blood existence. Once again Johnson guides us across her four streams: authors stuck in a single mode, the demography of Canadian Native population in the real world, stereotypical fictional portrayal, and Native readers who may not recognize themselves in the depictions.

One of the great statements in this essay that makes Johnson's smartass remarks art instead of sophomoric attitude is about the names of Native women characters: "Yes, there is only one of her; and her name is 'Winona.' Once or twice she has borne another appellation, but it always has a 'Winona' sound about it" (178–79). The phrase "it always has a 'Winona' sound about it" is highly inventive, since most character names in fiction are analyzed in relation to what they might symbolize instead of what they sound like. Most critics would make such observations about lines of poetry, regarding assonance, not the names of characters in novels. Quantifying the exceptions to being named Winona ("once or twice") grates wonderfully against the switch from numbers to sounds, creating surprise in the sentence—it starts out with a concept, an overused name, and ends with a sound, the Winonas, Ienas, Wacoustas, Ramonas, Wandas, and their many kinswomen. The damn thing's got a groove; it swings, man. While Johnson does not spell out the list here, onas, enas, and oustas float in and out of the essay with such frequency that this strongest of sentences is constantly reinforced without even being directly referenced.

Remember the old ploy of the subliminal Coke and popcorn ads at the theater? An icy soda flashes by on the screen before you can consciously register it, and pretty soon you find yourself standing in line in the lobby digging around for some change (bills now, I guess). Every Winona, Iena, Wacousta, and Ramona that comes up in the essay, whether or not we realize it, takes us back to those two wonderful sentences that marry sound and meaning. Christ, why can't we have more criticism like this today instead of the boring shit that tenures people? After tenure, at least, one would think literature professors might bust loose. The Johnson example illustrates what I am talking about when I tell students to write criticism in a way that would make their poems and short stories proud. This has nothing to do with abandoning strong analysis and engaged research—this is the heart and soul of it, especially the soul.

Smartassery is an art form, a technical achievement, a craft—not an attitude. Anyone with the money can buy a black leather jacket, but fewer can master a sentence like this one: "We meet her as a Shawnee, as a Sioux, as a Huron, and then, her tribe unnamed, in the vicinity of Brockville" (179). Here we have the naming of tribes presented in a parallel string of adjectives; then the parallelism is broken, and the shift emphasizes the change in status, "tribe unnamed," and the hilarious punch line, "in the vicinity of Brockville," an absurd gem since there is no Brockville tribe to match the parallel list of tribes that leads up to it. We switch from tribes to a city, just as we had been surprised in the other sentence when we went from numbers to sound. In Indian country we have had a lot of discussion of these identity issues in relation to literature but seldom with as much poetic verve as Johnson demonstrates here.

After discussing the Indian "girl's" fatal attraction to unrequited love, Johnson queries, "Will some critic who understands human nature, and particularly the nature of authors, please tell the reading public why marriage with the Indian girl is so despised in books and so general in real life?" (179). There is the sarcasm, one of the main weapons in the smartass's arsenal, that contrasts humans and authors by making authors some sub-category of humanity, thus, both acknowledging authors might be human but questioning this possibility as well. The satirist likes to have her cake and eat it, too. The main stylistic device comes through here strongly, the rapid navigation across the four streams, author, readers, depictions, social reality.

Would to god all smartasses would train themselves so well: "Then 'Winona' secures the time honoured canoe, paddles out into the lake, and drowns herself" (181). As simple as this sentence is, what might some of us give for academic writers to write an essay containing only one of these sentences that swings so effectively as do the three parallel present-tense verbs "secures," "paddles," and "drowns?" Those three particular verbs get the reader to do exactly what Johnson wants: give the canoe a helpful push off the dock and be done with the obnoxious maiden. That kind of parallelism, as scholars like Walter Ong have pointed out, creates a performance where a story is enacted rather than discussed. Certain critics get the canoe gliding across the water instead of just analyzing it to death. It involves craft. Less accomplished writers would botch the sentence by writing "Winona secures the time honoured paddle, paddles out into the lake, and drowns herself," thus killing the variation with the clunky repetition of "paddle." The simple formula of variation within the same, holding one thing constant like the present tense while varying each verb as in "secures," "paddles," and "drowns," is a level of musicality some writers never reach. It is no coincidence that "variation within the same" is one of the key features of oral performance—these written stylistic accomplishments originate in speech. Such language unites analysis and performance. It makes criticism matter—your reader is urged to consider the possibility of doing something about the ideas you present, enacting them since you have led the way by going to the trouble of enacting them yourself.

A complexity in the essay, one not always as skillfully handled in Johnson's poetry and fiction, is her observation that Charles Mair, author of *Tecumseh*, gets it right in relation to his title character and wrong in relation to the Indian woman Iena, succumbing, as all Mair's peers do, to the temptation to kill off whichever Winona-sounding character they are dealing with. Johnson recognizes here that criticism can be a mixed bag, and even an admirable author can sometimes disappoint.

Some modern readers might be thrown by the style of "A Strong Race Opinion" given that it smacks a little of yellow journalism with its florid ornamentation. Yet here Johnson seems to have control of her melodramatic language, consciously employing it to strong effect.

Notice what happens in the following passage. First, a digression. I am reminded of Brian DePalma's classic film *Carrie*, a rite of passage for those of us coming of age in the early 1970s. My family had an old Toyota pickup, a single car we somehow shared between my siblings and parents. Being sixteen and the oldest brother, I used to commandeer it for the Saturday night picture show, but the compromise was I had to take all my sister's friends. We'd pile half the neighborhood in the back; I'd park on the side of the drive-in least visible to the cops, kids would hop the fence, and I'd pay the single entrance fee and meet up with everyone at the snack bar.

Like all endless summers, it ended and eventually we got busted, but that's another story.

At any rate, we were watching the end of *Carrie* at the drive-in, and how could anyone not have seen it coming? All that schmaltzy music, the violins, the flowers, the carefully groomed lawns and cemetery grounds. In some ways I wish I were still that naïve, and maybe in some ways I still am.

Carrie's hand shoots up out of the grave, and I'm the only one in the back of the truck, loaded with my little sister's fourteen-year-old girlfriends, who screams, and I mean loud, and about as unmanly as any sissy-in-the-making could manage. Lori's friends all look at her like, "What's wrong with *him*?"

Notice, then, how Johnson starts out with all this florid language, floats you through the pastoral, then reverses your reverie with the jarring word "idiot" at the end of the passage, as if to say, "Gotcha, you idiot, you should have seen the hand coming!"

No, the Indian girl must die, and with the exception of "Iena" her heart's blood must stain every page of fiction whereon she appears. One learns to love Lefroy, the poet painter; he never abuses by coarse language and derisive epithets his little Indian love, "Iena" accepts delicately and sweetly his overtures, Lefroy prizes nobly and honourably her devotion. Oh! Lefroy, where is your fellowman in fiction? "Iena," where is your prototype? Alas, for all the other pale-faced lovers, they are indifferent, almost brutal creations, and, as for the red skin girls that love them, they are all fawn eyed, unnatural, unmaidenly idiots and both are merely imaginary make-shifts to help out romances, that would be immeasurably improved by their absence. (182)

Not only does Johnson jar us out of the sublime with the word "idiots," she reveals that she has self-consciously structured the sentence to do so by working up to the word "romances" in the sentence's conclusion. Here, style and subject are first happily conjoined, then violently ripped apart. Romantic works are discussed in the language of romance, only to be suddenly de-romanticized with words like "idiots" and "make-shifts" that undermine both the style and meaning of romance.

One might wonder, especially in relation to the kinds of things I have written before, in what sense can this essay can be claimed as Mohawk writing. I cannot speak on behalf of Mohawks, but I know if I encountered some Creek writer authoring the first work of Native literary criticism, and doing such a fabulous job at it, I would want to claim it as Creek. In further exploring what I mean by tribally specific aesthetics then, I recommend tribal literary critics fully claim as their own anything that demonstrates such a high level of artistic achievement. I say make excellence, especially originality, the central criterion as to what makes something tribally specific rather than some threshold level of beads and feathers.

This is another way of asking for what countless others have: that artistic rather than ethnographic criteria be applied to Indian creativity. Undoubtedly, some will see this as a contradiction with my earlier work in *Red on Red* where I explored Creek national contexts for certain literatures; however, I hope that careful readers will note the arguments I've made in various books regarding the way nationalism has the potential to free critics from fixed ethnographic and identity categories given the constant flux of the nation itself. I do not view the nation as an ethnographic concept. While "ethnocriticism" may have some value in Native literature depending on how critics apply it, I am most unabashedly not an "ethnocritic." As a critic shaped by my own attempts at fiction and a predisposition toward close readings of others' creative work, I hope for lively stories, wherever they might appear—in fiction, criticism, the class room, and elsewhere. While the Johnson essay has its inconsistencies as far as the application of its own argument for individuality in fiction, as a stylistically savvy work of satire (and mostly if not always as a success in terms of argumentation) it is a wonderful piece of writing.

The concluding paragraph of "A Strong Race Opinion" contains this sentence: "There are many girls who have placed dainty red feet figuratively upon the white man's neck from the days of Pocahontas to those of little 'Bright Eyes,' who captured all Washington a few seasons ago" (183). This is vintage Johnson, the stuff of her writing and her life which included performances in both pan-tribal garb and a costume gown. We have florid language contrasted with the less-dainty-than-it-might-seem foot resting menacingly on the enemy's carotid artery. And somehow this maidenly menace occurs in the same sentence that celebrates one "Bright Eyes," who was the hit of the Washington social season!

Whatever one might say about Bob Dylan's singing, before the end of the first measure of the song you know exactly who you're listening to. That, friends, is a stylistic accomplishment that cannot be said about every singer. For all the raspy, nasalized tonal qualities of his voice, he has a recognizable style. I may not like the way Willie Nelson plays pentatonic scales over every solo, but between that pentatonic approach and the sound of the old Martin he plays and strings up with nylon instead of steel, I know it's him on damn near the first note. Nobody with half a lick of musical sense is gonna hear Mahalia and mistakenly think it's Billie. (Although I love the scene in *The Talented Mr. Ripley* in which Tom is trying to learn jazz, so he can get in tight [!] with Dickie [!], and when he quizzes himself with the Chet Baker record, he can't tell if it's a man or a woman, a common mistake given Baker's high tenor voice.)

As do these singers, a few literary critics, not a multitude, develop a recognizable style, and so does Johnson in the sentence I just quoted, as well as throughout "A Strong Race Opinion." It is subjective to say, but for this reason I believe the essay is her strongest work—and it is this stylistic break-through that also facilitates a different level of complexity than is usually apparent in her writing. An essay about race individuality is also about stylistic distinctiveness, and it is the latter that gives her a language to explore the former. I obsessed over this endlessly in writing *Red on Red*—on what kind of language could best explore Creek literature—and I don't think I pulled it off as successfully as Johnson, but, believe me, I thought then about the relation between style and meaning and am still considering the subject.

To my way of thinking a musical voice is as important to criticism as an analytical one. When bebop fell out of fashion in the 1950s and 1960s, Miles Davis decided he wasn't going to play jazz for a roomful of two people and started strategizing ways to keep an audience by exploring fusion. He began approaching ways to make jazz accessible, even entertaining. The album *Kind of Blue* had been a breakthrough because the melodies were so simple many people who couldn't keep up with the bebop players could learn them, thus opening up the music even to those who didn't play or listen to jazz; entertaining listeners with easily remembered melodies, and inviting a new audience by making the album enormously accessible. The complexity of the melodic lines has to do with the way their simplicity is altered by the way Bill Evans's chords change underneath them. And however sparse or simple the notes, they swing by means of Miles's phrasing, an infectious groove that we still study as a model. Literary criticism and theory have enough problems without writing them in such a fashion that no one wants to read them. If we want readers to seriously consider our ideas, they better groove, man.

Works Cited

Johnson, E. Pauline. "A Strong Race Opinion: On the Indian Girl in Modern Fiction." In *E. Pauline Johnson, Tekahionwake: Collected Poems and Selected Prose,* edited by Carole Gerson and Veronica Strong-Boag, 177–83. Toronto: University of Toronto Press, 2002.

Womack, Craig. *Red on Red: Native American Literary Separatism.* Minneapolis: University of Minnesota Press, 1999.

Caught in the Current,
Clinging to a Twig

I want to begin by acknowledging a source: I could not unfold the story I am about to tell if it weren't for the fine introduction to Daniel F. Littlefield's 1992 biography, *Alex Posey: Creek Poet, Journalist, and Humorist.*

It had rained for several days by the time young Alexander Posey boarded a train in Muskogee to head for his hometown of Eufaula, Oklahoma, on May 27, 1908. He was thirty-four years old. The anomaly of the city of Muskogee, which had housed a U.S. federal court in the middle of Creek Nation jurisdiction, had been a harbinger of things to come. Only the previous year a voracious federal appetite had swallowed up Posey's entire nation: allotment under the Dawes and Curtis Acts had replaced the Creek system of communal landholding; the U.S. government no longer recognized the Creek constitution, which dated back to 1867; they had forced a bicameral legislature out of existence, and Creeks had to abandon tribally run schools, orphanages, as well as other charitable institutions—not by choice. Creek people, as far as the United States was concerned, no longer existed.

There was one small problem. Alexander Posey, and about fifteen thousand other people like him, were still very much around. Perhaps something melancholy fell with the rain that day as Posey looked out at the standing ditch water rushing by in a muddy blur, at stands of post oaks that in previous years might have had a sign tacked to them telling him how to cast his vote for principal or second chief, at impressionistic, fleeting patches of Indian blanket and other spring wildflowers, yellows and reds refracted through a rain-streaked window. The kind of blues that had caused him to open a poem with the question "When flowers fade, why does / Their fragrance linger still? / Have they a spirit, too, that Death can never kill?" (*Poems of Alexander Lawrence Posey* 95). Not just any old blues but Indian blues, the terrible fear of someone writing you out of existence, of someone taking over your story before it's finished, hell, before you even get a chance to tell it.

A year had passed and maybe some of the initial terror had faded, the uncertainty of not knowing what would happen once his government folded.

It could be fear had been replaced by bitterness, and maybe by the time the train had passed Summit, or Butler Creek, or Oktaha, Posey had recollected all the Creek stories his parents had told him to keep him from wandering off in the woods, tales of the tall man who whipped trees while chasing after you, the little people who'd get you lost, the tie snake who pulled you into the water. He had never been one to stay in the yard as told, but somehow he had escaped a terrible fate, he thought with a grin.

When the train stopped just a couple miles north of Eufaula due to flood water running over the tracks, as Posey stepped off board onto the gravelly right of way, he might have felt a rush of muddy reminiscence that had once caused him to pen the lines, "The broad Canadian, red with sunset, / Now calm, now raging in a mighty fret!" (67). Posey could not have known that he had detrained onto a landscape that a little more than fifty years later would also be drowned out when the state of Oklahoma would dam up the Canadian River and create the second-largest lake in its boundaries. If Posey could foresee the WPA projects in the 1930s, and Lake Eufaula in the early 1960s, inundations that would drastically change the countryside, he might well have wondered what Oklahomans had against free-flowing water.

By the time my dad grew up around Eufaula and Weleetka, my mom just north of Haskell, in the 1940s, they'd dammed damn near everything. Things changed that people don't think about unless they have lived before and after the creation of a lake almost as big as a county. My relatives talk of the way travel altered, how it took longer to get everywhere since you had to take a different route—the long way around the lake, as they say. Places my grandpa walked behind a mule and my dad dragged a cotton sack became homes to schools of bass and crappie. Old family settlement patterns, and the meaning of matching kin within particular landscapes, were set adrift. Some of the wildest land in Oklahoma would be flooded. Those dependent on hunting would have to find other means to survive. Once again, just as they had earlier in Posey's own day as statehood loomed, the ambitious prophesied a financial downpour—this time from a resort economy, hotels, campsites, and bass and ski boats.

Though dammed some fifty years later, the water was certainly flowing that morning when Alex stepped off the train, pouring out of the cottonwoods, escaping their green colonnades, and raising some serious hell with the railroad tracks. The conductor thought the road bed was too weak to support the locomotive. The wash out was about fifteen feet wide. Alex, young and impatient, had business to attend to in Eufaula. The next day he had plans to go upriver from town, put in a boat, and float back down.

He had undertaken such trips before and kept a nature journal that tried to capture the river he worshipped in some kind of language worthy of its beauty. He knew a certain kinship linked his love of the river and his love of his nation, a relationship he had tried to gauge in his journals but still hadn't quite gotten right in his thirty-four young years. Maybe this trip it would happen.

He and his friend Robert Howe had a plan. Perhaps the next day's river float gave him an idea. Get a boat, row around the washout—the rest of the way to Eufaula would be easy. Alex wasn't afraid of the river. He had grown up around it, swum, fished, floated, and written it. The river was no longer a place to *him*. It had become a character in Alex's writing, and characters are the only real friends that authors have. Characters who step into being inside a writer's imagination, rather than the real ones a person might have coffee with, are nonetheless dangerous for all their ethereal airs.

Some years ago now, the first day in a house I had rented after I moved back to Oklahoma, I found out why the names of characters, the names of novels, and particularly the name *Drowning in Fire* might have generated a good deal of heat in the way that Alex's character the Oktahutchee, the Canadian River, had generated a good deal of water on May 27, 1908. Before I could even move in the house it went up in flames in a conflagration that could have easily killed me, my partner, and my dogs. The kitchen was destroyed while the moving truck was still parked out front. The strange rescue of a twenty-six-pound black mutt named Gwendolyn ensued, a dog who had been in my life, and the life of my partner, for well over a decade. (She finally succumbed to cancer in January 2006. As a pup she attended the second Returning the Gift Conference, as some will recall, in Norman, Oklahoma, in 1993.) The attempt to drive Gwendolyn out of the burning house was not entirely unlike the rescue of a mule simply called "Old One Eye" in the novel. In the real-life version, the word "rescue" might be overly euphemistic since we had given the dog up for dead after broken windows and much blood and three trips I made inside the house that were like swimming through black ink.

Gwendolyn, on a schedule of her own, came out of the house when she was good and ready, triumphantly stepping onto the front porch like the star of a Walt Disney movie. I made the newspaper, the *Norman Transcript*, where many friends saw my name before they even knew I'd moved back home. I had told people in my family they could easily remember my mailing address since it was Eufaula Street, same as dad's hometown. Should be good luck, I told them.

Alex and Robert Howe, after many aborted attempts, found someone who would lend them a boat. It *wasn't* their lucky day. But how were they to know, and I imagine Alex, forever the prankster, was having the time of his life running around the countryside pestering neighbors who more than likely wagged fingers and tongues at such foolishness and told the boys to sit down, eat breakfast, and wait for the river to subside like any damn fool with half a brain would do. "*Legibus cey*," they must have said, as they pulled out a chair and bid the young men to chill out. "You can stay here tonight, go back tomorrow. We've got an extry bed, a cot on the porch, a pallet in the back room." That's how it works where I'm from when we know you and some-times when we don't if you act right. Those of you participating in this story, with a sense of things to come, might wonder if anything could be that important, shaking your head at the impetuousness of youth. But on the banks of the river that day, my friend, full of piss and vinegar and fun, you might have climbed in the boat, too.

So much depends on an oar. It's the little things you lose that cause the biggest disasters. When the guy in the stern lost his, the current caught the boat. The other boatman panicked and lost his oar as well. The boat started moving sideways toward the washout. It hit the railroad right of way fence with such force that it sank, and the four men jumped over the fence to keep from getting tangled in it.

They're only chest deep in water. Yet the current is so strong that they have no choice but to bob up and down, headed for the washout. The water running under the rails is full of ties and debris. To go under is certain death. Their only hope is to stay in the middle of the current and swim over the drooping tracks. Alex grabs on to Robert's hand. But that's the way Alex is, you know, sweet, sure, but also a real Rabbit who has a way of getting himself stuck to the closest tar baby within grabbing distance. The intimacy was short lived, however, as Robert reiterates that they must go over individually, sticking to the very center of the current, swimming over the top of the rails.

Joel Scott, an African American man who lived near by who had found the boat for them, is the first, and he goes under and dies, likely as not his neck broken. Robert, Alex's friend, is next, and he goes over the rails successfully, swimming out on the Eufaula side of the break. Tom Brannon, Joel Scott's friend who had also helped procure the boat, swims successfully over the rails. Now Alex is alone, the last to go.

He isn't ready, and Alex grabs onto a tree that is no larger in girth than an umbrella handle and just clings there. It's a wonder he doesn't uproot the thing. Alex wrote a poem once called "My Fancy." It's short. This is it:

Why do trees along the river
Lean so far out o'er the tide?
Very wise men tell me why, but
I am never satisfied;
And so I keep my fancy still,
That trees lean out to save
The drowning from the clutches of
The cold, remorseless wave. (85)

Not much of a poem, maybe, before May 27, 1908, when it took on new meaning, Alex clinging to a twig, eternity tugging at him with all its might. They say context is everything.

You can only hold on so long. In an old Creek story Rabbit goes to ask God for wisdom. God assigns Rabbit four tests, one of which involves bringing back an alligator; Rabbit totally screws it up the first time. The second go at it, however, he brings the gator back to God, dead as a doornail, just as promised. Instead of granting Rabbit wisdom, however, God just wants more and more and more—this time, a sackful of mosquitoes. How do you get mosquitoes to fill up a bag, even in Oklahoma, or Alabama, or Georgia, or Florida, or other such Creeky places, Rabbit pondered, but *come back with a sack of mosquitoes he did*. Now God wants a rattlesnake. Some Gods are never satisfied. Rabbit kills the rattlesnake by telling him he bets he isn't as long as a piece of wood if he were to stretch up against it or up agin' it as my grandmother might say if she were telling this story right now. In later years Creek Freudians would call this wood envy. Anyway, Rabbit plunges a thorn through the rattlesnake's head and brings God his snake on a stick, wondering what's this thing God has with all this dead stuff.

Instead of granting him wisdom, as promised, God tells Rabbit he's already too damned smart and predicts he'll always rip off old ladies, sneaking in gardens and chowing down on their cabbage. Rabbit says, "What the hell does that have to do with anything? Your stories never make any sense, God." God doesn't say who *she'll* be ripping off, maybe more Rabbits looking for wisdom. This isn't a story about Rabbit the trickster; this is a story about the capriciousness of God, about the scary shit you never saw coming when Oz turns out to be some snake-oil salesman turning gears behind a giant screen, and he has no idea how to get you back to Kansas.

Alex can't hold on forever. Robert Howe is limping up and down the bank, begging someone to run the two miles to Eufaula to get some rope to throw out to Alex clinging desperately to his twig, and, you know what, *no one will do it.* Forget the friendly Okies in the musical where the wind goes sweeping down the plains; these are a bunch of sick fucks who aren't going to step out into the lobby to buy some popcorn just when the guy on the screen might get his neck broke. Howe's begging has a new, poignant urgency, nothing like the gleeful romp around the countryside jokingly pleading for a boat that was only a few minutes and a few lifetimes earlier when *both* friends stood on dry land.

One spectator can't go because of a sore foot. Another has rheumatism. Tom Brannon's father says he's not leaving his boy's side. Somebody else says he's afraid to cross the river bridge downstream. Not exactly a bunch of warriors. There's quite a large crowd watching now, and Howe himself runs off to Eufaula in spite of a severe leg injury. God only knows what he was thinking on his run—if anything—other than faster. Maybe I should have taken Alex's hand. Could we have made it over together? Might I have given him the courage he needed?

It's possible the spectators get tired of waiting for Alex to break his neck or maybe they were never as bad as I make them out to be, and I'm just sending you running after more alligators, mosquitoes and snakes, but finally some-one came to Alex's aid. They find another boat and tie it to the right-of-way fence. The current is still very strong, however, and they can only get the boat within a few feet of Alex. The yokels have found some rope after all, one to tie the boat with obviously, and another to throw out to Alex. Alex tells his longtime friend W. C. Coppick to toss the rope out to him and pull him in.

"Are you scared?" Coppick asks. Coppick doesn't want Alex to grab the rope when he is panicked and let go. Alex now has one hand on the rope, the other on the tree. Those in the boat beg him not to grab on with both hands until he is ready. Alex grabs on, and the current sweeps him off his feet. It's like he's being towed by a ski boat, just four feet behind. It's not very funny to think fifty years later skiers towed behind boats would pass exactly overhead. Ex-hausted, Alex is unable to pull himself in. As W. C. hauls him in, Alex's grip on the rope slips.

Alex turns his head twice.

Once toward Howe standing helplessly on the bank, returned from Eufaula, the second time toward the washout, the current rushing through the hole in the road bed. Alex opens his hands.

Alexander Posey had been an unusual kind of writer. He started out writing poetry at Bacone University in Muskogee. For all that his poetry lacked at Bacone, it never got much better in later years. It was imitative verse that applied a sentimental European pastoral sense to Muskogee Creek country,

sometimes even populating Indian Territory landscape with Greek and Ro-
man gods and goddesses. Rather than naming the natural world that comprised his Creek environs, Posey invents a simulation of a place that he never
experienced personally but read about in nineteenth-century British sentimental poems.

A much more interesting literary development for Posey during his time at
Bacone was a fictional persona he created by the name of Chinubbie Harjo,
who shared Rabbit's love of inflicting suffering on others. In one of his Bacone
stories, "Chinubbie and the Owl," Chinubbie wins a storytelling contest by
reciting an elaborate lie about how he tricks an owl to keep turning his head
round and round until it twists clean off. This story prefigured things to come,
particularly with its complex narrative frame of stories within stories, the
story of the storytelling contest, and the actual story that wins it, a framing
device that will later brilliantly evolve into a body of literature that will become known as the Fus Fixico Letters.

In early 1902, Alex had become editor of the Eufaula *Indian Journal,* a paper
that is still published today in my grandmother's hometown, although it is no
longer an Indian-owned paper. Yet it still features many Creek Nation events.
Posey donned an elaborate disguise in which he pretended he didn't speak or
write English very well, and he sent in letters to the editor of the paper who
was, in actuality, himself. Earlier, at Bacone, Posey had read a wide array of
British, and even classical, literature. Unlike the hoax he was pulling off in the
paper with his illiterate letter writers, Posey was gifted in his use of standard
English in both its spoken and written forms.

Posey wrote these letters in a special dialect he called Este Charte (stijaati)
English, which simply means Indian English in Creek, the broken English of
someone who grew up speaking Creek as his first language. Students of African American literature might be reminded of the Jesse B. Semple letters of
Langston Hughes. Posey's own use of dialect is stylized, a form of caricature.

Posey used these letters to develop a political language best suited for cri-
tiquing the Oklahoma statehood process. Posey had eventually become convinced that the most viable future for the tribes was getting Indian Territory
admitted as a separate state where Indian nations would retain their governments and constitutions rather than simply being extinguished under the new
state of Oklahoma.

The fascinating aspect of the letters is Posey's attempt at inventing a spe-
cialized Creek literary language that deviated from normal speech because of
its caricaturized style, yet was immediately recognizable by Creek people,
many of whom knew those who talked something like Posey's characters. The

letters represent the most successful integration of fictional formats and political commentary in the history of American Indian writing.

Posey insisted on addressing a Creek audience in these letters, and when they became very popular in Indian Territory, he resisted making them more widely available in regional newspapers in the United States. Posey was trying to rally the tribes rather than entertain outsiders.

In all the ways that Posey's poetry failed, his letters succeeded. They create an extremely strong sense of place, evoking a feeling for the countryside around Eufaula: the town's streets and buildings, the speech of its citizens, natural details in the surrounding woods, the stomp grounds outside of town, Creek farming patches and Indian houses, a whole world, what the American realist William Faulkner, referring to his own fiction, called "his own little postage stamp of native soil."

During Posey's day the Creek Nation varied from Creek fullbloods, and some mixedbloods as well, taking medicine and dancing at traditional Creek ceremonial centers known as stomp grounds, to Creek Baptist and Methodist preachers explicating the gospel in Creek, reading out of Creek bibles, and singing out of Creek hymnals; from merchants and cattle ranchers leasing thousands of acres to subsistence farmers practicing Creek agriculture; from those who didn't speak English to those, like Posey, who had gone to Bacone and studied classical literature; from medicine men and town chiefs to tribal judges who worked for the nation and presided over court decisions; to Creeks with black skin and brown skin and white skin pure as the driven snow; and these represent only a few of the possibilities.

Is this, in fact, an example of what contemporary theorists would come to call hybridity? Well, today we would probably say yes. I strongly suspect, however, during Posey's time, that Alex himself just saw these things as the Creek realities that surrounded him. When he visited G. W. Grayson—a mixedblood friend of Posey's who looked very white and had also achieved a high level of education for his time—at his store in Eufaula, it's not very likely that Posey thought of Grayson as anything other than a Creek citizen, though surely he must have realized there were a lot of different kinds of Creek citizens.

We might begin then with the simple claim that self-consciousness about hybridity is neither ahistorical nor universal. Nonetheless, theorists often speak of hybridity, ironically enough, as if it were its own kind of essentialism; that is, they often speak of it apart from history. Today we might see Posey as an example of hybridity; however, we cannot be certain Posey saw himself in the same light during his own era.

What, then, is hybridity, and what is nationalism? The hybridity debates have to do with whether or not hybridity is an inherent, inevitable condition. I will concede that often it is, and that cultures are influenced both within and without their borders, that cultures are influenced *by* other cultures and assert their influences *on* other cultures. There are three problems with the way hybridity has been applied to Indian studies, however. The first is the assumption that Native people have only been on the receiving end of cultural assimilation rather than also influencing the European cultures that surround them. The second has been a recently theorized discourse in which hybridity itself becomes the main point—to the extent of obscuring Native intellectual history. The third is when critics assume that the inevitability of cultural hybridity makes any form of nationalism theoretically untenable. I will not delve into these three debates since I have addressed these matters in *American Indian Literary Nationalism,* but I will say something about them in relation to tribal sovereignty.

One particular aspect of nationalism important to Native Studies is the idea, and the practice of, tribal sovereignty. In its most literal legal terms sovereignty has to do with the government-to-government relationships between tribes and the United States, based on treaties. In its most metaphorical sense it includes all the ways a community imagines itself. You can win all the court cases in the world, but if you are not sovereign inside your own head it won't do you any good. One of the central places imaginative sovereignty thrives is within written and oral literatures through which communities present images of themselves to both their own members and the outside world—that is, within and across their borders. Essential to sovereignty is both a personal internal authority based on an individual's sense of what is right for herself and a collective sovereignty based on the needs of the larger group. These two sovereignties are as often in tension as happily co-existent; yet they are important interdependencies.

In my own definitions of sovereignty I concur with Robert Warrior, who claims in *Tribal Secrets* that Native American sovereignties must be viewed as open-ended processes rather than static definitions. Even in legal terms, where the definitions may be relatively more fixed than they are in metaphorical forms of sovereignty, tribes may hope some day for a legal status more empowering than that of domestic dependent nationhood as defined by the Marshall trilogy of Supreme Court decisions in the early part of the nineteenth century. Sovereignty, most people in Indian country would agree, whether on a legal front that protects homelands and jurisdiction, or on an imaginative front that allows the evolution of cultures, is essential to Indian survival.

Given the central role of sovereignty in Native American Studies, then, a key question is can one be a nationalist and, at the same time, committed to inclusivity, dialogism, alternative histories, diversity of perspectives, plurality, cosmopolitanism, global awareness, border crossing, and justice? Do the nationalistic aspects of sovereignty, at best, compete with diversity, and, at worst, make diversity impossible?

Considering our concerns with the effects of globalism these days, I would like to suggest that American Indian sovereignty is at the very heart of any meaningful discussion regarding transnationalism and border crossing because of the way in which tribes have almost two centuries of experience of having to mount legal defenses that involve defining the parameters of nationhood. The question "what constitutes a modern nation state?" and the issue of the degree of relevance of such states to today's world is central to both tribal and global studies.

Nowhere have these issues been more contested than in Indian country. Given that U.S. tribal sovereignty is defined as government-to-government relations, sovereignty embodies a constant movement between inside and outside, between and betwixt borders, in relation to tribes and federal policies, and even to nations in Europe where many treaties originated and, in some cases, governmental relationships still occur, a case in point being the Canadian tribes and their ongoing relationship with the British Crown. If the student of globalism is interested in the question of what are the ramifications of the modern nation state, where can she find a better study than Indian country? Is a community of 56,000 people, to use an example close to home, who do not have a land base but have jurisdiction in ten counties that they must also share with the state of Oklahoma, enough to constitute a nation? Obviously, I am going to argue that it is. In what ways do their borders intersect with the governments, Indian and non-Indian, that surround them?

Is a community of less than two hundred tribal people who are now landless, who have lost their language, whose tribal citizenship is based largely on remote ancestry, enough to constitute a nation of people? How much is enough? Are these, in fact, quantitative matters? Surely, within Indian country resides one of the most interesting debates in the modern world, concerning what it means to claim the validity of nationhood and what such a concept entails given the fluid borders of our planet.

Sovereignty is the very antithesis of an isolationist position and its definitions and interpretations have involved constant negotiations between inside and outside. No tribal literary nationalist that I know of claims that the value of sovereignty resides in its purity, its isolation, or its ability to go undetected.

A sovereignty that fails to interact across its borders would be no sovereignty at all. Tribal nationalism should be seen as central to any mature understanding of globalism and the fluidity of borders rather than some kind of obstacle blocking a superior postmodern enlightenment.

No doubt we must constantly challenge definitions of sovereignty. Critics might legitimately ask how effectively tribal governments and certain practices of self-determination have worked. We might seriously question, for example, social programs supported by federal funds or even certain forms of wealth redistribution through per-capita payments that have come about as a result of tribal operations, such as casinos, when social challenges seem as rampant as ever in some communities that receive such benefits. Money provides an inadequate solution if money itself is the problem and if an environment is created in which people cannot imagine any other answer to their problems than income. As we evaluate sovereignty we have to at least raise the question as to whether substantial change can come exclusively through tribal governments and federal programs.

We should study more grassroots movements within Indian country and even outside it. I have thought about Harvey Milk a lot recently because I reread Randy Shilts's *The Mayor of Castro Street* in anticipation of the much-touted Gus Van Sant film. Milk was assassinated one month before I graduated high school, and I was living near Sacramento at the time. Reading the book helped me understand why I felt so frightened then—it was for good reason. At any rate, the very meaning of so much of what Milk accomplished before he got elected to the San Francisco Board of Supervisors had to do with his engagement in forms of activism that didn't cost anything—most famously, his human billboards. He couldn't run big-money campaigns, so he had his friends make signs and line up along Market Street. Much of Milk's early work focused on a few blocks around Castro and Fifteenth, a microcosm, and people showed up at his camera chop to talk about things as simple as how to get a stoplight put in at a busy intersection near the school in their neighborhood.

One might suspect that if Milk's life had not been tragically cut short, and he had succeeded in city politics by attaining higher offices, he might have become less—not more—politically effective, as his needs would have naturally turned toward funding and a larger scope than neighborhood affairs (as it already had in his work as a city supervisor).

If change comes to Indian country, one wonders if it will come through funding or instead through grassroots efforts concentrated on work as simple as people helping find homes for stray dogs wandering their streets, volunteers planting community vegetable gardens in a local war against the life-threatening effects of bad diet, fluent speakers hosting language immersion classes that meet in people's living rooms instead of universities, individuals starting running clubs to encourage exercise, and so on. This kind of social organization duplicates age-old structures that have worked in Indian societies. Whenever I meet people trying to do something, almost the first thing out of their mouths is a particular disclaimer: "We don't have any money"— even for projects that don't require any. People tell me all the time they want to write a book, but they don't have any funds. I try to explain to them that writing doesn't work that way. You start a book with a story, not a bank account. I often suspect that if the people I talk to did have financial support, the *toknawa* would hinder, not help, their efforts.

All this is to say that we may very well have to reimagine sovereignty apart from funding and federal programs. Such a claim, however, has nothing to do with discarding sovereignty but with studying possibilities that give communities agency instead of more external control. I'm not talking about disbanding tribal governments or cutting off federal funding but thinking about ways to get people to imagine themselves managing their own lives and acting on those imaginings.

By the time Alex swept helplessly underneath the railroad tracks, and his body emerged on the other side briefly near the right of way fence, then disappeared, nearly one hundred people had gathered on the shore, watching. Some traditional Creeks believe that Alex was swallowed up by the very river he loved because he had gotten himself involved in real estate speculation after statehood, profiting by the sale of Creek-allotted lands. Some of the land he sold, perhaps, would itself be inundated under the waters of Lake Eufaula fifty years later.

Louis Littlecoon Oliver, a contemporary Creek author writing some eighty years after Posey, and a great admirer of his predecessor, sees a strange culmination of spiritual forces in Alex's life, even relating Posey's death to his vocation and choices of subject matter as an author. Oliver writes,

> There was a young Creek Indian person
> who attained an education
> and wrote beautiful poetry
> in English.
> Sad to say, he was taken away from us
> too soon.
> He attempted to cross the Canadian River
> when it was on a rampage,
> it swept him away to his death
> it is said

Had he not changed his name to
      Chenube Harjo,
   the river would not have taken him.
   Many will believe my thought.
The Harjos were strange and mystical people
      with possible animosities
from the Snakes, Alabamas, Espagogees, Seminoles.
      I'm not naming all the others,
      but you my people would know them.

I'm speaking about Alexander Posey;
      I believe a "hex" was put
         upon his soul
It is said he was not a fullblood Indian
      and estranged from his people
      by the Whiteman's ways.
His mother was the daughter of Pohos Harjo,
and a member of the Wind clan
      of the town of Taskegee
         it is said.
So Alexander Posey was born of
      Mixed and strange spirits
      and precious persons too,
that made him walk in the steps
      of two personalities
         it is said.

Littlecoon. I have spoken. (*Estiyut Omayat* 17)

A pool of water near the river bridge close to Alex's drowning became known
as Posey's Hole. In the next twenty-five years, ten people drowned there or
died from other accidents.

I wonder if Alexander Posey could have imagined four hundred Native
Hawai'ians in a federal penitentiary in Watonga, Oklahoma, in the heart
of the jurisdiction of the Cheyenne-Arapaho Nation, one of his Southern
Plains tribal neighbors within the territory? Not long ago, before I saw it
with my own eyes, I could not have conjured up such a vision myself until a friend of mine, a Muskogee Creek minister for the United Church of
Christ, cajoled me into going inside Diamondback Correctional Center to
meet with Native Hawai'ian men. Diamondback's name is strangely fitting. It

is like a space station in the middle of the prairie; its beacons light up the countryside for miles.

The reverend Rosemary Maxey is an interesting anomaly herself. She is descended from a long line of Creek Baptist preachers. Her call to the ministry was complicated by the fact that her particular Native Christian tradition does not ordain women. Unlike her male forebears she could not step behind a pulpit and proclaim the gospel in Creek as they had done for several generations in her family. She had to be ordained outside her own community. As a UCC pastor involved in peace and justice issues, she feels called to serve Native people. She has a large, expansive sense of those she is meant to serve—that is, those who constitute her brethren and sistren.

When she found out that, due to severely overcrowded prison conditions in Hawai'i, Native people were being sent to the privately contracted correctional center in Watonga, Oklahoma, she became concerned about the loss of contact these men would suffer in relation to their families and home communities thousands of miles away. Unlike ordinary prisoners, for these men, family visits would be an impossibility.

As Reverend Maxey began to visit and get to know the prisoners, she found out they were being denied their religious rights to practice traditional Hawai'ian chants, which prison officials had discredited as forms of martial arts, cult practices, and potential gangs. Reverend Maxey was centrally involved in a lawsuit in which the prisoners were suing for their religious freedom.

On Friday, June 11, 2004, I found myself in a prison yard with four hundred Native Hawai'ian men. It was 105 degrees out and most of them were standing in the sun. There was some shade up around the makeshift stage where prisoners and visitors from Hawai'i, whom Reverend Maxey had organized to come to the prison, were speaking, celebrating King Kamehameha Day. I wasn't entirely sure how I'd ended up there. Reverend Maxey is something of a tar baby herself. She gets you stuck to her causes, and the more you kick or try to bust loose, the harder you stick. This is a good thing because she is one of the smartest and most progressive-minded people within the Creek Nation today, and there is much to learn from being around her.

The prisoners, many of them musicians, were playing some really cool slack-key guitar stuff to get the program going. One of the prisoners began the event with the blowing of the conch shell. That sound, that invocation, brought us into a sacred place that transcended all the rolls of barbed wire and chain link, and I contemplated the way that Creeks used to have the same tradition at churches when they began services with a deacon blowing the conch. Reverend Maxey gave the opening prayer, which somehow managed to honor Hawai'ian deities, King Kamehameha, the Creek invocation of Ibo-fanka which ceremonialists use, and recognition of Hesaketemesse which Creek Christians refer to, as well as an acknowledgement of the very ground we were standing on within the jurisdiction of the Cheyenne Nation. This was something of a verbal feat, no matter the theological problems such a synthesis might imply.

The men were very kind that day, overwhelmed that anyone had gotten in to see them, and they kept bringing us water and chairs to sit in. Whenever a Hawai'ian man would bring her water, the Reverend Maxey would tell me to take note. Her day-long teasing ran along the lines of "When was the last time you ever saw a *Creek* man serving a woman?" She told me that she hoped that for once I was learning something.

Rosemary would continue to work at Diamondback, making the three-hour trip from Dustin, Oklahoma, every Monday. Truly she has earned the men's trust, and they call her "Auntie." Sometimes I think of her when I read things written about Diamondback by those who have never been inside, or even this essay, which could never match her real-life dedication, given the sporadic Mondays I accompany her when I'm able.

Hawai'ian UCC pastor Ron Fujiyoshi spoke of his own experience in prison in Japan for civil disobedience and his dream of more traditional forms of healing for Hawai'ians rather than retributive punishment.

It was getting close to my turn to speak, and I was scared shitless. I have never been in a more daunting rhetorical situation. It wasn't because of the usual fears one might have about visiting a prison, the possibility of riots, being taken hostage, the realization that prison officials have a policy against negotiation. It was because whatever I was doing felt so different than when I stand up in front of university students. I was listening to all these cool songs the prisoners were playing, the speeches that seemed directly related to life inside the walls, and I didn't have a clue what I might have to offer. I kept wishing they could just keep playing music, or better yet, I could sit in and play guitar with them. Forget the speech. Why did they need to listen to me?

My talk had to do with Chitto Harjo, a leader of the Creek resistance against Oklahoma statehood, who I compared to the line of various Kamehamehas who had fought against the annexation of Hawai'i. I began by commenting that as I looked in all four directions, I saw Cheyenne jurisdiction all around me. I joked, "We might want to remind Cheyenne leaders of some of the buildings that have been going up on their lands in recent years. Personally," I said, "I would have preferred an Indian casino." Not a laugh in the crowd, not one out of four hundred.

I had failed to measure the degree of these men's isolation not only in Hawai'i, where few of them led privileged lives that afforded them an education about the outside world, or even the inside world, but the fact that they had, literally, been dropped down, out of an airplane, smack dab in the middle of a state that many of them could not even locate on a map.

In fact, one prisoner, who interviewed me after my talk for a newspaper they were circulating in the prison, drew me a map of what he thought the state of Oklahoma probably looked like. He did it pretty well, had the handle stuck to an appropriately-proportioned pan. Then he said, "Now, can you put a dot about where we are at?" While I spoke many of them were chatting with one another, seemingly inattentive.

It was a difficult speaking experience. In the classroom, when you are bombing, you start pushing other buttons; you find something else that might work; you quickly shift gears. I didn't know what any of those buttons *were* there in the middle of the prison yard in Watonga. I doubt if I'm the only intellectual who might have a hard time relating to prisoners, and I think that is the very best reason for me to be there—few things worthwhile are easy.

After I finished and sat back down, I was able to relax some, and just visit with people around me. I was especially interested in the number of transgendered folk there and tried to say hello—just make small talk, which island are you from, that kind of thing.

The prisoners performed some amazing chants, as did the traditional people from Hawai'i who had come to visit them. I found this to be moving, especially since some of the prisoners had explained to me that they had not had the kind of traditional leadership they needed to learn how to do the chants as precisely correct as maybe they could have. Yet it was all there, the joy of it when Native people begin to feel a sense of themselves, a celebration of things that have of necessity been hidden in the past, a declaration, on their own terms, of what constitutes their identities. Inside such moments, I believe, are profound possibilities for realizing the ways in which nationalism, in this case an assertion of Hawai'ian and Creek sovereignties in the middle of Cheyenne jurisdiction with the ever-present Oklahoma barbed wire bearing witness, is not an impediment to transcendent borders but, for some of us, the very means of achieving them—a spirit, the poet called it, that death can never kill.

Works Cited

Oliver, Louis Littlecoon. *Estiyut Omayat: Creek Writings*. Muskogee, Okla.: Indian University Press, 1985.
———. *The Horned Snake*. Merrick, N.Y.: Cross-Cultural Communications, 1982.

Posey, Alexander. "Chinnubbie and the Owl." In *Chinnubbie and the Owl: Muscogee (Creek) Stories, Orations, and Oral Traditions,* edited by Matthew Wynn Sivils, 35–40. Lincoln: University of Nebraska Press, 2005.

——. *The Fus Fixico Letters: A Creek Humorist in Early Oklahoma.* Norman: University of Oklahoma Press, 2002.

——. *Poems of Alexander Lawrence Posey, Creek Indian Bard.* Muskogee, Okla.: Hoffman, 1969.

Shilts, Randy. *The Mayor of Castro Street: The Life and Times of Harvey Milk.* New York: St. Martin's Press, 1982.

Womack, Craig. *Drowning in Fire.* Tucson: University of Arizona Press, 2001.

Aestheticizing a Political Debate
Can the Confederacy Be Sung Back Together?

In my previous chapter about the last day of Alexander Posey's life, I tried to improvise off of Pauline Johnson's model, which vacillates between analysis and performance, and also bring in some satire in hopes of imitating the best of "A Red Girl's Reasoning" and "A Strong Race Opinion." Part of the reason for studying these authors, I would like to suggest, is imitating them, and this is the way we school ourselves in any craft. At the time of this writing I am trying to learn at least one of the horn solos for each cut on *Kind of Blue* on my guitar. How else are you going to learn to play jazz? To write? For a couple years when I first started writing fiction, I kept a journal of sentences I thought rocked the world. I tried to compose sentences of my own that sounded like those of my heroes. Some people might consider this imitative, but the real word for it is "training." A horn man would be goofy to think he was going to become a great bebop player without learning any tunes of Diz's, Bird's, and all the rest. I cannot imagine writing working any differently.

Let's review what we have covered thus far: gesturing toward a wholistic strategy, I have tried to approach art in these chapters so that narrative, music, visual works, and performance are part of a continuum instead of separate endeavors. One of our review questions should be this: what happens when fiction crashes criticism's party and vice-versa? I have attempted forms of critique that perform art rather than merely discuss it. Lived experience is as important to me as archival research, although the chapter to come, on Lynn Riggs's plays *The Cream in the Well* and *The Year of Pilár*, delve about as deep into the Riggs archive as anyone possibly can. Yet as the play I have written and my novella attest, my discussion of Riggs is also highly fictionalized. Even in the heavily researched nonfiction chapter on the two plays, I occasionally imagine fictional scenarios, locating Riggs's in my mind's eye, as N. Scott Momaday might say. In terms of affecting the literary world in some very small way, I hope for a reinvigoration of little-known works by bringing them not only into criticism, but into new fiction that reimagines authors and their characters. Simply put, I'd love to see a revival of interest in Lynn Riggs. As Justin does, I hope Lynn resurrects; and I'll be far less bitchy about it than Roe Náld. As far as cultural theory goes, to end with one final review point, I neither deny the reality of outside influences, nor give up on the possibility of a tribal aesthetic; instead, I have simply tried to examine whatever is most interesting about the artistic subjects I study.

Next, I want to examine the frustrating challenge of relating literature to the real world in hopes of seeing social change in our lifetimes: a highly idealistic task, though not an impossible one, and certainly one we should not abandon because of its difficulty. Alexander Posey's freedmen stories, more than any literature I have examined to date, allow me to connect contemporary concerns to art.

Alexander Posey's story "Uncle Dick and Uncle Will," about African Americans living just outside of Eufaula within Creek jurisdiction at the turn of the twentieth century, begins with the obvious: "Uncle Will was Uncle Dick's cousin" (49).

Let me put this one to you: if Uncle Dick and Uncle Will are cousins, then, friends, who are their nephews and nieces?

Warning: Think carefully before you answer the question.

Posey's narrative style in his stories about African American Creek citizens in "Uncle Dick and Uncle Will," "Uncle Dick's Sow," "Jes 'Bout a Mid'lin', Sah," and "Mose and Richard," combines the pastoral voice prevalent in Posey's poetry, here manifested in the narrator's depiction of a country idyll, with the dialect voices of the Fus Fixico Letters—in this case the speech of the African American characters around the settlements of Possum Flat and Coon Creek, outside of Eufaula.

"Uncle Dick and Uncle Will" opens with depictions of "wells of pure water" (49), as well as "open woods and pasture fields, which impart healthy and balsamic odors to the breeze" (49). Theirs is a "sequestered existence" (49), and the families who live there "prone to imbibe but little of the wide-awake spirit that is abroad in the world" (49). Whether or not the Afro-Creek community needs one, Posey's narrator also functions as master of ceremonies, telling us all we need to know, purportedly, about its inhabitants. Generously, we might note Posey's knowledge of classical rhetoric given his references—in poems, letters, and stories—to Greek myth, for example, and mark the similarity between his narrator and the commentary of the chorus. More realistically, we might see a darker edge to his pastoralism and narrative commentary, given his tendency in the freedmen stories to speak on the behalf of others who end up silenced in the process.

The emcee of this particular pow wow seems to be calling all the shots, and the jokes are less benign than the cornball announcer's one-liners. The characters may fall in line with Posey's own racist imaginings; for certain we can say the narrator stereotypes the freedmen as "simple people" (49), as indolent ("The other very important attribute—indolence—of this dark community is probably due to the fecundity of the soil" [49]), and as liars, some more artfully so than others ("he [Uncle Dick] was the incarnation of the ingenuity that fashions specious tales" [49]). As the narrator pulls the strings of his Afro-Indian puppets, when he reports on their herky-jerky doings, they become a monolithic They. In fact, They sound a good deal like the noble savage depictions of Indians written by white Indian lovers of the time, except that this particular They come off a little sillier. Although they are depicted as more noble than savage, still, the narrator's vantage point in relation to his characters is rooted in the kind of racialized assumptions of the ethnographic expert speaking on the subject of the "black mind." Thus, they seem a lot like nineteenth-century popular depictions of Indians. This conflation is more than coincidental.

The dialect is important because this is where, in a sense, the African American characters get to speak for themselves. They are still presented through a narrator, as are the viewpoints of all other fictional characters, even first-person ones. They reveal something important: how the narrator imagines them to be presenting themselves. Probably the most obvious characteristic is not the dialogue but the dialect—speech patterns so colloquialized it is sometimes hard to figure out what the characters are saying. A racist narrator or author might argue, "But that's what they really sound like." Realistic or not, of course, issues of who is controlling this speech, and the depiction it creates, make the dialect problematic.

The language of European pastoral surrounds, and often confounds, the integrity of the dialect. Expository sentences that lead into the quotations sometimes feel as if two ships have collided full speed ahead: "Through the dense fog, so characteristic of the low grounds along the Coon Creek at daybreak in wet weather, he descried the vague outlines of Uncle Dick's sow, uprooting his fine sweet potatoes. 'Dat dah ol' nigger's agawine ter hab trouble wid me dis bery moanin,' he murmured" (51). When Posey deals with Indian characters in his Fus Fixico Letters, he much more seamlessly integrates dialogue and exposition, assimilating everything, including European literary references and diction, into a powerful Creekness that turns it Indian. Here narrator and narrated speak two very different languages, the latter lacking the agency Posey gives his Indian characters to overtake and overwhelm Europe by asserting Indian powers of transformation on language.

If this were all there is in these four stories—that is, the suppression of Afro-Creek agency—I would never have dragged you all along even this far. Let me tell you why they are worth reading.

A close friend of Posey's, G. W. Grayson, held political offices in the Nation during the decades of the 1880s and the 1890s, when Posey published the stories. Posey skewered friends and enemies because of their African American ancestry—friendly gibes in relation to political allies, and virulent attacks in the case of enemies. In his introduction to *Chinubbie and the Owl*, Matt Wynn Sivils documents one of the worst statements of Posey's: "Our command of Creek is fluent and we are more or less familiar with English and Choctaw, to say nothing of our meager knowledge of stock quotations in Greek and Latin, but language fails us when we attempt to express our disappointment of the choice of the Union party for the next chief of the Creek people. All that we are able to say is that he is a nigger and a bad one at that" (20).

Yet new work has come to light that reveals that not only did Posey's friend G. W. Grayson himself probably have African American ancestry, and that some of his family had married African slaves passing the Grayson name and bloodline on to the freedmen community, but that Grayson himself wrote about these matters in his autobiography—evidently wanting his family to understand the extent of their relations, both black and Indian. Claudio Saunt's excellent 2005 critical history, *Black, White, and Indian: Race and the Unmaking of an American Family,* reveals that University of Oklahoma historian E. Everett Dale expurgated all references to African American relatives from the Grayson autobiography, and Saunt speculates about what was erased. In his biography on Alexander Posey, Daniel F. Littlefield, a scrupulous researcher and genealogist, documents that the Graysons of Coon Creek that Posey wrote about were an actual freedmen family Posey knew. Saunt has offered possible evidence that the freedmen and Creek Graysons are biological relatives.

For our discussion, then, we might broach the possibility that these four fictional works about the black Graysons of Coon Creek are a means of poking fun at Posey's friend, G. W. Grayson—something he, in fact, did at times in his Fus Fixico Letters, although not in relation to Grayson's African American relatives.

This, I must admit, is a guess, fraught with all the problems inherent in speculating about authors' intentions.

What Posey really meant, the stories' authentic Creek meanings, and their traditional interpretation—all of these are slippery slopes. I have, nonetheless, speculated about such things in the past when I felt there was a good reason to do so. In this case, however, I am interested in analyzing these particular stories as beginning, rather than ending, points. Rather than offering a "correct interpretation," I want to explore the ways in which we might become story-tellers ourselves, how we might tell stories about the stories, especially in relation to contemporary events in the nation that surround the freedmen controversy. I want to apply an artistic approach to a political debate—the possibility of looking at freedmen issues from a creative angle as much as from legal and historical claims. In some ways I'm just as interested in the least Creek, the least traditional, the least Indian possibilities for interpreting these stories.

Claudio Saunt has also provided evidence to the fact that some black Graysons in the Eufaula area were also Creek. Posey's freedmen stories to some degree are about his fellow tribesmen, not about a black community with no Creek ancestry or cultural connections, which is the way some Creeks view the freedmen today. That the community he depicts is comprised of Creek citizens is obvious because in one of the stories "Jes 'Bout a Mid'lin', Sah," he depicts the Coon Creek settlement voting in Creek elections. Today, some Creeks would argue that just because the group got to vote during this time period does not prove they were "real Creeks," an argument that I find lacking in terms of artistic imagination. Posey, I believe, knew that significant numbers of the freedmen had Creek ancestry, and also that Creeks of his acquaintance had African ancestry.

He certainly knew it in relation to Legus Perryman, and other political enemies he castigated in racial terms.

These stories about black Creeks, then, intersect with the history of a prominent national politician, G. W. Grayson, and also with the story of the nation itself, by virtue of its historical interrelations with African Americans.

All four stories are structured along the lines of paired characters who serve as foils to one another. Uncle Will, we are told, "was as unlike his famous kin [Uncle Dick] as an acorn is unlike a banana" (50). Will is circumspect in his storytelling; Dick is profuse. Will is the verbal artist who masters irony: "Learning that a certain one had reported that he was in habit of frequenting his neighbors' chicken roosts at night, he said, "De folks jus' now unkiver dat fac'? I's been a libin heah 'mos' fo'teen yeahs" (50). Dick, on the other hand, lies to suit his purposes rather than for narrative excellence.

Richard and Mose, two young school students in another of the freedmen stories, are set up exactly the same way, as foils to one another: "Mose was unlike Richard in nearly every particular" (64). Richard doesn't pay attention to school lessons and gets in fights, whereas Mose

> was not apt at cunning, nor quick to engage in conflict or dispute. He was lazy and easy-going. He liked, above all things, peace, shade and watermelons [!]. Richard could offer no inducement to cause Mose to

become his partner in what Uncle Dick called "tricks an' debilment." Even when Richard was the under dog in the fight, Mose would go about his business, as if he was not his brother and allow him to be beaten. But if to play at marbles was what Richard wanted, Mose could content him and beat him at his own game. (64)

If we read these doubled characters metaphorically as, Creeks and freedmen, there is no simple equation in which one is the "underdog" and the other his oppressor, since—as Mose demonstrates—he can just as easily be the victor, even if only at marbles. There is a lot more savvy to the story than some simplistic victimization of either party. The loquacious Dick is similarly polymorphous—not always a liar, he takes great pains to instill in his sons the value of education in the territory:

I didn't had dese chances w'en I wuz er boy, kaze dem whar slabe time; an' now 'fo' I sen' you to school dis mawnin', I wanter gin you dis little talk: I wants you to larn somet'ing, kaze de time done git heah w'en if you grows up ignunt, de white man' an' Mistah Injin gwine to git de best ob you; an dey may git de best ob you anyhow, but hit aint gwine hu't you to go to school. You mus' min' you' teachah, an' doan pestah wid de yuther chillun, but 'ten' to yo' own doin's. Now, Richud, I wants you to membah dis, kaze you all time up to some trick er debilment. (63)

Racial categories are polymorphous here, since Uncle Dick's advice is probably about black-looking Indians being subjected to the racism of non–black looking Indians. One of the fascinating aspects of the Saunt book is stories he tells about people who were at first on the Creek rolls, and then when the Dawes Commissioners saw them around their black-looking relatives, placed on the freedmen rolls—research that upsets, considerably, the contemporary argument that freedmen are not biologically Creek.

The racial shape shifting in the stories is reinforced by the fact that the narratives have their very own Choffee, the famous southeastern miscreant Rabbit, but here he shows up as a she and a sow. This is an important point, I believe, because while I want to examine the mutual destinies of Creeks and freedmen in these stories, I do not want to simply conflate them into the same tradition, nor negate the complexity of their history. I believe that freedmen also have a culture of their own (it does not follow that this provides a logical excuse for disenfranchising them, by the way).

The narrator takes great pains to develop the sow's character:

She was as notorious an animal as ever displayed bristles, and a constant annoyance to the whole Coon Creek Settlement. She was not a Berk-

shire nor a Poland-China but a mongrel, and of the most inferior sort. A
long sharp nose with which she could have easily quaffed the contents of
an ordinary urn, a back that looked much like the keystone of an arch,
hazel-colored eyes that rolled in devilish frenzy, and a wiry tail which
hung in a lengthy ringlet, were her most prominent features. (51)

This old gal's personal characteristics are well worth exploring. (I've always
liked her name in Creek, Sokha, one of those words that's just right.) Yet she's
not just Sokha, a genderless pig. She is named as a sow, most certainly not a
boar, and her gender is underscored: "In fine, she raised more trouble than
pigs" (54). She celebrates, it would seem, raising hell over motherhood. The
sow arises out of dreams: "One misty autumnal morning, Uncle Will, on
arising, looked out toward his potato 'patch,' to see whether or not his dream
during the night of seeing Uncle Dick's sow on his premises was veritable. To
his great dismay and consternation it was" (51). She has a penchant for busting
through fences and rooting up neighbors' food. Because of these unsavory
habits she is constantly chased by Will's dog, "Majah," which is supposed to be
"Major." In the latter regard, references to the previous war—the American
Civil War that fiercely divided the Creek Nation, and forged the destiny of
black and red Creek citizens for generations—occur several times in the story.

Uncle Dick is explicitly identified with the sow; both are cunning. The
narrator says, "[t]he remark Uncle Will once made describes her in a nut-
shell: "man, she's cunnin' as cousin Dick is an' bo'-bachd jus' like um'" (51).
Yet Will is also associated with the sow: "Uncle Will awoke one morning from
a dream trouble. He dreamed of yams and—Uncle Dick's sow—and the dream
came to pass" (55). The sentence before this tells us the sow "was partial to
such delicacies [*sic*] as yams and 'roastin' ears'" (55).

Uncle Will not only dreams of the sow; he dreams as if he *is* the sow in the
midst of one of her wild cravings. The foods are interesting because they are
African American southern foods which in this case, as with many other
dishes, are also Creek foods; corn and yams being especially notable as staples
important in the history of the Southeast.

The sow's nose is either chopped off with Uncle Will's hoe in one version
or badly bludgeoned in another. In her daring escapes she jumps off em-
bankments in a single bound—but with poise: "She had tastes approaching
refinement" (54).

That she is "no common sow" (54) becomes even more apparent when Will
confides "she lub liberty better'n de white folks" (54). (Is she *superior* to
white folks in her ability to conceive liberty or does she *prefer* it over white
people?) After one of Will's bludgeonings with the hoe, she "struck a bee line

for home. She had never realized until then that she had a home. Moralists might brood upon her misfortune with profit" (55). She is prone to racial hatred: "Her attitude towards 'sofkies' [Creek curs given to hanging around the sofky pot begging for scraps] in general was not calculated to breed familiarity. She despised them individually, collectively, *and as a race*" (54; my emphasis).

She even experiences a porcine reformation when in her old age her "career thereafter was smooth and uneventful. Realizing that she was leading a bad life and being a wise sow, she resolved to cut loose from her wickedness, and she did. She became a devoted mother and replenished Uncle Dick's larder with numerous fat shoats—some of them weighing not less than fifty pounds" (56). Her reformation includes a return to more conventional gender roles.

The sow destabilizes a number of categories and easy assumptions. The more familiar male Choffee appears here as a female sow. Choffee's rebellions are here in the hands (hooves?) of a female. She cannot be identified according to any particular breed, only as mongrel, yet she despises Creek curs who are similarly nondescript. Individual personality, to borrow Pauline Johnson's phrase, especially deviance, stands out more than any discernible race. The sow exists in both dreams and reality. Ambiguity abounds as to who owns the "tater" patch and the rights to avenge oneself on its porcine invader. Is cunning Uncle Dick the sow, or circumspect Uncle Will? When Uncle Will bludgeons her, is he beating a pig or walloping Uncle Dick by abusing his "property," the sow who had invaded Will's garden? Both beatings eventually occur, on pig and person, since Dick also suffers Will's abuse. Why do "white folks" love liberty so much, and why does the sow love it more? Why doesn't she know where home is when she seems to belong at Dick's place? What does it mean to hate "sofkies" individually, collectively, and as a race? Given the violence done to her, what makes the sow see the error of her ways and later return to motherhood?

The thing is almost as complicated as Creek history itself, especially in relation to the freedmen. I once heard a respected community historian say if someone explains Creek history to you and you think you understand it, he probably explained it to you wrong.

If Dick and Will, Richard and Mose, and, by extension, Creeks and freedmen, are possible pairings in the story, then we have this crazy sow getting between them and raising all kinds of hell. I'm going to venture that the impossibility of characterizing the sow according to breed can be related to the Creek confederacy itself. More than almost any other tribe, the Creeks are impossible to identify according to any one brand of genetics. Because of their geographical location in the Southeast, many tribes from farther east or farther south fled into the confederacy during the colonial period and afterwards.

George Stiggins, author of the autobiographical work *Creek Indian History* (written before Indian Removal but not published until recently), is a case in point. His community, the Natchez of Mississippi, were almost wiped out by the French in 1729. Several hundred of the survivors were sold into slavery in the Caribbean, but some of them ended up forming a town in the Creek confederacy. They spoke both Natchez and Creek, the language of their new citizenship. Many towns had similar stories and were bilingual. There are some groups, like the Euchees, for example, in whose case nobody is quite sure where they came from, and, because of their language, some speculate they are of Siouan origin. Omnipresent in Stiggins's account are African Americans in the Upper Creek towns, living there. They were important allies of the Red Sticks, and, obviously, they were also more than allies. Creek genetics is just about anything under the sun. DNA has never been the glue that holds the confederacy together.

What did hold the confederacy together as much as racial makeup was a strong matrilineal system in which clan and town identities could be passed on, whatever the racial background of the father. This, I believe, is why it is so important that the genetically polymorphous heroine of the stories is a sow, not a boar. Her sex, not her breed, is her key identity marker. In any Creek town, in spite of tremendous cultural, racial, and linguistic diversity, one could find members of one's same clan, inherited from one's mother, and this perception created a powerful national front that transcended pure genetics. Other national identities, such as the red and white town divisions specializing in war and peace, created a means of forging a national character out of tremendous genetic variability. The autonomy of towns was always in a very delicate balance with the will of the confederacy, and any single town had the dangerous potential to careen out of control, with uncles and cousins and majors and livestock in hot pursuit and doing a lot worse than bashing each others' noses in with farm hoes, as if that weren't bad enough.

As far as DNA goes, the confederacy might look a lot like

a razorback, but a fine one. The cast of her countenance would have led one to infer at a passing glance that she was disposed to delv [sic] deeply—cause a drouth in the bottom of a jug, or explore the mysterious depthe [sic] of a potato hill. Her eyes were a vicious brown and her color was sanguine or autumnal. Her tail would have set a saddler up in business selling buggy washers. She was swift and with it, wise. If pursued, she would run until she thought herself entirly [*sic*] out of danger and, then, canter a little peace [*sic*] further, to be sure. She was no common sow. She had tastes approaching refinement. (Posey, "Uncle Dick's Sow" 54)

In the history of the confederacy the term fullblood can be taken in its most literal sense: full of almost every kind of blood one could imagine. Yet these "tastes" approach refinement, and a strong national character forged itself out of radically destabilized racial categories. The trickster (I tried to make it through the book without saying that word) in "Uncle Dick and Uncle Will" is the DNA strand. The fact that both Dick and Will are identified with the sow is not really the point; any person of Creek ancestry could be her. And, to be sure, she's raised some serious hell.

You're not buying it, huh? Wait until you see how these stories end.

Each moves toward discord or alliance. In "Uncle Dick and Uncle Will," Will, pissed because Dick chopped off his pig's nose (what a dick!), drops his hoe and runs for his musket. Dick grabs the hoe and is hot on his cousin's heels. Rather than let Will gain entrance to his house and the gun, Dick lets loose with the hoe and wallops Will upside the head. Taking advantage of Will's near braining, Dick runs into Will's house and gets the musket for himself, emptying it on its fleeing owner.

Will keeps hoofing it (or "hubbin' it," a phrase I like, and that is the title of an old Bob Wills song) until he reaches a neighbor's, and the children run out of the farmstead, offering him, absurdly, to join them for a fish fry. Will's response is telling: " 'Go 'way childuns, wid yo' fis,' he quickly answered, 'I wants none ob dem t'ings dis moanin', sah. Cousin Dick been s'ot at me like we be no kin' " (52).

These stories are about recognizing the kinship of kin who are not easy to recognize. At times, especially recent ones, the confederacy has acted like the freedmen "be no kin," in spite of enormous evidence to the contrary.

"Uncle Dick's Sow," a slight variation on "Uncle Dick and Uncle Will," ends with Aunt Judy's incredulity at Will's condition:

"But, Uncle Will, whut been git at chew?"
"W'y dat ol' feller! Now is yo' satisfied?"
"Whut ol' feller, Uncle Will?"
"Dat whut I been had over de do!" (56)

The "ol' feller," of course, is Will's musket, placed above the doorframe, but it is also the kinsman who takes it up against him. The conflation here of weapon and shooter is anything but coincidental. Will, like the confederacy, is wounded (as has so often been the case) by its own weapons, its inability to recognize the meaning of tribal kinship, or to live up to the demands of community. These self-inflicted wounds are realities of Creek history. No doubt they have a complicated colonial backdrop, especially given the reconstruction treaty that some argue was forced on Creeks in 1866, requiring them to accept their former slaves as full tribal members. Yet the confederacy also has to recognize its responsibility as one of the oppressors of its Afro-Creek relatives through the institution of slavery, another reality of that same history. This chapter is mostly about a literacy response to the freedmen issue, but a serious question is a moral one. What are the responsibilities of a nation that once embraced the institution of slavery? Can it dismiss those responsibilities by simply claiming a biological, cultural, or historical difference from those it enslaved?

"Mose and Richard," a bit different kind of a story, ends with Uncle Dick in a rage when he discovers his two sons, the title characters, have been fooling him about going to school and learning reading, their only hope given the white and red racism that surrounds them: "if you grows up ignunt, de white man' an' Mistah Injin gwine to git de best ob you; an dey may git de best ob you anyhow, but hit aint gwine hu't you to go to school" (63). His sons have only learned the words, "go" and "cling," in school after letting on like they'd been learning much more. Dick beats the two boys mercilessly with his rifle rod, and, simultaneously, with the word "go." "You grab er hoe Monday mawnin'—whack!—and go up an' down dem cott'n rows—whack! whack—Dat's er good go fer you!" (66).

Mose gets the same treatment with the word "cling," and as he thrashes his kids with the gun rod we might remember it was Will's own, that Dick used on Will. A subtle connection is also made to the troublesome sow of one of the other stories: "I talk to you an' talk to you—whack!—but hit ain't do no good—whack! whack! Hit's jes wastin' pearls 'fo de swine—whack! I wants you to take dem books to de teachah—whack!—whack!—whack! an' cling to er plow Monday mawnin'—whack!—er I'll cling to yo' back wid er stick!!" (66). Dick's physical abuse of his sons is compounded by his own frustrations of the racist "white man" and "Mistah Injin" and his boys' failure to take his advice regarding education as a possible means of escaping racial drudgery.

The most telling—and hopeful—ending of the four stories occurs in "Jes 'Bout a Mid'lin', Sah." The story opens with a quintessential Posey pastoral scene at Bald Hill, also Posey's childhood home at the family ranch ten miles west of Eufaula. An African American neighbor, Jim Quobner, comes over and strikes up a casual conversation with the narrator's father. Jim reminds him that he did him a favor once by transporting a cow that the narrator's father bought from "cousin Shapah" over the river (59). Cousin Shapah, probably Sharper, a Creek family name, is an open signifier since the narrator does not specify whether he is Jim's cousin, the narrator's father's cousin, or all of theirs. One of the possibilities, obviously, that the story does not close off, is that the narrator and his father both have an African American cousin, the same one as Jim's.

Next, Jim reports the latest community gossip. Wootka Harjo (this would be Crazy Raccoon or Crazy Coon) got hit in the head with a ball stick at a Creek stickball game, and the medicine man, Ledifka, had to treat him. The slapstick in this anecdote is about as literal as it gets since Crazy Coon is hit upside the head with a ball stick. What is particularly interesting about the brief aside is the continuing open signification surrounding the anecdote. Jim could be reporting the local hearsay, but it sounds more like he is an eye-witness to these events. We have the possibility that Jim, a black man, was at a Creek ball game at the grounds and even, conceivably, a regular participant or member there. The story does not rule out Jim's participation, nor does it negate the possibility that Wootka Harjo himself, or Ledifka, could be Afro Creeks significantly involved at the grounds—even as medicine persons. One further possibility is that the nickname of the grounds member Crazy Coon, and its connection to the Afro-Creek community Coon Creek, draws attention to the relationship between red and black Muscogees.

The increasing segregation of Creek society, especially influenced in the early 1800s by its southern-allied Indian agent Benjamin Hawkins, and manifested in laws beginning in the 1820s that forbade intermarriage and took an increasingly dim legislative view of racial mixing, always met with varying, complex reactions among the actual citizenry.

Churches and grounds became increasingly segregated, yet there were, and are, always exceptions. This is necessarily true in a society where in, some cases, a church member or grounds member's racial identity would be ambiguous and hard to place in a single racial category. Some community members might easily be taken to be black people in certain circumstances, and, among white Oklahomans, often got treated as if they were because they looked phenotypically black, yet were perceived as Indians among Creeks— for whom, perhaps, they even looked Indian rather than black. More than people realize, much of this is in the mind of the beholder. These complications make attempts at segregation a real challenge, to say the least, and create lots of slippage.

Jim Quobner, then, may be a grounds member. And he may share a cousin in common with the narrator's father. And the narrator and his father may also be of African ancestry—how can we view it otherwise, since the story does not bother to correct these potential assumptions?

All of Jim's small talk in the story's opening has to do with him working up to the fact that he wants to borrow some bacon. The narrator's father seizes this as a political opportunity to win some votes for his favorite for the chief's office, John Moore. The Moore family has long been active in Muscogee politics, and the chief justice of the Muscogee Supreme Court, at the time of this writing, is Patrick Moore.

Jim, who also favors the Moore candidacy, claims to hold considerable sway over the Coon Creek community and promises to secure their votes for Moore. The image of the exchange, votes for a side of bacon, is a particularly "rich" one:

> Well, my father laid his larder under contribution to the amount of a magnificent middling, which had been smoked brown over slow hickory fire and packed away so as to retain its rich flavor. Streaks of lean and fat in almost equal proportion ran through the whole of it. (60)

What a beautiful, mouth-watering, symbol of moderation and mutuality. Have you ever tried to cut all the fat out of a piece of bacon before frying it? Impossible! Meat and fat are far too intertwined. Instead of gun-rod thrashings and buckshot, these two neighbors recognize that "equal proportion ran through the whole of it"; that is to say, where the freedmen leaves off and the Creek by blood begins cannot be separated one from the other. Whatever the arguments might be for disenfranchisement, segregating Creeks from freedmen is, in reality, an impossible chore in terms of any kind of rational basis. The bottom line is that it simply cannot be done, whatever the legislative efforts have been to the contrary. Genetics, and its interpretations, resists easy categorization. Our ever-pesky sow has shown up again since middlings—of course—are pork, not beef.

The story ends with good humor, what Gerald Vizenor might call compassionate tricksters. John Moore, the favorite of the narrator's father, loses the election. But that's not the point, is it? The story is about two neighbors who recognize their mutual destiny:

> My father did not allow himself to hope for a majority of the negro voters but he felt sure he had reason to be sure of one.
>
> The returns following the election caused my father disappointment. John Moore was defeated by an overwhelming majority. My father consoled himself, however, with the reflection that there were other election days in the future and the friends of John Moore had but to abide their time.

> A year or more afterwards, when my father had forgotten all about the stirring days of the campaign who should he meet but Jim Quobner, and what should Jim say but "I jacks, I jes tell yo', sah, dem Coon Creek niggers went an' turn right roun' on me!" (61)

Politicians come and go, but people at Bald Hill will still be left to either recognize their relationship with those at Coon Creek, as in this story, or deny it, as in the violent outbursts over Uncle Dick's sow.

Things have gone way downhill since this turn-of-the-century racial optimism depicted in "Jes 'Bout a Mid'lin', Sah." Today some members of the community at Coon Creek can no longer vote in Creek elections, since the freedmen were written out of the Creek Constitution in 1979. At one time Creek political parties, especially the politicians more closely aligned with the ceremonial grounds in the late nineteenth century, had a black constituency that helped elect them to office. Exactly opposite to what some claim as Creek traditionalism today, these traditionalists, like Isparhecher, for example, were running on platforms that vigorously asserted the full rights of freedmen (see, for example, Gary Zellar's *African Creeks*).

Perhaps it is still possible that a pesky sow could break loose in the national council chambers, even today.

The Posey stories are fascinating because we have a racist author (at least in terms of the Perryman slurs, comments in the Fus Fixico Letters, and the narrative stance in the very writings under discussion herein) writing fairly incisively, in spite of himself, about matters of race.

Stranger things have happened.

And if they can happen in 1894 and 1900, when these four stories were published, might we reach some kind of intellectual breakthrough today, especially given the way we pat ourselves on the backs for being so much more enlightened a century later?

One such literary breakthrough appeared on the scene a year into the new millennium. While I am not able to analyze it in depth here, I would like to point readers to Creek-Cherokee author Eddie Chuculate's well-written coming-of-age story "Yo Yo."

A young Creek protagonist, Jordan, an athletic junior higher, is surprised by new neighbors who move in next door to his rural Muskogee home. Yolanda, the African-American ninth-grader whose nickname provides the title for the story, is quite an athlete herself, a sprinter, and two years Jordan's senior. She is his senior in a lot of other ways, too, and not only does she provide Jordan his first sexual experiences, but he witnesses her much more advanced savvy about successfully moving back and forth between black, Indian, and white worlds. At footraces she is nearly Jordan's equal, a reality that disconcerts him to no end—the idea of a girl who might eventually best him at running and prove his equal in many other ways.

Jordan has to put up with a racist grandfather who gives him a bunch of shit for hanging around with Yo Yo and taunts Jordan about the possibility that she is his girlfriend. In this coming-of-age story, Jordan discovers there is much to be learned from Yo Yo's keener sense of survival strategies in the face of racism. Much could be said about the story, but when I teach it I always include the possibility that the intimate encounter between Jordan and Yo Yo is not simply about two junior highers but the last four hundred years or so of the Muskogee confederacy. There have been a lot of Jordans and Yolandas throughout much of Creek history, going back at least to the 1540s, when the first slaves started escaping from the de Soto Expedition (some historians have even speculated about contact between Africa and the Americas before Europeans came to the New World). The story holds out hope, I believe, that the confederacy can also come of age by embracing, rather than denying, its gorgeously rich multi-cultural legacy, a just cause for much celebration rather than an impediment, if viewed in a more imaginative light.

Two freedmen, Ron Graham and Fred Johnson, went to trial in the Muscogee Creek Nation District Court in September 2005. A key issue in the case was whether or not Creek freedmen who at one time had been recognized as citizens of the nation could qualify for contemporary citizenship when the criteria is now based on the "Creeks by Blood" roll rather than also on the Freedmen's rolls, due to the rewriting of the 1979 constitution.

Muscogee Creek Nation Supreme Court Justice Patrick Moore ruled that the District Court, in its final finding on March 17, 2006, acted "in an arbitrary and capricious manner" and "contrary to law" by denying the respondents/cross appellants, Mr. Graham and Mr. Johnson, "a fair consideration of their application when they first applied for enrollment as citizens of the Muscogee Creek Nation."

I am not qualified to examine the legal issues involved in the citizenship trial and its appeals. It is a morass of decisions and counter-decisions that make a literary type's head spin. Instead, I want to ask what happens when we look at the trial, and the freedmen issue more generally, from a literary, rather than a legal, perspective. I want to get beyond the usual questions, many of them unanswerable, that surround the debate: Are the freedmen really Creek or black in terms of blood? Do they participate in the Creek churches and ceremonies? Are they culturally black or Indian? Historically, were they ever part of the confederacy?

The debate, by the way is already aestheticized: Ron Graham, one of the appellants, is blood kin to the black Graysons, the real-life family depicted in Posey's fictional account, and Patrick Moore, the real-life chief justice, is related to John Moore, the real-life character who got cast in Posey's fiction and failed to get elected but engendered some serious friendships in the same beautiful middlin' story. The modern-day trial, in the most literal of senses, is literature.

Therefore, what if we consider the trial as art? For example, I would very much like to be part of the culture which, along with African Americans as its main inventors, gave birth to jazz—an argument, by the way, with a great deal of evidence given the call-and-response structure of stomp dance songs and their relationship to the pentatonic blues scale. Why are we always looking at the hole instead of the donut? I'll claim John Coltrane any day of the week as one of my musical cousins. Which is better, artistic excellence ("rich flavor . . . [s]treaks of lean and fat in almost equal proportion . . . through the whole of it") or simply running the pig out of the patch and waiting for the next outburst so the violence can be reenacted in a mindless cycle? In the latter scenario, we simply end up in a draw and each party's respective nose is missing: "'Yo' time done come now,' he [Uncle Will] ejaculated [as he threatens Uncle Dick]. 'I done lop off yo' nose er yo' done lop off mine'" (Posey, "Uncle Dick and Uncle Will" 52). Both Creeks and African Americans share the rabbit and tar baby story. Why not explore these interdependencies more broadly as the best that two-tribal groups have to offer as they participate together in responding to colonial histories by turning oppression into art?

Richly imagined, relations can be different: "The uncles in question were two of the oldest citizens of this neighborhood, but still possessed much of the vim and vigor of early manhood, Uncle Dick in particular" (49). And this comes from the racist narrator, prone to depicting lazy darkies simply overcome by too much easy living. How much more might be available to those who can dream into being a comic sow who just might root up a relative in the most unlikely of patches? An important issue, of course, is what constitutes the neighborhood? Coon Creek, the freedmen community, gives rise to Bald Hill, the Creek community, and vice versa, and some—like Jim Quobner and the narrator's father—have had the capacity to imagine that relationship; others have not.

Some folks back home, no doubt, might think me crazy for using four short stories, works of fiction, in order to analyze the freedmen controversy. Yet it is that very madness that attracts me—especially given the lack of imagination, of artistry, of creative chaos (one of the characteristics of the Creek Lower World) in the legal and historical arguments against the freedmen.

Is my interpretation of the Posey's stories inaccurate? Is it nontraditional? Maybe, but I'm not interested in accuracy and traditionalism in this case. I dream, instead, of a new narrative that recognizes the vitality of the freedmen community and creates a space for it within the nation. Accuracy and tradition, if they mean sticking to the old story that demands dispossession, do not capture my imagination—I am thinking like a fiction writer here. We should endeavor to tell a better story, aim for a higher standard of creative excellence—and when it comes to the freedmen case we should make art our aim because it demands a higher moral standard than history.

The contemporary implications of these four Posey stories are simply staggering. Saunt provides a good summary of the disenfranchisements of the 1970s and 1980s, worth quoting at length:

> In 1979, the Creek Nation replaced its 1867 constitution, which had enfranchised ex-slaves. Article II, section 1, of the new constitution reads, "Each Muscogee (Creek) Indian by blood shall have the opportunity for citizenship in the Muscogee (Creek) Nation." By restricting citizenship to people whose ancestors were on the Dawes-by-blood census and no longer recognizing the freedmen rolls, Creeks excluded the descendants of their slaves.
>
> In the 1970s and 1980s, the Cherokees, led by Principal Chief Ross Swimmer, similarly disenfranchised the descendants of their slaves, and the Choctaws followed suit in 1983. When Bernice Riggs, whose ancestors appear on the Cherokee freedmen rolls, challenged the disenfranchisement in the Cherokee Supreme Court, the justices ruled against her in a 2002 decision. The following year, descendants of Cherokee slaves asked the BIA to invalidate a Cherokee election because they were not allowed to participate. A regional BIA officer initially seemed prepared to consider the petition favorably and requested a response from the Cherokee Nation. "In this age of self-determination and self governance," replied Principal Chief Chad Smith, "I am shocked to find the contents and tone of your letter to be both patronizing and very paternalistic." After Cherokee leaders urgently requested a personal meeting with top officials from the U.S. Department of the Interior, the BIA summarily dismissed the election challenge. At the time of the dismissal, Ross Swimmer was a high-level Bush appointee in the Department of the Interior, second only to Secretary Gale Norton.

Between 2000 and 2003, a faction of Seminoles also disenfranchised their citizens descended from slaves. The story was followed closely by the *New York Times,* and on this occasion the BIA refused to recognize any government elected under such conditions. Although the Seminole Nation therefore had to restore the voting rights of the disenfranchised, it did succeed in excluding these marginalized citizens from educational and social service programs and from a $56 million payout due from the federal government. Of the Five Tribes, only the Chickasaw Nation did not participate in these modern-day disenfranchisments; it had never adopted its ex-slaves in the first place. (214–15)

People are going to be arguing until the cows come home about whether or not the freedmen are "really Creek." Everyone has a different opinion and no one agrees. A practical consideration has to be prioritized. Freedmen were legal citizens from the time of the Reconstruction Treaty in 1866 until they were disenfranchised when the Creek constitution was rewritten in 1979. After 113 years of citizenship, it was simply too late to kick them out of the confederacy. Some argue that the Treaty of 1866, which forced the nation to accept their former slaves, and other black Indians and black non-Indians, as full citizens was a colonial imposition. Yet by 1979, after 113 years of Afro Creek citizenry and hundreds of years of amalgamation of mutual destinies, it was impossible to disentangle Creeks and freedmen in any way that made sense or could be justified whatever the painful colonial histories may be that created the situation in the first place. The appropriate response to colonialism is not more colonialism, this time self-imposed by the colonized.

If one believes in sovereignty and citizenship, why impose a set of criteria not applied to any other group but those with black skin? Other Creeks seeking citizenship have to trace lineal ascent to the Dawes roll (as before disenfranchisement freedmen had to trace lineal ascent to the freedmen roll) not answer questions like some of those I've heard: can they prove their matrilineal side of the family is Creek? Do they participate at the grounds or the churches? Why do they only come around when they want something? Do they speak the language? And on and on, with everyone requiring a different set of criteria and no one agreeing. If these same requirements were applied to the entire nation, assuming anyone could agree on which ones provided the true test of Creekness, those few qualifying for citizenship could gather at a small country Baptist church barely big enough to fit its baptismal in the building.

An important historical reality is that a faction of the tribe has always supported the citizenry of Creek freedmen. Those who argue that the Treaty of 1866 was a colonial imposition overlook one important historical reality. If the Treaty of 1866 was forced on the Creeks, Article 2, which recognized the freedmen as citizens, was not. Loyalist Creeks who had sided with the union (and who made up the main body of Creek ceremonialists) fought hard to get the rights of Creek freedmen recognized in the treaty and for decades afterwards many of them continued to resist any threats to the integrity of Article 2. It is ironic, to say the very least, that, today, disenfranchising the freedmen is argued to be consistent with Creek traditionalism.

This mus(e)ing, that follows "Caught in the Current, Clinging to a Twig," illustrates, I hope, that my optimism about sovereignty studies is not a naïve belief that all sovereignties are optimal. When we sing around the fire and in the churches, a good number of our relations are painfully missing. They are absent by virtue of the segregationist turn Creek history has taken more than once, and they are present in the rhythms of the songs we sing, the tribalism of the stories we tell, and the physical features of many of the very faces who sing and tell them. If the confederacy sings itself back together it will be from once again, as it has before, singing to the tune of a committed citizenship that recognizes the reality of mutual destiny. More to the point, the recent Creek Nation constitutional reforms as the constitution is being re-examined at the time of this writing should also correct the tragic disenfranchisement of freedmen in 1979 by reinstating them as Creek citizens. Without it there will be no real reform and lots of missing noses. The historical record teaches us that factionalizing the nation has never been the answer. It didn't work during the Red Stick War or the Civil War, and it will not work with regard to the disenfranchisement of freedmen. The destruction will always prove greater than the net benefit, and such actions may potentially alienate the confederacy from other nations—tribal and nontribal—who, like our thought-provoking sow, love liberty.

As a novelist, literary critic, and musician I would love to walk away from this discussion given that I am probably among the least, if not the very least, of those qualified to talk about these matters—and I am the first to admit it. I am no Creek cultural authority, and never have claimed to be one. I am convinced, however, that a community puts itself in peril if it listens only to its experts. Weirdos, dreamers, and know-nothings—like me—may also inspire. I intend these opinions of mine to be the beginning point of a conversation, not as the final word on the matter. Let's talk.

Not enough Indian artists are talking about the things that matter. Novelists, literary critics, and musicians—such as myself—have a responsibility to deal with the real world, not solely with mysticism regarding love of earth and respect for all relations. One must also evaluate whether or not such philosophies are ever enacted. To conclude we should say nothing about these matters because we are "only" artists could produce a silence with disastrous results—and perhaps it already has. Art does not let us off that easy. It's hard, dangerous work. People have been known to get killed over it. "Don't shoot me, I'm only the piano player," is a famous copout. We should keep in mind, however, it was always meant to be ironic, not a model for artists. Too much Indian writing and criticism remains easily within the safety zone. Where is the risk, the vulnerability?

If freedmen Dick and Will are cousins, who are their nephews and nieces? By now, friend, you know the all-too-obvious answer. It is the Creek confederacy itself. Whether or not Posey intended it at the time of their authorship, especially given the racism apparent in his own writings, the stories are about any Creek person looking in the mirror and being willing to acknowledge the reflection that stares back at him or her.

Works Cited

Chuculate, Eddie D. "Yo Yo." *The Iowa Review* 31, no. 1 (Spring 2001): 61–77.

Posey, Alexander. *The Fus Fixico Letters: A Creek Humorist in Early Oklahoma.* Norman: University of Oklahoma Press, 2002.

——. "Jes 'Bout a Mid'lin', Sah." In *Chinubbie and the Owl: Muscogee (Creek) Stories, Orations and Oral Traditions,* edited by Matthew Wynn Sivils, 58–62. Lincoln: University of Nebraska Press, 2005.

——. "Mose and Richard." In *Chinnubbie and the Owl,* 63–66.

——. "Uncle Dick and Uncle Will." In *Chinubbie and the Owl,* 49–53.

——. "Uncle Dick's Sow." In *Chinubbie and the Owl,* 54–57.

Saunt, Claudio. *Black, White, and Indian: Race and the Unmaking of an American Family.* New York: Oxford University Press, 2005.

Sivils, Matthew Wynn. "Introduction." In *Chinnubbie and the Owl,* 1–24.

Stiggins, George. *Creek Indian History: A Historical Narrative of the Genealogy, Traditions, and Downfall of the Ispocoga or Creek Indian Tribe of Indians,* introduced and annotated by William Stokes Wyman, edited by Virginia Pounds Brown. Birmingham, Ala.: Birmingham Public Library Press, 1989.

Zellar, Gary. *African Creeks: Estelvste and the Creek Nation.* Norman: University of Oklahoma Press, 2007.

Lynn Riggs's Other Indian Plays

Some critics mention *The Cherokee Night* only in relation to Indian subject matter in Riggs's work. A notable exception is Riggs's most perceptive critic, Jace Weaver, a Native literary specialist and himself a Cherokee citizen like the playwright. Weaver views others of Riggs's plays that take place in Indian Territory as Native works, arguing, sensibly, that by virtue of their location and period that they have to be about Native people.

Weaver claims, for example, that Riggs's play *Green Grow the Lilacs*—published in 1930, a Pulitzer finalist that Rodgers and Hammerstein later turned into the musical *Oklahoma!* and opened in New York in 1943—is an Indian play and that its Indianness is less apparent in the Broadway production. Weaver gives reasons for the play's stronger Indian subject matter than that which the critics have given *Green Grow the Lilacs* credit for:

It is entirely possible that Curly McClain is actually an Indian. The nickname "curly" could have come about because he, as a mixed-blood, had curly hair, an uncommon trait among Indians. Further, it is at least marginally more likely that Indians would have been the cattlemen and the Amer-Europeans the farmers during the period. This adds a different spin on lines like "Territory folk must stick together" and "The farmer and the cowboy must be friends." This hypothesis is bolstered by the presence of other Natives in the Riggs text. When, for instance, the posse comes to get Curly at Aunt Eller's (a character Riggs acknowledged was modeled after his Amer-European Aunt Mary and his mother, Rose Ella), she chides Territory folk for taking the side of the U.S. marshal and calls them "furriners," a perfectly sound response for any territorial citizen, either White or Native. They defend themselves, however, in explicit racial terms. One states, "My pappy and mammy was *both* born in Indian Territory! Why, I'm jist plumb full of Indian blood myself." To which another responds, "Me, too! And I c'n prove it!" The possibility of Curly's Indianness is not undercut by the fact that he states he was born on a farm in Kansas; such a fact is not necessarily inconsistent with Native heritage (99–100).

While I have always appreciated the comedy of the line about being plumb full of Indian blood, I also find it jarring. A play that has dealt very little with obvious—or unobvious—Indian issues suddenly takes them up and then just as quickly drops them. By this point, of course, we are very near the end of the play, further problematizing the degree to which it deals with Native concerns since we have no further amplification of the statements.

I do not intend, however, to argue whether or not *Green Grow the Lilacs* is an Indian play. Already willing to acknowledge this point, I want instead to turn my attention to two plays of Lynn Riggs's that are very obviously Indian works that critics have largely overlooked.

The Cream in the Well, completed in 1940, is about a family from Verdigris Switch that is living within the Cherokee Nation in 1906 on the eve of Oklahoma Statehood. The family identifies themselves as Cherokees in the play, talks about their Cherokee allotments, discusses their daughter's education at the Cherokee Female Seminary in Tahlequah, debates the statehood frenzy with all its hype about progress and modernity, and faces racism as Cherokees from non-Indian territory residents. In other words, this is a Cherokee-authored play about Cherokee subject matter and should meet just about anybody's criteria concerning what constitutes Native drama.

The Year of Pilár, published in 1940, a little less obvious choice, does not take place in Riggs's own tribal community, and the play's central family claims to be Spanish (though such a claim in Mexico, of course, is fraught with complexities). The play, nevertheless, features a Spanish family from the ruling class and concentrates on their relationships with "their" Mayan workers in Yucatán in southern Mexico. One of the Indian characters, Beto, fathered by the rich Spanish patron who heads this family, is essential, not incidental, to the plot. Indian-white relations and the erosion of colonial society provide constant dramatic tension.

Furthermore, I know of no other work in Riggs's rather extensive oeuvre that deals directly with gay subject matter. In my own analysis of *The Cherokee Night* in my first book, I argued that this overtly Cherokee play has a *covert* gay subplot. *The Cream in the Well* and *The Year of Pilár,* however, require a different treatment. Gay issues are confronted head on in both, a striking feature that sets them apart from every other play Lynn Riggs wrote.

I might describe *The Cream in the Well* as Oklahoma gothic. More crudely, I call this one of Riggs's "Oklahoma Sucks" plays. Riggs spent a good deal of time thinking, and describing, the meaning of art in general, and in his work he maintained faith in an earlier era that constituted Oklahoma's, more accurately, Indian Territory's, golden age. A kind of noble savage theory applied to a state instead of a race of people, Riggs locates his idyll within the tradition of the pastoral.

Green Grow the Lilacs, Riggs claimed, depicts a kinder, gentler Indian Territory that would later become a more ornery one soon followed by an even meaner Oklahoma. This long-lost age of innocence, when the precursors to today's Oklahomans had actually been nice folks, Riggs maintained, had passed away by the time of his upbringing. Things had gotten ugly. Fast.

While a complicated theory that I have discussed at great length in *Red on Red,* suffice it to say that I have argued that the nice and mean territories reflect Riggs's internal psychological landscape, related to his ambivalence about the state, rather than a realistic depiction of the geography or its people. While a significant decline did, in fact, occur after statehood among the tribes in almost every facet of their lives related to their loss of autonomy through allotment under the Dawes and Curtis acts and the dissolution of tribal government, Riggs does not concern himself with tracing this kind of political regression. The downward spiral plays itself out most significantly in interpersonal relationships, and here I would like to focus especially on the dangers of sexual identity within the two plays.

The Cream in the Well is most decidedly not about the good old days when Curly was courting Laurey (and even in *Green Grow the Lilacs* a number of really weird tensions exist that might challenge the innocence critics, and even Lynn Riggs himself, ascribe to it). I have often thought that the best way to get oneself shot, stabbed, drowned, knifed, burned alive or some other kind of dead or near-dead, is to enter into any kind of heterosexual relationship in a Lynn Riggs play. You'll be a goner for sure.

In *Green Grow the Lilacs,* the honeymooning couple barely escapes a crowd that wants to burn them alive, a farmhand knifes a fellow worker; the bridegroom goes to jail, escapes, and is pursued by a mob.

Nobody said marriage was easy.

In *The Cream in the Well,* written much in the same spirit of Riggs's play *A Lantern to See By,* the characters face unabated meanness at every turn that seems to be part and parcel of the spirit of place in these plays' settings. One could almost coin a brand-new word like "Oklapression" to describe both the oppression and depression that Riggs associated with the state (I won't, though, since we already have enough of these in Native literature). A friend of mine always ends the statement "I grew up in Oklahoma" with "and it liked to have killed me." Perhaps the same could be said of Riggs and many of his characters.

The Cream in the Well is about an affluent Cherokee family, not unlike Riggs's own, whose patriarch is wealthy enough to lease land to other territory residents. Riggs's non-Indian father was a prominent citizen of Claremore. Riggs's father—like Will Rogers's father, Clem, who was Cherokee, and another affluent man around Claremore and within the nation—was involved in cattle, wheat, and banking. The two families knew each other quite well, although Will was already off beginning his show business career on the vaudeville circuit during the time of Lynn's upbringing.

What the two men, Lynn and Will, thought of each other provides an interesting case for speculation. Given their public prominence and radically different personalities, I like to imagine what must have transpired between them the few times they found themselves together and how they might have reflected on these encounters. In my imagination, Lynn's interior monologue about Will would go like this:

> I had known Will but not so well. He had already left Claremore and for the vaudeville circuit by the time of my childhood. But my first time in Hollywood, after I had left home and run away to New York, Will and I wound up on a movie set together. I was just a kid learning the ropes, and he helped me get a little part as an extra. Will liked Oklahomans, but I never did quite fit the bill, so we remained aloof. Will took to men he could rough it up with or sit around fantasizing about the last days of the open range with. I could do all that—I mean I could hold my own mounted on a horse with any of the best of them—but talking about the old cowboy days didn't hold much of an attraction for me, not in terms of trail rides and cattle drives and such, though I'd impressed Will a time or two with my guitar and trail songs. I was more interested in what made people tick, something I found difficult to articulate—the harder it was to describe them, the more they captured my imagination. Any fascination I had regarding cowboys had to do with whatever was most hidden among them. And inside them. Especially inside them. This was not a Will Rogers conversation.
>
> Will wasn't exactly the type of fellow who I could bounce ideas off of about serious theater, either, though he knew a helluva lot about how to entertain a crowd. He always eyed me kind of suspiciously, more because I came off as an effete artist, and I never bothered proving myself otherwise out on the polo field or in the roping chute, though it would have been easy enough to do, all except the rope tricks. This was the only thing I ever agreed with my father on, who had no patience for Will's twirling. Dad always said if you were dancing with your lariat you weren't catching no cows.

Will may have seen me as—hell, I don't know—pretentious or some kind of threat to the aw-shucks image he worked so hard at all the time. It probably wouldn't have helped his act too much if people saw him with another Claremore boy who was more comfortable talking about the new theater of poetic expressionism than cow punching in relation to some cornpone school of political commentary. People might get the notion that not all Claremore folks were born so naturally chock-full of country wisdom, that their hillbilly boy wonder might be faking it. I didn't mind the act; I enjoyed it as much as the next urban American, reading his columns faithfully. One thing I always admired Will for was that he spoke Cherokee, and I didn't, something that always made me sad and a little jealous.

The crazy thing was, in spite of it all, how much we did have in common. Our fathers were both cut from the same bolt of cloth, except mine was white. They wanted us to stay home and go into cattle and banking. Neither of us obliged them and neither ever lived in Oklahoma again once we'd run off as teenagers, even though both of us would talk and write about the territory and state for the rest of our lives; it would become the center of our art; if, in fact, you call what Will did art.

I'll admit the *way* he pulled it off was art; that guy was born to perform. He was a genius at extemporizing; although, over the years, he was basically finding new ways to work the same material. But on any given night he could look out over the footlights and take the pulse of a performance hall in one well-cast glance. He was astounding in his ability to relate to a live audience, or, for that matter, a reading audience, to somehow tap into something that everyone immediately perceived as authentic. I've written some damn good plays, if you ask me, but often as not they've gone against the public grain, whereas Will embodied America's consciousness. I found his first name fitting—the way one man so represented the will of the people.

Maybe that was the difference between me and him; I don't know. He tapped into what the public wanted to hear, and I fought that same impulse. And, of course, none of my plays had paid for a barn the size of the Hearst Mansion the way his films had. That would be another big difference. He came from a rich family that just kept getting richer. Whatever he might have said about the politics of the Great Depression he knew very little about the matter from personal experience. What could better suit Americans, for whom the expert's authority is always a matter of self-declaration, not lived reality?

Experience, the best teacher? This is what America wishes it believed.

I'll tell you what haunted me most about the plane crash. Wiley Post, like Will, had been away from Oklahoma for a long time, but he died with his watch set to Oklahoma time, three hours' difference from Alaska. The watched stopped, on impact, at 8:18 P.M., Claremore time.

The family in *The Cream in the Well*—to return more directly to Riggs's play—in spite of its affluence, finds itself struggling. Their only son has left them to join the navy, and they feel his absence keenly around the farm. Mr. Sawters, the father, is having a hard time finding enough help to keep the place going. Unlike traditional Cherokees living in really isolated areas and surviving off of subsistence farming, hunting and fishing, this is a farming *operation*.

Mr. Sawters is the kind of guy that many of my poor Indian and white relatives worked for or farmed on shares for. Please do not misunderstand me—this does not diminish his Cherokeeness any; he represents a faction of the tribe that, historically, always played a big role in its leadership and destiny (although this is not exactly the direction the play is headed in—that is to say an examination of Cherokee factional politics does not seem to be its aim).

Clabe, the son, was aided and abetted in his decision to join the navy by his sister, Julie. Julie had objected to Clabe's choice of girlfriend, a young non-Indian woman too "small town" and uneducated for Julie's tastes. She believes her brother could have done better. Julie is something of a blueblood, and this will connect her strongly to Pilár in the next play, as we shall see.

Julie's snubbing of Clabe's white girlfriend is somewhat ironic given the way that Indians were viewed in the Territory and later in Oklahoma early in the century, but not inconsistent with the kind of Cherokee family that is represented in the play from this particular faction of the tribe. Julie also encouraged Clabe to go away, supposedly, because she hoped that he would avail himself of greater opportunities than those available to him around Verdigris Switch in the northeastern part of the territory.

Clabe's acquiescence to the very strong demands of his sister seems rather a mystery given that he is a natural-born farmer who loves the land and the life of rural farm labor. This play, like most of Riggs's writings, has a strong gothic sensibility and moves toward the revelation of an ugly secret that will reveal the true reasons for Clabe's departure.

The play is in two acts, and each act might be seen as a kind of Cherokee *Who's Afraid of Virginia Woolf?* (Albee's play was published long after Riggs's, I realize, and this description is meant to convey a feeling about the work rather than a historical comparison.) In other words, the play is about the dinner party we all wish we never had or wish we never attended.

In rural Oklahoma, of course, they are not called "dinner parties." We could probably more accurately call it an "invite," accent on the first syllable. Gard and Opal, the ill-fated young couple and guests of the Sawterses, farm for the Indian family on the share system, a common cropping arrangement in the territory. In Gard's and Opal's case, this reflects an Indian reality especially relevant to the turn of the twentieth century, before statehood. Non-Indians had no legal rights in the territory, including land ownership, so they had to lease land from Indians. Mr. Sawters has designs on young Gard. He hopes to ask him to hire on in the fall to harvest the Sawterses' crops, too, which is largely the reason they are being invited over to supper.

The couple live across Big Lake, a recurring place in Riggs's fictional landscape upon which he bases another play which was, in fact, titled *Big Lake*. This lake actually exists close to Verdigris. One has to keep in mind that the play takes place in the years before all the WPA damming projects of the 1930s, when Oklahoma decided they would no longer allow running water anywhere within their boundaries. During the time of the play lakes were much more of a rarity in Indian Territory, although creeks, rivers, and watering holes abounded in Eastern Oklahoma. Lakes have a heightened presence in Riggs's plays, a fact easy to miss today since those of us from the state associate it with abundant lakes, a rather common landform. In Riggs's dramatic landscape Big Lake has a particular suicidal pull; it is a place of drownings.

The couple rowing across the lake toward a very unpleasant dinner party have a complicated history with the Sawters family. Opal was Clabe's girlfriend before Julie sent Clabe away to look for better opportunities. Opal's husband, Gard, had been interested in Julie before he married Opal. Gard suspects that Opal still loves Clabe. In other words, this is just about the dumbest idea for a fun evening this side of the Arkansas River.

The Sawters family has received a letter from Clabe, which they read as Gard and Opal approach in the rowboat. In the letter Clabe has announced that he will never return to Oklahoma again, and, he says, if the family wants to know the reason, they can ask Julie.

I might pause here to add a brief biographical note about Riggs's own aversion to Oklahoma. He could not stand being stranded in the state more than a couple days at a time. He had an ongoing secret arrangement with his New York literary agent. If he was called back home, and it turned into an extended visit, the literary agent would wire a fabricated emergency telegram, inventing complicated scenarios which required Riggs's immediate return to Santa Fe, Hollywood, or New York—whichever Riggs lived in at the time. Riggs only returned to Oklahoma very reluctantly. He politely accepted a couple of literary awards from the state but did not show up within its borders to claim them. He did not attend his father's funeral in Claremore. For Riggs, as a Native writer in the 1930s—and I think this resembles the feelings of another Indian writer of the time, D'arcy McNickle—home represents lack of intellectual opportunities and the inability to grow as an artist—and much more threateningly a gloomy oppression that kills off all forms of human liberation.

One central theme of the two plays is certainly the pain of returning home. Contrary to the homecoming impulse that many critics have written of in relation to contemporary Native fiction, Riggs's work is marked by a more skeptical view in terms of successfully returning to a homescape largely marked by mean-spiritedness rather than reintegration back into the community. This might be one of the primary reasons for reading his plays today, their resistance to contemporary formulations in Native work that sometimes risk becoming formulas. The fact that their Indianness is evasive makes the Riggs plays interesting or, at the very least, different than more contemporary writings.

Meanwhile, back at the ranch, back at the Sawterses' ranch that is, as one might easily predict, things get ugly right quick once Gard and Opal arrive. At the center of the storm is Julie, Clabe's sister, malicious in rather singular ways. Most significantly, she can put bad thoughts into people's minds.

The Cherokee, and southeastern Indian, notion of witchery, of the witch who can shoot objects into people, might be of some interest here. I do not mean to mislead, however. That kind of Cherokee traditionalism does not surface in the play in obvious ways. Unlike *The Cherokee Night,* the "Cherokeeness" of the characters is not discussed very much. The play does not proclaim itself to be about Cherokee identity or other things Cherokee.

Ironically, because it is about a Cherokee farming family going about its everyday life, the "Cherokeeness" of the play may be even more convincing than that of *The Cherokee Night,* given the naturalism in *The Cream in the Well,* at least regarding Cherokee matters. Other aspects of the play are far less convincing because it suffers, as does so much of Riggs's work, from melodrama, more specifically from sensational violence that deflects serious attention from the inner workings of the characters. Cherokee identity, however, is presented in a much more straightforward fashion, albeit in the context of the freakishness that so often surrounds everything Riggs wrote about.

As I have said elsewhere, the truly bizarre nature of Riggs's writings has to do with the fact that he evidently did not feel free to discuss same-sex relations, so he ends up on a lot of diversionary paths where he substitutes manifestations of violence for naming the closeted condition of the frustrated men and women who people his landscape.

Regarding *The Cream in the Well*, I make the comparison to witchery even though the Indianness of the play proves subtle in terms of any attention given to Cherokee traditional culture. Julie's cruelty, something of the sort often associated with witches, involves intentionally causing substantial bodily or spiritual harm to others. Only one overt clue, however, suggests Julie's witchery: before the dinner party we see her mysteriously walking around the house with a pitcher of lake water.

Other than that strange detail, which will, in fact, become significant later on, Julie only intimates her witchery by her meanness. Other gothic atmospheric elements abound in the play—for example, there is an old organ in the house, and various family members stop by and play weird tunes on it, à la Lurch in the Addams Family. The Sawterses, however, are more creepy than they are kooky.

The culmination of Julie's spite occurs while a storm brews out on the lake, a rather heavy-handed symbol for the one inside the house. The lake is choppy, so poor Gard and Opal are unable to row back home and escape the unlucky dinner party. They have to spend the night with the Sawterses.

As if to rub Opal's nose in her losses, Julie has Opal bed down in Clabe's room for the evening, but first hangs up a photo of Clabe over the fireplace before settling Opal into her quarters. Then Julie will not leave and let Opal get some sleep, instead staying in her brother's room as if to stake her own claim for Clabe. She proceeds to scare the daylights out of Opal by talking about the storm on the lake and suicide by drowning. The idea of Julie putting thoughts into people's heads looms large here:

OPAL. I feel fine. Only there's— [*Something is on her mind: she goes restlessly to the window.*] This wind gets me jumpy.

JULIE. Does it?

OPAL. It always has. Sometimes it 'pears to me it lives out there on the lake.

JULIE. What?

OPAL. The wind. Its home is there. It never goes anywheres else, it seems like. But at night it comes clawin' and scratchin' at the winders.

JULIE. It doesn't seem that way to me. If you said lake—I could agree with you. It must be cold at the bottom of the lake. Cold as death. I think about that sometimes.

OPAL. I wish you wouldn't talk that-a-way!

JULIE. Goodness, don't be afraid, Opal! Nothing's going to hurt you.

OPAL. [*Too emphatically.*] I'm *not* afraid!

JULIE. Well, I've often thought—in spite of the chill and how lonely a
way to die—if things ever got too bad, you could easily row out in the
middle and jump out of the boat.

OPAL. [*On edge.*] Don't say that! Please, Julie!

JULIE. Why, Opal. I'm not talking about you. I'm talking about myself.

[OPAL's *thin, little mouth is getting under control. Her really savage will
comes to her rescue in time.*]

OPAL. I think you mean me. (183)

Next, the two women have it out over Clabe, Julie still maintaining that she
did not want Opal to marry her brother because Opal was not good enough.
Opal responds stereotypically for a white Oklahoman of her time, giving us
insight into the racism of the territory:

JULIE. [*Coolly.*] If you must know you weren't good enough for him.

OPAL. [*Contemptuously.*] Where I come from my family wouldn't have
spoken to the likes of you, Julie. Virginia people have their pride you
wouldn't know about.

JULIE. Really?

OPAL. Maw liked to died when I told her about Clabe and me. You
should've saw her face! She thinks to be part Cherokee Indian is the
same as bein' part nigger. (184)

The racist denigration of both Indian and black identities relates, of course, to
the fact that some Cherokees had African ancestry that some whites, and some
Cherokees, held against them. In both *The Cream in the Well* and *The Year of
Pilár*, a relationship exists between race and gay identity in which the latter is
equated with the ultimate form of banishment, it being far more transgressive
than race. All things queer involve an ostracism so extreme as to be largely
unthinkable, far beyond degrees of racially based social inferiority since they
are unnamable, unlike race issues, which the conversation between Julie and
Opal demonstrates.

While *The Cream in the Well* takes up the cause of the tortured sibling
driven by incestuous desires, and *The Year of Pilár* heralds the Indian underdog against his colonialist oppressors, neither play advocates on behalf of
same-sex desire even though the subject is broached in each.

The way the racial hierarchy figures here, as expressed by a non-Indian,
non-African American, territory resident, contradicts Uncle Dick's freedmen
viewpoint which places African Americans on the lowest rungs of the social
ladder, a hegemony he warns his sons about. Yet "white" (as opposed to

"black") Oklahomans who claim to be "part-Indian," rather than Indian, have often been known to use this excuse to explain why their relatives did not identify as Indians because, they claim, Indian status was "worse than" being black. This is a commonplace romanticism that diminishes historical realities and says as much about the person rationalizing an uncertain identity as it does about actual social conditions. The diversity of tribal factions, their relations to each other within the tribe, and their relations to the outside world is a shifting dynamic—individuals vary in regard to their opinions about the status of blacks, Indians, and Afro-Indians, and, in fiction, as E. Pauline Johnson might remind us, individual personality is one of the medium's many charms—thus the contradiction between Uncle Dick and Opal. As is often the case in *The Cherokee Night,* Riggs over dramatizes race in *The Cream in the Well*—in this particular case because race takes on larger symbolic meanings that have to do with the experience of various kinds of social outcasts, and these two plays will include gay pariahs in each of them.

In the contest of wills between Julie and Opal, an idea emerges that will become increasingly clear and eventually fully articulated in the play: Julie busted up Clabe and Opal because she wanted Clabe for herself. Although she is in love with her brother, Julie has never admitted it, and she clings to her illusions about sending him away for better opportunities.

This is where the play gets really weird, as if things were not already weird enough. We will see this same theme repeated in *The Year of Pilár.* I said earlier that these are not only Riggs's other Indian plays, but they are Riggs's gay plays—the only works in his oeuvre that I know of which deal with gay subject matter overtly. That's the good news.

The bad news—and it is very bad news indeed—is that both plays very clearly link gay identity with incest between siblings. This is not subtext, nor is it hidden between the lines, and neither is it a matter of decoding or nuanced readings. Sexual relations between brothers and sisters who have also been involved in same-sex relations are what we're talking about here. Both plays build toward a culminating moment when these characters' doubly tabooed desires are exposed, and that moment is the very crescendo of the play, a huge orchestral roar that drowns out all the other movements that lead up to it.

We have not yet quite arrived, however, at this final revelation, although Julie's desire for Clabe has been hinted at in a number of different ways. Julie, used to winning every battle she mounts and successfully exacting revenge, finds herself quite undone when Opal produces a bundle of love letters from Clabe that she "just happens" to have on her person. This sends Julie over the edge, and she reacts like a jilted lover.

Julie gets even meaner than Opal. She goes for the jugular. Opal is haunted by fear of her own mental instability. Her family, it turns out, has a streak of insanity running through it. They had pretended as if the mother (the same one, by the way, with the racist formulations about Cherokees and African Americans) had died when, in reality, they had put her in the mental institution in Vinita.

Julie gives Opal something to ponder by telling Opal that insanity is hereditary. Opal, in an extreme state of agitation, runs out onto the boat landing screaming about going home—and who wouldn't after dinner with the Sawterses? She tries to get into the rowboat, falls, hits her head on the oarlock, and slips in the water and drowns; hers is a death that has already been foreshadowed by Julie's morbid talk of the lure of the lake's waters.

Opal's death means that Julie has successfully killed off her competition for Clabe. She says to his photo, "Is this what you wanted? How do you like it?" (192). She wreaks part of her revenge on Clabe himself for choosing Opal instead of her and for writing the letter that denounced her.

The Sawterses lay Opal out in Clabe's bedroom, and she finally gets some sleep, but this time the sheet is pulled all the way up over her head. Even as Gard sits up with his dead wife's body, he proposes to Julie, threatening to tell Julie's "secret" unless she marries him. Gard probably does not realize the full extent of Julie's secrets, as far as her incestuous desires are concerned. He is smart enough, however, to figure out that if Opal took a nosedive into the lake, Julie probably had something to do with it. Julie's unspoken secret provides a strong parallel to Clabe's queer secret, which will be revealed later in the play. However much Gard may know about Julie, his is a singular marriage proposal—marriage by blackmail, one of the many problematic heterosexual relationships omnipresent throughout Riggs's work. Julie admits defeat, and the next time we see her in the play she has acceded to Gard's proposal.

The second act of the play depends on the same structure as act 1, but this time *Who's Afraid of Virginia Woolf?* becomes *Guess Who's Coming to Dinner?*—except that the surprise lover is neither black nor heterosexual, and the family has already met him. The prodigal son returns home to share Thanksgiving Day with his family, and we will find out that he has fallen a lot lower than the pigsty. Clabe's return surprises the Sawterses because in the letter in which he renounced Julie, he also vowed never again to come back to the farm. Mr. Sawters, who has fallen into a chronic depressed slump because of Clabe's departure, feels much renewed by the prospect of his returning son. He will have more help running the farm, and he never could understand why Clabe left in the first place, since his son had a natural affinity for rural life.

This is also a homecoming for Julie, given that she has stayed away since Opal's drowning and her subsequent marriage to Gard. As one might predict, the dinner sets in motion another disaster, but it plays itself out quite differently. In act 1 we see a focus on revenge. Act 2 develops a corollary theme: the idea that witchery, ultimately, dehumanizes the witch. Julie, in fact, shows up for the dinner a much diminished version of her old self. Haunted by her past, she fears her brother's return, especially given the letter he wrote to the family, in which he blames his absence on Julie. Unsure what Clabe accuses her of, she would just as soon not find out.

Gard, Julie's husband, is drunk. Not a little drunk, but completely shitfaced, to the point that the Sawterses finally have to put him to bed, symbolically linking Gard with death since they laid out his former wife in the same house. He has also paid a price for his meanness. He wanted Julie; now he has her, and he has to live with her. As the old cliché goes, be careful what you pray for. Gard failed to show up to help the Sawterses out at threshing time, and they get in a fight over this—he makes up for his absence during their dinner-party thrashing time. Gard has also done little with the land he rents from the Sawterses, so the family has received almost nothing in crop shares from him. The Sawterses desperately need Clabe to stay home this time and take over the farm.

Clabe shows up, like Julie, much worse for wear. He is "dark and hefty, and used to facing tough situations. But there is more to him than male arrogance; he is haunted and bitter, his mind complicated by dark passions and an almost-violent necessity to survive" (204). Clabe's darkness, obviously, is not merely a matter of being dark-skinned but is reflective of an inner turmoil, the cause of which, the play will reveal, is incestuous desire—but, as with many of Riggs's plays, we will be left wondering if it is really something else.

Close parallels can be drawn here to Riggs's own life. When Riggs had the nervous breakdown at University of Oklahoma (OU), everyone assumed it was because a young woman he was dating had dumped him, not unlike the story the family has construed about Clabe and Opal, one, in fact, that Clabe may be complicitous in, since it provides him a cover. Likely there were other reasons for Riggs's own meltdown at OU, as his October 14, 1923, letter to Witter Bynner attests,

Dear Witter Bynner—

Can you advise me, please? Are there any competent psycho-analysts in this country—ones in which absolute trust could be placed? I am in terrible straits, dear W. B., and, since I've removed all the possible physical causes for such a state, my mind only is left.

I would never consider writing to you in such a fashion but nothing at all interests me, nothing gives me pleasure, nothing seems worth doing—in fact, I find it almost impossible to do anything—can't seem to concentrate. Morbidity—

I have sent a collection of lyrics called "Rhythm of Rain" for competition in the fall Yale contest. Here is "Roland" which I did this summer last before complete disintegration began. It is not the one I mentioned some time ago. Will you write me soon? Please.

Yours,
Lynn Riggs

Oct. 14, 1923
731 De Barr,
Norman, Okla.

This, from a young man who was one of the most active OU students on campus—one of his plays had been produced there; he had been on a singing Chautauqua tour representing OU; and he had edited university literary publications, participated actively in fraternities and honor societies, attended every single football game, and much more. Can anyone doubt that there was more at stake than dating issues?

In the official story provided by OU friends and other acquaintances—and which is repeated in his biography—Eileen Yost, charming, Irish, dark-haired, and beautiful, wanted to marry and Riggs had no money. Hod Byer, a geology student who did, came along and swept her off her feet. I suggest that we question the official story, especially the cause-and-effect reasoning it provides.

What might replace the Camelot tale will always be a matter of speculation, but I believe that one possibility is that Riggs thought that Eileen would be the woman who would save him from his homosexuality. When the girl of his dreams, who was everything he wanted, dumped him, that may have been a major letdown. More important, in the case of an intelligent man like Riggs, he may have realized that Eileen was not the cure, and he did not have the support he needed at age twenty-four—and, most likely, at any age to come—to reach the simple conclusion that no cure was necessary.

The happy-go-lucky OU student, supposedly a little depressed because his girlfriend preferred money over poets, had a dark side. In another letter to

Bynner, dated December 6, 1922, a year before he left under strange circumstances, Riggs writes of his junior year at the University of Oklahoma, "I'm sick of this school. It's as tawdry and inconsequent [*sic*] as Eddie Guest. There isn't a man here on the faculty that [*sic*] inspires me to be anything bigger than I am. The students are all right, cordial and all that, but common-place and narrow. I don't believe I'll ever get a degree—it isn't worth it."

I suggest a healthy skepticism in relation to official biographical explanations. Further, I want to suggest such a strategy for interpreting the plays as well. One conventional way to analyze Riggs's plays is tracing causes and their effects—for example, linking the sibling incest to the resulting haunted bitterness we see in Clabe, who is torn up, according to this line of reasoning, by the transgression. Another way of reading a Riggs play, however, involves looking at the less obvious—even the unlikely—factors behind the characters' malaise.

One thing is certain; Clabe has returned home deeply cynical. Although he still feels connected to the land and has some suggestions for improving the farm, his navy experience, and what he has seen of U.S. domination overseas, has caused him to re-evaluate all the hype about the benefits of Oklahoma statehood.

It is ironic that an Indian critique should emerge from an Indian's experiences overseas in Europe, although it is more of a literary irony than a historical one, given all the Indians since the time of early contact who somehow ended up in Europe and had all kinds of things to say about both the Old World and the New. George Copway (Ojibway) even wrote a book about his 1850 trip to Europe, entitled *Running Sketches of Men and Places, in England, France, Germany, Belgium, and Scotland* (1851).

Regarding the turn of the century optimism concerning Oklahoma, the feeling was that the territory would turn the corner and find itself in the middle of a new history, a great moment of enlightenment, progress, and, most importantly for any Okie worth his salt, increasing fortunes.

No one better captures the feeling of the statehood frenzy than John Joseph Mathews in his 1934 novel *Sundown*, although its time period is a little bit later than the Riggs play, since it takes place in the early years after statehood, when faith in modernity complements the oil boom in Osage country. Optimistic ideology seems powerfully supported by the earth itself, as gushers shoot gas and oil up into the sky. Okies are not inclined to see black rain falling down all over as a bad sign the way other folks might. There will be oil. And blood.

In *Sundown* an exploding gas well that some claim lights up the countryside all the way from Pawhuska to Tulsa underscores the near-insanity in the community. The locals try to put out the flames by shooting at them with their rifles in a futile effort to separate the fire from its gas source, a potent symbol of technological progress uncontained and out of control.

In Riggs's play, Mrs. Sawters says to Clabe, "Is anything wrong?" Clabe responds, "Wrong? In this best of possible worlds, what could be? Haven't you heard it yet?—it's the Millennium? The country's on fire with progress. Indian Territory's on the high road to statehood. Everybody's going to be rich and the old U.S.A.'s about to become heaven on earth. It must be so because T. R. says it's so" (206).

Clabe himself seems all about questioning the official story, given his ironic endorsement of Teddy Roosevelt. If he represents any kind of politics—and, again, overt politics are not often evident in Riggs's plays—Clabe's is a politics of skepticism, since he constantly threatens to contradict the story of why he left the farm and remains bitter about new social developments in the territory since he has been away.

John Joseph Mathews himself had a very developed political philosophy in *Talking to the Moon* (1945), in which he critiqued U.S. naïveté in terms of thinking America could forever dominate global affairs. American triumphalism, Matthews argued, divorced itself from the natural world, in which a close observer would note that life forms are in flux, moving from states of youthfulness and virility to senility, not staying forever at the height of their powers. Robert Warrior has extensively, and perceptively, discussed Matthews's unique synthesis of environmental and political philosophy in the book *Tribal Secrets: Recovering American Indian Intellectual Traditions* (1995).

In Clabe's case it is obvious that something other than U.S. political domination is eating at him. Although Clabe's friend Blocky has driven Clabe out to the farm, and Blocky, whose mental prowess seems to match his name, represents the frenzied progress, since he wants Clabe to join him on a career track of reading law and eventually seeking political office; these dialectical moments, however, seem to be rather brief side trips around the play's eventual denouement, which culminates in brother and sister facing a terrible secret. Upon Clabe's arrival, in fact, he and Julie have embraced, to use the exact language of the play, "hungrily," and transgressive desire seems to overshadow territorial politics.

The family, apparently oblivious to the real reasons for Clabe's haunted condition, determine that he is sick—but not because of the incestuous tensions in the household. Instead, the Sawterses express dismay that Clabe feels so out of touch with the exciting spirit of the times. Mrs. Sawters, an exception, understands, at least on an intuitive level, Julie's role in Clabe's malaise and has many times tried to thwart Julie's meanness and plans for revenge. Mrs. Sawters has special insight into Julie's character because Mrs. Sawters had grown up full of hatred herself and can anticipate Julie's next moves.

The nature of Mrs. Sawters's bitterness during her youth remains ambiguous, a somewhat less-than-convincing aspect of the play given the way the subject is broached but left undeveloped. While Mrs. Sawters suspects the worst in Julie's motives, she has not fully understood, or at least not admitted, the incestuous tensions in her own house. Julie's hatred will prove to be self-hatred, driven by shame over her secret desires. Riggs links incest to homosexuality because both must be hidden. Julie's bitterness, instilled by guilt, is inflicted on others in spiteful actions.

Mrs. Sawters, sensing imminent danger and knowing Julie's potential for cruelty, confronts her daughter. She has guessed correctly that Julie will try to send Clabe away again. Mrs. Sawters knows that if Clabe leaves a second time his departure will destroy her husband. Mrs. Sawters intends for Clabe to stay put.

Riggs certainly knew these pressures to stay in Claremore well, and he dealt with the problem by leaving forever. In addition to all the weird psychological angles we find within the play, there is the real-life claustrophobia of rural Oklahoma families that tend to hover over their broods long after the chicks find themselves ready to venture away from the farmyard. This is a world where going away, as Riggs did by the time he was eighteen—first to be an extra in Hollywood (in a Will Rogers picture no less), then to New York city, then coming back home to Claremore only to run off to Norman to attend university—is equated with being very queer indeed. Not to mention the community's all-encompassing ban on gender nonconformity of all stripes (which is not to say, of course, that gender nonconformity did not exist). A symbolic incestuousness in rural life in Oklahoma, manifested in family pressures to stay home as if married to each other, underscores the more literal incest in the play.

From an Indian perspective, even going away from Claremore to Norman is a radical departure. Consider Chal Windzer, and his two Osage buddies from the more traditional faction of the tribe, leaving the Osage reservation for the University of Oklahoma in John Joseph Mathews's *Sundown*, a novel that takes place very close to the period when Riggs attended OU and was published little more than a decade after. This is a major journey geographically, culturally, psychologically, and in every other way; it is so traumatic, in fact, that none of the three finish college. This is still the case today for many Native students from Oklahoma attending OU. The dropout rate is phenomenal.

And many will never even have a chance to drop out, being unable to even conceive of going there in the first place. Riggs, of course, was a very different Indian from Chal and his two friends, but the journey to Norman still constitutes an immense expanse one has to cross—and I speak from personal experience, having grown up in a family whose people often haven't finished high school, much less gone to university.

Someone like Riggs, who had early on ventured as far as New York and California, must have already been a real weirdo by the time he was eighteen, as far as Claremore was concerned (however, he might be honored in the state today—especially if you're willing not to mention anything about his being gay). Ironically, his effeminacy, travels, intellectualism, and other aspects of his "queerness" may not only have *caused* him to flee Oklahoma, it may have *enabled* him. Home folks would likely have said, "That figures."

We must remember that this was an earlier generation; now many, if not most, older people in Eastern Oklahoma have lived out in California at some time or other, and migratory patterns have changed things so that going back and forth became the norm. Yet even today many folks might leave, especially for military service, but return to rural parts of the state and live out the rest of their lives.

Clabe, our fictional character, never wanted to leave in the first place. The Sawters family knows only that his reasons had something to do with Julie, who seems to be the epicenter of every mean storm. They know she has always thwarted Clabe's intentions. Mrs. Sawters puzzles over Julie's hunger for Clabe's presence, yet Julie always wants to send him away at the same time. At ten o'clock at night, after bedtime, we know Mrs. Sawters has made good on her threat to stop Julie this time because the lights are still on in Clabe's room, where Mrs. Sawters is pleading with Clabe to stay. Julie has been waiting at the bottom of the stairs for the door to open and allow her to get in the final, imperious word. Clabe comes down and defiantly tells her that he is staying on the farm.

Julie asks Clabe why he wrote the cruel letter denouncing her the previous spring. Julie still clings to the illusion that she sent Clabe away to keep him from Opal, to borrow her words, from tying himself down to a "foolish, stupid little nobody who'd shatter every hope [he] had in life to be happy" (216).

Clabe realizes Julie's witching abilities, the way she can shoot thoughts into people's minds; in fact, he had never wanted to leave the farm but had succumbed to her influence over him. Clabe ups the ante by threatening to tell Julie's secret, to reveal why she wanted him out of the picture in the first place.

He leads up to naming Julie's illicit desires with a story. Clabe has been kicked out of the navy on a "bad conduct" discharge. The family, of course, does not know this and Julie is learning it for the first time. Clabe reminds Julie of the expensive brooch he sent her while he was overseas, which, it turns out, was purchased just before he was booted out of the navy:

CLABE. [*Impatiently.*] O God, Julie! Can't you realize I tried every way I could think of to blacken my name, and ruin my character! There are plenty of reasons for my disgrace. All good ones! That brooch you're wearing, for instance . . .

JULIE. It's beautiful. Until . . . your letter that time—I always wore it to remind me of you.

CLABE. I sent it to you out of pure malicious contempt.

JULIE. Clabe!

CLABE. Wouldn't you like to know where I got it? You must have guessed it cost a pretty penny. A lot more than you can save out of a sailor's pay.

JULIE. You stole it?

CLABE. No.

JULIE. [*Numb with foreknowledge.*] Where, then?

CLABE. Oh, I bought it all right. [*With significant but understated emphasis.*] There are ways open to the young.

JULIE. You—made money off of women?

CLABE. No. Not women. All sorts of creatures hang around the ports on the look-out for whatever they can find. They're lonesome and they're desperate. But some of them have money—and are glad to pay for their pleasures. [*As JULIE turns away, sickened.*] I didn't care one way or the other. When you're bent on destroying yourself— you'll do anything—and gladly—just so it fills you with disgust.

[*JULIE takes off the brooch, in revulsion, drops it on the table.*]

JULIE. How can you look at yourself? How can you bear to remember such things!

CLABE. I *don't* remember them—hardly ever. I've learned a little secret. Even to think about evil is death. I've learned that. (216–17)

Not exactly a happy little gay picture. In fact, we will eventually learn that the shame of incest has made Clabe, to use his own words, "bent on destroying" himself, so he searches out behavior that, in his mind, disgusts him equally, and he can further his ruination through sex with men. And unlike Hardy's maid, there's no undercurrent of giddy glee here from the discovery that being ruined is just about the best thing that could ever happen to a girl. The speech that follows on the heels of this one brings out into the open another subject the siblings have never discussed: their mutual attraction:

> CLABE. The needs—yes! There's only one way to wipe it all out—make it like it didn't ever happen, any of what's happened. *Give in to what you are.*
>
> JULIE. [*Breathless, knowing the answer.*] What do you mean?
>
> CLABE. The thoughts you've thought, the needs that are killing you! Give in to them.
>
> JULIE. [*Appalled—low and tortured.*] You're my brother. Don't say such a thing to me!
>
> CLABE. I'm saying it.
>
> JULIE. No. I can't! It's more evil . . . sin that could never be wiped out.
>
> CLABE. How do you know?
>
> JULIE. It's in the mind, it's in the blood. The whole race of man is against it.
>
> CLABE. Not all. Let's say it out plain, and see if it can hurt us. We're in love with each other. We always have been. It's taboo, they say. Who says so? It's happened like that. We fought it, both of us, fought each other, turned our sickness and disgust at ourselves toward others. Look at Opal, Gard, Paw and Maw. Look at us! Jesus! We were wrong . . . and ignorant. But now we know. *All there is to know.*
>
> JULIE. [*In quiet agony.*] Horrible. . . . Maw told me once—hate on one side of a coin. Turn it over. On the other side, love. But *this—this—* love. No, it can't be!
>
> CLABE. [*With tense conviction, pleading.*] Yes! It *can* be. *Any* love ever offered to you has things against it. Sometimes things that frighten you to look at. But at least it's something positive. It declares you on the side of life, instead of the side of violence and death.
>
> JULIE. [*Tortured.*] I can't see it.
>
> CLABE. [*His eyes on her unbelievingly, but fearfully, aware of the answer.*] Are you so committed to darkness you can't make one step against it? Julie! Can't you cross a border that has no existence none whatever? Are you lost that far! (218–19)

Today we might read much of this as camp, at least the line, "*Any* love ever offered to you has things against it" (as well as the stage directions demanding many ambiguously defined tortured states from the actors. I wonder what the director did with *those*?). As far as the "any love" line goes, we can almost hear

Humphrey Bogart saying, "Sure, I know we got some things going against us, kid, you being my sister and all, but whaddaya say we give it a go anyhow?"

These lines, of course, were not camp to Riggs, but the stuff of high drama. The comparison is a little extreme, but think of filmmaker Ed Wood. Nobody believed in Ed Wood's movies like Ed Wood. He thought he was making art. Riggs was never that naïve, and he never made anything as bad as *Glen or Glenda,* but I wish to point out that there are two kinds of camp: camp that is camp because it was meant to be camp and camp that is camp because it was meant to be so very serious, and we look back at it from a different vantage point than the way it resonated with author or audience or both at the time of its creation. In the case of the incest passage here, I believe we are talking about the latter kind of camp, not the former.

This is not to say, however, that the lines do not have their own complexities. Although the topic is obviously incest, are we also talking, on some level or other, about queerness? Could incest provide a smokescreen for other things on Riggs's mind? When Clabe says, "Can't you cross a border that has no existence, none whatever?" surely there is something subversive going on here. An audience would be forced, even in the 1940s, to *hope* Riggs is talking about gay relations, not sex between a brother and sister.

Julie thinks of a way out that will save both of them from the impending disaster of their mutual desire. She will walk out on the thin ice of Big Lake, break through, and drown herself. Clabe offers to join her in mutual suicide, but Julie believes he must stay and help the family, especially Mr. Sawters, who has placed so much hope on Clabe's return.

Julie's goodness, supposedly, comes through in the end by virtue of her self-immolation, the first time we see her thinking of someone other than herself. It is a sacrifice, unfortunately, that seems to negate any hope for the power of queerness. In fact, in her last words to Clabe she emphasizes that he too must do his part: he must change, and he must forget. She repeats his line that "even to think about evil is death."

Killing off deviance, however, never boded any better for Riggs as an artist than it would for the characters in *The Cream in the Well.* He had a strong desire to write plays that went against the grain, yet he backed down every time he started to succeed, changing the subject like a sleight-of-hand trick whenever it got too close to revealing queerness.

After weakly protesting Julie's suicide, Clabe gives in and agrees that her drowning benefits the whole family. In the end the brooch, the piece of jewelry Clabe bought from his earnings from hustling men, confirms the hypothesis that the incest theme may merely afford a diversion for other issues. As (heterosexual) Julie breaks through the ice with her Scarlet Q, so to speak, she may be the queerest character in the play—even if she is heterosexual—if we think of deviance in the broader senses that many theorists conceptualize it these days. Loving something but sending it away, burying and denying desire, have engulfed Julie from the play's beginning to end. We are told that the brooch, light as it is, is still heavy enough to drag her down to the bottom of the lake:

> JULIE. Listen to me. Forget me. *I never existed.* It's best.
>
> CLABE. Best?
>
> JULIE. Yes! Even to think about evil is death. You said so. Hang on to that. Forget everything—you—me—my life—the rottenness—every-thing horrible.
>
> CLABE. Yes. [*Spent with the effort, relieved and wan,* JULIE *slowly and deliberately goes to pick up the brooch and fasten it to her dress.*] What are you doing?
>
> JULIE. This goes with me.
>
> CLABE. You can't wear it now—that—that—*thing!*
>
> JULIE. I will, though. Like a badge. Like a banner. Where I go, it must go too. There'll be nothing left to remind you—of it or of me. *Even the memory of evil is death.* We both know it now. [*She pauses by the door, looks down at the brooch.*] See—It weighs nothing at all—such thin silver, a thimbleful of stones. [*She envisions it clearly, dragging her to the muddy depths. After a moment—she is not afraid.*] But it's heavy enough. Like a weight. (220–21)

Julie is more martyr than deviant, hers a transgressive state that fails to free any-one from terminal creeds, binaries, static definitions, or rigid societal roles. Sibling incest, of course, isn't easy to celebrate, and probably shouldn't be, ac-cording to most cultures. Still, deviance of any sort is drowned in the play. The symbolism of all the weight culminating in the tiny brooch, and the brooch be-coming a badge, I believe, involves a degradation of the object of art, as its beauty is replaced by the mundane and the authoritarian—the jewel becomes anchor; the fashion statement morphs into lawman's badge. It is to be cele-brated "like a banner" only to whatever degree one sinks it into oblivion, never to be seen again. It goes in the opposite direction of art, a reverse transcen-dence, from deviance to convention, and it represents the lopsided equation dis-cussed in other parts of the book where too much value is given to conformity.

I wonder if Riggs ever wrote a play that told the truth, then tied a rock to it and sank it in Big Lake? Just what kind of a brooch hurried it toward the weedy bottom?

Next we have the inversion of the earlier witching of Opal and the culmination of the theme that witchery turns itself back on the witch. Julie could not witch Opal out into the lake without some of that bad medicine rubbing off on herself. In the process of putting suicide into Opal's head, Julie has also put the notion in her own thoughts. This is why witchery, ultimately, is a form of sterility: harm can only be inflicted on others by inflicting it on oneself, too. Gandhi and other pacifists have argued this profound simplicity—that any act of violence, no matter how noble the cause, will make the oppressed an oppressor and compromise justice. He will become the very thing he protests when he takes up violence as a solution. Whether or not one agrees that pacifism is always a viable alternative, it is a powerful argument. Julie's violence against Opal, by necessity, will turn back on Julie.

In order to go home, the play seems to say, one must kill off one's queer self. *The Cream in the Well*, like many a Riggs play, shows the wear and tear this erasure has on people's bodies and souls. In relation to Riggs's own experience, this play could just as easily be titled *Why I Won't Move Back to Claremore*.

A fascinating aspect of both *The Cream in the Well* and *The Year of Pilár* is that instead of killing off the gay characters in the plays, Riggs gets rid of the women. Needless to say, this is not an improvement. Feminist readings of these plays might be rich in terms of considering why these women are cast as witches and the reasons they have to be killed.

The play ends ecstatically, with the whole family rejoicing over Julie's disappearance since, except for Clabe, they do not yet know she has drowned, but only that things are a helluva lot more peaceful in her absence:

BINA. I don't know why you act so funny. [*No answer.*] But I think there must be a good reason. [*Puzzled at the thought.*] I feel somehow *you're* good, too, Clabe—not mean like you used to be. Do you mind my sayin' so?

CLABE. No.

BINA. I've noticed it ever' since you come home. [*Softly, secretively.*] I don't know where Julie's gone—and I don't care. I don't. And I think it's good I don't care. *Good*—not bad. Do you think I'm awful?

CLABE. No.

BINA. [*Like a care-free child.*] Oh, I feel so good tonight—like a load was lifted off of my shoulders! [*She goes toward the organ.*] I don't know— maybe it's the weather.

CLABE. [*Remembering* JULIE's *words—softly.*] Tomorrow will be clear and bright.

BINA. [*Gaily.*] Uh huh. Bright as a daisy. I bet it will. [*Then, slightly abashed.*] Blocky's nice, aint he? [CLABE *nods.*] I hope he comes to see us like he said he would. [*Then, quite crazily, at that dizzying prospect.*] Oh! For once in my life, I jist don't care if I wake up the whole blame house I feel so *good!* [*She hammers out some gay runs and chords.*] (221–22)

One cannot help but wonder about the appearance of the G word twice in the concluding passage—once in the final line—and whether or not this is coincidental. It meant something different back then, but the word was in circulation among gay people by this time, and may have even begun to be understood in its own special sense as well as its general meaning having to do with frivolity.

The family's euphoria may wane, at any rate, whenever Julie washes up on shore, or, then again, it may not. They could always lay her out and see if Gard proposes again. Or she may never surface, having been dragged to the cold depths by such an evil weight. Bina's own future marriage to Blocky is hinted at, so Gard may have some competition if Bina is on his mind, but then again Bina and Blocky, as even their similar names attest, probably deserve each other.

As always in Riggs's work, heterosexual bliss is highly problematic given the deaths that contextualize the potential future engagement of Bina and Blocky, both of whom are the dunces of the play. If heterosexual marriage triumphs, it is the marriage of two idiots, full of neither sound nor fury—unless one takes their mindless prattle for passion.

Although the centrality of Native people may be more questionable in *The Year of Pilár,* since much of its focus is on a non-Indian family, the play's very strong parallels to *The Cream in the Well,* its location in Mayan country, its exploration of Indian-white relations, and the prominence of the Mayan character Beto make a convincing case for significant Native subject matter. (Although I would admit that such Indian perspectives leave something to be desired by modern standards in Native literature, which features Indian characters telling their own stories as central to the work.) The choice of the Crespos as the focus of the play, rather than Beto as the viewpoint character, might seem to link this particular play somewhat more closely to the work of the Santa Fe Anglo writers rather than the Native authors contemporaneous to Riggs: Mourning Dove, John Joseph Mathews, and D'arcy McNickle. Yet the play does not fit easily into either camp.

Furthermore, the tragedies that befall the white Crespo family are strikingly similar to the ill-fated lives of the Cherokee Sawterses. A cynical argument might be made that Riggs's Indians simply fill in as needed whenever he wants to dramatize favorite themes of forms of authority that kill joy, or that stifle one's natural inclinations.

I would argue, however, that Riggs is interested in Indians as Indians even though only a handful of his plays make this obvious. Phyllis Braunlich's statement—that Riggs's refusal to turn his Cherokees into Indians easily recognizable by the public only strengthens his work—is compelling (*Haunted by Home* 12). I find the strongest argument for this naturalism within *The Cream in the Well* itself: as in *Big Lake*, and as in *Green Grow the Lilacs*, the Cherokee sense of place and Cherokee nationhood are evident in the concrete naming of recognizable places within the nation and stage directions such as "*Indian Territory, 1906*" more than in some kind of ethnographic scrutiny of Cherokees.

Riggs chooses to dramatize his concerns about forms of oppression that kill the human spirit within Cherokee country. He could have set these dramas elsewhere, obviously. That choice should concern us as we attempt to understand Riggs's plays. In drama, as in all literature, place means something, as do national boundaries. When an author chooses to name the place of his concerns as the Cherokee Nation, then readers cannot easily dismiss the Cherokee Nation from their analysis of the plays.

In earlier works I have argued that Riggs's sense of doom in *The Cherokee Night* reflects Riggs's internalized homophobia as much as any historical reality for the Cherokees. Riggs, however, also cared about Cherokees as Cherokees, not merely as symbols. His closetedness, however, creates tremendously complex problems of representation for him.

Riggs chooses to set *The Year of Pilár* in Mayan country—during the time of land reapportionment, no less—and all of this means something, something Indian, in spite of the many weird angles that confuse issues. The play takes us away from Cherokee country. It does not, however, take us away from Indian country by virtue of its very location. It takes place on Mayan land, in this case Mayan land under the control of wealthy non-Indian hacienda owners—a situation that is about to change because Mayans are soon to get the land back, which is the focal point toward which the play's dramatic action moves.

While the internal psychological circumstances which engulf the white Crespos bear some resemblance to the Indian Sawterses of the previous play, I wish to note an important difference. Unlike *The Cream in the Well*, *The Year of Pilár* takes up a singular subject unparalleled in twentieth-century Indian literature at the time of its writing: it focuses on the return of Indian land. An author would not broach this theme again until decades later, when Leslie

Marmon Silko, in *Almanac of the Dead* (1991), would represent land redress as future prophecy rather than as a historical reality in a particular geography in southern Mexico the way Riggs does.

Although the family's psychologies might bear some resemblance, the political circumstances surrounding the Sawterses and the Crespos remain quite different in light of the inversion of power that occurs at the end of *The Year of Pilár,* when the Crespos and non-Indian *patrones* throughout Yucatán are driven off their haciendas and Indians take their land back. This certainly differentiates the Crespos from the Sawterses, who are posed on the brink of Oklahoma statehood and who will wait almost another thirty years—beyond the scope of the play's setting—before they even witness the partial restoration of Cherokee government under the 1934 Indian Reorganization Act (applied in Oklahoma in 1936), much less the return of Cherokee land, which Cherokees still await today.

Now, having qualified the play's similarities, I will proceed with my cautious naming of the parallels between the white Crespos (to whatever degree any Mexican, no matter how wealthy, is purely white) and the Indian Sawterses. There is Clabe Sawters's exile from Oklahoma; there is the Crespo family's exile from Yucatán to New York during the Mexican Revolution. There is Pilár Crespo, the aristocratic blueblood daughter who kills joy in everyone around her because of her overbearing demands that her family follow conservative Mexican tradition, and there is Julie Sawters's own sense of superiority when she demands that her brother leave Oklahoma because he might marry a girl beneath him if he stays.

Both women appear as domineering and outside gender norms: they defy their respective Mexican and Oklahoman fathers, and, in fact, take over the running of their families—one demanding a brother's exile from Oklahoma, another demanding a family's return to Yucatán, and in both cases against their fathers' respective wishes. Thus, their adherence to tradition is mitigated by the fact that they would rather impose it on other people than follow it themselves, since they reject the strong patriarchal traditions of both Oklahoma and Mexico. (I realize the arguments about southeastern Indian matrilinearity have a certain relevance, but anybody who lives in Oklahoma has experienced certain gender inequities that abound in both Indian and white culture in the state.)

There is Clabe Sawters, the wayward son who leaves home and returns in defiance of his sister, and there is Trino Crespo, the wayward son who leaves home to go Native, shacks up with a handsome young Mayan lover of his own sex, assists Mayans in taking back the land, and repudiates his rich white family—also to the shock and horror of his sister.

There are Don Severo Crespo, a failed surgeon, and Mr. Sawters, a failed farmer. In the Oklahoma play we have sibling incest between brother and sister; in the Yucatán play we have brother and brother incest. Both plays contain strong elements of gothicism and the eventual revelation of an "ugly" secret: in each instance the incest is intricately linked to gay identity—gayness, as well as incest, being the ugly parts.

In spite of all these similarities, however, the sweep and range of *The Year of Pilár*, with its much more developed exploration of colonial as well as interpersonal relations, make it a more difficult work to interpret than *The Cream in the Well. The Year of Pilár* still has me stumped.

The play opens in 1937 New York City, where the Crespos have lived in exile for nearly twenty years since the Mexican Revolution. Doña Candita, the mother, longs to return home, but her husband insists on staying. Convinced that if he only remains in New York long enough he will gain recognition as a great surgeon, Don Severo seems to have reconciled himself to actually working for a living rather than commanding a hacienda, resignedly accepting his fall from privilege. Don and Doña, their titles, emphasize that they are heads of the household, and parental authority—almost always gone wrong—is an important concept in Riggs's plays.

The sons and daughters of this family are a study in contrasts. Pilár, truest to form, has not accepted her father's resigning himself into the working class (upper working class though it may be). Pilár still believes in the authority of family tradition and its arm of enforcement, the Catholic Church. For Pilár, family means, more than anything else, proper breeding—claiming the purest (in Mexico this means non-Indian) bloodlines, as well as possessing a sense of one's privileged status and behaving accordingly.

Chela, Pilár's sister, is a cabaret singer who hopes to get a lucky break in the night clubs of New York. Pilár does not approve of her sister's foray into show business. None of their Spanish ancestors were torch singers. Fernando, another sibling, fills the role of the rich kid who rebels against his parents. A communist, he idealizes worker organization—although he knows little about labor, never having done any.

Trino paints. At the time Riggs wrote the play he was in his longest relationship, that with the painter and dramatist Ramon Naya, a Mexican citizen. Riggs hoped to get Bynner—or anyone else, it would seem from the evidence in his correspondence—to help Ramon obtain legal status in the United States. Ramon's impact on the play is obvious in terms of the help he must have given Riggs with the Spanish language used in the dialogue; Ramon's influence can be seen elsewhere in the more overt political orientation of *The Year of Pilár,* a deviation for Riggs.

In the 1930s Riggs was writing during the most radical decade of American drama—the time of the Federal and the Group Theater, a decade of agitprop, labor plays that supported union organizing, and so on. Yet Riggs, like many other playwrights of his time, in response to the radicalization of the theater, preferred exploring personal relationships rather than political ones. Modernist and activist plays were somewhat at odds during the decade, in spite of the proliferation of each.

Ramon Naya, unlike Riggs himself, was more politically oriented in his philosophy and work. The overt politics of *The Year of Pilár* make it quite different from any other play in the Riggs oeuvre. It is too simple, however, to equate Trino, the fictional Mexican painter, with Ramon Naya, the Mexican painter living with Riggs at the time of the play's composition. When Trino is first introduced onstage, the directions read, "A sullen and searching fire is in him" (6). I have analyzed such statements as a reflection of Riggs's own interior landscape, especially in earlier interpretations of *The Cherokee Night*. Trino probably contains elements of Naya, Riggs, and the intersections of their volatile lives together, as well as unaccounted sources of creative inspiration that go into any character—the individuality that E. Pauline Johnson argues for in fiction.

Pilár oversees the affairs of the household, not Trino, Fernando, or their father; and her ruling hand, evident everywhere in the New York apartment, demonstrates her authority both at home and abroad, since she has taken over even before the family returns to Yucatán. She subverts Mexican patriarchy and perhaps matriarchy as well, since she orders her mother around, too. She demands her brother's obedience, just as Julie demands Clabe's. When Trino hangs up one of his own still lifes of flowers, Pilár jerks the portrait off the wall and demands that Trino replace the somber ancestral portraits that hung there before. Like Julie, she is another witch figure, except here the witchery is politicized: "Her mind has the keenness and the violence of her Conqueror forefathers; her emotions the fierce range that will devastate others—or herself. A bitter directness and a resolve to do a dangerous act possess her at the moment" (8). Pilár embodies male colonial authority.

Trino had not wanted to hang his painting in the first place, but his more free spirited and egalitarian sister Chela had urged him on before Pilár came into the room and discovered the change. Trino's criticism of his art has to do with its inability to effect political change:

CHELA. Oh, it's beautiful!
TRINO. Pretty, I guess. But what of it?
CHELA. You're an artist, that's what of it!

TRINO. It doesn't seem to matter. With the horrible things going on in the world. [*Genuinely troubled.*] This morning—did you see the headlines? How can Spain go on—our own people, brothers almost— how can they have the heart to struggle on against such odds? The Fascist powers allied against them. Bombs from the air tearing them apart. It's sickening! (7)

Her brother Trino will grow increasingly politically active as the play progresses, but Pilár's concerns do not include the fight against fascism; if anything she is given to cultivating her own inner fascist. She has a plan to force her father, Don Severo, to move back to Yucatán. Convinced of his weakness, evidenced by his failure to effectively exercise the privilege he was born into, Pilár determines to make up for her father's lack of resolve by taking charge herself.

Pilár is a staunch conservative, yet her defiance, obviously, is not the stereotypical Mexican daughter's response to her father's authority. According to Pilár, Don Severo went to New York only to show up a rival family in Yucatán by becoming an accomplished surgeon, not to protect his own family by fleeing the revolution. Pilár further challenges his authority when she openly criticizes her father's marital fidelity. For Pilár the blueblood, her father's real sin is not that he has broken the bonds of marriage but that he was "screwing whatever [he] could find" (11), and by this she means having sexual relations with Indians, a point that will be made quite clear later in the play.

Pilár is for aristocratic tradition and against New York, which symbolizes wanton abandon to her, especially in regard to the proliferation of both modern and popular art forms there. It was probably that very wanton abandon, of course, that set Lynn Riggs's sights on the city at an early age, since New York was the first place he had fled to at eighteen. Pilár argues that her family must flee to Yucatán because they have become too New York, a lifestyle that is beneath them. New York is a city of cultural decay, where a good family is diminished by degrees every day they remain:

This afternoon I was at the del Hoyos. You should see what's happened to them! The great del Hoyos are trying to be New Yorkers. Their drawing room is full of drunken bums, cheap cafe society, maudlin, jittery imbeciles, just like the rest of New York! The girls drink like fish, Clotilda takes heroin. Grace is gone out of them completely, their manners are the manners of pigs, they stink with filth and decay. My God, is that what we're going to turn into? No, no! I won't have it! Look at us. Poor *mamacita*—her head buried in the church—like an ostrich. Look at Trino, thinks he's an artist. Good

God, who'd spit on an artist? Grandfather would roll in his grave. And Chela sucking around Broadway with her tongue out after lecherous Jews who might give her a job. (10)

Pilár—here, at least, an equal-opportunity bigot—wants nothing of New York and the avant-garde. As we saw earlier, even a still life of flowers is too much for her, only portraits of dead relatives—stiff lifes—will do.

Pilár demands that the family return to Yucatán post haste before they slide further into a New York state of mind. Like *The Cream in the Well,* the play concerns itself with what happens to those who dare to return home—interesting themes given that Riggs himself never did. The plays become Riggs's way of explaining to himself why he can never go back. The two plays, however, do not merely duplicate each other. Julie sent Clabe away from Oklahoma to see the world. Pilár, like Julie, dominates the family by steamrolling over them. Unlike Julie, however, she sends the family away from the outside world and back to their birthplace.

Don Severo accedes to Pilár's demands after the worst of Pilár's accusations, which include exposing his "screwing whatever [he] could find," in Yucatán's jungles, as mentioned earlier. She tells her father, "[You are] [p]assing on your sickness and incompetence to fill the world, to overwhelm the world and destroy it! For you *are* sick, and you *are* incompetent!" (10). Part of the body of evidence she has amassed against Don Severo includes spying on him at the hospital where he works: "I've been to the hospital, I've talked with Dr. Easton, and I know. You'll never be a great surgeon. You won't even be passable. . . . You're a failure, a failure" (11).

Pilár, like Julie, immediately regrets her mean-spiritedness after abusive outbursts but cannot control them nor keep further incidents at bay. Even she characterizes her authoritarian bouts as "rotten," and her demands take a toll on her: "PILÁR turns away from watching him, looks at her family. In her face is no arrogance, no triumph, only the spent, almost pleading, almost tearful look of the disciplined and the proud after a hard victory" (12). Although she feels bad for a spell, she seems to recover her spite quickly enough, and she has the overall constitution of a cigar-puffing Latin American general. By the play's end, however, it will become clear how much of a toll these god-like edicts have taken on her, and once again the theme of witchery diminishing the witch will culminate in her suicide; she will pay a high price for her hatred.

Two of the siblings, Fernando and Chela, are more deeply rooted in New York—one by his commitment to labor agitation, the other by virtue of her determination to make it in the entertainment world—and do not want to go back to Yucatán, but they have no choice once Pilár has issued the edict. Trino's reaction will prove the least predictable once the family returns home.

Upon arrival at the Crespos' old hacienda in Merida, Cuco Saldivar, the plantation overseer, has ordered a band of Indian musicians to play and welcome the family home. At this point the play's Indian themes come sharply into focus, and we are introduced to Beto, a young Mayan man of nineteen years (in the play he is always referred to as a "boy," a reflection of the patriarchal world that surrounds Indians). Beto exemplifies, among other things, Indian resentment of white authority—a subservience marked by a repressed anger, always in danger of brimming over, and hidden behind an obedient façade. But in Beto's case the anger is less suppressed than it is in other, more docile, Indian workers. He talks back to his overseers. This creates a strong irony in the play because Beto slowly reveals himself as the Indian most committed to nonviolent alternatives when land reapportionment goes into effect and violence ensues.

Ordered by Cuco to dance for the amusement of the Crespos as they celebrate their triumphal entry, he refuses. He is a dangerous Indian, more savage than noble, as are all Indians whose idea of a good time is getting land back instead of dancing for tourists. Beto dares to say no. This no, though quietly spoken, will resonate loudly throughout the entire play (I cannot help but think of Elijah Harper's infamous no to the Canadian Meech Lake Accord. It's a pity we know so little of these revolutionary moments here in the United States).

Cuco queries, "You're glad to see the Crespos, aren't you?" to which Beto replies, "No. They are nothing to me" (13)—a significant reply since the play will reveal that Don Severo Crespo is Beto's father, making Beto's refusal to do a dance shuffle for the white family all the more significant. At every turn in this play, art—in this case dance—is wrapped up in asymmetrical power relations.

The rest of the Indians, in spite of Beto's refusal, compliantly provide the subservient backdrop that Cuco demands of them. Cuco's wife interprets Beto's incalcitrance as "uppityness" because she believes Beto is making the most of his white blood.

Cuco rats on Beto for his refusal to dance Indian; he reports to Don Severo, "Oh! I may as well do this now as later. One of the boys—I've just had a little trouble with him. This one. He was insolent. . . . I asked him to dance the *jarana* and he refused" (17). Indian art—dancing, in this case—is controlled by outsiders.

Don Severo calls Beto over, and in a further act of defiance, Beto refuses to give his name to a white man—to, in fact, *the* white man, the hacienda owner whose worldview would have Beto understand that he also owns Beto. Beto gives his first name but not his surname. His surname, of course, in reality, is Crespo, although he has grown up only as "Beto," fatherless.

Rather than punishing Beto, Don Severo drops the matter because he intuits the real reason for Beto's reluctance to give his last name—as has his son Trino, who responds to the awkwardness of the moment by walking up to Beto, introducing himself, and shaking Beto's hand. Rather than rescuing his father from embarrassment, events of the play later reveal that this friendliness may simply be due to Trino's attraction to the handsome young Mayan. Pilár goes into a frenzy because her brother has condescended to shake hands with an Indian, thus compromising the authority and privilege of the entire family— and perhaps Pilár also sees the "hookup" in the works.

Before the family has unpacked their bags, or even gotten inside the hacienda for that matter, one member defects: Chela announces she is returning to New York. She gives a number of reasons, but the most concrete is this: "Something horrible hangs in the air" (18). Every aspect of the land intimidates her—the cultivated hemp, the open fields, the sea, and the jungle. Yet something else also seems to gnaw at her:

> PILÁR. Why do you want to escape? Everything is here—everything!
> CHELA. If there's something inside you you like, you can bear it. I hate everything I am, every thought I ever conceived, everything I ever did. It's *myself* I want to get out of!
> PILÁR. You're sick.
> CHELA. Yes, it's sickness, if you like. But I'll cure it—or die of it—in my own way. That way isn't to be found here. (19)

Everything in me tells me that this is Lynn Riggs describing Lynn Riggs, a reflection of his perception of his "sickness," and a restatement of the "Why I Won't Move Back to Claremore" theme. If Chela had any self-respect, she would have the internal strength to remain home and resist the oppressive environment of her family's authority, as well as the oppressive aspects of Mexican culture, to fight the good fight. Without those inner resources, however, she must flee to an environment where she can deal with one thing at a time. Riggs himself could not face the strictures of his family combined with Oklahoma's homophobia.

I am not grasping at straws here: these fictional pronouncements closely match Riggs's writings about himself. In the second (December 3, 1923) letter to Witter Bynner after the nervous breakdown at OU, a short month after

Bynner had intervened and spirited Riggs away from Norman to Santa Fe, Riggs writes, "You wanted to know the truth so here it is: feeling much better, thanks to you, only it will take several decades to overcome wrong habits of thought, won't it? I'm beginning Decade 1——."

Bynner includes a handwritten note to himself at the bottom of the letter: "He was on the edge of melancholia. Had to leave college. I worked hard to strengthen his spirit—perhaps I was in time." Evidently, Riggs's prediction that his wrong habits of thought were going to take a lifetime to overcome was not mere fancy.

Riggs made a poignant journal entry almost two decades after the OU disaster. For the rest of his life Riggs, evidently, felt the symptoms of collapse constantly pursuing him, and took great pains to stave off a relapse when he felt the disaster coming on again. This entry is from February 22, 1940:

"It's not what happens—it's the way you feel while it's happening."

In 1922—I took just a course—or maybe 2—at school—so I'd have time to nurse my gr-r-r-eat poetic talent. Result: emptiness, confusion, life closing in. At last (other things contributing, naturally) complete breakdown fall of '23, flight to Santa Fe, and all of early '24 getting back my sanity.

Now—I've almost done the same thing again over a period from 1937, through 1938, and even *all* of 1939—a longer period of disastrous retreat. The exact pattern repeated. *This is not to happen again.*

> 1922—It began
> 23—Got worse
> 24—Continued
>> Recovery began:
>> 25—With *conscious*
>>> effort to *exteriorize*.
>>> (Went on climbing and
>>> had some success)

Now:

> 1937—It began
> 1938—Continued—(+ hell!)
> 1939—Continued

So: if I'm to learn, this is it.
Great effort necessary

but 1940 is to begin the new
lift and the new cycle.

But it won't *just happen*.

The return in *Of Mice and Men* is good. George and Lennie are fleeing,
fleeing the stalking posse coming nearer and nearer—and then safety:
the ditch. Then they breathe, they drowse in the beauty of the night, and
dream. But there is here a warning and a premonition. And at the end
the flight, the posse, the quiet place—and death.

Hmm . . . not one word about Eileen, the Irish beauty, who dumped him at
OU and caused him to fall apart, according to the official story. Incidentally,
Eileen Yost has a page of caricatures in an independent monthly humor
magazine in March 1924, a periodical founded by Riggs himself. She would
have written this immediately after Riggs was rescued by Bynner and spirited
away to Santa Fe. She titles the sketches and commentary "Men Who Have
Rushed Us." Under one inking of a geeky-looking guy she calls Edgar, she
writes, "Has treble voice and a girlish figure. Makes all teas and openhouses. Is
of rougish [*sic*] mein [*sic*] [I gather this is a reference to makeup] and thinks
everything is 'cute' " (13). Given such scant "evidence" we move into the realm
of fiction if we guess that maybe Lynn thought more of Eileen than she
thought of him; still, it is an interesting leap to see Riggs as more courtier than
lover. Eileen, obviously, didn't hold out much hope for "Edgar" as a serious
date. Later Riggs would become just such a companion to Bette Davis and
Joan Crawford, relationships that are well documented by Riggs's own correspondence with the two women, and even published gossip columns. The Yost
caricature seems a little mean, and it represents a mere fraction of what the
average Oklahoman could dish out in words if not in actual violence.

Riggs wrote his journal entry many years later, during his years with
Ramon, and one cannot help but wonder what went on in that relationship.
By all indications, especially Riggs's own letters and journals, it was volatile.
Riggs's desperate struggle to hold himself together is heartbreaking, as is the
fear that he constantly lives with that he could once more fall apart. The
journal becomes a forum for his mantra, in which he convinces himself he
will survive. Chances are extremely high that his fragile emotional life did not
lend itself well to stable relationships with Ramon or anyone else.

To return to the play's treatment of these matters, in contrast to a character
like Chela—who, like Riggs, wants to escape her "sickness"—Pilár experiences different agonies. As does Julie, she always feels bad after inflicting a

vicious assault on her victims—but not bad enough to consider alternatives to the verbal violence that tends to re-enact, rather than challenge, the patriarchal authority she both adheres to and transgresses. Pilár's privilege includes exempting herself from her own rigid morality.

As many a Bette Davis or Joan Crawford movie from these decades will tell us, a protagonist can be a "bad woman" (her badness always being related in some way or other to her independence), but by the end of the story she will either be reformed or dead—"bad" girls get it in the end. That was the formula, and Riggs certainly does not deviate from it in these plays. Various family members and friends comment on Pilár's usurpation of power normally reserved for men:

> DOÑA CANDITA. [*With secret guile.*] You depend on yourself too much.
> PILÁR. Grandfather did. On himself alone.
> DOÑA CANDITA. But he was a man. You are a woman. The rules are different. (25)

Cuco, the plantation overseer, finds himself increasingly attracted to Pilár, and one of the female characters warns him, "A woman is supposed to keep her mouth shut, except to say, 'Yes.' . . . Would you look at a girl who smokes in public, swears in public, wears her hair like a harlot, and doesn't know the way decent women are supposed to behave?" (19).

Doña Candita herself has plans of marrying Pilár off to Cuco, since he owns a successful cigar factory, and his pedigree meets with her approval. When Doña Candita mentions this to Pilár, she replies, "I could give myself to a man, I think. But I shouldn't care to marry one for life" (26), causing her mother to have a conniption fit. Pilár, well outside Latin American norms considering the symbolic significance of virginity and marriage for women, does not quite come off as the Virgin of Guadalupe. Furthermore, "I could give myself to a man, I think," is not exactly the statement of a flaming heterosexual. Yet Pilár also succumbs to very conservative forms of authority, and, like Julie, arranges, to have herself killed off to pay for her "sins."

On returning home, siblings Trino and Fernando enact an interesting role reversal. Fernando finds a girlfriend within about thirty seconds of setting foot on Yucatán soil—one of several of the play's less-than-convincing fortuities—and he seems to have found something more interesting than labor agitation, since he becomes apolitical thereupon.

Trino, on the other hand, develops a political consciousness that will lead him deeper and deeper into the Mayan community's struggle for land, eventually culminating in Trino's "going Native" and moving into a traditional

Mayan *jacal* with Beto. Trino, the only sibling not born in Yucatán, none-theless feels the pull of the place more acutely than his siblings. We might guess that the pull of Beto has as much to do with it as that of the land. Later we find out at least one person, Pilár, thinks that the two of them are pulling on each other.

Beto schools Trino in the Indian struggle and in the cultural differences that separate Indians from whites, yet Beto predicts that Trino will fail to under-stand or overcome this gulf himself. It is a complicated relationship in which love alone does not guarantee its success, given the potential for cultural conflict due to racial difference and hostility due to homophobia. (One won-ders, of course, how Mayans might see same-sex relations and the challenges of Riggs—or Ramon, his collaborator—knowing anything about this.)

A rather long conversation, which takes place at the outset of Trino's and Beto's burgeoning relationship, needs to be quoted in its entirety. It takes up this very subject: how well, if at all, an outsider can understand Mayans. I am not enough of an essentialist to believe that Riggs, because of his Cherokee ancestry, had some kind of special insight into the "Mayan mind," and I think what Beto says to Trino might even indicate Riggs's own skepticism about overestimating the possibilities for insight into other cultures, experience born of Riggs's many years around the "Indian experts" that hung out at Taos and Santa Fe:

BETO. There is strong blood in your veins.
TRINO. No, Beto, not in mine. Listen, Beto, my grandfather was a ty-
    rant, an oppressor. It's no wonder he was at home here. Slaves to
    command—to torture if it pleased him—forcing them to work like
    beasts to fill his own money-bags. Women slaves to enjoy at night.
    The rich gluttonous old Spanish bastard! It's no wonder he was just
    like that with that old despot, Don Porfirio Diaz. They were birds of a
    feather. You should hate them—hate us all—hate *me*.
BETO. We don't hate. We Mayans have never hated.
TRINO. It would be better if you had. Look at these ruins—at the ruins of
    Chichen Itza, Uzmal—a dozen cities, their walls down, their story in
    dust. The Toltecs crushed and buried your temples under their own.
    The Spaniards came, and put yokes around your necks, hating your
    freedom and your beauty. A little hate would have saved you. The
    machete was in your belt—and you wouldn't use it!
BETO. Hate kills the people it inhabits.
TRINO. And the people it's directed against, Beto?

BETO. No, we don't die, Trino. A horse, covered with iron to protect him, his feet sharp shod, his nostrils snorting, goes into battle.
Against what? Nothing. No enemy. What happens? He sinks in the
spongy grass, the marsh. The *cenote* filled with reeds and rushes
swallows him. Nothing has happened. All is as it was before.

TRINO. Do you like your lot, then?

BETO. We bear it. We are grass.

TRINO. Trampled underfoot, bruised and bleeding—you bear it!

BETO. Yes.

TRINO. And you—you personally, Beto—do you like your lot?

BETO. Who am I—personally?

TRINO. Flesh and bone! Hope in you—or not in you!

BETO. I don't know such words. I work. That's all I know.

TRINO. You should hope and struggle and fail—and rise up and fight and
conquer!

BETO. What should I conquer?

TRINO. The earth.

BETO. [*With a mounting asperity.*] Like your ancestors. And what happens after they conquer? They decay. Look at those haughty ones and
wonder. Look at yourself. Who are you to instruct me?

TRINO. Don't be offended, Beto. If you are not my friend, I have no
friend. [*BETO looks at him quietly a moment, then turns away.*]

BETO. [*Softly.*] We have no right to be friends.

TRINO. Why not?

BETO. I feel it.

TRINO. I am white and you are Indian. And this is Mexico. Is that it?

BETO. Perhaps.

TRINO. But the land is yours—soon, Beto. The government is giving it
back to you. They have said so. [*Gently.*] I ask for your friendship.
You are my superior.

BETO. You think of high and low. You are not to be trusted.

TRINO. Why do you say it?

BETO. You will betray me. And not know how you have done it.

TRINO. No, I won't, Beto.

BETO. To you some must be above, some below. It's in your blood.

TRINO. [*Narrowly—like an accusing challenge.*] We are not so different.
The blood, I mean. You have white blood, Beto.

BETO. [*Deliberately—also knowing the secret.*] You should know that.

TRINO. Yes. I know.

BETO. [*In deep controlled protest.*] It doesn't make me white. I am Mayan! An Indian only!

TRINO. Yes, you are Indian—but— [BETO *goes away, dark, troubled*
deeply.]

BETO. [*After a moment—quiet again, measured.*] But I have half your
sickness, Trino. Half. So I can understand you enough to be your
friend. I will be your friend, Trino. I can't help it. (30–32)

Beto, as in Christ's prediction of Peter's denial, and of Judas's more malicious act, announces Trino's inevitable betrayal. The Oedipal symbolism,
since Trino will not recognize the betrayal until it is too late, is also evident.
When the treacherous moment comes to pass, it will strike at the very heart of
this relationship—that is, at its most human element: the love between the two
men, a dimension of the bond between them that Trino will prove incapable
of imagining. The discussion of hatred, we might guess, relates very closely to
issues of self-hatred in terms of sexual orientation. We cannot unravel same-
sex desire from the political dimensions of the play—Trino's impending denial
will go hand in hand with his inability to understand the position he occupies
due to white privilege, and more importantly with his inability to rethink the
world in terms of something other than hierarchical and oppositional categories. Trino responds to oppression by replacing it with another system of
hierarchy: "You are my superior."

"I'll take my turn and grovel now," he seems to be saying. "That will be fair,
right? Then we'll be even. I will have demonstrated my remarkable capacity
for sensitivity or at least had to have suffered as much as you."

One is struck by the various essentialisms in the passage: its universalizing
abstractions about the Indian mind, Indian simplicity, Indian pacifism, Indian endurance, and so on, as well as the totalized rapacious white Other who
provides the contrast to the noble Indian. The passage's ending considers
factors of blood quantum, but fails to draw any conclusion as to what they
mean. Beto first says that although he is half white he is all Mayan, but soon
after concludes that his white blood constitutes a "sickness."

Could Beto's "sickness" consist of his desire for Trino, for a white *man* rather
than his own white blood? One might consider *The Cherokee Night*, in which
blood quantum determines which characters can feel their Cherokeeness more
strongly than others. Among his young friends, Gar, with the higher blood
quantum, proves the Indian most haunted by his heritage. Like Beto, he is a
halfblood. And like both Beto and Trino, his sadness cannot be explained by
racial factors alone. Gar is the queerest character in *The Cherokee Night*, even
though his possible homosexuality is not made in any way explicit.

To carry the speculation further, could Riggs imagine himself as a "real Indian"? One wonders if he saw his gayness as an inhibiting factor, something that kept him from being a "real Cherokee." In his letters he occasionally refers to himself as a Cherokee to white friends. Yet we also know the reality of his life, his having fled Cherokee country forever. He seems to have replaced contact with Cherokees with a pan-tribal consciousness—he was a supporter of Pueblo water rights, for example. Many non-Indians—artists of the Santa Fe colony—however, had also taken the same position.

Riggs, given his time among Mabel Dodge Luhan's crowd, had to have become quite familiar with the unique "friend of the Indians" philosophical consciousness that developed around Taos in the 1920s and 1930s. The artist Georgia O'Keeffe and the writers D. H. Lawrence and Mary Austin were three important members of the community. In their understandings of their encounters with Native peoples, Jungian-like notions of universality— the idea of transhistorical archetypes that humans share across cultures and time periods—are very important. The notion of fusing with another culture in a process of transformation that goes beyond the intellect and into the realm of mystical communion is paramount. In terms of the somewhat naïve belief in complete cultural accessibility, there is something very American about this notion that Indian spirituality is akin to the democratic ideal, in that it should be equally available to any sincere seeker.

Similar ideas to the ones made famous in D. H. Lawrence's "spirit of place" philosophy were also an important part of the intellectual environment of the Santa Fe and Taos artists, such as the notion that the Americas possessed a unique spirit somehow unavailable in Europe, and that anyone who spent enough time on the continent would be changed if he or she were only open to these forces. Modern America's disavowal of the spiritual influences that came out of the American soil was part of what caused the alienation of modernity. Indians, more in touch with the "spirit of place," had a lot to offer Americans and especially Europeans, who had not had the advantage of the transforming qualities of the New World.

At one point in the play, Trino tells his brother Fernando, who wants to bribe Indians at the hemp mill to sing and dance for him by giving them wine, "[T]hey have it [something better than booze] already—the thing you ought to crawl on your knees to get" (34). Trino, of course, is not talking about superior wine, but the worldview articulated by Beto in an earlier passage. One theme of the play is the spiritual bankruptcy of the aristocracy in relation to the purity of the Mayans.

Whatever Riggs might have lacked in terms of a traditional Cherokee up-bringing (so far I have found these matters difficult to scrutinize, given available autobiographical evidence, and have found conversations with contemporary descendants less than revealing), he may have tried to make up for with ideas from the Indian sympathizers at Santa Fe and Taos as well as his own attempt to forge some kind of pan-tribal consciousness.

An October 18, 1925, article in *The Daily Oklahoman* is titled "Oklahoman Is Member of Santa Fe Artists' Colony: Claremore Youth Becomes Close Friend of Witter Bynner in New Mexican Literary Group." The article, written a little more than a year after Riggs was sent there after his nervous breakdown, provides a sense of how the colony was perceived in the 1920s:

> Down Santa Fe way there is a colony of artists and authors who have made of the ancient New Mexican town a western successor of Greenwich Village. It is there that one must go nowadays if he would rub elbows with genius. Oklahoma has sent one of her talented ones to this land of shrines and missions—Lynn Riggs of Claremore. When Witter Bynner, the poet, lectured in Oklahoma some four years ago he met young Riggs then a student at the University of Oklahoma. He was much impressed with the Oklahoma boy and it wasn't long until there was a poem in the *New Republic*, entitled "To a Young Inquirer," written by Bynner and dedicated to Lynn Riggs. Two years ago Lynn Riggs went to Santa Fe to be with Bynner and the rest of the group that has made the place the mecca of the literary minded. A few miles out on the canyon road, the ranch of D. H. Lawrence smiles off into the white sands. Stephen Graham has found something in this country to hold him. Mary Austin is there. Willa Cather is one of the colony at times, and when she visits Santa Fe she neglects everything else. It is said she enjoys the folklore of the natives and to collect curious relics.
>
> And what is it that holds these people to Santa Fe? The question is answered when one rambles through this ancient city, for the glamor of the old is over all. It is one of the most picturesquely historical places in our land. The story teller finds a wealth of material and an authentic background for his work in Santa Fe. Indians still in a primitive state, ancient cliff dwellings at Rita de las Frijoles, the far-famed pottery maker, all furnish subjects of rare interest. One of the most typical Indian pueblos is that of Taos, some few miles north through the exquisite but dangerous Rio Grande canyon.

The article also reveals, with a good deal of chagrin, that the local Indians there who pose for artists later come back to be paid, destroying the artists' notions of their subjects' authenticity. The article obsesses over the requirement of an exotic subject for artistic endeavors. Riggs's plays, similarly, emphasize the bizarre as much as the everyday. At any rate, Riggs had already made enough of an impression in Oklahoma by the age of twenty-six, when this article was written, that the state was keeping tabs on him. It is interesting to note that Bynner dedicated a poem to Riggs and that Riggs, the article claims, went to Santa Fe "to be with Bynner."

This may have been the kind of reportage that Riggs was worrying about when, in a September 16, 1929, letter to Walter Campbell, who was writing a story about him for *Southwest Review*, Riggs says, "And while I think of it, will you please leave Witter Bynner out of the story[?] For years that poor man has been getting clippings about me, which somehow hoping to improve the story of me have dragged him in. And especially in Oklahoma, it's been done to death—of course there are implications back of it which are slightly embarrassing, as you'll know. So do you mind killing this fictitious overtone by ignoring it[?]"

In Yucatán, Pilár seems to have similar suspicions about Trino and Beto. She asks the two men, "[A]re you lovers already?" (33). Given that this is the first day of the family's arrival, and the two men have barely met, this is a strange question that may relate to Riggs's own paranoia about such matters—as the careful instructions to Campbell might attest.

However Riggs might have viewed the Santa Fe art community, the play seems to recognize the shortcomings of the self-proclaimed Indian expert. Trino tells Fernando, "Good God, I used to respect you! Jesus, you and your paternalism! Your generous nature! You'll give them wine! The Good God Bountiful! The good god-damned fool!" (35). Trino's wine represents, as much as anything, his cultural misapprehension: he thinks he has something Indians don't know about yet, and Trino is not aware they make their own cane rum (34). In short, he thinks he knows more about Indians than Indians know about Indians. Fernando is the Indian expert, the anthropologist who writes a book based on a summer's fieldwork.

Riggs, probably, did not fall for the Santa Fe romanticism hook, line, and sinker. He had a falling out with Mabel Dodge Luhan, whose love of Indians, quite possibly, did not include queer Cherokees who had the good fortune of attracting handsome young men. In a taped interview a decade after Riggs's death on January 4, 1968, one of Riggs's lifelong friends, Spud Johnson, told OU professor Arrell Gibson, "Mabel asked him to stay there, and they had a cozy time together. Then Lynn had a friend join him, a boy from the University of Denver, who came to stay with Lynn for a while. Mabel took an instant dislike to this boy and from that moment on, although Lynn stayed on in Taos and had a house, she wouldn't even speak to him." I am reading this passage, obviously, in a queer light that to me is rather obvious, although some may see something entirely different, choosing to interpret the permanent Luhan-Riggs rift as her simple dislike for a friend of Riggs's. Admittedly, if Riggs didn't get along with Mabel, he was in good company, given the multitude of people she pissed off, gay and straight. For the purposes of interpreting the play at hand, however, we might speculate that the experience, or similar ones, may have weakened Riggs's faith in white beneficence. The pervasive kitsch of Santa Fe and Taos tends to inflict people who live there long with an increasing cynicism. A person can only take so many Kachina dolls and Kokopellis, after all, before going postal. If he experienced homophobia in the arts community, especially after escaping it in Oklahoma, Riggs may have landed in yet one more place where he felt like both an insider and an outcast, not entirely unlike his Oklahoma world. No wonder he was unhappy.

And, of course, Riggs probably did not seem like much of an Indian to the Taos crowd. He may have found himself in the infuriatingly ridiculous predicament of enduring non-Indians (and some Indians, too) who deemed that Cherokee tribal citizenship, if they even understood such a concept, was not enough of a measure of authenticity for them.

His first day back home in Yucatán, Fernando, much to Pilár's dismay, goes slumming—successfully. As Julie rejects Opal, Pilár rejects Fernando's choice of Ninon, whose family has lost all their money as well as their reputation. Although the blueblood Pilár disowns Fernando for refusing to follow her orders to abandon Ninon, Fernando's defection is small potatoes compared to what awaits the family when Trino eventually takes up residence with Beto, a triple transgression as we shall soon see. Following Pilár's weird, premature accusation about Trino and Beto being lovers, romantic events seem to be happening at an accelerated rate. Either things are really hopping in the hemp fields, or Riggs might have worked a little bit more on the pacing of his play, since the family seems to have stepped off the ship into a country lit up by romances.

While Fernando becomes increasingly comfortable with life as the patron's son and soon forgets the communist agitating that had consumed him in New York, Trino gets more vocal about the sins of his fathers and the injustices that surround him. He tells Josefa, a friend of the family,

> Good God, these are men—with feelings—not inanimate objects, not
> so many picturesque Indians in a Rivera painting! They work like
> dogs, and live on a starvation diet of beans—and not enough of

them—to put cake in your mouth and silk on your backs and gold chairs to sit on. . . . They sit there on the hemp mill—the very symbol of their oppression and slavery—and make a song. . . . There are people, and I'm one of them—who'll never rest till you're all down, down in the dirt where you belong! Get out, get out—all of you—and leave a little privacy to your betters. (39–40)

The passage foreshadows Trino's role as traitor to his race, which will culminate in land reapportionment at the play's end, when he opposes his own family. Art, increasingly, provides less and less solace to Trino—take his criticism of the idealized Indians of the Rivera mural, for example—and he seems to have set aside his own painting for more direct engagement with life. From Trino's viewpoint, at least one art form, song, is negated by poverty, represented by sitting on the hemp mill in destitution. Trino seems to endorse a binary opposition, art or politics, not the synthesis of both.

It is not only painting that Trino tends to place in oppositional camps, as when he pits art against action. As Beto has predicted, while siding with the Mayans and even concluding he upholds their philosophy, Trino's orientation toward dualistic thinking remains unchanged, and he still sees white and Native realities in hierarchical terms that involve superiority and inferiority, just as others of the ruling class do. In Trino's mind, Indians are simply superior to whites; he has reversed the categories, not challenged them. A more radical paradigm shift that questions the very nature of systems of power that privilege one group over another seems outside Trino's philosophical range.

Fernando has the capacity to understand that he and Trino are a lot alike—both Fernando's disdain of Indians and Trino's respect for them depend on assumptions based on knowing more than Indians, speaking for them, and clinging to concepts of possession. Fernando says, "And what do you think you are now, my brother? Are the Indians yours? Do the down-trodden belong to you now that your brother has deserted? You were here. Have you a better right to be here than we have?" (40).

In a typical Riggs-style melodramatic turn, Fernando's command for a young Indian man to play music results in the obedient musician being macheted to death by another Indian who is less than amused by the minstrel show. Beto, who resists violent responses to oppression, recognizes the way in which colonization often results in community members turning on their own rather than recognizing the real sources of their oppression: "No matter who fights, what brother against what brother—it's the Indian who dies" (41).

The scene recalls an earlier one, since Beto himself had been asked to dance—and refused—at the family's homecoming. Beto, who we might have expected to be the most radicalized Mayan, given that he refuses orders from his "superiors," is, nonetheless, a pacifist—a nice complexity of the play.

Eventually a break is incorporated into the play's structure that adds a much needed sense of temporal credibility and finally allows a reasonable amount of months to pass, given the substantial sequence of events that occur. Riggs breaks up scenes 5 and 6 by an intermission, and when the curtain opens on scene 6, seven months have elapsed since the family's return to Yucatán. Fernando and Ninon are being married, which Pilár has opposed from Fernando's earliest interest in the young woman. Pilár has refused to let them wed in the cathedral, and, as with everything else, her word is law in the family. She wants to keep the wedding out of the public purview since Ninon and her mother have fallen from grace within the Yucatecan aristocracy.

Fernando plans to go away to work in the chicle jungles and take Ninon with him, since his marriage prevents him from advancement at home. Though she does not directly banish her brother as Julie did Clabe, Pilár's full endorsement of aristocratic mores is certainly part of a system that makes it necessary for Fernando to leave. The family's experience of diaspora has not abated since their homecoming to Yucatán: Chela ends up in Havana, Fernando is in the chicle forests, and Trino eventually "shacked up"—so to speak—with Beto in a Mayan community away from the family hacienda.

By the end of the play, Pilár, the last sibling remaining with the family, will herself face the most devastating removal of all of them: a departure from home—and from life—that involves a final understanding of the tragic consequences of power and the way in which supremacist viewpoints inevitably destroy those who assert them. Until this realization, however, she strikes out at individual family members, blaming them for the family's decay—believing, for example, that Chela's departure on their first day back started them on a downhill spiral from their aristocratic manners.

Pilár has a marriage proposal from Cuco, the family's long-trusted friend who managed the hacienda during their years in New York, and, given that Cuco is made of the right stuff (money and blood), the family approves of the match. Pilár finally gives in after the eighth proposal (I have already commented on her marked ambivalence about heterosexual union). Cuco advocates marrying and traveling to Europe. The Cardenas government, however, has already begun dismantling estates in Veracruz, and those in Yucatán are certain to be next. Cardenas is arming Indians to assist the military in land reapportionment.

Pilár, who feels like she brought on the family's troubles in the first place by demanding their departure from New York, determines to see them through the political difficulties at home rather than run off to Europe on a honeymoon lark. In addition to refusing to go overseas, Pilár insists on stalling Cuco for three more weeks while they wait for the end of the Church bans to be married. Cuco has no reason to believe that she will make good on her word since she has imposed yet another obstacle, a frustration that eventually will lead him into a state of desperation in which he seeks libidinous comfort in less respectable community members—simply put, the town prostitutes.

The play's most surprising "marriage," however, involves no official ceremony. Trino has moved into Beto's jacal, a traditional Mayan dwelling roofed with palmetto leaves. Trino has taken to Indian life, affecting Mayan dress and attitudes—or so he would think. The stage directions say the two men "are shirtless, having had their showers, and look cool and comfortable. Their trousers are rolled up sloppily, and they have on *alpargatas,* the Yucatecan sandal" (52). In fact, they seem very "coupley" indeed as they eat and talk about their work together before Pilár and Doña Candita appear at the door.

Needless to say, two men farming to support each other, rather than wife and family, is not something the Crespos are used to. Whatever social roles Mayan gay men, or their equivalent in Mayan culture, experience, would probably be unfamiliar to this family—and, one can only guess, to Riggs, the playwright. While Latin American culture outside the Indian world has also always had its share of same-sex activity—generally more accommodating to men inside certain parameters that maintain machismo authority than to women—two men living together and supporting one another economically would not be seen as the usual pattern.

Trino has been gone for a month, and the two women have come to check up on him. Trino's family is dismayed to learn he has actually been doing some work: lifting rocks and clearing fields for corn. This will not do. Trino, as far as his mother and sister are concerned, has gone to seed, one might say, and his mother complains about the waste of good aristocratic privilege which she sees as disrespectful to their forefathers who worked so hard so they could be better than everyone else (54).

Along with the work, Trino has also taken on a Mayan worldview, or at least his perception of one. When asked why he lifts rocks, Trino tells his mother, "[f]or a new *milpa.* Beto and I have cleared away a new piece of the jungle. Now we're piling up the *mojoneras,* laying corn, green shoots. Eventually— harvest, food in the stomach, happiness in the heart. That's the way it goes" (54).

This is the only marriage we see in the play that actually seems happy at the outset; sadly, it is destined for an even greater disaster than the failed heterosexual unions because what will be rejected in this case is the very possibility of the marriage itself, the potential of two men loving each other, rather than the shortcomings of a particular couple.

Riggs, as Braunlich notes in her biography, had a tendency to isolate himself with his partner early in his relationships; this happened with Ramon. Lynn's and Ramon's friends complained during the couple's strongest years together that they never saw them anymore. The two men seemed to have retreated to the sanctuary of their home. One might compare the depiction of simple work and life inside the jacal with Lynn and Ramon's best times together. Riggs's friend Spud Johnson wrote a letter to Betty Kirk on July 13, 1937:

> Enrique [Naya's original name, which he changed, was Enrique Gasque-Molina] doesn't like dogs, but does like perfume[!] . . . Lynn's entire life and habits have been completely changed since our return from your charming but upsetting adopted country. Among other things, they've turned into hermits, see very little of Lynn's old friends, including my- self, don't go out socially at all, have stopped drinking and smoking— and even writing and painting as far as I can make out. All very odd indeed. (qtd. in Braunlich 151)

Trino, a Mexican painter as was Ramon, has also quit painting. The political and personal are linked here, I believe: Trino ceases painting because he sees it as less meaningful than direct political action, but he also may have simply found that his new relationship with Beto has overwhelmed his painting:

> DOÑA CANDITA. You aren't painting anymore.
>
> TRINO. Painting? Rot! What good is it?
>
> PILÁR. I liked your painting, Trino.
>
> TRINO. I don't remember it that way, Pilár.
>
> DOÑA CANDITA. You painted so beautifully!
>
> TRINO. Flowers in a vase—flowers alert—flowers dropping their petals— flowers dead on their stems!
>
> DOÑA CANDITA. I have kept them all.
>
> TRINO. [*With his first show of violence, but quiet and controlled.*] No, mother! Don't keep them! They're sickening and they're a lie! Burn them, *mamacita,* burn them! Don't have such lies about you. Open your eyes and see! (54)

One is struck by the lack of consideration of alternatives. Rather than quit painting, Trino could create something more meaningful than flowers in different states of repose. Again, we see the art and action dichotomy, as if the two forms of experience are mutually exclusive. Of course, this also marks a historical split in the 1930s theater world: between the modernists who want to explore the interiority of their characters and the activist playwrights connected to a lively decade of U.S. social movements that supported labor, and other kinds, of organizing. This political disparity lived under Riggs's own roof—Riggs was more interested in developing character, Ramon in engaging causes.

The personal nature of the men's relationship is no less problematic than the artistic. In spite of the profundity of the men's passions, so consuming that they overshadow Trino's art, their relationship cannot be sustained in fact or fiction. Riggs's longest-term relationship, with Ramon, did not last more than five years, and even so it was on again, off again. I suspect that Riggs's own inability to accept the idea of two men loving each other had something to do with this. And then there was the social pressure from the outside, and the passage just quoted shows Trino's frustrations with various pressures from himself, family, and society.

To have two plays in the Riggs canon with such strong parallels that both equate gay identity with incest seems telling, and more than coincidental. I cannot imagine Riggs possessing the healthy sense of self necessary to sustaining a positive relationship. There is much evidence I could supply from journals and letters about Riggs's unhappiness, but let me simply offer a Riggs poem that I think conveys Riggs's pain as potently as anything I know of. It is called "Dark Song":

> The dark street,
> the shut door—
> yours to keep
> as before.
>
> Moon unclear,
> no hand turning.
> Rain not near.
> The wide brow burning.
>
> Walk at will,
> cry to night—
> sleep seldom,
> sleep light.
>
> Never strive
> to erase

what is so—
in the face.

in the flesh,
in the stream
redly run.
Man in dream

multiplied—
the leaden feet,
the dark song,
the dark street.

You are heir,
as many another
to such pain—
brother, brother.
(*This Book, This Hill, These People: Poems* 28)

Given that Riggs's journals and correspondence seem to evidence both his personal pain and his volatile love life, I believe the poem has some autobiographical elements. If Riggs brought such unhappiness to his intimate relationships, it is likely he drove lovers away rather than creating an environment in which partners could live together. This might even be reflected in *The Year of Pilár*, and its depiction of artist/Indian personalities in a doomed sexual relationship.

To return to the play, then, Doña Candita has come to bring Trino back to his own people, but Trino refuses to return:

TRINO. [*Quiet and sure.*] Death is in that house, Mother. The walls are cracking. In the darkness of night, haven't you heard the shifting of stone on stone?

DOÑA CANDITA. It was built to last forever.

TRINO. So were the temples of Uxmal, the mighty pyramid of Chichen! But the jungle—the living vine—the crawling vital piercing tendrils creep at the base, at every crack—and make of their splendor a jumble of stones for lizards and vermin to breed in! Life is in the earth, mother—in the earth and the people of the earth—not in the arrogant stone!

PILÁR. You're hurting her!

TRINO. I'm sorry [*Fiercely.*] You put her up to it, Pilár! (55)

I want to concentrate for a moment on the political forces behind the image of the living vine. This work's attention to colonialism is the most overtly political of all of Riggs's works. This is likely Ramon's influence on *The Year of Pilár* as well as on Riggs, since Ramon, in his own plays such as *Mexican Mural,* addressed political issues more directly than Riggs. Ramon's contributions to Riggs's plays that take place in Mexico are not merely a matter of speculation. Naya was born in Merida, Yucatán, where *Pilár* takes place, and in a June 12, 1937, letter to Witter Bynner, whom Riggs begs for help in getting Ramon a visa so he can stay in the States living with him, Riggs says, "I'm not going to tell you, Hal, that the American drama (whatever of it is represented in me) will die on its feet if Enrique has to go back—but I'd like you to know that—in the most literal fashion he's a big help to me. My new play is laid in Mexico— and the next one beyond this is about the Mexicans in and around Lamy" (qtd. in Braunlich 149).

In 1939 Riggs and Naya collaborated on the play *A Cow in a Trailer,* and their life together also included discussing and articulating theories of drama. "The Vine," referenced in the long quote from the play as "the living vine," was a major theoretical statement formulated by Riggs and Naya and first written of in a letter to Paul Green on March 5, 1939. A fifteen-page manifesto, it lists thirty-five points about the exigencies of modern theater. The name comes from the poem "The Prophet" by Pushkin. Riggs and Naya interpret the poem by saying, "[I]n the poet's concept it seemed as if he stood on a great height out in space viewing the world and seeing the strong, yielding, but always upward, always affirmative, and always green impule toward the sun. Our theater, green and resilient as a vine, must also thrust toward the sun."

The idea of affirmative plays centers this particular philosophy. Riggs hoped to jump-start his and Ramon's ideas into a dramatic school, and his theater friends Mary Hunter and Andrius Jilinsky had already encouraged the beginning of such a movement. In their explanation of the vine philosophy, Riggs and Naya observe that the poet-playwright faces resistance at every turn, from all involved with the stage, from producers to audience members, which results in artists compromising their work. Riggs and Naya say, "[T]he first step, we feel, in making such a [freer] theater a living actuality, is to produce a clear and exact body of theory—in the way revolutions are made."

In spite of the manner in which the word "revolution" colors the statement, and might even stir up associations of the radical politics of the 1930s, Riggs did not see political didacticism as the main thrust of the playwright's work (and this was the close of a decade, of course, when the Group Theater, agitprop, WPA theater, and so on, were foregrounding politics onstage and even using plays as a means of political organizing at workers' rallies and so on. Riggs's statement comes at a time when the most radical decade of American theater was just beginning to decline, leading up to the staunch conservatism of the McCarthy era a decade later).

It is likely, in addition to reflecting the waning of politicized theater, that Riggs's summary of the vine philosophy had downplayed Naya's more overt activist politics—which Naya, also a playwright, brought into his scripts in works like *Mexican Mural*. From Riggs's letters one gets the sense that he tried to micro-manage every aspect of Ramon's life—from controlling publication of biographical statements about Naya (he allowed none), to using his influence to get Ramon fellowships, to taking care of his visa status, and managing his bank accounts. It is not hard to imagine him toning down Naya's politics in the vine statement.

Riggs and Naya say that their theater will provide "a place of creation, not destruction." They claim that too much destruction already exists in real life and that evil is not fought with more evil; it is challenged by life, not death. In short, they say, "our theater will attack nothing." They go on to write, "We shall not set out to startle people. . . . We cannot too much repeat: we have no worldly battle to fight." Yet such a theater will grapple with the hard things in life. The difference is that the aim of the work will be healing. Given the many violent, sensational distractions in Riggs's plays, which as often as not work themselves out in bleak rather than affirmative endings, one might wonder exactly what he means. Just who is healed at the end of *The Cream in the Well* or *The Year of Pilár*?

The letter lacks any dramatic examples that might illustrate the theory, but Riggs and Naya go on to say that they seek a theater that is non-photographic and non-journalistic. By this they seem to demonstrate a commitment to impressionism over realism, since Riggs states the movies can depict literalism well enough given that they have cameras that can record. Riggs and Naya endorse new forms such as modern dance. They say theirs is "not to be a theater of ideas but a theater of feeling."

Evident in the vine philosophy lies a contradiction between examining hard realities, a need for gritty realism, a commitment to political scrutiny that would be an unavoidable part of this process; and, on the other hand, an impressionistic, affirmative, theater of feelings. This inconsistency may represent Riggs's and Naya's disagreement on the subject. I think *The Year of Pilár* is more political than other plays in the Riggs oeuvre because Riggs wrote it during the years the two men lived together, and Ramon did more than provide words in Spanish. The letter to Paul Green, which Riggs and Naya hoped would launch the Vine School of theater, may also constitute a personal statement about the two men working out their differences in the form of some kind of compromise.

Riggs does not wholly give in to Ramon's influences. Both *The Cream in the Well,* with its brief criticism of U.S. expansion (a mere couple of lines in the play), its skeptical view of turn-of-the-century optimism, and its sarcasm about the statehood frenzy in Oklahoma, and *The Year of Pilár,* with its more developed politics and commentary on colonialism, contain a tension in which eventually politics fall by the wayside and are replaced by psycho-drama in the form of the two plays' incest themes. Gay identity is also broached as a subject, only to be replaced by more pressing concerns.

That said we should now turn to the full articulation of Trino's and Beto's same-sex relationship. When Trino insists that he is happy and Mayan life suits him well, his mother lets it go at that, an exemplar of the "don't ask, don't tell" policy. Pilár, however, refuses to give in, and seems fully determined not only to undermine Trino's willingness to perform manual labor but to spill the beans on the two men's other activities and make sure her mother hears about it. This is not a little mean, and is more akin to Julie's tendencies to torture people than any commitment to truth telling.

> PILÁR. [*With contempt.*] Lifting stones, sweating in the fields like an ox— what good is it?
> TRINO. [*Sharp and sultry.*] That isn't it! How little you understand! I'm allied with something at last—can't you see it?—allied with something and it's no longer death. I'll help all I can to wipe out the stench of rottenness in the land—the stench our fathers left behind them!
> PILÁR. Fernando talked that way in New York. Thank God he got over it!
> TRINO. And how did he get over it? Why? His own pollution—and a piece of flesh he wanted! And he's forgotten everything!
> PILÁR. [*With deadly emphasis.*] You'd do well to do the same.
> TRINO. Is it on that side you bark now? I seem to remember you hated his marriage, you thought it beneath him.
> PILÁR. [*With sharp insistence.*] His marriage was a mistake! I say so still. But a natural one. *Not like you, my brother—not like you! Fernando's mistake was a natural one!* (56)

A low-class marriage, according to Pilár, is not as bad as a queer union. Pilár does not like her family doing work—whether Trino with a Mayan man or

Fernando with a working-class Mexican wife, but she can deal with that more easily than gay marriage. Her blue blood, it would seem, is not absolute, and she recognizes degrees of transgression, especially when she needs to cut herself some slack in following the rules. Somehow, she has been chosen to impose them on everyone else, not to live by them.

Trino's tragedy involves his inability to understand his own investment in colonialism, which continues to haunt him in the way he hierarchizes the world. When he talks about "wiping out the stench our fathers left behind them," this would include Beto, who the play hints from the outset was fathered by Don Severo—a fact, as we shall see, that Trino has always known. As Beto observed earlier, Trino can only see the world in oppositional terms, and neither personal relationships nor human community can be built solely on opposition. Trino is already setting himself up for his Peter-like denial of Beto, a treachery that Trino has sworn off, being unable to imagine his own capacity for re-enacting the sins of his fathers now that he has "gone Native" and gotten all goose-pimply for Indians.

After a brief stage direction that tells us Pilár and Trino are "powerless to stop," the mean-spiritedness reaches its apex:

> TRINO. What do you mean?
> PILÁR. [*With heated contempt, her meaning still veiled.*] Can't you even talk to your own family anymore without others present? Why is this? Are you a coward alone?
> TRINO. Nearly all men are cowards alone.
> PILÁR. [*With cutting passion.*] There's a reason for your bravery now, little brother! And I know what it is! I'm not blind—and I won't be silent. This sore will see the light, do you hear? You have Beto, that's what it is—you have Beto and you're not afraid! My brother's a *puto*, a stinking *puto*! (56)

Riggs uses the Spanish slang for "fag," literally a male whore (rather than the feminine "puta"), which mediates somewhat, though not much, the risk he takes here for his mostly English-speaking audiences. The use of "puto" for gay male is widespread throughout Mexico, an immediately recognizable term with clear implications. No doubt this is one of Ramon's contributions to the play's language.

This play differs somewhat from *The Cream in the Well* because Trino's sexual relationship with Beto also means an incestuous relationship with his half-brother. Clabe's sexual relationship with Julie is also incestuous but not homosexual. Beto is a half-brother, unlike Julie who is a full sibling to the object of her desire. The gay relationship between Trino and Beto, in some weird way, might be seen as a little less incestuous, though "less" and "more" incestuous, in this case, become absurdities on any kind of quantifiable level.

Why the equation of gay identity with incest? Discerning whether Riggs himself equated them—always a slippery slope because of issues of intentionality, or even determining the meaning of these themes within the plays—is not easy. By clouding both subjects, however, Riggs at least finds a way to bring the gay issues into the play in a manner he could not in his other works. In order for the plays to be produced publicly, Trino and Beto cannot get away with their desire any more than Clabe and his men around the docks can, or Clabe and Julie can. "Trino," of course, is short for "Trinidad," and the trinity in this play is Trino, Pilár, and Beto; Clabe, Julie, and the waterfront trysts are the trinity in the other. Pilár, in her insistence on assuming all family roles simultaneously—father, mother, and sibling—is symbolically incestuous if not literally so.

In *The Cream in the Well*, at least on a literal level, Riggs keeps the queer stuff separate from the incestuous stuff, since Clabe's sexcapades occurred around the docks with European, and possibly American, men he is unrelated to and his sister is the opposite sex. On a metaphorical level, however, Clabe and Julie's speeches bring together the incest and queer themes, especially given Julie's own symbolic queerness. All of this, like most everything in Riggs's plays, is weird, pretty confusing, and difficult to get a fix on, as is Riggs himself. In this sense one certainly has to give Phyllis Braunlich credit for her biography *Haunted by Home*. Riggs is no easy subject to figure out.

In *Pilár*, much more so than in *Cream*, the gay and incest issues are politicized, and embedded within the discussion of colonialism. When Pilár says, "Can't you even talk to your own family anymore without others present?" we could capitalize Others, since she means Beto. The irony is that Beto is family on at least one level and possibly two: he is her half-brother for certain, and he may be, as she herself believes, the husband of her full brother.

Pilár's aristocratic notion of *sangre pura*, that somehow the family has had a colonial history in Mexico "uncontaminated" by Indian blood and culture, is a falsehood; Beto is a case in point. The Faulknerian theme so important in *Absalom, Absalom!*—regarding whether the white southerner can recognize his dark offspring, with all its literal and metaphorical possibilities—takes on additional "shades" here, with the incest and gay themes thrown in to further complicate things.

Beto's prophecy, sadly, comes true next, but we find out the prediction plays out a little differently than anticipated. The denial we have been waiting for is not only about race, about repudiating one's Indian brother, nor simply the denial of one's Indian self—that is, the strange ability to look in the mirror and fail to recognize one's own Indian face, a tragedy that is central to Mexican history. Here we have the further negation of loving that Indian brother in a same-sex relationship, a gay betrayal.

After Trino slaps Pilár and demands that she take the accusation back, he says,

> TRINO. [*Sickened.*] You make me sick at my stomach. [*With accusing power.*] Would I have an affair with my brother? Would I? Not with my brother—or with any man!
>
> PILÁR. [*With superb contempt.*] Brother!
>
> TRINO. Yes, *brother!* Beto is my brother—*your* brother.
>
> PILÁR. Recognized by whom?
>
> TRINO. By me!
>
> PILÁR. That doesn't make it true!
>
> TRINO. Close your eyes to the fact, if it pleases you. The fact is still there.
> (57)

While acknowledging Beto as brother, Trino denies him as lover. Given that the play does not hedge any on the reality of Trino's and Beto's biological relationship, which even Don Severo will soon own up to, one wonders if a weakness of *The Year of Pilár* is that the play, ultimately, suffers from the same malaise as Trino, who must hierarchize some form of supremacy in opposition to its inferior counterpart. Thus the play will eventually reconcile itself to interracial brotherhood while denying gay relations.

Riggs downplays the possibility of love between two men when Trino enacts Beto's prophecy that Trino will repudiate the relationship. The play links same-sex desire to incest, and, evidently, the former is more odious than the latter—a position also strongly reinforced in *The Cream in the Well*. A Mayan brother can be acknowledged; same-sex lovers cannot. Trino, as Beto foresaw, remains locked inside a supremacist mentality—in this case heterosexual supremacy, a philosophy he clings to even when his own experience, presumably as Beto's lover, has the potential to teach him otherwise.

During the Judas moment Don Severo walks in with the government's dispossession notice in his hand, the official writ that will cause the family— what remains of it, anyway—to flee their home once again. The gay/incest themes are further embedded in the politics of the play's colonial setting since the family is dispossessed the very night of the gay revelation.

Beto and Trino, the latter having been recognized by the Cardenas government as an Indian supporter, have been chosen by the officials to assist in the partitioning of all the haciendas. Trino, like the artists in the non-Indian Taos community of the twenties and thirties, occupies the position of Indian supporter. The authorities have chosen Beto to dismantle the hacienda at Techoh, the Crespos' land where he resides. The queerest characters, Beto and Trino, while representing various levels of transgression, are also agents of land redistribution, arguably demonstrating some connection to the positive potential of deviance in this tricky play, in which it seems uncertain whether gay identity should be celebrated or forever erased. Searching for an internally consistent, cohesive philosophy is elusive, given that the play's scores of ideas constantly exert changes on one another.

Don Severo, oddly enough, emerges as the most compassionate character, and we find out that it is at his recommendation that the government chose Trino and Beto to help carry out land reapportionment. Don Severo can be given credit for more than simply hoping two family members will procure him a better deal—Severo is destined to lose all of the land anyway. Don Severo seems to have learned something from his many failings. Unlike Thomas Sutpen, Severo acknowledges his dark son. Even Pilár seems moved by his compassion:

> DON SEVERO. I'm proud of you both. [*Quietly, simply, with deep feeling, but without self-pity.*] Being a father is a lonely thing. He is halfway between past and future. Weary of the past, and fearful of the future. And the present is empty.
>
> [*TRINO comes over, puts his hand on his father's shoulder, in unspoken sympathy. After a moment, BETO does the same. Tears flood up into DON SEVERO's eyes. PILÁR comes in, quiet and gentle.*]
>
> PILÁR. I've come to apologize to Beto.
>
> BETO. [*Sincerely.*] It doesn't matter. Don't think of it.
>
> PILÁR. [*Gratefully.*] Thank you, Beto. [*Turning to her father—gentle and compassionate.*] Father—your son.
>
> DON SEVERO. Yes.
>
> PILÁR. My brother.
>
> TRINO. You admit it?
>
> PILÁR. [*Her voice very low.*] Yes. What else can I do? [*She looks from one to the other. She feels the strong and poignant bond between the three, she feels her loneliness, her inability to enter into that magic. Like a little child—wistful and alone.*] I've interrupted! You don't want me. I'll go. (59)

The resolution of this scene may strike us as more than a little pat, since only moments before Pilár thought the two men were sharing a bed and seemed quite unready for the family reunion that occurs here. Did the notion of Trino's and Beto's intimate relationship disappear without a trace from Pilár's mind after the revelation of the family's genetic link to Beto? To what degree has Pilár become sympathetic to the two men's living together? Is she sorry or simply outfoxed? Rather than staying and working out the complexities of this newfound nuclear family, she simply leaves pouting, complaining she is unwanted.

Like Julie, she will make the ultimate self-sacrifice, supposedly proving her goodness in the end, although one might wonder how her eventual suicide lessens the family's troubles, contributes to its future survival, recognizes newfound relationships, makes up for Pilár's own shortcomings, or redeems the sins of her colonial ancestors. Will Pilár's suicide advance land redress in any way, or does she simply give up in despair over the possibility of living her life as an ex-owner? Such questions become increasingly unclear as the play moves toward its ending.

One might even wonder what, if anything, the suicide does for Pilár, beyond relieving her of the troubles of existence. It may be a cliché formulated in beginning writing classes to warn young writers about melodramatic pitfalls; nonetheless, as a general rule it holds up all too often that suicides in literature frequently serve as copouts. Writers sometimes do not know how to handle the complexity of their subject matter and allow difficult tensions their continuing place in the work, so they simply kill off the character(s) who are hardest to figure out. This happens time and again with Riggs's people when sensationalism replaces character development.

Tennessee Williams, a Riggs contemporary (we might say he really achieved recognition about a decade after Riggs, in the 1940s), also suffered from the limitations of his time, but the gay undercurrents in Williams's plays lead him toward a revelation of his characters' interior (and exterior) lives; in Riggs's plays, the same undercurrents lead him away from his characters. It is hard to point to a Riggs character that is as well developed in terms of revealing motivations, hopes, and fears as an Amanda or Laura or Tom or Blanche. Riggs's plays turn on plot, especially its more sensational manifestations, not on explorations of consciousness or even in-depth treatments of social milieux. I believe Riggs's double challenge, nay, triple challenge, of trying to reveal something about what it meant to be gay, Indian, and Okie, all at the same time, was simply overwhelming to him; and some of it, of course, was simply untenable in the theater world of his time. Hell, it's overwhelming to me, and I don't live in the climate of fear that surrounded Lynn Riggs.

The Crespos hear on the radio that on one of the neighboring haciendas Indians have risen up and killed the owner and his family. The Crespos' flight has become much more urgent. The family packs and prepares to leave, but Indians are drinking, singing, and firing off guns outside. Of all the times to visit, Chela returns at this very moment from Havana, where she has been singing in night clubs. In a campy scene straight out of *Reefer Madness,* Chela announces her degradation as a night club floozy who has taken to smoking dope, and she sparks up a big old hooter as the guns fire all around her, taunting Pilár by telling her she gets high to help her cope with prostituting herself. It couldn't get any better if Chela were to hand Pilár some of her stash and say, "This bud's for you."

While the scene outside might seem clichéd—the proverbial Natives are proverbially restless—it ends up that Beto and Trino have negotiated the family's safe escape from the menacing Indian crowd. Whether or not the gang is pacified, however, Pilár has determined that she is not leaving without offering her body as a "living sacrifice," to borrow Saint Paul's phrase, to the mob outside, although what happens to Pilár is probably not what Saint Paul had in mind.

Trino reveals more of his "friend of the Indians" attitude—that he knows best for the Mayans, and their future lies in revolt rather than the kind of patient resistance Beto advocates throughout the play. He tells Pilár,

TRINO. The Mayans have always accepted authority from above, meekly. Now there's no authority above them—for the first time in centuries. There'll be abuses at first. It's inevitable. The *politico* crooks and dispossessed *hacendados* will scheme their guts out to get back what they've lost to ignorant Indians, accustomed only to the labor of the body. But the idea of the right to power goes to starving cells quickly. And it won't die so easily in their veins. *They'll learn to fight.* (64).

All this from a guy whose total experience in Yucatán spans seven months, only two of which have been in a Mayan community. Summer fieldwork doth not a Mayan make.

While Trino finds his niche during the Indian revolt as an aide-de-camp among the Mayans, Pilár is swept into a vortex of which the most devastating effect on her is her loss of control. She has no authority among Indians who have recently risen to power, and she no longer has control over her family, since all her siblings have defected. Chela is only stopping by on her way to New York and a Broadway career (Thought I'd say hi—sorry about losing the hacienda—but I'm going to be in a musical!) and does not plan on seeing the family again. They probably ran out of munchies.

Pilár, in her desperation, momentarily drops a little of the coy mistress act, and seeks solace from Cuco, wanting him to hold her. Cuco interprets this as a breakthrough, and brings up the marriage question again: surely Pilár will marry him, he insists, now that the family is dispossessed and she needs support. Pilár, however, hedges yet again and says they must wait until they get settled in town. Cuco can bear no more of her stalling tactics, and he reveals he has been seeking sexual release "in the mires of women—any woman—white, yellow, black, *any* woman I could find—night after night——!" (67). Pilár responds, "Take me," but when Cuco tries she says, "not here——!"

"First, you say you will, and then you won't," the old swing singer used to croon in the aptly named "Undecided." Well, it is in her mother's bedroom that the conversation is taking place, after all, and there is a riot outside, but Pilár is more concerned about her mother's altar and the pictures on the wall—her Spanish ancestors are watching. Cuco smashes one of the portraits.

> CUCO. [*With bitter contempt.*] . . . These—these are between us. Not only the living—the dead!
>
> PILÁR. Yes, yes!
>
> CUCO. I might have known. It isn't to be. You're free—free to lick the feet of the dead—who don't give a damn! They *don't*! The dead have betrayed you! and the living don't want you. Your family doesn't. *Nor do I*! I wouldn't have you now.
>
> PILÁR. Cuco!
>
> CUCO. I can see your fate. No one in Merida will speak to you, you know that. They'll say I refused to marry you, because I had you before marriage. Josefa will see to that. You won't be able to stand it! Ninon and her mother couldn't—what the tongues did to them. You can't either. You'll have a walking death, whispers always in your ears! Your last chance is gone. Your grave is dug for you.
>
> PILÁR. [*Her voice dead.*] Yes. You've said it all. Get out.
>
> CUCO. [*Weakening.*] Pilár!
>
> PILÁR. Get out!
>
> [CUCO *goes to the door, unlocks it, opens it, turns.*]
>
> CUCO. I can't leave you.
>
> PILÁR. You will leave me.
>
> CUCO. [*Agonized.*] Say it—I'm a toad, a snake, the lowest—disgusting, crawling——!
>
> PILÁR. You're a Latin, Cuco. A high-born aristocratic Yucatecan—the privileged, the inheritor of all good—the ultimate dream, the triumph of the blood. [*Her voice shaken with realization.*] *Like me*— Cuco. Save yourself if you can. Get out before it's too late.

CUCO. What will you do?

PILÁR. What does it matter? (68–69)

I'm intrigued by the idea of licking the feet of the dead but afraid to Google this on the internet since it probably really exists a Yahoo! away in our techno world. Unlike Gard, who forces a marriage with Julie at the most inopportune moment—the death of his wife—Cuco is unable to follow through with his meanness. After he leaves, Don Severo and Doña Candita try to get Pilár to hurry along and escape while they still can. Pilár, however, vows to stay behind rather than save her life by fleeing. Pilár, like Julie—who demands Clabe forget everything about her once she drowns herself, and that he erase the memory of his own queerness—tells her family they must forget her as well.

Doña Candita wants to stay with her daughter, but her husband forces her to leave; unlike Pilár, who challenges her father's authority at every turn, Doña Candita is a dutiful Mexican wife who must obey. Pilár is a bundle of contradictions. She defies her father, but she upholds the collective authority of the fathers, the patriarchal conservatism that she so values. Insisting that others adhere to these conventions, she, however, never follows the rules herself. Like Julie, Pilár, in a sense, emerges as the queerest character in the play, even if she is heterosexual, given the many levels of her gender deviance and other forms of resistance to authority.

After the Crespos have fled without Pilár, Beto comes with a saddled horse and a lantern to help her escape. Pilár insists on staying behind to be killed. Beto undercuts her dramatics by telling her that the Mayans have no intention of killing her. Pilár, still calling the shots, next commands Beto to turn the Indians against her, still hoping someone will murder her. One might wonder why she is so determined to die—certainly it is not over the loss of Cuco as potential husband. More likely she does not want to continue in a world where her family will no longer rule the region, and she will no longer rule her family.

Yet the play resists such a cynical reading. Pilár tells Beto,

PILÁR. [*Desperately persuasive.*] Yes, Beto! You're gifted, you're wise. You see things the way they are. Understand this, then. Not till I die—not till all such people as myself are dead—we, the ones who've lorded it over the weak and lowly—not till all of us are in the grave can a stricken people sing again, be free again! *You must see this!* (70)

Beto reluctantly agrees and says, "It may be so" (70). Pilár, it might seem, has had an epiphany about her own investment in colonialism and feels sorrow now instead of a sense of privilege. What she calls for, however, seems implausible given that the death of all colonizers and their descendants is another means of opposing and hierarchizing relationships (not to mention pretty unrealistic). Romanticism pervades here; this primitive offering suggests Pilár is some sort of fertility goddess whose death will cause a profusion of growth in the spring.

Beto, fathered by Don Severo, is himself one of the descendants of colonialism, as, metaphorically, are all indigenous people, since no one has come away from the last five hundred years unscathed by colonial attitudes if not bloodlines. These facts significantly challenge the efficacy of Pilár's sacrifice, intended to eliminate the tainted and leave only the pure. Pilár's newfound "either red or dead" attitude simply ignores the complexities of colonial history, especially in Mexico, where even the population that is considered non-Indian—that is, the vast majority of Mexico's mestizo citizenry—has a good deal of Indian blood and a considerable legacy of indigenous culture.

Once again, then, why must Pilár die? Further, what brings her to an end that seems so inconsistent with her character and the way she has charged through the thick and thin of things up to this point? Beto, in spite of having acknowledged Pilár's argument, cannot allow her to remain behind. The crowd has reached a fever pitch, and, evidently, become more dangerous than he let on earlier. He tells Pilár, "there's drunkenness there, a fever—any moment something may happen, they may begin to——" (71). Pilár interrupts his unfinished statement, and the stage directions are interesting:

> PILÁR. [*In a thrumming excitement, knowing the answer.*] May what, Beto?
> BETO. They may break loose—their passion, their anger, their lust! No one could protect you! Come with me, quickly—now!
> PILÁR. [*Sensing what to do now, controlled, hard, quiet, deliberate—her voice as of old low and imperious.*] Go to the rail where the horse is tied. (71)

Well, we should have known. The Natives *are* restless after all. Beto seems to have revised his earlier opinion that they would not hurt Pilár. If this—Pilár's choice to be fucked to death; and putting rape into the context of choice, and Mayan land reformers in the role of rapists—isn't problematic (and sexist) melodrama, I don't know what is. Riggs's plays very frequently go over the top, into a realm of excess that seriously threatens their artistic viability. If Pilár is simply paying for the sins of her ancestors, why the "thrumming excitement"? How can an oppressive history be wiped clean by volunteering for rape? If

Pilár has seen the colonial light, why does she reassume her authority and privilege ("her voice as of old low and imperious")? Perhaps it is because she is still calling the shots. Perhaps violent rape by Indian men will confirm for her everything she believes about her superiority. Perhaps because a future in a modest working-class house in a small Mexican town instead of a fortress commanding a vast horizon is not her style. OK, you're right; I'm guessing. Is there some convincing way of reading this play? She may not be out on thin ice, exactly, but one is struck by the parallels between Pilár's and Julie's absolute and suicidal wills as Pilár walks out of the hacienda and into the scene of her brutal rape:

> BETO. I don't dare leave you.
> PILÁR. [*Sharply authoritative.*] Do as I say! I am still your master. Go. Wait for me. Do this.
> BETO. [*After a moment of effort, in which her dominating will wins.*] As you say, Pilár. I am accustomed to obey. It's too early yet for me to change. [*Lifting the lantern.*] This lantern . . .
> PILÁR. [*Firmly, sensing the symbol, seeing what the end is to be.*] Keep it. I shan't need it. There's light enough.
> [*Quietly he goes, turns along the corredor, passing the open window, disappears. The voices of the Indians surge up. Loud again, uncontrolled.* PILÁR *watches* BETO's *departure carefully, holding on to her high and desperate courage. Turning, she notices a few pictures still on the walls— those pictures that are her past, the past of her race—all she has held dear. She moves to them, takes them down in a quick movement, stares at them. Painfully, she drags herself away from their hypnotic and weakening influence, and throws them crashing into the middle of the room. Now she turns, faces straight back to where the firelight is leaping, and the ghostly and menacing shadows move and cry out. Quietly, she moves straight through the door, straight toward her fate, her immolation. Angry voices accost her—jibing, earthy voices. More shots. At the same moment, the muted music of the radio dims down, and a voice is distinguishable.*]
> RADIO VOICE. . . . . Buenos noches, señoras y señores. You are listening to the voice of Mexico! [*The music swells up, the triumphant concluding bars brassy and stirring.*] (71–72)

How can a rape be a redeeming sacrifice? Just who is being appeased? Certainly not the victim. Just what is being sacrificed? Who volunteers for a rape? How does a rape pay for one's own shortcomings or the terrible injustices committed by one's ancestors? Trino has repudiated still lifes and even more cutting-edge art for a life of simple labor, and Pilár has smashed portraits, but where does that leave us in relation to art and its intersections with activism? It would be a mind-boggling understatement to say the ending of Riggs's play is puzzling.

Since the stage directions literally announce that the lantern is a symbol, we might pay attention to this peculiar light that Pilár rejects as she voluntarily walks out into the crowd she hopes will rape her. Let us turn for a moment to Riggs's Oklahoma play, *A Lantern to See By.*

One of the interesting facts about the play is found in a newspaper clipping among Riggs's personal papers that tells about a boy who killed his father with a pinch bar on August 31 [I could not make out the year] in Oologah (Beinecke Rare Book and Manuscript Library. Yale University. Call Number YCAL MSS 61. Box 8, Folder 162). The young man, Jodie Harris, shares a first name with the protagonist of *A Lantern to See By*, Jodie Harmon, who commits the same act. More bizarre is the fact that Riggs collected clippings about family members who kill each other, including husbands who kill wives and vice versa.

One such example is a cousin of Riggs's in Sapulpa; she shot her husband, but before the murder she had gone and picked out a new suit she wanted him buried in. Needless to say, the court convicted her easily, and she might as well have picked out a new outfit for herself as well. Riggs turned this murder among his relatives into his only novel, *An Affair at Easter*, which he was still working on at the end of his life. A central theme in the novel is the fearful possibility that the accused might tell all the town's secrets on the stand; some of these are gay secrets. Murdering heterosexuality is a constant Riggs obsession committed many times over in his plays, certainly far too many to be mere happenstance murders of those of the opposite sex with an ax to grind (mostly on each other and far too literally).

A structural device in some Riggs plays is the shivaree, or the play-party, not altogether unlike the masque or costume ball of European theater. Such a party, which occurs in act 3 of *A Lantern to See By*, is attended by Jodie Harmon and a young woman named Annie, who has worked for the Harmon family since their mother's illness and death. Annie, at times, has acted like Jodie's girlfriend, but, more often than not, Jodie seems more like the girlfriend. His effeminacy provides a constant source of comment throughout the play, especially in terms of ugly jibes from his father, who publicly humiliates his family and physically abuses them at home. In a loud public harangue, he demanded his wife, Thursley, have a daughter; when the wife later gave birth, she died in the process.

Annie has come to the party to ask John for the money he owes her for taking care of the family in the mother's absence. John Harmon has withheld her pay because he knows as soon as she gets it she will run off to Muskogee. Jodie comes on the scene with a lantern just after Annie has unsuccessfully confronted John Harmon for her money. Jodie has romanticized himself as Annie's protector—and love interest.

The way Annie sees it, she doesn't need any protecting. She has her sights set on the big city, not life with a fruity farm boy. John owes Jodie money as well. In an act of defiance Jodie had left home and gotten work, but his boss gave the money to John Harmon instead of directly to Jodie. Jodie fancies bypassing patriarchal authority by collecting his rightful wages from his father and moving off to Muskogee with Annie. He does not know that Annie has been playing him all along for whatever advantages she can gain, and her trip to Muskogee will be a solo flight.

Most unfortunately, *A Lantern to See By* also takes up the rape theme, and just as problematically. It comes to light that John Harmon has been coming into Annie's room at night and having sex with her. Annie cannot make up her mind whether she has actually been raped or she let John Harmon get away with the sex.

Jodie, in an ugly way that suggests the viciousness of his father, accuses Annie of leading John Harmon on. Annie blames Jodie, saying, "You wuzn't here t' pertect me" (179). This is an ugly world in which everyone is an oppressor—including Annie, as we soon shall see. This is a problematic depiction—a rape victim who is the source of her own victimization.

Annie sends for John, and Jodie confronts his father in the lamplight, just outside the smoke house. The stage directions read,

> [*He sees the open door of the smoke-house and starts toward it. He pauses,
> looks about, gets the lighted lantern he has set down by the house, and
> with it in his hands goes into the smoke-house. He hangs the lantern up.
> It sways. His shadow jerks grotesquely in the block of light streaming
> from the door. After a moment,* JOHN *comes out of the house. He sees
> the light in the smoke-house and comes forward. Half-way across the
> open space he stops, staring inside the open door.* JODIE *comes out,
> forgetting the lantern, and confronts his father.*] (180)

Light, illumination, confrontation, as in *The Year of Pilár*, lead up to a fatalistic ending. Jodie demands that his father give him his pay so he can leave with Annie for Muskogee. John Harmon refuses, insisting instead that his son go back to work and continue to turn over his wages. Jodie does not back down, and John threatens to take a chain to him, the same as one of the violent brothers, a chip off the (father's) old block, had threatened to do earlier to their horse, Daise. There is a constant rivalry between the macho brothers and Jodie, whose effeminacy seems threatening to them.

John Harmon is linked with the lantern: he snuffs out everyone else's light. He is also associated with a snake, and one does not have to make any kind of Freudian leap to find phallicism in this passage, given that Jodie's mom died in childbirth:

> JODIE. I'll choke you to death like I would a snake. Fer you *air* a snake . . .
> Maw that you killed with yer ways, a-makin her have children one
> after the other the way you did—she must a knowed whut you
> wuz! . . . She musta knowed you uz a snake, a snake a-crawlin through
> the bushes from ever sound it heerd to keep from gittin stepped on
> Snake, snake! That's what you air! With the ways of snakes! You killed
> Maw who wuz a light a-shinin. An' now this you've done to Annie!
> You won't never do nuthin else! (181)

John's masculinity, one that thrives on snuffing out femininity in Jodie and also in women, douses any queer illumination in whatever ways such light might manifest itself. The outburst against killing women through reproduction, of course, is no metaphor. I think of my grandparents' generation and Oklahoma women who had thirteen or fourteen children.

Further, while all the male siblings in the Harmon family work their asses off for John, they are a constant source of labor for women who must cook and clean for them. Not only are women's bodies severely taxed, but any kind of femininity is despised in men as well.

Of the most bizarre of Lynn Riggs's autobiographical anecdotes—and, believe me, there are a good number of competitors—is the one about Bosco the Snake-eater. In Riggs's childhood, a carnival came to Claremore, but Lynn and a girl friend had ten cents they planned, instead, to spend on a movie. They were lured, nonetheless, inside the tent of "Bosco the Snake-eater," after which both children sat on the curb and vomited (Braunlich 29). I have imagined this story as a scene in a film, one that I connect strongly to Lynn Riggs's father:

> [*The scene opens with a full shot of the Claremore Theater at a distance. Its
> cupolaed roof casts a shadow over the streets of the town. Cut to a
> newspaper heading underneath a photo of workers painting golden trim
> on the railing of the second story theater terrace. "Make it gay, but not*

gaudy, boys!" Eddie Lyon, builder of Claremore's Orpheum Theater, is
quoted, admonishing his workers as they put on the finishing touches
just before the Grand Opening. Cut to the theater marquee which reads,
"One Show Only, Bosco the Snake-eater." A close up of the people
milling out of the entrance, holding up their hands against the sun's
midday glare. The camera pans with the couples as they move down the
wooden sidewalk away from the theater, at the intersection stepping
down to a dirt street over which yellow dust hangs in the bright, blind-
ing sunlight. The glare has not let up any, and still the theatergoers hold
their hands against the light, though their eyes have long recovered from
the darkness they came out of. They step around a boy of some thirteen
years or so, seated on the bottom step, knees drawn up to his chest. Close
up on the boy. The boy rocks off his heels onto his toes, leans over himself
and heaves, violently ill. Just before we can see him vomiting, cut to his
Stetson-hatted father. The camera shot is from a low angle, and the
father is looming over the youngster, turning away in shame, casting a
shadow over the boy, the street. His face is half-shaded by the white low-
crowned Stetson.]

FATHER. [*Disgusted.*] Rollie Lynn Riggs, rise up from that sidewalk and
leave off with your foolishness. [BOY *spits into the dirt, disgusted by the*
filthy taste in his mouth. He doesn't move.] You just had to see Bosco
the Snake-eater, didn't you? Well, I myself knew better, but I says let
the boy have his fill if he thinks he can take it. I never heared the like,
your whining night and day, weeks on end, until the theater opened.
Now, here we are after a mule's age of your driving me plumb to
distraction. Onced you got inside, cain't hardly wait for the show to
start. The lights go up, and Bosco struts onto the stage, throws off his
purple cape, and spins and spins with that old python snake wrapped
around his neck. Not enough to even scare a little girl out of her
bloomers, but I thought you was fixing to crawl under your seat,
hiding your eyes, then peeking out of your fingers like you waddn't
half-growed up already. Turned white until I thought you'd quit
breathing. He got that snake all unwrapped, and then you couldn't
keep from looking any longer. That "python" waddn't no more than
a swollen-up bull snake some poor widow woman caught down in
her storm cellar amongst the fruit jars. Bosco, the Hungarian Snake-
eater, my eye. Some drunk they found from over Oologah way, most
likely will sober up sometime tomorrow! That snake swaying back
and forth in front of Blotto's face and him breathing corn liquor all

over it, pry clean stunned it into submission. Blotto closing his eyes, and the drunk python slithering into the closest thing he knowed as a snake hole, considering. And Bosco or Blotto or whoever opening up wider and wider, letting him unravel, the same way he lets whiskey course down his gullet. Until that snake's little tail was the only thing left poking out and waving a little bit and Blotto gone all cross-eyed. I liked to have laid a death grip on you, boy, just to keep you from running out of the theater. And after months of "Daddy, don't forget you promised to take me to see Bosco!" What a waste of a nickel!

In light of all this fact and fiction, in *A Lantern to See By*, Jodie's threatening to choke to death his father, John Harmon the snake, is richly nuanced. When examined alongside Bosco, we have not only an image of revolt against heterosexual oppression—as when Jodie confronts his abusive macho asshole of a father—but queer self-hatred, when Lynn pukes at the sight of what he feels himself becoming, a cocksucker. Riggs's throwing up afterwards is certainly telling, an act that may have foreshadowed the self-hatred he would have to live with the rest of his life.

In the play, John throws a crowbar at Jodie, the one he had hit him with earlier. Jodie retrieves it, however, and in this reversal of power he experiences the rush of hearing his father, now a pitiable figure rather than his abuser, begging for his life. During the bludgeoning, the lantern gets knocked down and flickers out. Annie's reaction to the monster slaying, the killing of the snake who has been raping her, is deeply disturbing. She reveals that she had planned on continuing the sex to get money for her trip to Muskogee. She is incensed that Jodie has killed off her potential source of income. The sense in which John was raping her becomes increasingly clouded.

Jodie's justification for the murder is that his father destroys whatever illumination is in others: "I had to. He'd a-killed me—all my life—slow. He's been hanging over me threatenin, so I couldn't see right, from bein so afeard of him. He's dead now. I'm glad" (183).

After Jodie's show of strength, Annie calls Jodie an effeminate weakling, and she claims John Harmon was the real man in the family, a strapping hetero hunk: "He wuz a man, he wuz a man with guts. An' you killed him! You! You! You aint a man. Weak little runt! Weak! Weak! He wuz strong. He coulda broke you with his two hands—" (183–84). Annie's rapist, then, is presented as her hero.

Of course, this is surrounded by irony since Annie is so desperate to escape rural life in Claremore that she will do anything to get money to leave, including trying to turn rape to her advantage. This is another "Why I Won't Move Back to Claremore" play. In capturing the meanness of Oklahoma, however, one wonders if these plays do not exploit a whole set of terrible prejudices against women. Do the plays effectively challenge meanness or do they become mean in their own right?

The final revelation is that Annie, like Pilár and like Julie, is the proverbial "bad girl." She does not merely want to get away, she has all along planned on becoming a prostitute in Muskogee because prostitutes get to dress up and go to dances! This, she fancies, is preferable to the domestic drudgery of cooking and cleaning every day on the farm. The play presents an oppositional world with few alternatives between rural monotony and the life of a painted lady; this may partially reflect the fact that the opportunities for women in Eastern Oklahoma at the turn of the twentieth century were not outstanding—thus the extreme opposition of farm slave and whore. Annie says, "It's better'n being here! They don't kill themselves a-workin. An' they have clothes. An' dancin! I wanted to have things! I won't now—not ever! I'll have to go back home" (184).

Annie tells Jodie she hopes he hangs, surely a reality check in terms of Jodie's romantic notions about being her boyfriend, and she runs into the party crowd screaming that Jodie killed John Harmon so that the fun seekers will turn Jodie over to the sheriff. Jodie offers no resistance and freely confesses the killing. His final words:

> JODIE. [*Wearily.*] I aint gonna run away. I'll go to Blackmore an' give myself up tomorrow. In the mornin—early. I'm t'ard. Mebbe I'll be better tomorrow. [*Lifting his head.*] I'm glad I done it. It's better that a-way. My mind ud got dim. It didn't light my way so's I knowed whur I uz goin. It's brighter now—a little brighter. (186)

Jodie kills off his heterosexual oppressor, the source of much of his fear and hatred, yet the play suggests that the most likely result will be his hanging, although some of the old folks speculate that John's meanness might help mediate Jodie's cause at the trial—either way hetero authority prevails. Riggs called the play "A Tragedy in Three Acts," and Jodie's future, to use the play's central metaphor, is dim at best. I am also interested in the idea of extinguishing light and the diminishing role of art in *The Year of Pilár* and *The Cream in the Well.*

Metaphors of light and darkness struck Riggs at the very core of his being, reaching back to his earliest memories, I believe. Shortly after his emergency exit from OU and his escape to Santa Fe, he wrote Bynner on February 6, 1924, during a brief return to Claremore:

Dear Hal—

I am here at last—in a snow-drift, literally and metaphorically. Can you imagine a head that visualizes instead of reasons, and the vicious gone terribly toward disaster? That is mine. However, in a great world it's a small matter, isn't it? And please don't worry about helping me—you have done that. I have met great kindness at the wrong end of life that is all. And if I *should* shuffle back to earth, I should be pleased. Straining toward the beauty of the immaculate is your business. The forces of earth rise to crush the weak things, the tortoise without a protective shell. This latter complication (which you know about, dear Hal) would have been little difficulty had there not been earlier unresolved ones. You would understand if you were here in this squalor and dirt and misery and harshness from which I have never been absent. What little work I have done in poetry has been not realization but a feeble attempt to escape from a birthright. So the sonnet I sent you in New York about "I have sung of beauty where I have seen no beauty" remains my truest utterance. The rest are lies—dramatized. I cannot write otherwise than this. You would not want me to write jovially I am sure. Hal—it isn't right, it isn't fair, to have carried the world as a terrible stone about one's neck through a life-time, *to have gone timidly and hopefully through a jungle where no light shone (for what good is a light if you can't see it?) and to have come at last to the deep shadow where even the mind will not work, and the jungle beasts are transformed marvelously into terrible things inside.* (My emphasis)

Returning to *The Cream in the Well*—since we have light and jungle metaphors in an oppressive environment linking us across various writings now—we have a vicious sister, Julie; a brother, Clabe, who has turned tricks on the waterfront in order, he tells us, to degrade himself; and meanness that emanates from both siblings' self-hatred due to their illicit desires—a meanness inflicted on all those around them that leads to a final suicide that Julie argues will cause the incest, and, by association, the queerness, to be forgotten. In this work, the themes of racism, territorial politics, and turn-of-the-century optimism make brief, momentary appearances that seem more to reveal the characters' dysfunction than to emerge as developed social critiques.

In a second play, also connected to light and jungle metaphors, we have a diasporic family whose return home is marked by an inability to escape the disastrous consequences of the oppressive relationships that have characterized their history in Yucatán. Here we also have siblings moving toward some inexorable personal catastrophe, every aspect of which complicates their po-litical history. We have a deeply politicized play, in which the personal and political do a very close two-step together. We have the seeming *appearance* of a gay relationship that one sibling, Pilár, believes to be factual, and another sibling, Trino, vehemently denies. Beto, who might give the definitive word on the subject, remains silent—although he has a good deal to say about Indians, whites, and comparative philosophy. What we do know, however, is that Beto predicted a betrayal, and, when it comes—by process of elimination—it must be a gay betrayal: Trino fully acknowledges that Beto is his brother, so only one thing is left in explaining Beto's sense of betrayal: Trino's inability to acknowl-edge the men's love for one another. Beto believes his white lover has betrayed them by denying their relationship. Rather than making the betrayal explicit, Riggs leaves it up to the audience to figure out what is left to deduce after betrayal of blood relationship is eliminated as a possibility.

If Beto's prediction is indeed fulfilled by his lover's betrayal, then the incest is also a reality. Somehow these startling revelations are simply dropped as the play focuses exclusively on Pilár's immolation at the end. We are then left to wonder how volunteering for a rape erases a colonial legacy and what the hell happened to the relationship between Trino and Beto. The two men are politically allied at the end as they oversee land reapportionment, but are they still intimately allied as lovers? The two-step has lost one of its partners, same-sex desire. These false starts and stops simply leave us wishing we found out more about "the thing" between Trino and Beto. Maybe this is Riggs saying, essentially, "I wish I could tell you more about these two guys, but I can't. I don't know how."

In a third play we have an effeminate farm boy whose brothers and father constantly torment him about his delicacy. He likes to believe he has a girl-friend, Annie, but we find out, in no uncertain terms, that she never saw him as a romantic interest (like Eileen Yost's mean disdain for "Edgar"?). Jodie's "girlfriend" has suffered sexual abuse from the boy's father, John Harmon, but she cannot decide whether this was rape or she allowed the sex. She deter-mines that whichever the case, she is going to figure out a way to make money out of it.

Although a woman does not sacrifice herself at the end of this play, a young man who acts like one will almost certainly either be hanged or incarcerated until he dies. Jodie feels that his hanging, or lifetime imprisonment, is well worth the freedom that entailed obliterating the man who snuffed out all light in himself, his mother, and Annie. The light in Jodie is a queer illumination—he is a farm boy who works alongside his mother after the men's work is done (for which John beats him), refuses to inflict violence on farm animals, uses terms like "purty" to describe the particulars of natural beauty around the farmstead, talks only around women, and goes by the nickname of "funny boy"—and death or incarceration is the price for the expression of his deviance. It is Jodie's character, however, that we are meant to sympathize with.

Beto, the Mayan, is the only person in any of these plays who may imagine the possibility of love between men—and this is an unarticulated conclusion astute playgoers might only figure out by a process of elimination, since his sense of betrayal cannot involve a denial of the blood relation that all family members come to acknowledge. Once the play's audience members reach that determination, however, they then have to deal with incest. One is tempted to try to formulate some theory here about colonialism as incest, but what would it be? We might consider ideas about the asymmetrical power relations in most incest cases, such as an adult abusing a child. In these plays, however, we have incest between siblings driven by their own desires. Clabe even argues for the legitimacy of incest, claiming the taboo is an arbitrary social construction. Why are the gay incest plays also Indian plays? There are so many disparate ideas that a unified theory that compares colonialism to incest seems impossible. Finally, there is Pilár, walking out into the riled-up crowd of overstimulated Mayans who will rape and kill her.

If we don't know the destiny of these characters, do we gain any more of a sense of the future of art as reflected in all the discussion of painting and activism? What was Riggs trying to do here? Many of his poems in the volume *The Iron Dish*, published in 1930, start out with accessible images yet move toward a frustrating inscrutability by opening themselves up to more and more possibilities that do not form any obvious pattern, and this play, as well, does not lend itself to an easy analysis. "One Who Never Died" begins thus: "With poems neither lance-like nor blanketing / Nor a known shape" (30). If someone tells you something about Lynn Riggs, and it makes sense, he or she explained it wrong. *The Year of Pilár,* more than any other Riggs play, has me stumped. And that is why I cannot let it go.

Works Cited

Braunlich, Phyllis. *Haunted by Home: The Life and Letters of Lynn Riggs*. Norman: University of Oklahoma Press, 2002.

Johnson, Spud. Interviewed by Arrell Gibson. January 4, 1968. Western History Collection. University of Oklahoma. Lynn Riggs Papers. Box R-43, Folder 4.

——. Letter to Betty Kirk. July 13, 1937. In *Haunted by Home,* 151.

"Oklahoman Is Member Of Santa Fe Artists' Colony." *The Daily Oklahoman,* October 18, 1925, sec. 8-C.

Riggs. Lynn. ——. *A Lantern To See By*. In *Sump'n Like Wings and A Lantern To See By*, 105–86.

——. *This Book, This Hill, These People: Poems*. Tulsa, Okla.: Lynn Chase, 1982.

——. *The Cream in the Well*. In *Four Plays*, 155–222. New York: Samuel French, 1947.

——. *The Iron Dish*. Garden City, N.Y.: Doubleday, Doran, 1930.

——. Journal entry. February 22, 1940. Beinecke Rare Book and Manuscript Library. Yale University. Lynn Riggs Papers. Box 8, Folder 163. Call number YCAL MSS 61.

——. Letter to Paul Green. March 5, 1939. Beinecke Rare Book and Manuscript Library. Yale University. Lynn Riggs Papers. Box 2, Folder 46. Call number YCAL MSS 61.

——. Letter to Walter Campbell. September 16, 1925. Western History Collection. University of Oklahoma. Walter Stanley Campbell Collection. Box 36, Folder 8.

——. Letter to Witter Bynner. December 6, 1922. Houghton Library. Harvard University. Archival microfilm. "Twelve Letters to Witter Bynner." Call number bMS Am 1891 (707).

——. Letter to Witter Bynner. October 14, 1923. Houghton Library. Harvard University. Archival microfilm. "Twelve Letters to Witter Bynner." Call number bMS Am 1891 (707).

——. Letter to Witter Bynner. December 3, 1923. Houghton Library. Harvard University. Archival microfilm. "Twelve Letters to Witter Bynner." Call number bMS Am 1891 (707).

——. Letter to Witter Bynner. February 6, 1924. Houghton Library. Harvard University. Archival microfilm. "Twelve Letters to Witter Bynner." Call number bMS Am 1891 (707).

——. Letter to Witter Bynner. June 12, 1937. In *Haunted by Home*, 149.

——. *Sump'n Like Wings and a Lantern to See By: Two Oklahoma Plays by Lynn Riggs*. New York: Samuel French, 1928.

——. *The Year of Pilár*. In *Four Plays*, 1–72.

Weaver, Jace. *That The People Might Live: Native American Literatures and Native American Community*. New York: Oxford University Press, 1997.

Womack, Craig. *Red on Red: Native American Literary Separatism*. Minneapolis: University of Minnesota Press, 1999.

Yost, Eileen. "Men Who Have Rushed Us." *Whirlwind* (March 1924): 13.

Uncle Jimmy's Personal Emissary

James Riggs, a bachelor in his forties, brightened the lives of the Thompson and Riggs children. When Aunt Mary went into town to work to support her six daughters and two sons, she left them in his care. The children of Bill Riggs were often there, too, with gentle, musical, unique Uncle Jimmy (who appears in Lynn's play A Lantern to See By*).*

The family did not have much, but Uncle Jimmy managed to have popcorn on hand, stick candy, which he bought in five-pound bags, and apples by the bushel. In the evenings each child who had behaved well during the day was rewarded with a stick of candy. Occasional exploration to pick up pecan nuts or gather blackberries provided special treats. While the children enjoyed snacks, Uncle Jimmy hammered out tunes on his old dulcimer and taught them to sing the old songs that Lynn learned to love.

The best times of childhood for Lynn were spent with his kindly uncle and his cheerful, high-spirited girl cousins. . . .

Lynn's play The Boy with Tyford Fever *uses incidents remembered from age eleven, when he had suffered from the common and dreaded disease of typhoid, of which his mother had died. One day when Lynn was acting cranky, Juliette [his stepmother, also Cherokee, like his biological mother] ordered him to go to the "dog house," but his father noticed his flushed face, felt his forehead, and found he had a high fever. On this one occasion his father interceded for him. When Juliette refused to nurse the sick child, Bill Riggs sent for Aunt Mary. It was she who took turns with Bill, sitting up twenty-four hours a day for several days until the fever left Lynn.*

Bill helped his older brother James (Uncle Jimmy) finance the building in 1909 of the St. James Hotel across from the Claremore Missouri Pacific Railroad station and train yards. Jimmy added for his sister Mary a boarding house and dining room at the side rear of the hotel, where she cooked for boarders and hotel guests. Often in the evenings at the hotel, Uncle Jimmy and the family would sit on the porch and sing together. The railroad section hands, who stayed in a bunkhouse at the yards, came over to sing with them, teaching them more folk songs from all parts of the country. . . .

A life-threatening experience, apparently a sunstroke, sent Lynn's Uncle Jimmy indoors in 1910, shortly after he completed the St. James Hotel. He took up residence in his room there and, wary of the sun, did not leave the place for twenty-four years. His sister Mary persuaded him to come out on May 5, 1934, for her seventy-third birthday party. On that occasion he took his first automobile ride to her home, as reported in the Claremore Progress on May 6. One of his nieces drove him around the area, showing him all the new sights, which included Lake Clare- more, the Hotel Will Rogers, and Oklahoma Military Academy (for- merly the Eastern University Preparatory School). He saw the Will Rogers Airport, named for a boy that he had trotted on his knee and chased to "tan his hide," the son of his close friend Clem Rogers. Al- though, during the ride to Mary's, James Riggs insisted that the car go down alleys to avoid traffic, he enjoyed the trip so much that he decided to see "anything and everything" at age seventy-seven.

Phyllis Cole Braunlich
Haunted By Home: The Life and Letters
of Lynn Riggs, *27–31*

The Sun Stream

Keeping a painful dream
Alive, keeping a stilted
And decorous desire, he came
To a place where rocks tilted.

The sun stream
Smote him from that cliff
So that he wallowed in pain
And at last cold and stiff,

Unable to go back
Or to rise,
Lay with that golden fluid
On his eyes.

Lynn Riggs
The Iron Dish, *52*

Uncle Jimmy led me up the steps of the St. James Hotel. Aunt Mary, his sister, came out the screen door carrying a bushel basket and setting it down in front of me. "Here, Lynnsey," she said, "dump your sack." I shook the burlap seed bag until the last walnut, hickory, and pecan fell out. Me and Jimmy had been busy all day in the creek bottom, picking. I plunged my arm in to see if I could still reach the bottom of the basket. Aunt Mary rested on the porch swing away from the heat inside the hotel, hoping for an outdoor breeze. They had the front and back doors open for a draft but no luck.

The countryside had been dead still all day. Bright and cloudless, shade was scarce. People stayed on their porches; dogs crawled under them and dug holes in search of an inch of cooler ground. The paved sandstone walkway leading up to the hotel had taken on the color of the sky bearing down on it; the rocks shimmered with sunlight.

Mary picked up her palm leaf fan. "Lynnsey, run in and get my glass of tea," she said. "I'd start cracking those nuts if I was able to move." Inside, I threw the last chunk of ice in her glass from the icebox like I knew she wanted it. The ice man wouldn't be around again until Wednesday. Back on the porch I handed her the sassafras tea, and she held the glass against her forehead with one hand and fanned with the other.

"Sister, you got one arm cooling you down and the other working up a sweat," Uncle Jimmy said. Aunt Mary grunted, and kept fanning. Uncle Jimmy turned to me. "Yessir, you got a mess of nuts there. You must have had a team of field hands heppin' ye."

"No, Uncle Jimmy, you know it was just me and you," I said. "We don't need no field hands, do we?"

"Let's see which weighs more, you or the basket. That oughta tell us something." Uncle Jimmy squatted down, his back straight as a board, and grabbed on to the handles, lifting with all his might. "I'm a liar if there ain't forty pounds of nuts you got there. Now hold on tight to your overall straps."

"How come?"

"There's no prize for gathering without the official weigh-in." No sooner did I have a grip on my front straps than Uncle Jimmy had picked me up by the back ones and lifted me clean off the ground. I hollered for him to set me down.

"Suspicioned as much," Jimmy said. "Not an ounce over forty-three pounds. You might have to take off another pound or two for all that field dirt on you. Boy you gone and outpicked your own weight. Ain't that something? Looks like I don't have a choice in the world. Where is that stick candy for prize-winning pickers? I'd have to put you down to think clear where I put it, I guess."

"It's on top of the china hutch, Uncle Jimmy. That's where you always keep it!"

Uncle Jimmy turned loose of one of my straps in order to scratch his head and think. I dangled wildly over the porch; the train station across the street swung toward the sky. "The china hutch," he said. "I'd a-never thought of there." Just then my mother came into view, stomping her leather shoes on each wooden step as she climbed toward us.

"Put that boy down, you damned fool," Mother demanded. "You'll split the seams on those brand new overalls."

"Watch your language, Juliette," Jimmy said. "We got guests here at the hotel. Clabe just got out of the navy, but he might never of heard of a woman who could cuss worse than a sailor, even in Oklahoma. I was just funning with the boy nohow."

"Set him down this minute," she insisted. My feet touched gently on the creaking boards. "I'll be out in a minute," Mother said as the creaky screen door slammed behind her. Jimmy winked at me and sat me down in the porch swing. "That's the meanest damned Indian I ever knowed," he said, "and I known some mean ones. I hope you turn out a sight nicer. And I have just the thing for it, too—something that would sweeten up a copperhead snake."

Uncle Jimmy went in, and I ran over to the window, watching as he reached to the top of the hutch. He came out with a stick of candy, striped yellow and black, in his mouth, his dulcimer sticks in one hand, and the instrument itself in the other. He handed me the yellow-striped candy, already sticky from his mouth, and stuck out his tongue, streaked black as coal.

He set the dulcimer on its stand and started striking it with the mallets, making some chords, some melody lines in between. The chords were wild-flowers, Indian Blanket, when they first come out of the ground in spring, and the single notes were the breeze making them sway back and forth. One of the railroad section hands sitting on the balcony started to sing about Shenandoah Valley. Then I could hear him coming down the stairs to join us.

When he came out on the porch he was buttoning his overalls over his white shirt. He'd just gotten cleaned up and his hair was wet, black and glistening. "Why, hello, Clabe," Aunt Mary said. "How's civilian life treating you?"

"I'll take the navy any day over laying track in this heat. Where's your guitar?" Clabe asked, turning to me. It was inside in Jimmy's room. When you play at the movie house the whole town knows you mess around with music. Directly, I'd go in and get it soon as I'd took care of that stick candy. Jimmy fiddled around for along time before he really got to playing anyway. He was still whistling, waiting for the right tune to come to him. The section worker sat down on the hotel steps. "Jimmy, you got any more of those church hymns for us?" he winked. "You look flush," he added. "Kind of early in the day isn't it? Or does singing spirituals do that to a man?"

"I got too much sun," Uncle Jimmy said. "Me and the boy picked up all these pecans. Here, I got a song that will sanctify you from head to toe." Jimmy spit over the porch rail. When he started singing he looked like a scarecrow stuck on the end of a broomstick, except a scarecrow don't bob up and down none. Somehow his high tenor voice came out steady in the middle of all that commotion,

> Come on over Daisy, don't be shy
> I'm a-gittin hungry for some of your pie
> Slice me some rhubarb, better yet berry
> But nothing tastes fine as a piece of your cherry

"How does a forty-year-old bachelor know a song like that?" the railroad worker asked.

"I've tasted all different kinds of pie," Jimmy said.

Mother threw the screen door open so hard that it slammed in front of her instead of behind. "James Riggs, they'll run you outta Claremore. They can hear you clean over to the railroad station."

"That's just across the street," I said. Mother grabbed a hold of my arm. "I'll have no sass from you, young man. You get this way every time you come over here." She glared at Uncle Jimmy. "They must be beginning to wonder what kind of a boarding house this is." Jimmy didn't look up from his dulcimer playing, and he was still bobbing on the second verse of "Daisy," which he'd kept up just as loud. Mother ran the railroad worker off the porch, telling him to stop acting like a vagrant.

"Wait a minute," Jimmy told him, his mallet pointed at Mother, "She's leaving. You, on the other hand, have paid to stay here." Clabe stood in the street wondering which one to listen to.

"Juliette Riggs," Jimmy said—each syllable of her name like a hammered dulcimer note, sweet sounding but forcefully struck—"you're welcome on my porch anytime, but it *is* my porch, and a little music never hurt anyone."

"You're forgetting who paid for this porch," Mother said, "and the hotel attached to it. Your brother—my husband, in case your sun-addled brain has boilt to mush—has an interest. Until it's paid back we have some say around here. You can check the papers at Farmers State Bank and Trust and see whose name is on them. Stop by your brother's desk on the way out. The president of the bank is always glad to see kin. Seems they kindy disappear-like after you give them a loan."

"Never miss a payment," Uncle Jimmy said and struck up another dulcimer song,

> Just because you think you're so funny
> Just because you think you're so hot
> Just because you think you've got something
> That nobody else has got
> You ran around and spent all my money
> Then laughed and called me old Santy Clause
> Well, just because you think you're so funny
> Just because, just because

Mother drug me off the porch. At the bottom of the steps she jerked my candy out of my mouth and threw it into the dirt. I could still taste it while she hauled me away. I started to cry. She marched through the dust without looking back. She told me to shut up or I'd have to go without supper and spend the night in the dog house, an old chicken coop where our setter Roy hunkered for shade behind our house. It didn't have any chickens in it. We had moved to Claremore when I was six, and the chickens were on Daddy's farm out in the country over by Big Lake.

As we marched down the elm-lined dirt streets of the town, I reached into my overall pocket to feel for the sandalwood with the pearl inlay beneath my fingertips. It went in a woman's hair, but I wasn't sure if you would call it a barrette exactly, or something else. The Syrian peddler had kept it in a box that looked like Mother's silverware container. He said it came all the way from China. He'd asked me if I wanted it for my mother, but I wanted it for me. I needed a place to hide it since no one would believe I should have it. It took me a month of nickels I saved up from playing guitar at the Saturday movies with my voice teacher, who accompanied me on piano. She got a dime, being grown up and all.

I was headed up our whitewashed concrete steps when Mother said, "Stop." She told me to empty out my pockets. "I'm going to wash these overalls. Jimmy has gotten you filthy. You'd think a grown man would know better than to play outside with kids." I froze. I didn't want her to see the barrette.

"Hurry up," she said. My pockets were always full of something, from kite string to birds' nests and everything in between. When I hesitated, she said, "Damn his hide if you ain't got more of Jimmy's candy. You'll end up a toothless old buzzard just like him, which is why no woman from here to Vian will even set foot near him."

Mother started undoing my straps, and I said, "Let me at least get on the porch before I pull off nekkid."

"Well, get on up in there if you're so high-toned modest," she said. She was right behind me, so I took the barrette out of my pocket and popped it into my mouth while she was coming up on the porch. When she saw my bulging cheek, I thought she'd make me spit it out. "I knew as much," she said, "Jimmy bribing you with horehound. You're fool enough to do anything for that man for penny sweets. Worse than a dog begging for scraps." I managed to wiggle out of my overalls without opening my mouth. "You'll be up early tomorrow cultivating for your daddy over at the farm. Set the wind-up. Don't make me come over to that hotel again looking for you. You live here, you know."

Inside the house Mother had all the shades pulled to keep cool, and it was dark everywhere. It smelled like camphor. It was hot inside, and I itched all over. I had been sleeping in the backyard on a cot to get out of the heat whenever it didn't rain. I was covered with mosquito bites, knots from ticks I pulled, bumps where fleas had bit me, and chigger bites on my legs I'd covered over with clear fingernail polish to smother the mean little bastards.

I liked my cot outside better than tossing and turning on top of my bed, covered with sweat, and my sister telling me to keep still. Some nights I'd get under the house awning out of the rain and count the seconds between the thunder booms and lightning flashes until my father dragged me in out of the storm. On such nights I wanted to run all the way to the lake and see the bolts of electricity hit the water. Light would explode, I reckoned, and I'd be able to see every willow branch waving over rough water splashing against the black roots that held up dug out banks; then everything would disappear back into darkness before a person could get a good look.

On calmer nights I liked listening to the coyotes. Not a one of them sounded the same, just like people. They would get the town dogs howling right a long with them like they wanted to run off and be coyotes instead of hanging around houses. But it only took a minute for the dogs to realize they were dogs and shut up. You noticed things like that when you slept outside. I was partial to night noises, the ruckus that cicadas make in the trees, screaming so loud you'd swear they had lungs. I knew they had a language, but I hadn't figured it out.

Listening to bugs sing was like floating on water. At Big Lake I would float on my back and look up at the sky rising and falling as the clouds shimmered above me, light coming and going as they covered and uncovered the sun.

Back on my cot at night I floated on cicada music. They carried me off to my dreams and flew me back from my nightmares. I collected the transparent hulls they left behind them, what was left of cicadas who'd gone back into dreams themselves.

Sometimes Mother sent me to the dog house for punishment, but I didn't mind. Sleeping outside in the chicken coop wasn't a sight different than the porch to me. Only thing was I didn't get supper. Roy was there with me, and I liked sleeping with him since he didn't get to come in the house. He lay next to me in the night until he got hot, then crawled off till he wanted up against me again. A person wouldn't even need a sheet if it weren't for mosquitoes.

Earlier in the afternoon Aunt Mary had come over and hung some netting over my cot when she saw how bit up I was. That's how Mother knew I had been at the hotel; Mary had told her. I went into the room where me and my sister Jelly slept. She was already in her bloomers even though we hadn't ate yet. She was sitting up on the mattress tick in the dark, sweating, her brown curly hair pressed to her forehead. "You better getcha something to eat," she said, "before Mother puts it up." In spite of her blue eyes and curly hair, Jelly was dark—much darker than me. She showed Indian, like Mother. One of the real children. The only thing I knew of my real mother was the funeral notice in father's drawer.

"I want my book," I said to Jelly. I got my copy of *Deadwood Dick,* my favorite cowboy story, from under the bed and left the room. Deadwood Dick had just discovered a cave to hide in when I left off reading the night before when it got too dark. Mother wouldn't let me take a coal oil lamp on account of I'd stay up all night reading. I grabbed a hunk of cornbread off the top of the wood stove, poured some buttermilk into a cup, put the cornbread in it, and got me a spoon.

I hurried out the back door into the last of the light. I called Roy over and scratched behind his ears. As always, he wagged his tail, then sauntered back over to the dog house and crawled inside the coop after I give him some cornbread. He was used to crawling in there out of the rain or the sun. I pulled the netting apart and climbed in, reading, eating a little, laying on my side. I could hear Father inside the house. He'd just come in from the farm. Mother was fixing him something, the leftover eggs and potatoes on top of the stove. She wouldn't want to start a fire.

Father came out on the back porch and called me in for supper. I held up my cup of corn mush and hollered, "I had some already." Father went back inside, shaking his head. I opened up *Deadwood Dick,* to the page where the outlaws had discovered an underground lake in their hideaway cave. They were singing "Ole Joe Clark" as they splashed around and scrubbed days of grime off of each other from their long run fleeing the law. And then I saw stars behind the pages I held out in front of me and the sound of the men's voices from deeper and deeper inside the cave. I dropped the book and tried to pick it back up and finish the page I was on.

When my sister shook me awake the next morning, Uncle Jimmy was saying, "Swim with me, Lynnsey," as the outlaws looked on, nodding their approval, but when I opened my eyes I saw our little banty rooster, perched on the clothesline, crowing into the sun and bobbing back and forth on the swaying cord, moving in and out of focus as the mosquito netting that surrounded me turned in the breeze and shifted the vision.

"You forgot this," my sister said, squinting in the bright morning light and poking the alarm clock in through the opening.

"Go away, Jelly. It's too confounded early."

"You'd of slept in all morning."

"The sun would have woke me up."

My father came outside and said, "Get up, son. Come in here and have breakfast," the same as just a few hours ago except it was dinner then and now it was morning. I knew I'd be faced with more eggs and potatoes. I was sick of them. I wanted a piece of chicken, a fried drumstick. I'd rather sleep in later than eat. I stuck *Deadwood Dick* in the back pocket of my overalls, then buttoned the straps over my bare, peeling shoulders. I stood up. The pockets were rough against my bare chest. It felt good.

Though I had easily pocketed *Deadwood Dick,* the alarm clock would be more of a problem. I was always hiding things. Inside, Dad made me put on a shirt after Mother told me I was getting too dark to be respectable. "You'll be as dark as your sister," she said. "You can't go around white folks looking like that."

Dad pulled out his time piece from his bib pocket and scratched his bald head. "Your mother's right. No use burning up alive out there," he said. "Fact of the matter is Jimmy's feeling poorly from all that nut gathering yesterday. Mary come over this morning and told me."

"He's sick?" I said, worried.

"That man never was cut out," Mother said.

"He just needs to mind to the hotel, that's all, instead of foolishness with the boy. If he had kids of his own he'd know better. Don't you worry none, Lynn; you won't be behind that plow forever. I got a place at the bank for you, just like I got that hotel for Jimmy. In the meantime, you gotta learn to work instead of acting like a fool, and plowing will learn you that as quick as anything."

I sat down and broke open a biscuit. I spooned some gravy on one of them. "Pass me the jelly, Jelly," I said to my sister. That was the joke in our family, repeated by everyone except my mother. Jelly passed it across the table without saying anything. I spread the huckleberries on the other one and said, "Jelly's on my biscuit."

"Tell her to get off," Father said while lighting his briar pipe. Dad poured me some coffee. Jelly acted like she didn't hear us. I put a lot of cream and sugar in until the black disappeared and the light took over in the little brown whirlpool I made with my spoon.

"You're making me sick, heaping up sugar like that," Mother said. When Father went out to harness the mule I hurried out the back and retrieved the alarm clock from my cot, headed for the wagon, and stuck it in a half-empty seed bag in the wagon bed, well before Father had even begun leading the mule over. I was pleased. I could feel *Deadwood Dick* in my back pocket when I sat down next to Father on the front seat.

As the mule pulled up the steep road into the Tiawah Hills, I looked up at the baggy spider webs growing in the tops of the post oaks as we bounced along. I wondered what was in them, why so many spiders had gone to all that trouble. How did they escape once they had spun their balloon-shaped webs? Or did they work from the outside? How did they get back in? A house with no entry or exit. There might have been more to it if I could ever get up there to see them. I didn't ask Father, who only spoke of banks, wheat, and cattle.

After the road turned away from the railroad tracks, we crossed Otter Creek. "The key is to start out small and build," Father was saying. "Why, many's the man who had to make due with even less than you at first. Take that allotment land of yours, for example."

"Down by the spring?" I asked. There was a place you could see water bubbling up from below the ground, and it was colder than the rest of the stream. Uncle Jimmy had put a metal collar in, and you could dip the spring water and drink it just like it had come out of a well. It wasn't muddy like the rest of the creek. Rumor had it that he kept beer cold in the spring, but I never seen any. The collar was a metal barrel. I liked to climb over the side and jump in it, the shock of landing up to my neck with an icy splash that took my breath away down in the creek bottom where no cool air stirred in the thick woods and sweat dripped in your eyes in spite of all the shade. My feet would hit bottom just before my head went under. I could feel the bubbles under my toes where water pushed its way up through the sand. It was like swimming in seltzer, the kind they use at the soda fountain.

I pictured splashing around in there with scoops of strawberry ice cream all around me. I liked to stand in the collar up to my eyeballs and look out at the slippery clay banks and canopy of trees that blocked out the sun, the breeze, everything. Jimmy didn't like me getting in the collar and stirring up the clear water. "People drink out of there, you know," was what he always told me, but I never knew of anyone to come down there other than me and him. He claimed some renters who had leased an Indian allotment hauled water from there. I'd jump in anyway, quick as I got down there and get my overalls off before he could catch up with me. I could no more stay out of that collar than a preacher keep quiet about sin.

"I'll admit that piece of land is a little wild," Father said, "but there's a lot a man can do with no more than an axe and a good mule. There's that flat spot those Indian boys already had half cleared to play baseball before the commission assigned that to you. They done got most of those stumps out. You could put that in winter wheat and graze some cows on it too. That spring, dammed up, would make a good stock pond. You can cut wheat and sell some feeder calves. Before you know it you'll be leasing a larger place. Most likely from me. And that's not a very far piece from owning your own."

"The spring," I said, worried.

Father took this to mean I thought he had a good idea.

"That's right, boy. Now, you're thinking. That's already a fine start. You can work a teller's window at the bank to keep you busy during the winter."

"Couldn't we keep the spring like it is?" I asked. This was me and Jimmy's favorite crawdad hole. He made metal two-pronged gigs he attached to slender cane poles, and he was teaching me how to stand over the streambed and spear crawdads before they could dart away. Jimmy went into a trance, turned still as stone, before he let loose with a lightning-quick thrust of his spear. I couldn't breathe until the gig head came out of the water with the crawdad squirming on the end of it.

"A spring-fed pond like that won't go stagnant. You'll have some pretty bass and brim in there instead of these old mud-hole catfish in the dirty creeks around here. Make for some mighty fine fishing," Father winked.

I could already fish down there. Jimmy kept a loaf of old bread on the bank that we'd bait up with or we'd catch grasshoppers for the bass. It was a hidden world. And there were plenty of smallmouths, not just bottom feeders.

Father and I passed the Cherokee Baptist Church just south of where the railroad tracks met up with the road again. It was so lonesome, its roped bell to call believers hanging limply in its white wooden frame, the outdoor pews under the open-air arbors empty, and the wood-framed houses surrounding the church ground for fourth Sunday camping-in unoccupied. "Sad as a church on Monday," that's what Jimmy said.

After we clanked over the wood bridge we came up on our field, the first one I had ever plowed. Father had high hopes, but I took an instant disliking to walking behind farm implements. Father gave me a penknife for a present when I came in from putting the mule up the first day. I finished it alone, from harnessing him at dawn to pitching hay to him that evening.

I had nothing personal against the mule; it was the part that came in between hitching him and putting him up that set my sights on a better line of work. I'd already seen enough dirt clods to decide I didn't want to study them the rest of my life. Father had shown me how to bear down on the plow handles and slow the mule on the tough spots. I figured it a waste of time, skinny as I was, to throw myself at a metal and wood contraption that had no intention of digging deeper into the earth simply on account of me.

While Father watched I worked harder than the mule himself, but as soon as he left I'd just hold on to the handles and coast. The mule drug me along as I searched the end of the field for any signs of Deadwood Dick's gang stepping out of the tree line. I needed some entertainment, and I didn't have enough money saved up to run away. I don't think the plowing turned out that much different; we'd get the seed in, and the corn'd come up like it always does. If it didn't there was always bugs or weather that could be blamed.

Today I had to drag the cultivator; corn was already in. Father was headed for the bank as soon as we got rigged, and he saw me started on my first row. He'd come back later with a sandwich on store bread and check my progress at noon. Father had parked the wagon in the shade. I always had to tell him to stop under a tree; he'd have burned us all alive otherwise. I got a tin bucket and went out into the pasture for the sorrel mare, the oats held out in front of me.

If it was me, I'd never fall for such an easy trick. They must like oats something terrible. We were switching out before Father went back to town, him driving the mare to the bank, me the mule in the field.

I tied Dolly to the side of the wagon, reached in, and pulled out the half-empty feed sack with the alarm clock in it. I set it inside the barn like I was putting it away. I got started on the first row while Father finished hitching Dolly to his wagon. When I could see no more than their dust cloud and the two of them had disappeared into the next section, I hollered, "Whoa," got the mule stopped in the middle of the knee-high corn row, and he stood there with his ears twitching, wondering why he'd had the good luck to quit so soon. I went into the barn and wound my alarm clock some more. It didn't like much since I'd already cranked it up good after I woke up. I set it for 11:15.

Then I went back to plowing. I had to create a good deal of excitement to get that mule convinced we were on a special work schedule. He was a one-speed mule, and I had a two-speed day ahead. He'd already stopped after just starting and that sure didn't perk him up any either. I hollered, slapped the reins around, whooped like an Indian, and sang all the verses of "I Ride an Old Paint," each in a higher key than the one before. I imagined going up a fret at a time on my guitar after each chorus of "Ride along, ride along real slow, the firey and the snuffy are rarin' to go." I had a good ear that way. I learned "Old Paint" from the cowboys who had stayed at Uncle Jimmy's boarding house on the way home from cattle drives and the Kansas City markets. They told about the open range in the Territory, running cattle over thousands of acres before it was all allotted out into 160-acre parcels.

Some days I'd stir up a hornet's nest with the plow, and judging by the way they stung me and the mule both they took it personal. Such times the two of us made considerable progress on staying awake behind and in front of the plow and reaching the end of the row in record time. Today it was just my singing.

Something started working because I could smell wet leather against horse flesh; the mule was lathered, and the harnesses were creaking. Weeds were flying from the cultivator shovels, and we were skinning the field of second-growth cockleburs and horse weed the way you'd pull a squirrel from his hide before he hit the frying pan. I had to ease up on my vaudeville act some since the mule was fixing to break into a trot. And I needed to listen. It had got hot, and I knew we were well into mid-morning. I didn't want to miss the alarm when it went off.

If you get quiet enough, you can hear all kinds of things such as the train siren slowing down miles away at the edge of town, the fire that crackles in a neighbor's field where trash is burning, even the buzz of heat, weaving in and out of the corn stalks in shimmering waves of color.

Or silence. Like when the cicadas stop, and you wonder what's gonna happen next. That's why I nearly jumped out of my skin when the alarm clock rang out. I'd been listening so hard for it that I was bound for distraction. The ringing brought the mule back in focus, his ass bobbing up and down in front of me. At the end of the row I walked him to a stand of willows next to the road ditch. I realized my mistake when I saw the mule swatting at mosquitoes with his tail: willows, water, mosquitoes.

I didn't have enough time to be picky. Leaving the mule hooked to the cultivator, I ran to the barn to turn the alarm clock off. It stopped ringing before I could reach it. So I wound it up some more. Couldn't have lost more than a minute. I took it back with me in the shade. I sat against a fence post in the dirt. The mule nosed around in some clover, chomping it against his bit. A wood tick crawled up my arm before I could get the cover of the book open. I'd had them in a lot worse places than that. Looking down the road Father would return on, I gave myself thirty-five minutes, allowing for enough time to get the clock back to the barn and the mule in his row.

Deadwood Dick was showing a new gang member how to shoot from the hip. The Mexican bandit had barely escaped the revolution into the safe arms of the United States. Straightaway he consulted widows and pretty young women who had aided the outlaws as to their current whereabouts. The Mexican Bandit's sole purpose in locating Deadwood Dick had been setting his eyes on evil as pure and unrelenting as the black mark on his own soul.

Deadwood Dick, sensing a man of similar interests in his Mexican compadre, took extra time to school the bandit as to the use of side arms. One hand on the Mexican's hip, he raises the other slowly, directing the bandit to lift his weaponed hand, too, in unison. His stubbled cheek is against the bandit's smooth brown face as he directs the sighting of the pistol. The outlaws are cheering, waiting for the gun to go off in the hands of the two new friends.

I heard the church bell ring instead of the pistol's report. It was the middle of the week—surely there was no church service. Had someone died? I marked my spot in *Deadwood Dick* with a twig, and walked to the fence line where I could see the church at the bottom of the hill. Wagons had pulled onto the grounds, and I could make out the vague shapes of people climbing down from them, walking toward the camp houses, some towards the church arbor. I heard singing. Some of them must have already been seated. I knew the tune, "Come Thou Fount," except it was in Indian—Cherokee, I reckoned, since that's mostly what we was around there.

There was no organ or piano, just voices, women's and men's, running neck and neck with the cicadas. I had never heard anything like it, an aching sadness that made you glad to be alive. Heaven sounded real, like somebody's house everyone in town had been to at least once, even though I couldn't understand the words of the hymns. I leaned against the fence, and held onto the top strand, straining to hear better. The post had broke off at the bottom, and it swung back and forth as I listened. Laziness. They should have put in a cedar post; they last longer.

And then someone tapped me on the shoulder. First I screamed, then I let go of the fence, and it twanged like a guitar string. I turned around to see my father's flashing eyes, an alarm clock in one hand and *Deadwood Dick* in the other.

"Time to get up," Father said dryly. "You'll be late for church with the Indians." Then he slowly tore *Deadwood Dick* down the center of its spine. I grabbed for the book, which he tossed in the ditch. He pulled off his belt, and I got strapped, but not very enthusiastically because any fool could see I'd still made my way through quite a bit of the field, and my father would have been late for work had he whupped me and then sat down afterward to give one of his speeches, lining out all I was supposed to learn from the lesson and how to become a man who mattered in Claremore. Father didn't like leaving the bank's money by itself for very long and that saved me.

On the ride home in the late afternoon my talkative father said nothing about cattle prices; Indians who had their restrictions removed so they could sell their allotments; neighbors late on loan payments; hands he might line up to help him cut wheat at harvest; or scorn for Clem Rogers's son, who was gallivanting all over the countryside twirling a rope alongside minstrels and snake oil salesman while the family was sitting on top of a wheat and cattle empire back home that could use his help. Father planned on beating the Rogerses at their own game by raising serious children who didn't run away for something as foolish as vaudeville.

Mother met the wagon in the yard. "Mary has driven me to distraction," she snarled, holding on to the horse's reins below the snaffle bit. I don't know why she did that, since the horse wasn't going anywhere. Father had them to where they would stand dead still while he was bridling them up or unhitching them at the end of the day. The horse had its ears back, waiting for her to let go. "Jimmy is no more than sun-addled, but Mary insists on calling on the doctor. She wants you to fetch him while she stays with Jimmy. I told her you had bookkeeping chores on your accounts before you went to bed."

Soon as Mother thought she had stopped the horse, who had no intentions of going anyplace except the barn to get his bag of oats, she turned loose of the reins and climbed up on the running board, grabbing a hold of my arm.

"I can get down myself," I said, jerking my arm away.

"I'm not here to help you," she said. Father must have told Mother about my reading instead of plowing. I climbed down and started undoing the traces.

"Can't you see I'm busy?" I said, when she grabbed my arm again.

I felt the hot sting of her hand across my face. "I'll take care of this one," she said, leading me toward the house while the mule stood in the middle of the yard waiting to be put up.

"That boy still has work to do," Father said. "You take care of your own business. I'll see to the boy. Put up the mule, Lynn. Then go to your room.

You'll skip supper tonight. I'm going over to the hotel. I'll walk so you can get the horse in. I'll ride Jimmy's horse if the doctor is needed."

I watched Father disappear down the dusky street. Mother stood and glared at me for a spell before going back into the house. After I got the mule put up, I headed for the back door. Mother blocked my entrance into the kitchen, her hands crossed over the top of her apron. "Where do you think *you're* going?" she said.

"To my room," I lied. I was going to look for some tape to put *Deadwood Dick* back together. I had kicked through the ditch weeds until I found it. I was aiming on sleeping outside on the cot once I got it fixed.

"He told you to skip supper."

"I can do that in my room as well as anywhere."

"You'll sleep in the chicken coop," Mother said, not moving an inch from the doorway.

"Fine," I replied. I'd yet to figure how an adult reckoned making a body sleep outside was a punishment. I had the book in my back pocket, even if it was unrepaired. What else did I need?

Minding Mother without an argument made her madder yet. When I turned and looked up at the stars, yawning, she slammed the kitchen door so loud the cicadas let up their racket for a second, startled. I didn't think anybody could shut *them* up. I was sweating all over, and no breeze was stirring. I could feel my head starting to throb, and I had no stomach for beans and cornbread or much else—certainly not the sweltering kitchen, and least of all Mother.

I could feel chigger bites around my ankles starting to itch, which they did every confounded moment you waddn't occupied with something else to keep your mind off them. The grass in the backyard was going to seed. I had been skipping the back and just mowing the front. The white-seeded stems, taller than the rest of the lawn, were still as fence posts in the hot night. I followed the path to the chicken coop, worn from years of feeding and collecting eggs, I reckoned, back when hens were housed in it.

I undid the latch of the door; it was a big X frame with chicken wire tacked on it, and I pulled it toward me, creaking on its hinges. "It sounds like a donkey braying," I thought; then I started to get dizzy, falling against the door which slammed back shut. I heard the latch click into place. I looked at my fingers. They were poking through the chicken wire. Some of the wire had popped out of the frame, but the cross boards kept me from falling through. Watching my fingers awhile as I held onto the chicken wire, I waited for my head to stop swimming. Like one of Deadwood Dick's men, clutching the bars of his jail cell as the sheriff looked on laughing, I peered into the coop from my side of the chicken wire. That would be like looking into the jail cell instead of out of it, though.

I undid my hands from the wire, turned and leaned my back against the coop to get my bearings for a minute. I looked up at the Big Dipper, and each star was resting on one of the wood shingles sloping down our chimneyed roof.

The spell passed as quick as it came, and, all at once I was pulling the door open again and walking through the dusty coop as if nothing had ever happened. Had I fallen just moments before? I had my cot on the raised floor where the nesting boxes were, under the tin roof, to keep them out of the rain. I pulled the cot out into the open part of the coop under the stars. After I got it drug out, I went back to the nesting boxes and got my candle and the matches. Lighting the candle, I dripped wax on a tin feed scoop, then anchored the candle in the soft meltings. I sat my lamp holder on the cot and took a seat myself, taking off my shoes. Between the starlight and the little flame that lapped softly over the sides of the feed scoop, there would be just enough light. To keep them out of the feathers and dirt, I hung my overalls on the metal-hasped clipboard hanging on a nail, where Mother had kept track of her egg money before we stopped raising chickens in town.

Sitting there on my cot, it took everything within me to keep from scratching my chigger bites. I couldn't resist brushing a chicken feather over them, which only made me want so much more. I sighed. I walked through the feathers and made my way outside the coop. I pulled a twig off the sweetgum tree in the backyard and brushed my teeth with it. Had it not been for Mother, I would have gone in and got a little baking soda. When it was late enough maybe I'd sneak inside.

Back on the cot I sat on the edge and brushed the dust off my feet before laying back in my underwear and holding *Deadwood Dick* between me and the stars.

His men had a bad case of cave fever—on the edge of mutiny, they had been hidden there so long. The Mexican bandit had soon forgotten his loyalty to Deadwood Dick and led a group of rebels to sleep just outside the mouth of the cave, risking exposure, even lighting a fire against the express orders of Deadwood Dick himself.

The Mexican had waited for his band of mutineers to fall asleep under the delicious moonlight they had been deprived of for so long. Lying next to him, one arm thrown back invitingly in repose, was the youngest member of the gang, Fearless Frank, who had never let Deadwood Dick down before the Mexican showed up.

Fearless Frank's head rested on his saddle, his dark hair tossed like stardust, a long loose strand laying against his smooth, fair throat, pulsing innocently. The bandit moves to his knees, stealthily making his way over to Fearless Frank. He leans over the sleeping youth and gently unbuttons his way down the boy's calico shirt, pausing when he stirs. When Fearless Frank's chest starts to rise and fall again, the Mexican reaches in tenuously and follows the leather thong down the boy's sternum and firm belly until, just above his belt, his fingers clasp the gold pouch resting snugly where his shirt is tucked in. The bandit pulls the pouch out, his eyes glinting with greed, and unsheathes his Bowie knife, making fast work of separating the money from its owner.

I went over to the nesting box and brought the other half of the book back to the cot. How could Fearless Frank have joined the Mexican and left Deadwood Dick alone in the cave? I looked for the dog-eared page where I'd first met Fearless Frank:

Around the camp-fire were grouped half a score of men, all rough, bearded, and grizzled, with one exception. This being a youth whose age one could have safely put at twenty, so perfectly developed of physique and intelligence of facial appearance was he. There was something about him that was not handsome, and yet you would have been puzzled to tell what it was, for his countenance was strikingly handsome, and surely no form in the crowd was more noticeable for its grace, symmetry, and proportionate development. It would have taken a scholar to have studied out the secret.

He was of about medium stature, and as straight and square-shouldered as an athlete. His complexion was nut-brown, from long exposure to the sun; hair the hue of the raven's wing, and hanging in long, straight strands adown his back; eyes black and piercing as an eagle's; features well molded, with a firm, resolute mouth and prominent chin. He was an interesting specimen of young, healthy manhood, and even though a youth in years, was one that could command respect, if not admiration, wheresoever he might choose to go.

One remarkable item about his personal appearance, apt to strike the beholder as being exceedingly strange and eccentric, was his costume— buckskin throughout, and that dyed to the brightest scarlet hue.

"Why, you see, it is to attract bufflers, if we should meet any, out on the plains 'twixt this and the Hills."

He gave his name as Fearless Frank, and said he was aiming for the Hills; that if the party in question would furnish him a place among them, he would extend to them his assistance as a hunter, guide, or whatever, until the destination was reached. Seeing that he was well armed, and judging from external appearances that he would prove a valuable accessory, the miners were nothing loth in accepting his services.

I was clutching my chest, grabbing for the missing gold, and Father was lifting me off the cot. "My god, he's burning up," Father seemed to be saying. "Here, feel his forehead." Standing in the door of the coop, unmoving as if she was still in the same place blocking my entry into the kitchen, was a dark blur against a white apron, the apron flapping around like laundry in the wind, though no wind was blowing. Behind her was the chicken coop door swinging on one hinge. When she spoke, her voice came from the bottom of the well in the front yard—Mother herself was no more than a sheet blown up against the door frame. "He didn't do enough work today to get hot," the voice said.

"You've got no business putting him in a poultry shed," Father said. "I'll mind to his plowing; you keep to your own business. You oughta have enough sense to figure you don't put a near-growed boy knee-deep in chicken shit, much less a sick one."

I'd never heard Father forbid Mother before or say "shit," which I always figured was a word bankers couldn't use. It frightened me. Because Father seemed scared himself. Father jerked a towel off the clothesline and sat me down by the well. As he lowered the bucket, I slumped over and fell in the grass. "Lynnsey," Father cried, sitting me back up against the well frame. He lowered the bucket as fast as he could. He looked like he was making ice cream backwards. I laughed and fell over again.

Father wrapped the wet towel around my neck and laid a washcloth against my forehead. Mother was slinking around the well like a hound dog looking for a chance to suck eggs. I wished somebody would run her off for good.

Father picked me back up, and the roof of our house was rolling, the chimney swaying back and forth like it was being conjured by a snake charmer, soon to rise up and take its place in the Big Dipper. "At least the doctor's still at Jimmy's. How'd you both come up sick on the same evening?"

"We planned it that way," I mumbled. "I don't need a doctor. What happened to Jimmy?"

"He had a temperature of 105 degrees, and his heart nearly pounded out of his chest. He was unconscious, and your Aunt Mary, little as she is, managed to throw him in a bathtub with a block of ice until the doctor got there. The doctor says she saved him from brain damage, maybe death."

"Is that what I got?"

"No, Jimmy went back in the sun today, working on that pole barn behind the hotel. I don't know why you're sick."

"Do I have what killed mama?"

"Of course, you don't," Father said, looking away. Mother wanted to put me to bed with Jelly, but Father shook his head no. I thought I heard the word "contagious." They were like the movies. You had the captions the screen actors stood on top of, but you knew they were saying a whole lot more. Father carried me and laid me down on the porch and came back with my cot. He told Mother to beat it with the broom and put some fresh bedcovers on it. When she asked why, he just glared at her. Father set the cot in the front yard for Mother to get ready.

"The whole world don't need to know he's sick," Mother said. The next thing I knew Father had one foot in Dolly's stirrup, and how she got there saddled I'll never know. Mother was still arguing when he rode off at a trot, and before he disappeared down the dark street I could see he had Dolly at a gallop, like one of Deadwood Dick's gang instead of a banker.

A little breeze had started up, and the porch swing was creaking. Guinea fowl were roosting in the catalpa tree in the front yard. They were the neighbors'. Mother was batting them out of the tree with the broom instead of beating the cot, and they landed on the ground squawking and flapping their wings, Mother running behind them telling each one she was going to wring its neck.

I thought any minute one of the guineas was going to turn around and chase her back in the house. She still hadn't got my cot set up when the doctor came up the front steps carrying a medical bag in one hand and a little black pocket-sized book in the other, stopping since I was laid out at the top step where he couldn't get past me. Mother set her broom against the tree and watched from the front yard. Father brought the cot up on the porch and laid me on it, so the doctor could get to me easier. The doctor slowly ascended the stairs. I figured I couldn't have been too bad off as long as it was taking him. He bent over to sit his bag down and had a thermometer shaking in front of him, and it was in my mouth before he had straightened back up.

"One of my tricks," he winked. "Betcha don't even remember opening your mouth." He was frowning. I wiggled the thermometer, so he would know I wasn't dead.

"One of my tricks," I mumbled. He grabbed it out of my mouth, not laughing, and read it. "Get a washtub," he told Father. "We're putting him in a cold bath before he gets any hotter." The washtub was already on the porch. Father began carrying buckets from the well and dumping them in. The doctor told Mother to take my clothes off. "Wait until the tub is ready," I said, wanting to delay my exposure in front of Mother and the gang on the porch, but she was already jerking my shirt over my head.

When Father lowered me into the tub, I thought of Fearless Frank splashing around with the outlaws, but he had to keep me from jumping out as soon as I felt the steel bottom underneath me and the water sloshing around my waist. My teeth started chattering right away when Father sponged the water over my chest and back. Mother told Jelly to go back inside and stay in bed, since she kept poking her head through the front door to see what was happening.

"Get his head wet," the doctor said. "That will cool him down the fastest. Has anyone here had typhoid?" the doctor asked.

"His mother had it."

"That was eight years ago," the doctor said. "I mean recently."

"Jimmy's got a fever," Mother replied, as if the doctor hadn't just been over there. She had her broom again. Maybe she was going to sweep up the rest of the guineas or try to run the doctor off. One of the birds had come back and perched on a higher limb, out of her reach. I bet it was asleep, its head tucked under its wing.

"Jimmy has heat stroke," the doctor said without glancing up at Mother. He was thumbing through his little black *Merck Manual.* "The fever will stay with the boy another two weeks or so, depending on when it started. If he gets rose spots on his chest the second week, he has typhoid for sure. Not everybody gets them. Most don't. He could still have typhoid if he doesn't get them. The real danger is toward the end of the fever if he starts bleeding with the diarrhea. You want to keep him on liquids when the diarrhea starts, but I'll be back around before then."

"I'll stay over at Jimmy's," I volunteered, "since we're both sick."

"We've got to keep you away from people," the doctor said sternly. "Now that Jimmy's cooled down he'll be all right, but hot weather could bother him for a long time. He'll need to stay indoors out of the heat. No more foolishness," the doctor said, eyeing me knowingly. That worried me. Everything me and Jimmy did together was outside.

Although it was too dark to see Aunt Mary, I could make out her plumed hat floating down the street because of its white feather bending in the breeze. "Dressed for a party," Mother sneered. "And here it is the middle of the night."

"It'll be a party if we don't get some of you off this porch," the doctor said. He was the only doctor I'd ever known to talk. "We need to let the boy get some rest. Just keep him cool and watch his temperature."

Aunt Mary unfastened her bonnet from her head and set it on the porch swing. She eyed Mother like she might be dumb enough to sit on it—or come after it with the broom, since it had a feather on top. She took off one of her white gloves. Mother rolled her eyes. "Who's watching Jimmy?" Father asked.

"Mrs. Barnhurst," she said. Mrs. Barnhurst was an old lady with no husband who boarded on the second floor of the hotel. "Jimmy's better now. He wants me to leave him alone, says he's had enough of women for a long while."

"Look to me like he's always had enough of 'em," Mother said.

"Pickins are mighty thin around here," Aunt Mary said, snapping her other glove as she pulled it off her arm. "It's bound to get a sight worse since he claims he'll never go outdoors again. You cain't hardly court from a door frame. This won't improve his bachelorhood none. He'll snap out of it soon enough, I imagine." Now that she was ungloved, Mary turned toward the doctor. "Got a smoke?" she asked him. "Looks like I'm gonna be here awhile. It's just a front porch, but it's a sight better than a chicken coop," she said, glaring at Mother as she threw the glove on the porch swing with its mate.

The doctor handed Aunt Mary a cigarette and lit it for her. "How long have you been smoking?" he asked.

"Every since I could make fire," Aunt Mary smirked.

"You heard the doctor," Mother said. "Clear out of here."

"I heard no such thing," Aunt Mary replied.

"Thanks for sitting up with the boy," Father told Aunt Mary.

"You go to bed," Mary said, directing him inside. "You've got work tomorrow."

Mother followed behind Father and left us on the porch.

"I can take Lynn over to the hotel in the morning, doctor. Two sick men are as easily cared for as one."

"No, he'll stay here," the doctor said sternly. "Typhoid is easily spread." Aunt Mary blinked. No one in my family had ever said that word. I wouldn't have ever heard tell of it myself had it not been for my sneakiness. Aunt Mary kept Mama's jewelry in a music box in her room at the hotel. I used to get in there in order to see my mother's things, touching them to try and remember her. At noon when Mary got busy feeding guests there was an hour or so when she couldn't keep up with me. That's where I first saw the barrette with the pearl inlay.

The fever had cleared my mind. I hadn't bought it from a Syrian peddler; I'd stolen it from Aunt Mary. I figured I had as much right to it as anybody, since it used to belong to my mother. Folded in the bottom of the box, with a brooch sitting neatly on top of it, was a newspaper clipping from the *Claremore Progress*. When I took it out and read it, it gave typhoid fever as the cause of death. Father had brought the music box over to the hotel after Mother tried to throw it away.

"In that case I'll stay right here on the porch with him," Aunt Mary said. "You never can tell; they might even let us in the house if it storms," she said.

"Suit yourself," the doctor said. "He's just as well out here as long as it's dry. If it gets damp out bring him in." Aunt Mary was already wringing out the washrag and wetting it in the bucket, paying no mind to the doctor as he left. Aunt Mary was knocking a tin pail against the porch rail to shake any spiders out.

"We don't need any fiddleback bites," she said. "We got enough trouble around here as it is." The doctor had disappeared.

"What's that for?" I asked."

"No telling when a person might need a bucket," she said, sliding it under my cot.

"Read to me," I begged.

"What am I supposed to read?" she asked. "Nothing out here but moon-light."

"Well, then read that," I said, still able to grin a little. I leaned over the cot and pulled the half of *Deadwood Dick* I had in my back pocket out of the overalls strewn on the porch. Aunt Mary looked at what was left of the book, but she didn't ask. "You better enjoy it," she said. "In a few days *Deadwood Dick* will be the least of your worries." She lit a kerosene lantern and sat it on the rail next to her chair. Bugs had already landed on her pages. A locust dive-bombed her tied-up hair and fell on the porch with a thud. "I'll allow you might be too sick to read here in a day or two," she sighed. "But you need to get some sleep before the sun comes up and it gets too hot to rest. So I'll make it short":

> Fearless Frank took in the situation at a glance, and not hearing the cries, he rightly conjectured that the one in distress had again become exhausted. That that person was in the thicket below seemed more than probable, and he immediately resolved to descend in search. Slipping from his saddle, he stepped forward to the very edge of the precipice and looked over. The next second the ground crumbled beneath his feet, and he was precipitated headlong into the valley. Fortunately he received no serious injuries, and in a moment was on his feet again, all right.
>
> "A miss is as good as a mile," he muttered, brushing the dirt from his clothing. "Now, then, we will find out the secret of the racket in this thicket."
>
> Glancing up to the brink above to see that his horse was standing quietly, he parted the shrubbery, and entered the thicket.

It required considerable pushing and tugging to get through the dense undergrowth, but at last his efforts were rewarded, and he stood in a small break or glade.

Stood there, to behold a sight that made the blood boil in his veins. Securely bound with her face toward a stake, was a young girl—a maiden of perhaps seventeen summers, whom, at a single glance, one might surmise was remarkably pretty.

She was stripped to the waist, and upon her snow-white back were numerous welts from which trickled diminutive rivulets of crimson. Her head was dropped against the stake to which she was bound, and she was evidently insensible.

With a cry of astonishment and indignation Fearless Frank leaped forward to sever her bonds, when like so many grim phantoms there filed out of the chaparral, and circled around him, a score of hideously painted savages. One glance at the portly leader satisfied Frank as to his identity. It was the fiend incarnate—Sitting Bull!

Aunt Mary had skipped ahead. I imagined Frank himself tied to the pole, his arms pulled behind him, the defiance in his eyes as his captors took turns wielding the buckskin lash against his bare back. The fever was returning, and I groaned. Aunt Mary wetted my hair and wiped my face. The sheet I had pulled over me felt like a scourge against my hot skin. It was soaking wet. Aunt Mary wanted to take it off and put a dry one on me, but I held on to it. "Turn loose, Sitting Bull," she said, "It ain't a tug-of-war."

When I woke up the next morning, the sheet twisted around my feet, Aunt Mary was asleep on a cot next to mine. Father might have felt sorry for her and brought it out in the morning. I felt a tremendous thirst, and my throat hurt. I sat up to go in the house and get a glass of water. The washrag fell off my head. I don't know how it could have stayed there all night—maybe Mary had just gone to sleep. I bent down to pick it up off the porch, and the wood slats spun out from under me. I looked up to figure things out, and the porch roof did the same thing, swinging under my feet. I was the center of a turning Ferris wheel. I pitched over onto Mary's cot, and she was up on her feet putting me back to bed so fast that she could have raised dust. I couldn't see how she even had time to wake up.

"Don't you get out of bed again," she said. I knew she meant it. "It's bad enough to have a fever without diving off the porch." She didn't say typhoid. "What do you want?"

"A glass of water," I managed. My throat was parched. Aunt Mary nearly ran into Mother, who was on her way out the screen door.

"What's all the ruckus about?" Mother demanded. "You're indecent, in that nightgown out here for all the world to see."

"I thought you wanted me to take off my party clothes," Mary answered. "Well, they're off."

"Is Jimmy coming over?" I rasped.

"Jimmy has taken a vow never to go in the sun again," Mary said. "It's going to be a long time before you see Jimmy, since I'm not letting you off this bed, and he refuses to come out of the hotel."

I couldn't believe Jimmy would volunteer to stay inside. I knew women were behind this. Aunt Mary must have tied him to his bed. But Mary was here. I figured he'd already be over to check on me. I might have to go over to the hotel and untie Jimmy.

The heat woke me up in the afternoon. Gar Sixkiller was standing over my cot, holding a bottle of medicine. I felt like a steer with grub worms fixing to be popped, everybody working over me. Gar was shirtless and barefoot in his brown dungarees, and when he reached the bottle of quinine over to Aunt Mary, his long, black hair fell over his chest. He had two letters in his other hand, and Aunt Mary tried to take those, too, but Gar backed away so he could present them hisself.

"Good god a-mighty, you're not an English butler," Aunt Mary chided. Gar flashed his sharp, gleaming teeth and wiped the sweat out of his eyes. "You've sweated on my letters," Mary said. She held one up, and sure enough, the ink was blurred.

"I have a message from Jimmy," Gar announced, his grin now as wide as the front porch, though he was still standing stiffly like a royal attendant.

"Can we receive it sitting?" Aunt Mary asked mockingly. Gar had gotten a job at Jimmy's hotel, and he sure took it serious-like.

Deadwood Dick had once robbed an English butler who he almost shot, and would have, except for the butler's bravery guarding his master's fortune. I had seen Gar twice—the previous summer when he had worked in Father's hayfields, and more recently when he came by the hotel every day looking for work, and Mary finally just give up even though she started out telling him she couldn't have a fullblood in a white hotel. Gar had told her he was looking to work outside, and she had just glared at him until he left. But he was back every day. And it wasn't long after he started painting the porch rails that he'd worked his way inside, serving guests. For that he wore a shirt, a white one he pulled off every night and scrubbed with a bar of lye soap out back at the pump. I worked the handle for him.

"When will Jimmy be here?" I asked.

"Jimmy is at the hotel cooking," Gar said. "He says he's taking over in the kitchen."

"Jimmy couldn't cook in the middle of a barn fire," Mary sneered.

"Jimmy sent the cook out to hire help to finish the pole barn for the guests' horses. He has asked me to go with the cook over to Verdigris to hire Lester Proctor, since I speak Cherokee. Jimmy says he won't work outside anymore."

"His brain is baked," Aunt Mary said. "Along with yours, Gar. What will the cook do? We can barely pay her, much less more help." Jimmy was always complaining about the cost of any worker inside the hotel, telling Mary she should be able to take care of her end just like he kept up with the outside without hiring anyone to help him. It wasn't like him to want to hire more.

"The cook is showing Jimmy how to fry chicken for supper. When they get the chicken fried, me and the cook will be on our way to Verdigris."

Aunt Mary jumped up. "Gar, you stay here with Lynn." She looked at the bottle in her hand. "Wait a minute, Lynn, I need to give you this quinine. Gar, go fetch a glass from the kitchen." When Gar came out, he had a glass of water and a tablespoon. Good thing Mother wasn't there to see him inside the house.

Aunt Mary poured the quinine into the glass of water. I turned my head away. I would have put up more of a fuss, but I didn't want to look like a baby, so I picked up the glass and gulped the water down as fast as I could before I tasted it. "I'll be right back," Mary said. "Gar, you run over and get me if he needs anything."

I had never seen our porch so busy, what with the doctor coming over and now. As Mary hurried off, I laid back down. "Gar, could you damp my hair?" I asked. Gar pulled up a chair next to me. He took the washrag, which was draped over the bucket, dipped it in the water, and wrung it out, his sinewy biceps straining with the effort.

When he bent over me, his chest was inches from my face as he ran the washcloth over my hair. He smelled like talcum, like he had just bathed. His hand was cool and wet on my forehead. The sheet was still over my waist, thank god. The hollows under his arms, his chest, two hills covered with the grassy down of a teenage boy, the sunken valley of his slender belly, and the stream ran down the sides of my face. "I better wring it out better," he said.

"Have you ever heard of Sitting Bull?" I asked. I figured he might know.

"Isn't he one of those wild Indians?" Gar said. His hand was resting on my stomach as he wetted my forehead.

"He's an Indian in a book," I told him.

"I heard tell some Sioux came here once to talk about moving to the territory," Gar said. "They liked the Creeks better than us. But they never came back."

I was trying to keep from staring at him. "How come they call you Gar?" I asked.

"My teeth," he grinned, showing them to me. He liked his teeth; that much was for certain. I liked them, too. "I open sody bottles for people. Gar have sharp teeth. They bite through fishing line."

When Aunt Mary came back on the porch she had a note in her hand. It was a day of messages.

"From your uncle," she said, handing it to me. "I told him to walk over and tell you hisself, but he won't set foot outside the hotel. Was a time I never could get him inside the place; now I can't get him out."

"Dear Lynnsey," it started out after I got it all unfolded. It was written in pencil on lined yellow notepaper. It was a big piece of paper for a small message, most of the page wasted. "A person sees things. when he's too hot to recognize anyone around him even his own self. What I seen don't bear repeating. I do know I'll never allow myself. to get that hot again please come see me since I'll never set. foot outdoors. So help me god. Uncle Jimmy."

That's when the pain started. My stomach. Tender to the touch. It hurt where Gar had put his hand.

The fever dreams came to me then, endless repetition of the last line I had heard before dozing off, floating between sleep and wakefulness. I would force myself awake by sitting up because losing my mind scared me. It was bad enough to think I might go crazy, but the prospect of repeating the same line millions of times, unable to stop, was more than I could bear. In sleep I heard Jimmy singing over and over, "A-takin' that herd to Baxter, by God! A-drivin' that herd to Baxter, by God!" I would get myself half-propped back up on the cot enough to call back my own words, but before I knew it I would be asleep again, except now it was "in the narrow grave just six by three, they left him there on the lone prairie." It was the opposite of counting sheep to go to sleep. I was going to sleep where I couldn't stop counting sheep.

It could have been days later, or just after the doctor's visit, for all I could tell. I heard voices in the yard. I rose up on my elbow. Esther Connelly, my schoolmate, came up on the porch first. The rest of them was standing in the grass with their lunch sacks in their hands, the boys shifting from foot to foot and spitting in the dirt, the girls whispering to each other. "Come on," Esther kept growling to the crowd behind her who were too spooked to get close. Esther cleaned the blackboard and helped hand back papers at school. She would have liked it if the teacher drowned or got married, and she could take over. Esther was like a sheepdog trying to herd terrapins no more than anyone ever listened to her, but she never got discouraged.

"We made you a card," Esther said, inching barely close enough to give it to me unless I grew new arms. I had reached about as far as I could when Esther pulled the card back. "What's that?" she pointed. "On your chest?" I looked down to see for the first time the signatures the disease had left on my flesh, one a fiery lightning rod, the other a manger floating on a pink cloud. The lightning rod was touching fire to the manger. Light shot out all over from where it had been set afire. The pictures on me didn't bear a lick of resemblance to any flowers I had ever seen, and the doctor had no right to call them rose spots. If he knew no more than that he should keep his opinions to hisself.

Suddenly the porch was full of kids pushing each other out of the way to get a closer look at me, as if I had been hand-painted by God. Esther told everyone to back off, so they all squeezed in closer. I was looking up at gawking faces. I opened my shirt up all the way for them to see. I was being lapped up like gravy in a dog bowl. I pulled my shirt clean off. The boys were in the front row, and they had pushed the girls to the back.

Esther, who I could no longer see, asked, "Will you be able to play guitar at the movies this Saturday?" Dunc, a cowlick-headed boy from Verdigris Switch who only had one strap left on his overalls, said, "Maybe he'll be dead by then." I motioned with my finger, and Dunc pushed his way over to my cot and leaned toward me so close I could smell the pomade in his hair. His pink earlobe was almost touching my lips, his loose overall flap resting on the rose spots. I made like it was my dying words, drawing him closer. His ear was a seashell I could have run my tongue inside. I rose up on my elbow and said just loud enough for those gathered around him to hear, "When I go I'm taking you with me." Dunc jumped back and my schoolmates parted like the waters of the Dead Sea as Dunc ran down the steps, crying. My throat hurt, but I laughed as kids were backing up and falling all over each other to get off the porch.

Ellen dropped the card, the second of my letters, before running. Until my illness I had never got notes or letters from anybody. As they made their way down the street, Dunc had stopped crying and was letting on like nothing happened. I heard him say, "Let's go and see his crazy uncle standing in the window," as they got farther away.

Two of my classmates had left lunch sacks on the porch. I was hungry, but things just poured out of me faster than I could put them in. I stuck my foot on the card and slid it over without even getting up. I was worse than lazy; I was lazy gone to seed. The card was cut in the shape of one of the roses that had turned to something else on my chest. It didn't open up, only one-sided. Figured. I would have made it fold out into a full flower, blooming as you opened it. I turned the card over and read the poem Mrs. Sawters had written in a lady teacher's neat spiraling loops:

> More than the scarecrow frightens off the thief
> More than Moses' rod parted the Dead Sea
> The prayers of all your loving chums, friends who sit in class
> Will scatter crows and waters part until you safely pass

What I needed to pass right then required the bed pan. The outhouse was too far away. While crouched behind my cot, I traced the outline of the pink blaze on my chest. Now I knew I had typhoid for sure, even if no one would say. It was this same dysentery that killed Mama, tore her guts up, bled her. The sky beyond the porch was a dark anvil.

By the time of the first thunderclap Mother would be dragging me inside by the ear if I didn't get up soon. She was taking the clothes off the line before they got drenched; sheets were snapping in the wind, and the temperature was dropping fast. Mother was screaming for me to go in, flapping around with the blowing laundry. She clawed at a sheet that had wrapped around her face.

I started to drag my cot to the door. I hadn't moved it but a couple of feet before I was worn out. I could only think of falling on a bed. I left the cot on the porch. Mother would yell. I opened the screen door, and I didn't remember anything of how I got there between the time the door slammed and I found myself in the middle of Jelly's straw-tick mattress. She was in school. Rain was falling hard on the tin roof. Even with the rain pounding I could hear Mother's leather shoes stomping on the floor as she wrestled the laundry in the living room. The room was hot, and I smelled bleach from the wet sheets. Sweat was running in my eyes. I should have been in school like Jelly. I was alone.

It was still raining the next morning when the third letter came, soiled by muddy raindrops. I had been up all night cramping with the diarrhea. I had nothing left but my guts, and there was some blood. I couldn't go to the outhouse because I was afraid of what would happen to me if I got wet. Jimmy, for the first time, was afraid of the sun, and I was scared of water. Jelly had left me, too, since they didn't want no one around me. I guess they wanted at least one kid that waddn't dead. She was staying over at Jimmy's hotel, where I should have been. Mother came in to get the bedpan in gloves up to her elbows. "You would be better off in diapers," she said when I made her sit it down again. Father came in as I was crouched over the pan.

"He's bleeding some," Mother said.

"I'm going to get the doctor," he replied.

Then they left me. I had got my mind back since the fever stopped. But not my book. It had been in those overalls and Mother had done the wash since. This was the first time I got out of taking a bath in the leftover laundry water since I was sick. If Mother found my book in the pocket it might be out on the trash heap, soaking wet and ruined by now. I had no way to get it without a drenching if that's where it was. I got up to look for it, but the doctor had come in the front door, so I pretended like I had been laying down. He entered my room carrying a red chihauhau dog in one arm; she sniffed the air suspiciously, her large, doe-like eyes shifting nervously as if planning an escape route. The doctor sat her on the floor, and she jumped on my bed, spinning wildly by my side then plopping down next to me with a whimper. It was like a hummingbird had landed—something you'd never expect to see lying still. She rested her head on her front paws. I imagined her heart throbbing like the beating of wings.

"I told you at the front door," Mother said, "I don't allow dogs in the house. Put her outside." The doctor wasn't listening. "I'll take a broom after her," she added, "need be."

"Helen is my assistant," the doctor finally replied. Mother left the room. The doctor winked at me. "Helen specializes in carrying diseases away and disposing of them," the doctor said.

"What if she takes one on she can't get rid of?" I asked. I didn't believe the fool doctor, but I asked anyway. He must have thought I was an imbecile or no older than Jelly. Maybe he thought my mind was done gone from the typhoid.

"I take them out of her when we get back to the office," the doctor said. "This is from Jimmy," he added, handing me the folded-up note. "Jimmy has took up residence behind the second floor window. I guess the front door was too close to the light. He raps with his knuckles when people walk by. No one can hear him, and they just go on now they've stopped gawking. I would have never seen him, but he opened the window and threw this at me."

The doctor reached in his pocket and pulled out a pecan. "Addled as he is, he's a dead aim. I didn't appreciate his use of my head as a target. I hollered at him to leave off this nonsense, but he wouldn't come outside, even in this dark sky," the doctor laughed, shaking his head. "I said, 'I'm not moving an inch until you come down those stairs.' Jimmy threw another pecan at me, then a note in a shoe box. I got it unfolded and seen it was for you. Helen got a little wet in front of the hotel, and when I put her and the letter in my satchel she got it muddy.

"I trust it is still legible?" the doctor said, handing it to me. I opened the envelope without tearing it up much, and the ink hadn't run.

> By the time you read this it will be raining. Don't let on to the others. Our sickness coincides so. we got to make plans. I always knowed we suffered from the same disease. I take my meals inside the hotel with Gar. Please come over and eat. With us soon as you are well. I will say then what happens when the sun has you or may bee you already know from your fever. The window is almost black now.

"I'm going to give you some opium," the doctor said, "to relieve the pain of the diarrhea and help you get some sleep. Until we get this stopped," he said, tapping a syringe, "it's still liquids only." He was eyeing the lunch sack on the other bed. From the schoolkids on the porch. I didn't know how it got inside the house. "We're trying to avoid any more intestinal hemorrhaging," he said to Father, standing in the doorway now. The doctor tightened the rubber hose around my arm. I watched the needle pull back, take some of my blood with it, then the little black plunger give it back.

———

Mary says you can't hardly get from one end of the hotel to the other without tripping over him he hangs around the front door all day and tries to call people over who pass on the street. He won't let as much as an elbow out into the sun so often as not they can't see who's calling from the shadows by now naturally the whole town has discussed it enough that he don't need to step out into the sunlight and show hisself it's got to where they cross over to the train station so they can pretend they don't hear him folks got no patience for someone who was near dead if he survives to tell about it and Jimmy's told so many of them that they've beat a new path to the drugstore who's ever seen Jimmy inside the hotel he never even as much as sat down to eat in there before he got heat touched as soon as he got a plate fixed he useta pick it up and walk out in the front of the hotel plate in hand lean up against the peach tree and whistle while he was eating in any weather short of a tornado if it was raining he'd stand as far as he could toward the edge of the porch without getting wet the boy took on too many of his habits sleeping and eating outside the only time Jimmy came in was to go to bed and in the summer he didn't do that kept the kid awake half the night talking out there on the porch you'd a thought he lived there. Now he wouldn't go out if the place was afire.

When the voices grew fainter, the room tilted, like in between the frames when you turn a kaleidoscope, just before you get to the next picture. When they all came back in focus, Helen the chihauhau stood up on her hind feet and did the Mexican hat dance next to me without a hat. "Steady, Helen," the doctor said, placing the stethoscope up to her hummingbird heart. "She has taken the disease now," said the doctor. "So we might as well gather on the porch since the rain has let up for a spell."

He held out his hand, and I arose. Jelly had come in from school, and she took mine, and we made a procession down our hallway. The pictures of Mama and her kin were back on the walls, and I smiled. Mama had diamonds in her teeth when she smiled back from her portrait. My stepmother tried to take her picture back down, and the doctor barked, "It stays up, Juliette. Doctor's orders. He'll have a setback fever a hunnerd and four." Mother's hand snuck back in her apron. The doctor pulled us into the living room and up to the front door. He turned loose of my hand and grabbed on to the doorknob. Instead of opening, the handle stretched away from the door like pulled taffy. I grinned. The doctor set Helen down on the floor. She pawed at the door, and it swung open.

People had gathered on the porch, adults this time. Father was holding an open bank ledger, erasing a sum. Gar was fanning Uncle Jimmy to cool him off, even though rain was pouring off the end of the porch. Aunt Mary cradled an armful of fresh-cut willow boughs. Mother was out in the rain, again chasing the guineas, running them in the direction of the lightning flashes, her broom spinning above her head like a weather vane. Uncle Jimmy stepped forward to lead the singing. "Lord, god it's a-ketchin'," he sang, directing the others with one of his dulcimer sticks, and they joined in one by one.

Father set down his ledger on the porch swing and led the second chorus, "You can't trade a fever for a rick of wood."

Gar carefully placed his fan next to the bank ledger and sang, "A fever can rise only as high as Claremore Mound."

Mary managed to find room for the willow boughs which smelled fresh cut and wet. "God-all-Friday, you got Tyford fever," she sang, leading verse four.

Helen stamped her feet and yipped, "He don't neither, gave it to me!"

Mother ran up on the porch and took the broom after Helen, singing, "Mr. High-and-Mighty thought he'd never catch it." That ended the singing when one of the guineas got between Mother and Helen and flew up in Mother's face, causing her to drop the broom. The guinea run Mother off of the porch and treed her in the catalpa, where Mother squawked and flapped on a sway-ing branch. Helen made a leap all the way over the porch steps and jumped up and down at the foot of the tree trunk, baying like a sixty-pound blue-tick hound while the guinea flew at the trunk. I held Jimmy's note out in front of me and read it to the assembly for Jimmy's approval. My throat hurt. I coughed.

"Go on," Jimmy said.

> Learning to write is well. nigh impossible at my age. A bachelor may have a will but what good is it if a man gains the whole world but has no one to pass it on to? If you learn. to write. better than I can I will leave you the hotel, Lynnsey. You can leave it and keep from burning up maybe. Damn her eyes she oughter done you better than that anyway.

Mother cawed up in the catalpa tree. When I looked back down a scorpion was crawling on Jimmy's note. I held the piece of paper over the porch rail to wash away the scorpion in the downpour. Instead of being swept off the paper onto the ground, the scorpion grew larger as it climbed up raindrops skyward. It stopped raining, and the scorpion fell with a splash into a grassy puddle. I ran out to the barn and came back with a pitchfork. I anchored its tail down with the tines. I lassoed its body the way Fearless Frank roped wild buffalo, except he called them "bufflers," and I tied off to the porch, stretching the scorpion out between pitchfork and lariat like a header and heeler does a steer at a jackpot roping. None of Will's show twirling—working cowboy stuff. Gar was rubbing his chin, studying my technique approvingly. He had an Indian's beard, the kind you could grow until the day you died and it would only get so long, a wholly different kind of business than a white man's whiskers. Full-bloods grew everything in patches, from corn hills to their wild little beards. "That's good," Gar said, observing my roping.

"Did you use a double-hitch on him?" Father asked.

"That tail will make a right smart hat plume," Mary beamed, "if I can shrink it down to size."

"This won't get you out of your chores any more than that fever," Mother sneezed from up in the tree.

"Lord God it's a-ketchin'," Helen barked hopefully, but she soon forgot about Mother and was lunging at the front end of the staked-out bug as Doc was trying to round her up before she got too close to the twitching speared tail.

"Leave *that* disease alone," Doc yelled, but it was too late. Helen had agitated the bug so that its writhing had severed it from the pitchfork. The tail end was alive, just barely, and shrunk down to Mary's hat size.

The tail made a little hop, not very scary at first, towards me. I backed toward the porch steps, afraid to turn my back on what was left of the bug.

Each step I took backwards, the tail's leap increased in speed and height. I stumbled on the steps, and the tail landed on my shirt collar. Mary batted at it with a willow bough, and I felt a stinging slap on my rose spots when she missed the bug entirely. I buttoned my shirt back up.

I felt the scorpion just edging over my shirt collar and touching my neck when I woke up screaming in Jelly's bed.

Except it felt like months later. Something was different about the light in the room, the light of another season, longer shadows, another sun coming in through the window. There was a knock on the back door. A voice called out for Mother. It was Gar. Mother didn't let fullbloods in the house, which was why Gar had come around back.

I could hear my tongue-tied cousin Chet stuttering a whole wagonload of nonsense. Chet wasn't allowed in either, along with Mary, who wasn't an Indian or an idiot, but acted like both according to Mother. Maybe the only thing Mother and Mary had in common was that Mary had her own dose of the high and mighty, as Father called it, where Gar was concerned because he was a dark Indian and where Chet was concerned because he was bad luck, especially around babies.

Chet's birth was marked. The morning Chet was born Mother had seen a brood cow licking her long dead calf, flies buzzing around its swollen tongue, the stupid cow carrying on as if she had just delivered. This was in the field of Chet's daddy. Chet was about the only thing Mother and Mary agreed on. I don't know why Mother didn't let Jimmy in the house. She didn't need a reason for him.

Gar must have given up on Mother because he started calling, "Lynn," and Chet started in raising a ruckus—as if Gar needed any help. Chet could get everything between Claremore and Oologah in a single sentence. You could understand the stuttered words once you got as used to him as we all had, but nobody else knew how to put any of it into any order that made sense. The less he made himself understood, the more Chet talked. He seemed to think spreading it thicker would make up for how little it meant. If Mother was here she would say, as she always did, "Lord god, it's an idiot and an Indian," and refuse to go to the door. Father and I always answered.

I sat up on Jelly's bed and thought about standing, but nothing happened. The rough splinters of the board floor felt good on my bare feet, and, sitting up, my back hurt from laying around so long, but I felt good otherwise. I was hungry. I wanted a piece of salt pork. I craved salt and gristle.

I found myself on my feet. My shaky legs were crossing the room, and it was like I was mounted on them the way you would ride a horse, the horse carrying you rather than your own body. I was of a mind to tell my legs to get back into bed, but I decided against it. I walked down the hallway past the portraits of Mother's relatives. My own mama, and her kin, had long ago disappeared off the walls. I wondered if my own photo had already been removed. I looked in Father's room, and it was still sitting on the nightstand. Maybe I was coming back.

I made it all the way to the screen door. I felt like my legs somewhat belonged to me now, so I opened the door wide against Mother's orders. I had been around Indians all my life; both my mother and stepmother was Indian; I didn't see what difference it made if they were in my living room. Gar wasn't much darker than Mother, but Mother had set her mind on higher things.

Gar and Chet didn't come in, even though I invited them. Chet was shifting from foot to foot; he'd bunched up like a horse does when he can't make up his mind whether or not to jump a ditch. "She ain't here," I said "Come on in." I was about to take Chet's hand and pull him through the door when I saw the yellow Jersey cow with a corn-husk mattress on its back tied to the front porch.

"What you got there?" I asked.

"A cow and a mattress," Gar said, as if Claremore had been founded for no less than the transport of beds on the backs of cattle. "How long you been in your right mind?"

"Where are you going with it?" I replied, since I didn't know the answer to Gar's question.

"I'm moving in with Jimmy," Gar said. "I'm going to run errands for him since he won't go outside. Mary said all the beds were took, so I brought my own. I wanna borry your wagon the rest of the way."

"I can run errands for Jimmy myself," I insisted, "soon as I'm better. Father isn't here to borry you the wagon." I couldn't imagine Mary letting Gar move in the hotel.

"Jimmy said to have you hitch up and drive us over."

"Drive over?" I said. I couldn't remember how long I had been in bed, if it had been weeks or months. "Don't he know I'm sick?"

"'pears not," Gar answered. "Come over and see for yourself."

I went to my room and threw off the nightshirt. I was a pale skeleton, but I was no longer spotted. I glanced in the mirror at the hollow-eyed, shrunken reflection. It wasn't me, but it stared back just the same. I would be outside with Jimmy again, get some sun, darken up. The pants and shirt I put on felt good, much better than the cast-off bedclothes now lying in a heap on the floor. Mother would tear into me for leaving them there, which is why I didn't pick them up. My head itched, and I wanted a bath.

"Gar," I said, and he came inside, poking his head in me and Jelly's room. "Fetch me a twig off the sweetgum."

"That's the way," Gar nodded happily, and lit out for the back door. He came back, this time stepping into the room, and he placed his long brown fingers over my open palm. I could feel the leafy twig between us. I waited as long as I could before I took it. I went into the kitchen and poured some baking soda into my palm, brushing my teeth. I spat out the back of the house. I wanted to get rid of as much as I could.

I hadn't buttoned my shirt yet. So I started in on the top button, but my hands were shaking. I guess whatever had started in my legs hadn't spread up to my fingers yet.

"Let me help you with that," Gar said. Gar squinted down at the buttons, concentrating. I felt considerably poked and jabbed, but I relished pain that come from some other source than dysentery and fever. It felt good to hurt regular. "I never done this on no one else," Gar apologized.

"That's all right," I said. I took his fingers and moved them down to the last of the buttons. "I'll work on this one while you finish up," I said. I had touched his palm and now the other side of his hand. He pulled me over to a chair where he sat to do the final button.

When we got out on the porch I had to sit down on the swing. It looked so ordinary now—rails painted an ugly gray, concrete steps, a tin awning Mother claimed wasn't befitting of a banker's house. I was just as determined to get to Jimmy's, but my body had as much recovery as it could take for one day. "I'll never make it to the barn," I told Gar, "much less hitch up a mule and take a hold of the lines. You do it."

"It's not mine for to do with," Gar insisted. "We'll have to get along with this cow, I reckon. Chet couldn't get the hang of carrying the mattress the way it flops all over or we would have brung it ourselves. I'll carry you. Jimmy wants to see us."

Gar took a hold of me, swung me up, and I got my arm around his neck, but I couldn't see how we'd ever get all the way over to Jimmy's. Still Gar seemed plenty determined, and I guess by then there waddn't all that much of me left to lift. He carried me off the porch. I seemed to remember now the doctor having announced some days, or maybe weeks, ago my fever had broken. I couldn't recollect the last time I had been crouched over the bedpan, a position I had practically learned to sleep in.

I laid my head against Gar's neck. "Your hair is wet," he smiled. It was from washing up a little. I closed my eyes for awhile. I didn't want any distractions. I could feel Gar untying the Jersey with one hand. I felt the sun on my back and Gar's own heat pressed against me as he clucked for the cow to start moving.

"Steady the mattress," Gar shouted to Chet. It was like navigating a ship what with all to balance, carry, and steer. Instead of righting the load Chet took after the cow with his long hickory branch. He had nearly pulled down the whole tree, I guess, to get enough bough to keep from getting kicked. He was paying more attention to his hickory limb than the cow. It took two hands to manage the "switch," but Chet swatted the cow instead of balancing the mattress, and the cow jerked violently. Gar almost dropped me and barely kept hold of the lead.

"That cow's gonna kick your brains out," Gar said, "If you got any. Leave off with that hickory, and throw the mattress back on." Chet and the mattress wrestled about a day and a half, until finally the mattress gave up and ended up back on the Jersey. Chet had cussed up a blue streak, but with him you couldn't tell a string of curses from a month of sermons. Only Chet knew for sure he was cussing; the rest of us just had to take his word on it.

I closed my eyes again in order to concentrate on Gar whenever the envoy got back underway. Gar smelled sweet like tobacco. We must have come to the railroad tracks because I felt the cow balk. My face bumped against a tin of Garrett snuff in Gar's shirt pocket. It made me want a pinch though I didn't dip. I wondered when Gar started.

The back of Gar's shirt was wet from all his exertions. Gar leaned farther into the street and pulled the cow toward the tracks. I held on tighter. Gar tried sweet-talking her for a spell. "Come on, Flossie," he cooed, then said, "Aw, the hell with it. Chet, give her some of that heat!" Chet hesitated since he'd just been yelled at for working his branch, but once he understood he took after her, mumbling joyfully with each stinging lash since he'd given up the main trunk in the street and was down to a switch.

Gar's soaked cotton shirt was the only barrier between his skin and mine. With my eyes shut the shirt wasn't there, since I'd already seen him without it. My face was getting wet. I had my lips where I thought they oughta be. The snuff can was the pouch of gold hanging from Fearless Frank's neck. If we passed the stone-hewn schoolhouse, which we must have, the wheat elevator, the cotton gin, the row of white houses with screened in porches coming into town, I never knew it. It was just me and Gar hitched to a cow that was doing everything she could to keep us from ever getting to Jimmy's hotel—better than if someone paid her to stop us. Even Chet was doing his part. Every time he righted the mattress the Jersey stopped, and every time Chet fell back to give her a switching the mattress slipped off, and that's how we stuttered down the street, Chet dealing first with the mattress end of the cow and then the tail end.

Gar was starting to smell like pitched silage, a sweet fermentation I imme-diately took to. My lips moved against his shirt. My tongue darted out. I wrapped my arms even tighter around his back, pulling my face closer against him. Gar was dragging the cow with all his might. I wondered how long he could last.

Gar had changed. He had muscled up over the summer out in the country's hayfields, pitching up seventy-five-pound alfalfa bales into wagons. I had been there when he bucked hay for Father, on back of the wagon as a matter of fact where I drug the bales into the bed after he heaved them onboard. Dad had to stack them, but I helped a little. I was mostly along to see how it was done until I got bigger. Gar had them thrown aboard faster than I could drag them back. We both came in that night covered with straw dust, me sneezing and wheezing.

Mother had me go in the house and wash at the basin, but she wouldn't let Gar inside. Father and her argued, and he told her to have some decency, but, as usual, he gave in. I poured water from a galvanized iron bucket into the tin basin, plunged my face in, and swabbed with the washcloth hung over the side. After I got the straw dust out of my itching eyes, Mother had me take the basin full of dirty water out to Gar in the yard—her notion of decency.

"Sorry," I apologized to Gar, as he took off his shirt. He shook his head back and forth to get some of the chaff out of his ears. He took the washcloth I offered him gratefully and breathed a sigh of relief when he wiped the dust from his eyes. I held his shirt while he ran the rag in circles over his face and chest.

"That's the first I've seen clear all day," he said.

"Me, too," I had replied, watching his silhouette as it got darker. When he finished Gar threw the washrag into the basin of dirty water.

"Tell your ma thanks," he said. I handed him the shirt. "No sense putting that back on," he added, rolled it up, then disappeared into the night, swallowed by the din of cicadas and darkness. I picked up the washrag and smelled it, searching for some trace of him, but it was lost in the burning scent of lye.

Now I had a hold of him in broad daylight on Claremore's main street. A clock chimed the noon hour, so I knew he had made it as far as the brick state bank where Father would be inside working. Boots were clomping up its wooden sidewalk toward the door. I opened my eyes for appearance's sake. The carrot-topped Emmett twins, Banger and Pounder, were sitting on the bank bench, throwing a penknife into the dirt, trying to make it stick. "Red on the head like the dick of a dog," Gar chanted below his breath.

"It's my turn," Banger was saying, trying to grab the knife.

"Don't think for a minute I won't stick you," Pounder threatened just as Mrs. Emmett walked out of the front door of the bank looking like she had something hidden on her. That's how white people always look like coming out of a bank. They might as well wear a sign: "Rob me, I'm loaded." If Indians wore a sign it would say, "Rob me fast; I'm fixing to spend it within the next hunnerd yards."

"Let's get going, boys," Mrs. Emmett said, as if they were always fixing to stab each other. She was in a hurry with her loot. Banger had a hold of Pounder's arm and twisted until he almost had his feet lifting off the ground before Pounder turned loose, and he somehow managed to throw the knife, but it went wild in a sideways arc. I couldn't believe it; the knife stuck when it landed in a nice easy loop in front of Chet's feet. Chet picked it up and folded it, handing it to Mrs. Emmett. Even Chet wasn't that stupid. Anyone could see them two wasn't meant for steel blades.

Both of the boys started in wanting it back, and I was hoping to get out of there before they had their own mother wrestled to the ground. Banger's attention had turned to us, though. "Look at that near-growed boy carried like a baby," he said, as if knifing his brother made him more grown up than everyone else.

"That Indian is too dark to be his mama," Pounder chimed in.

"That's not very neighborly," Mrs. Emmett said. "That's Mr. Riggs's son, and he's no more of an Indian than we are. He's been sick." She didn't mention Gar or Chet. "Nice to see you out, Lynn," she said, as if mattresses were herded past the state bank on a regular basis. When you are the banker's son people don't ask as many questions.

Mr. Lawyer Hoskins, a friend of Father's, came out of the bank. He could ask as many questions as he wanted. Gar had started our envoy back up, so Lawyer Hoskins had a full view of the ass-end of our proceedings.

"Whoa!" he called out. "There are laws governing the undue use of milk cows as beasts of burden!"

Gar stopped, but he didn't turn around. I could see over Gar's shoulder that this made Lawyer Hoskins mad. He came forward for a closer inspection. He was the only man in Claremore who ever carried a briefcase. When he bent forward to get a closer look, his spectacles liked to have slid off the end of his nose.

"What's your destination with this illegal load?" Lawyer Hoskins asked. He thought he was borned funny. He didn't know bullies don't make people laugh, generally speaking.

"I'm bringing my bedding over to the hotel," Gar said. "Moving in to help Jimmy."

"Moving in?" Hoskins laughed. "Did you ever know an Indian to stay at that hotel?" he asked, his eyes on Gar.

"Yes," Gar said, not bothering to explain who that might have been.

"No sooner will you get to that hotel than Mary will turn that cow right back around."

"Jimmy wants me to move in."

"Jimmy is sun-addled," Lawyer Hoskins said. "And it must be catching. On the other hand, we haven't had a parade since the Fourth of July, so feel free. We'll get to see you coming and going. Maybe a goat cart will join you on the way back, or a little red fire truck. Carry on with your load."

"That's just what I aim to do," Gar said. "This boy ain't seen his uncle since they both took sick."

"His father might be interested to know you've drug him out of bed. Maybe I should go in the bank here and get him."

"Tell him we're over at Mary's," Gar said, leaving off the Miss. "If he's inersted."

Gar picked me back up, gave the Jersey a tug, and said, "Come on, Chet." We were moving again. The hotel faced the red-gabled railway station. I could see as we got closer that people had gathered for the 5:15 Katy from Muskogee.

Chet was a fool for watching a train arrive. It was the wheels turning as it went by that put him in a trance. When one was coming in he'd run up and down the tracks until it got there and stop dead still the minute it passed, a finger pointed at the spinning, clanging iron rushing by him. As soon as the train stopped it was like nothing ever happened; it held no more power over him.

A little boy with a satchel followed on Chet's heels. I knew any minute Chet would bolt and start running the tracks as soon as he heard the whistle on the edge of town. The boy was tugging on Chet's overall pocket, which was always hanging out. "I'm going to Sapulpa, mister," the boy said. "Whur are you off to?" Chet didn't want to be bothered; he had his head cocked for the train. If we lost him we might get to the hotel easier, since it wasn't entirely clear if Chet was herding the cow or we were herding Chet. Maybe Gar had all of us on a lead rope, pulling us toward Jimmy.

Chet started in on his Tower of Babel train schedule. Where his knowledge of all the train stops and its times came from I never could figure out, since he had never ridden it. He also managed to get in every person he'd ever known who had been onboard and why. The little boy had a hold of Chet's turned-out pocket like he was part of our procession. Chet took his hand away.

"Getta low now," Chet said, trying to shoo the kid off, but he had grabbed back on. "Train's a-comin' been comin'. Inola's a stop long running 6:15 am of a breakfast. Jess rode it to see Brad off to school in Norman ain't light out that early he kept following Brad to Norman. Daylight's later in winter fifteen minutes to unload and put on new bags pull the cross arm down before it leaves I seen the black greasy f-f-f-f-fireman come in and drink from a bucket a water. Is your mama in Sapulpa better grow on over to the station Talala is the furthest Dunc ever run off to but his uncle was waiting and rode him back to Claremore tied to the seat of his buckboard. Katy and Frisco cross tracks at Muskogee that Inez girl they say couldn't be accosted for the same night Suggs Aker was seen lighting off the train at Watova where there isn't a stop and walking into the woods when they run cows off the track he might drink some it leaves at 4:37."

The little boy looked up at Chet, but he never turned loose. "Are you feeble-minded, mister?"

"He gets agitated when the train comes," Gar said. "And you're holding him up." Gar just wanted the kid to go away. Chet usually was a sight worse. His speech improved considerably around trains. They cleared Chet's mind for a single subject and freed him somewhat from his stammer. Apart from the railway station whatever came out was a language best suited for Chet and no one else. It was like the forward motion of the train carried Chet's mind in a single direction that followed the tracks of passengers and freight cars.

The whistle sounded, and Chet dropped his willow bough. What had once been Chet's pocket in the little boy's hand was now an empty grasp. By the time the kid's arm fell to his side Chet was running the tracks; we had lost him. The kid sat down his satchel and switched hands. "That man ain't right in his mind," the boy said, picked the satchel back up, and walked toward the raised platform where other passengers waited.

Nobody was on the porch of the hotel. We walked around back where the building pushed out into a wide gully, then the back of the alley. On the other side was the half-finished pole barn, cedar posts scattered in the caked dirt. "I can walk now that we're here," I said. I didn't want Jimmy to see me carried.

Gar put me down. "Hold on to this cow while I set the mattress out of the dirt. She won't go nowhere." A massive sandstone kitchen on the ground level held up the top floor of the hotel. On the second floor was a door and a tiny platform where a stairway zigzagged its way to the ground, a rickety one built out of barn lumber. It led to a second platform before making its way to the ground. From its crest to the bottom, the stairway was like a crooked waterfall following an uneven streambed.

Gar drug the mattress over to where the stairs descended and leaned it up against the wall of the hotel. He walked the Jersey across the gully and tied her to one of the posts that held up the pole barn. He threw her some hay. "She'll stay put for a spell," he said.

Mary came out on the platform, her sleeves rolled up, and an iron skillet in her hand that she was scouring. "Oh, no you don't," she hollered, waving the skillet like she aimed to brain one or both of us. She bounded down the steps without touching the handrail, a regular circus tightwire act on that staircase. She landed in the middle of her overgrown honeysuckle tendrils as if she'd skipped the middle platform and the steps in between. The honeysuckle had wrapped around a rusty tin drum where she sat her skillet. Mary charged out between two dusty lilac bushes, headed straight for us.

"Hand over that boy," she said.

"I don't have him," Gar replied.

"Don't give me no lip; ain't got time for it," Mary threatened.

"Where you been, Aunt Mary?" I asked. Once she was gone there was no one around to take care of me, unless you counted Mother or Father.

"Me and your mother had a little disagreement," Mary answered, "over what might be referred to as proper medical care. She wanted to lock you up in the room; I wanted to keep you out on the porch and see to it you got in from damp weather. You seem to have recovered without me. More than likely without her, too. Jimmy might as well still be sick. I can't take his foolishness in here, trying to drive out the slightest sign of daylight. Much more of this and we'll have to get him a room at the nuthouse in Vinita. I reckon they can find one plenty dark in there."

"He's not crazy, Mary," Gar said. "Just sun struck."

"Don't start in with the Indian nonsense," Mary told him. It appeared they had argued this before. "What are you doing with that mattress?"

"Jimmy asked me to move in with him," Gar confessed. "And he says he has to see Lynn."

"You'd think the man was dying the way he's gathering his loved ones around him. He's helpless enough without you living here like his nurse." But Mary sounded less than sure. I was surprised she didn't tell Gar she couldn't afford to upset her white guests.

Then I heard Jimmy's voice. For weeks I had only known it in my dreams. A muffled cry of "Is that the boys?" was coming from the second floor of the hotel. Jimmy sounded like he was lost in the dark.

I wanted to run and see what was the matter, but Mary seemed undisturbed, and she hollered at the top of her lungs, "We're not at your beck and call! Come out and see for yourself!"

"We got that barn to finish," Mary said, "and here I can't get him out the front or back door." A hand appeared in a second floor window, motioning us to come in.

"How long has it been since you ate anything?" Mary asked.

"This morning," Gar said.

"I don't mean you. I know you'd never miss a meal."

"I had some broth last night."

"I mean real food, not what your mother fixes. She could kill a healthy man, much less a sick boy. Come in here and eat."

I was still looking up where the hand had been. It appeared again, beckoning us in. Sitting down to eat first didn't seem like such a bad idea. I needed to garner some strength.

"Pick him back up, Gar."

"Says he can walk hisself now." Gar didn't seem to be taking no more mess from Mary. We walked into the kitchen. It was walled and floored in natural rock, field stones farmers had been glad to get rid of when the hotel was built. Walking to the table was like stepping down a creek bed of even stones— Jimmy's idea, and I'd helped him plane them. Mary seated us at the pine table Jimmy had built. I remembered the day he came back from the sawmill. I had handed him the boards off the back of the wagon, and we made the table right out in front of the hotel. Me and Jimmy sanded and varnished it, carrying it up on the porch in between coats so it didn't get rained on. It seated twelve people. The hotel didn't usually feed any more than that.

"Alright, let's get some food inside you," Mary said. I could smell pinto beans. More often than not I was sick of beans, but I would sure eat some right then if they were set in front of me. There was some meat sizzling and Mary must have put her scoured skillet to use. It smelled like a fried pork chop. I knew what that would taste like, breaded, salted and peppered.

I watched Mary in the kitchen, and she pushed some logs to the back of the chimney and shoveled the coals toward the front. She put some unshucked roasting ears right on top of the coals. I thought I might fall out of my chair before I got something to eat. My head was swimming, and I started to imagine those ears of corn grunting while they rolled around in a mess of butter like shoats in a mud hole.

Mary came out and filled two glasses with buttermilk, and Gar sat down beside me. Mary didn't say anything. He usually ate out back with Chet. I didn't understand. Mary was acting like an Indian. If there's one thing you can count on if you're at any of your Indian kinfolks' that acts like Indians, they'll feed you or anyone else that comes into their house, white or Indian alike. If they're eating, they'll offer you some, and you better take a little, too. It was only whites who didn't sit down and eat with Indians. I couldn't figure what all had happened at the hotel in the few weeks I had been away.

It don't take corn long sitting on live coals like that, which I reckoned was the reason she put them there rather than waiting for water to boil on top of the wood stove. Mary brought them out heaped up on a platter and set them in front of me and Gar, some of the husks still smoking. I didn't wait for the butter, and I burnt my fingers on the blackened shucks. Mary had a white porcelain bowl of steaming brown beans on the table, too. "Eat some beans while the corn's cooling off," Gar said. "It ain't going nowhere." Gar spooned some beans in my bowl, then his. He was blowing on his.

"Better get you some of that corn," I said.

"I gotta hold off on the corn," he replied.

"Still too hot?"

"We ain't touched medicine yet for that," he said quietly.

"You been sick, too?" I asked.

"He means Indian medicine," Mary said, setting down a plate with the pork chops. "Now, hush and eat." Gar speared one on the end of his fork. He wasn't shy about pork, whatever he had against corn. "Go slow and don't take too much," Mary advised. "This ain't your last supper, though we were beginning to wonder. You and Jimmy need to stop conspiring to take sick at the same time—you could work in shifts if you don't mind so the rest of us can still tend to our business. It looks like you got your mind back at least. I'm not so sure about your uncle."

"They say a person who is touched by the sun sometimes takes the fire into his mind even after his body recovers," Gar said. "You can cool down the flesh, but the thoughts go on burning."

"All I know is the bills don't stop on account of a sunstroke. I've given up and let Gar take over where Jimmy's concerned," Mary told me. "I don't have time for your uncle's foolishness and a hotel both. Someone's gotta keep the place going. If Jimmy wants a nursemaid Gar can run after him. I've got other things to do. Gar, you'll have to stay in Jimmy's room, though. You're not taking up a guest room that I can let out."

"Me and him done considered that," Gar said. Somehow, in the few weeks I had been sick, Gar had taken my uncle from me. I wondered who I belonged to now. The sadness I had begun feeling had to compete with starvation from weeks of liquids and little solid food. I was finishing up with ripe tomatoes from the garden and red juice was running all over my plate. I chased after it with a piece of cornbread. I could smell thick, green, entangled vines. Some strength came back to me; my hands had quit shaking. I could have fallen over backwards in my chair I was so full, and I wanted to sleep. My head was nodding when I heard Jimmy's voice, "Lynn, are you coming up?" He must have been standing at the top of the stairs.

"Why don't he come down?" I asked sleepily.

"He's got his room fixed to where he likes it," Gar said. "We'll have to go up." Gar seemed to know all about Jimmy these days.

"I'm full as a little old tick," I said. I stood up from the table when I could have just as easily crawled under it and went straight to sleep. At least the world didn't spin anymore, and Gar and Mary didn't look like they were standing on the other side of a dream, the way I'd seen everyone who hovered over my cot. When we got to the stairwell I almost stumbled over a box at the bottom of the landing. More were stacked next to the china hutch. "Who's moving out?" I asked, thinking one of the long-term boarders was leaving.

"Jimmy's moving all his things into the room he has fixed up," Gar said. "And some of it is mine." I looked at Mary, and she shrugged. "I'm finished taking care of him," she said. "If he's quit working outside, I'm quit feeding him. I work for paying guests."

"He's working indoors now," Gar said.

"That's women's work. We need a man around the place. That barn has to be finished for one thing."

"I can do the outside work," Gar answered.

"How are you gonna do that when he has you waiting on him hand and foot or running all over the countryside on account of he's so scared of daylight?" Mary offered her hand up the stairs, but I told her I was fine. She grabbed on to me anyway, and Gar was behind me. Everyone was pulling me toward Jimmy.

"I'll get him to go outside again," I thought, but I was starting to wonder. Surely Jimmy couldn't stay away from the spring, where there were perch to catch, crawdads to gig, wild onions to pick in the spring, and no bossy women anywhere to be seen. It was only a matter of time.

Someone had painted yellow daffodils against a white background along the whole length of the stairway handrail. The hotel had never had much in the way of decoration. It offered people a bed, something to eat, and a place to clean up, rather than sweet smells and pretty knick knacks. Gar saw me looking. "Painting's kind of Jimmy's new specialty," Gar said.

I had a hard time imagining Jimmy with a little hand brush painting delicate flowers on rough-hewn pine. I'd seen him drive fenceposts with a sledge hammer, brain a hog and hoist it up on a cross beam to bleed it, pull out tree stumps with a mule team, shoot a squirrel in midair as it was leaping for a safe branch, but I'd never known him to paint tiny flowers or spend any more time inside a building than it took him to sleep at night. Often as not he slept outside, and he was the one who spoiled me for the sounds of crickets in the grass, cicadas in the trees, coyotes howling in the fields. We had spent more nights on the hotel's front porch than inside either one of our houses. Every morning we would wake up to Mary pounding one of her rugs she had thrown over the porch rail with a broom and her cussing, "Dammit, this ain't a bedroom." Or she would say to me, "Ain't you got a mother?" and Jimmy would stretch and yawn, saying, "Yeah, that's the problem."

At the top of the stairs I put my hand on the doorknob where I'd seen Jimmy beckoning us from outside. "He's not in that one," Gar said. "Too much sunlight."

"But I saw him," I protested.

"He only waved us in from there," Gar said.

"Why didn't he wave from his own room?" I asked.

"He caint," Mary replied disgustedly. The door was open to one of the rooms where Gar walked in and disappeared. The only light was from the hallway. Jimmy was standing close enough to the door where I could see him winding an alarm clock. I had wanted to see him for weeks, but I hesitated in the hall. "Well, you're here now. I'll leave you men to yourselves," Mary said with amusement, then left to go down the stairs.

"Where are your windows, Uncle Jimmy?" It felt like there was no way out of the room, even with the door open.

"Come in, Lynn. What I have isn't catching. You've already had it." Jimmy was paler in just the few weeks since I'd last seen him. He looked too white for my liking. I thought he would be red, but the sun must have passed out of him. He had his hair slicked back neatly like he was going out, instead of his usual porcupine appearance, and he was dressed up in a vest with a watch fob, like a businessman.

"Going somewhere?" I asked.

"He takes care of the guests now," Gar answered for Jimmy from somewhere in the room, "on the inside." That was Mary's job. No wonder she was complaining.

"Here, I'll show you something," Jimmy said. I stepped just inside the door. Once in the room a minute I could see Gar sitting on the bed against the far wall. Jimmy put down the clock on top of a dresser and opened a drawer, pulling out a woman's nail file. Where on earth had he gotten that? I remembered the barrette I'd hidden long before I took sick. I had been reading *Deadwood Dick* then.

Jimmy stepped quickly to the other side of the room. I heard the soft little rasps of the file scratching glass. Except there was no window anymore. It was painted over black. Both of them were. "I'll just let a little in so you can see." Jimmy stepped back from his efforts. He had a lot to work around, so he'd scraped a zigzagged lightning bolt just big enough to let in enough light to reveal that the window was hung with pictures of my mother, a champagne cork dangling on a string, a swatch of calico, a blue fan painted on cardboard, a yarn Santa Claus with the bell missing from his tasseled cap, a string of beads made out of pecan shells, and a cattail tied with dusty magenta ribbon.

Jimmy brushed off his hands. "That's how quickly you can get some of it on you," he said.

"Black paint?" I asked.

"Sunlight," he answered. I stepped closer to Jimmy's collection. In the center pane hung a snapshot of my mother by a fountain, water overflowing. Jimmy stood next to her, and he had Mama's bonnet, and Mama had Jimmy's best low-brimmed Stetson. Both acted like they was fixing to throw the other's hat into the fountain. It was a standoff. I was sitting on the ground, not old enough to walk, reaching up toward both hats. Father must have taken the picture.

"I'll get that painted again once you leave," Jimmy said, meaning where he'd let in a little sliver of light, and between that and my eyes growing accustomed to the dark I'd been able to see the things hanging in the window.

"I can stay and help," I offered. "We can sleep on the porch tonight."

"Gar can help me," Jimmy said, "here on the inside."

"The porch is shaded," I added. "Nights have been cool. Good sleeping weather." I threw that in even though I had barely known my nights for some time, since I had fought my way through dreams in another world that had its own weather unknown to the general population of Claremore. Jimmy might have been there, too, or maybe he hadn't ever come back.

"Sun falls on it in the morning," Jimmy frowned. "You ought to know that. Gar, come here, and you can do something for me." Gar rose off the bed. He had grown taller this summer, as tall as most Indian men. He hadn't quite filled out into his lanky frame yet; he still had some catching up to do with his body. I felt like a skinny little runt. "Come over here and look out from this line I scraped in the paint." Gar bent toward the window, his hands clasped behind his back. "What do you see?" Jimmy asked.

"The back stairs," Gar said. "Some of the landing if I look down."

"You knew that was out there before you painted it," I told Jimmy.

"I was beginning to forget," Jimmy replied sadly. "What's the spring like?"

"I haven't been there since I took sick."

"I want you to go down to the spring and come back and tell me about it."

"Today?" I asked.

"It don't need to be today," Jimmy said. "You ain't full well yet."

"What do you want to know about the spring?"

"You need to learn to take in everything," Jimmy told me. "Gar ain't much for describing it, though he's a good hand at most everything else. I'm going to have you tell me about it on a regular basis." I didn't know exactly how I'd do that. By the time you cooled off in the spring, once you started walking back home through the thick woods where no breezes stirred, you forgot how cool you'd been by the time you come out of the tree line, sweat dripping in your eyes. The hotel was even farther. I might forget what all I seen down there or get distracted by the heat. Maybe I'd have to bring something with me and write it all down. Or could be there was some way to commit it to memory like I done at school with facts and figures. Except most of those I ended up forgetting soon as I recited them back. I'd have to learn me some way to see things and remember.

"What do you think of my window?" Jimmy asked, proudly.

"I never seen that picture of my mother." It was the first window of its kind I had ever known, but I wasn't sure I oughta say that.

"You wouldn't sit still, but she refused to take the picture without you in it. Your father kept saying, 'He don't pose,' and your mother kept saying, 'It ain't that kind of picture.' We was always trying to have some fun, me and her, even during picture taking. You seemed to know better than to behave."

"What's all the other stuff?" I asked.

"Odds and ends I had Gar gather for me from outside."

"You aiming to start a collection?" I said.

"It's for recollection," Jimmy replied. "I don't want to forget. Some things are not needed, others are."

"Cain't you recollect the spring?" I asked, worried.

"It changes all the time," Jimmy said, "and I want you to keep up with it."

I hadn't thought about the spring changing much other than getting too cold in the winter to go down there. I guess if I studied it I'd have to admit when the leaves fell off the trees you could see through the woods different. It looked like now I was going to have to keep up with such doings. How'd Jimmy figure I'd be any better at it than Gar? What if I was a sight worse?

In the other blackened window frame were all the pictures of Mama that had been taken down in our house. Gar had been a crow, scavenging. How had he gotten these pictures? It had been years since I'd seen them anywhere except in my dreams, since they were thrown out so long ago. They must have been over here at the hotel all along. I walked to the window and stood there a long time, catching up. I had almost forgotten them.

I was standing there lost in the pictures when Gar said, "Is it time now, Jimmy?"

Jimmy sat down on the bed next to Gar. "Yes," he said. I wasn't paying much attention since I was studying my mother.

"I have your book," Jimmy said.

I wheeled around to face him. "You have *Deadwood Dick*?" I said, full of wonder. I had given it up for the trash heap, and I would be grateful to see even its two split halves.

"*Deadwood Dick*?" Jimmy laughed. "I think you're ready for something else." Jimmy went back to the dresser and threw the nail file in the top drawer. He pulled out a thin paper book, more of a pamphlet. It wasn't hard or soft bound, just folded. He walked over to the window and handed it to me.

A brown cover about the color of a feed sack and something like the same material had the words "Speaking Outside the Territory" written on it. I opened up the soft, floppy cover and a title page further explained "A Guide for Proper English and Books that Cultivate."

"A lady by the name of Alberta Halverson wrote that. She taught over at the Cherokee Female seminary. White woman from back east. She used it in her classes. She forgot it here at the hotel, then moved back home, and we didn't hear from her again."

"This is a book for girls," I said, disappointed.

"I never learned no more than I growed up on around here," Jimmy said. "You might want more than that." Jimmy had the dulcimer sticks in his hand now. The dulcimer was on its stand, pushed against a far wall. Jimmy carried it over to the bed and sat it down in front of Gar. After Jimmy took his seat next to Gar, he slid the dulcimer in front of himself, so he could play it. He patted the spot next to him. I came and sat down, the three of us together, and that's how we sung, all of us:

> Oh, bury me not on the lone prairie where
> The wild coyote may howl o'er me, where the
> Rattlesnakes hiss and the wind sports free,
> Oh, bury me not on the lone prairie.

While they were singing, I went and grabbed my guitar, which was standing in a dark corner. I kept it at the hotel since Mother didn't like music. Hadn't touched it since I'd been sick, even though a lot of music had gone through my head—notes that had hung in the room like motes of dust floating in a sunbeam, thousands of them but none that made up any one particular song. When I picked up my guitar, I figured it had to be out of tune considering the weeks it had gone unplayed. Sitting back down next to Jimmy and Gar, I made a D chord and let the open A string hum along, caught the F-sharp with my thumb on the low string, so I was ringing out all of them from top to bottom to check the tuning. All by yourself, an out-of-tune guitar isn't so much of a problem. With someone else playing along, the mismatched notes make waves of sound when something isn't right.

The D chord I played sitting next to Jimmy came out as nothing less than pure light.

Lightning

A Play in Two Acts

Act I

Norman's little frame train depot—early evening.

A steam locomotive is approaching a small one-floor station that flies an Oklahoma state flag from its wood-shingled roof. The station master opens the door and peeks out, then pulls a luggage cart out the door and onto the platform. A young woman in a bonnet—who is seated on a wooden bench on the platform and holding hands with her nervous boyfriend, who keeps pulling a watch and chain from his vest pocket and putting it back— suddenly stands up. A car starts to honk its horn in the dirt parking lot behind the building. People climb out of their cars and gather on the platform. Three young, rowdy farmers who've ignored the posted warnings to keep away from the tracks have pulled up near the rails and are draped over the hood of an old, rusty Model T—a country car, done in by caked red mud—laughing noisily. They look toward the direction of the train, and one stands up, takes off his fedora, waves it, and hollers.

FARMBOY

Here comes the Chief!

The FARMBOY tugs on his overall straps, beaming, as if he has just guided the train in from the night. As the whistle and steam wind down, the sound of cicadas in nearby trees mingles with cheerful voices as the arrivals are found and greeted. A young man is struggling off the train with a large trunk. A porter offers a hand, but the deboarding passenger seems protective of his cargo.

LYNN RIGGS

No, thanks.

He holds a silk handkerchief to his face against the dust, stirred up by arriving cars and wagons.

236

EILEEN YOST

Lynn Riggs, over here!

EILEEN is standing off from a cluster of laughing college men who have not been paying attention to her, the arrival of the train, or those disembarking. LYNN looks toward the voice, but ignores EILEEN, instead noticing her male friends, easily identified by their shining fraternity pins on vests and shirtwaists, and he begins dragging his burden toward them, grinning. LYNN speaks under his breath, admonishing himself.

LYNN RIGGS

Talk and smile. Don't act like a seed clod.

A booming voice, that of a sandy-haired youth in uncomfortably tight trousers, starched white shirt, black tie, and a Pi Kappa Alpha vest, yells confidently for LYNN to join them. The other brothers join in.

FRATERNITY BROTHERS

This way, Riggs. Step up old bird, and we'll try to get you back in time for house dinner! Have to put some weight on you or you'll never make All-Conference quarterback! Ha! Ha! We never pledged a poet before, but times are hard! You wouldn't be thinkin' of high-tonin' us and joining up with another fraternity, would ya? Welcome to the Varsity—that's what we call the U—you'll get used to it!

A frenzy of winking, back slapping, fierce handshakes, and arms thrown around LYNN's shoulders commences. EILEEN watches LYNN, who winces as a brother slings another arm around him. EILEEN, who is dressed in a white blouse and a blue skirt, uses the distraction as an opportunity to pull a hand mirror out of her bag and adjust a matching blue ribbon in her hair. She stands back smoking a cigarette while two of the fraternity brothers, BUN and TRUCKY, hoist LYNN's trunk on top of a roadster and strap it down. EILEEN grinds her cigarette under her high heel, walks over to the car, and waits for BUN to open the door, but he ignores her. LYNN hurries over and offers her a hand as she settles onto the seat. TRUCKY winks at LYNN.

TRUCKY

You sit next to Eileen. That'll keep you from joining up with the Megs.

BUN

Mr. Rollie Lynn Riggs, I present to you Eileen Yost, president of Delta Gamma sorority, and the girl whose name is most likely to get top billing in every brother's date book.

EILEEN glares at BUN, who is starting the car.

TRUCKY

She probably had to cancel a date just to be with us tonight. She sure keeps up the boys' morale, doesn't she, Bun?

BUN

Sure. Eileen, who did you stand up this evening?

EILEEN YOST

Oh, it's so hard to remember. What with library dates, Saturday morning and Saturday afternoon dates, dances on Saturday nights, Sunday breakfast dates, church dates, dinner dates, afternoon dates, sandwich dates, and evening church service dates. And that's just the weekend. Tomorrow . . .

TRUCKY

We get the picture. You're booked through Christmas.

> *The red dust shines in the car's headlights as they start down the dirt road toward the university. LYNN, squeezed between TRUCKY and EILEEN, holds his hat on his lap. EILEEN smiles at him.*

EILEEN YOST

Pay no mind to those two. They're windy as a couple of old coon dogs.

> *Lynn returns her smile, relaxes a bit in the back seat, and stretches his legs.*

EILEEN YOST

How was the train ride down?

LYNN RIGGS

Uneventful. We crossed your big, muddy river so many times I thought the train was going in circles.

BUN AND TRUCKY

What river?

EILEEN YOST

These foreigners! They couldn't tell the Canadian from the Cimarron.

> *EILEEN sighs in exasperation.*

EILEEN YOST

Both born outside the Territory.

LYNN RIGGS

Ah, U.S. citizens. Yes, I must agree—they are an indelicate dose of poison. Having become one myself a few short years after my birth, through no fault of my own, I'm sure of it. Yes, most indelicate.

EILEEN YOST

What a generation we are, Mr. Riggs! The doctor smacked our backsides—speaking of indelicate—and we drew our first breath outside the United States, in the Territory. But we were weaned on a new country, not of our choosing. The university, as a matter of fact, is only two miles west from the old border of what used to be Indian Territory.

LYNN RIGGS

The Chickasaw Nation, to be more precise.

TRUCKY

Hey, Bun, they're conspiring against us.

BUN

Yeah, me and Truck pay tuition. You two get it free because you're Oklahoma residents. Your lovely university isn't so high-toned it won't take our dough. Even from foreigners. Our money is the same as yours.

EILEEN YOST

Same money, different source. A beer-baron daddy in Wisconsin for our man Truck, and a string of Iowa grain elevators in the family of His Royal Bun. Perhaps we could have just as easily christened them bread and beer.

TRUCKY

How come you don't keep quiet like the other sisters?

EILEEN YOST

Because I don't have to.

> EILEEN *lights another cigarette. They turn south on University, a tree-lined avenue with a cement sidewalk, where college men carrying books for their girlfriends avoid oncoming cyclists.*

LYNN RIGGS

Any fatalities?

EILEEN YOST

No, but it's said that the real excitement was during the territorial days when the sidewalks were wooden and girls were always ripping their dresses on protruding nails. Frat boys would let loose with a catcall every time they heard the sound of tearing cotton. That tradition, thankfully, has passed away with the advent of cement. Although rumor has it that a certain rival sorority actually sends its sisters to stand on the sidewalk in hopes a young male cyclist will run one of them over. I prefer dinner and a movie. Now if

Rudolph Valentino was pedaling gaily along, I might throw myself in front of him, but why bang yourself up for a frat boy?

Ah, the old boardwalk. They say it used to be better than an alarm clock. Every morning you'd awaken to the old familiar plunk, plunk, plunk that told all within hearing distance it was time for classes to begin.

LYNN RIGGS

Here we are, Boyd Street, brick paved even. It's like a magic passageway from one world to another, from downtown banks and cotton gins to books and dreams.

TRUCKY AND BUN

And football. Here's Boyd field.

A full moon hangs over the small cluster of university buildings. Boys are coming in, pulling off pads and helmets after an evening of scrimmaging. In the distance, a new stadium is under construction. No permanent stands have arisen yet, but steel bleachers have been erected on the east side, and temporary wooden ones are being built on the west.

TRUCKY

This year is the first they've had those form-fitting leather helmets, thigh pads, and cleats. Coach Bennie Owens insisted if we keep facing off with giant Swedish farm boys like the Cornhusker linemen, we better put something on our light Oklahoma men. Before that, they just wore thick mole-skin britches and horse collars for shoulder pads. Maybe shin guards if they were lucky. They grew their hair out to soften concussions and just butted heads like old billy goats.

LYNN RIGGS

Not entirely unlike waiting to be run over.

The car turns down an elm-lined avenue, one of the two or three streets that have houses on them. BUN *pulls up to the fraternity house, where a resident catches a football and is chased around the flagpole by his frat brothers. On the porch, a group is playing bridge; others are lounging in chairs reading the sports page by kerosene lamp. The young men in the front yard charge up to the car, whooping and pounding on its hood when it stops in front of the house. One of them raps noisily on the window with his knuckles.*

FRATERNITY BROTHER

Hey, poet. Open up. We wanna take a look atcha.

LYNN climbs out and looks around. The FRATERNITY BROTHER *raises a football for a quick toss.*

FRATERNITY BROTHER

Poet, go out for a pass.

LYNN makes a run past the flagpole but fumbles an easy catch. Looks are exchanged between the men in the front yard. LYNN, *embarrassed, recovers and ambles over to the car and offers* EILEEN *a hand stepping out.*

EILEEN YOST

Thank you. I see someone around here still knows his manners. The sorority is just around the corner, so I'll be on my way. I'm afraid you'll have to defend yourself against the brutes, Mr. Riggs, without my assistance.

LYNN RIGGS

Well, my dear. This ride has exceeded all the joys of a severe toothache.

EILEEN YOST

Yeah, a real jaw-buster.

LEROY BOGGS

Hey, that's some kind of talk for a new pledge. Leroy Boggs's the name.

LEROY offers LYNN *a friendly handshake after introducing himself.*

LEROY BOGGS

I'm headed for the shower.

He picks up the football and winks at LYNN *before trotting up the front stairs. He tosses it underhand to* LYNN, *who catches it with both hands.*

LEROY BOGGS

We'll make a wide receiver out of you yet.

He is up the stairs in two bounds and in the house.

EILEEN YOST

Oh, gosh. I have to come in and get the list of names for the homecoming committee. Then I really must be off. New girl moving into our place, too.

BUN

I'll get you the list out of the office. But first let me take Riggs to his new room.

TRUCKY

Grab aholt, poet.

The two of them labor toward the house with the trunk.

In the foyer lies a guest book opened on a large white pedestal where visiting parents, mostly, have signed in. A looming oil painting of Senator Irvin Morrisson, class of 1910, is hung over the fireplace of the living room. Smaller framed photos of oil men, politicians, preachers, and professors— all former house members—line the walls. There are no Indians.

They turn down the hall, and LYNN's *room is at the end.* EILEEN *stands back as the men enter the small room which consists of two short wood frame beds, a single shared nightstand between them, and a room to the side whose door is cracked just enough to reveal a porcelain sink.* LYNN *drags his trunk to the foot of the bed on the unoccupied side of the room, adjacent to the tiny cupboard of a closet.*

The door of the bathroom swings open unexpectedly, and out steps LEROY, *barely covered in a skimpy towel and dripping water on the wood floor.* TRUCKY *motions toward the hallway, trying to get* LEROY's *attention, but* LEROY *is looking at* LYNN's *trunk, considering how much space it takes up in the cramped quarters.* LEROY *shakes water out of his dark, curly hair like a dog coming out of a creek. He looks at* LYNN, *eyes flashing.*

LEROY BOGGS

Hope I didn't get you wet none, poet. Mighty small quarters, ain't it? If you're gonna take to romancing the sorority sisters right away, we may have to write down a schedule. Then again, you can't get these nice campus girls within a mile of your room. And there are house rules. But if you're nice to old Truck here, once in a while a little something can be arranged. Poet, do you have any talcum powder in that trunk of yours? I seem to be all out.

> LYNN, *mouth agape, watches the little trail of water dripping off of* LEROY's *chin onto his chest. He tries not to stare at the bulging towel barely draped over* LEROY's *waist, and, instead, forces himself to look at the big wet footprints coming from the bathroom.* EILEEN *is standing in the hallway, hand over her mouth, stifling laughter until she can hold it no longer. She steps front and center into the room.*

LEROY BOGGS

WHAT IN THE NAME OF MIKE?!

> LEROY *looks around the room in a panic for something he might throw over himself, all the while backing toward the bathroom and clinging desperately to the skimpy towel, lest it should fall off during his hasty retreat.*

EILEEN YOST

Now that we're all on such very intimate terms, Mr. Riggs, I do believe I can begin calling you Lynn. Yes, and I shall always think of Leroy Boggs and the exact moment we all became so very well acquainted. Why, thank you, Leroy, for this little ice breaker. Everyone has always said that the Megs were the friendliest fraternity on campus, but I'm beginning to think otherwise. Now, Lynn, get the man his powder. You see, Lynn, your fraternity brothers are just like deer hunters. They are forever masking their true scent.

Basement of the fraternity house—one month later.

LYNN holds a letter in his hand. LEROY comes in the room.

LEROY BOGGS

These basement digs aren't so bad.

LYNN RIGGS

It's not the arrangements; it's the cooking and cleaning I have to do to keep them.

LEROY BOGGS

C'mon, you're not the first brother hard up enough to do house duty to pay the rent. There's always someone down here living on the cheaps and pulling KP upstairs. It's not like you got a rich daddy back home like Truck and Bun does. You'll be back upstairs with me in no time.

LYNN RIGGS

My father is, in fact, a man of means.

LEROY BOGGS

Hey, I didn't mean nuthin' by it! Whatcha got there, news from home?

LYNN RIGGS

Yes, the most recent announcement of my failings, served up like a brown existential porridge.

LEROY BOGGS

I'll remember that one next time I'm calling plays: "Calvin, you fake hard to the right, like a brown existential porridge."

LYNN reads the letter to LEROY.

LYNN RIGGS

Dear Son:

I will no more support your college expenses than I did your previous venture in Hollywood. You tell me that your mother and I have no business reporting on your affairs. Preventing a life of dreaming idly, playing guitar, writing poetry, and traipsing off to the West Coast for an insubstantial role in the moving pictures is more than our affair: it is our duty. I talked to Maud the other day, and she sees all the seeds in you that were apparent in Will as a boy; only Will had foolish notions of riding the open range after there was no more range left to ride. Like Clem with his Will, I could never get you to plow a field without finding you'd snuck off to read a book out in the end rows where you thought I couldn't see. Only Will had that darn trick rope in his hand instead of the volume of some poet who had caught his fancy. Will never made it past his beloved Deadwood Dick, like you did. One showman from Claremore is enough. And now we see, and I hope you see, what has become of Will's sense of loyalty after years among show people. You rode 1600 miles only to be cast as an extra in a film no one has ever heard of since. Your mother and I hoped and prayed that Norman represented a gradual return, but now I am tired of waiting. Come home at once, where sure opportunities in cattle or wheat or the bank are guaranteed by family and friends, rather than vague dreams that must be chased from here to Norman—or to the Pacific Ocean for that matter.

Sincerely,

Your father

LEROY BOGGS

Well, poet, looks like the well has run dry back home. Whatcha gonna do for funds? I know you ain't about to go back.

> *LYNN opens his trunk and pulls out a leather portfolio for keeping legal papers. He digs through it and holds up a document that reads "Cherokee Allotment Certificate."*

LYNN RIGGS

I haven't mortgaged this yet.

LEROY BOGGS

What is it?

LYNN RIGGS

My Cherokee allotment.

LEROY BOGGS

Will you still be Cherokee if you sell it?

LYNN RIGGS

I'll get it back. I'm just going to borrow money off of it.

The barn at UNCLE JIMMY's *farm—many years earlier.*

An overcast fall day is marked by a weak sun that has been trying to emerge from behind clouds. JIMMY, *a middle-aged man in overalls, with the bib unfastened and straps dangling, stands next to a barn, smoking a cigarette and examining river cane leaned up against the slab board wall. The man hands one of the canes to* YOUNG LYNN, *bending down and showing him a forged metal point on the end, a small three-pronged spear.*

UNCLE JIMMY

That's what you gonna poke that crawdad with. Gar Sixkiller's old man learned me to make these and told me all manner of thoughts about creeks. Real sharp, so be careful and don't trip with it.

YOUNG LYNN *takes it slowly, cautiously.*

YOUNG LYNN

How'd you make it sharp like that, Uncle Jimmy?

UNCLE JIMMY

I forged it in a f'ar. Then cooled it off and put an edge on it with a stone.

They walk toward the creek, YOUNG LYNN *ducking through a barbed wire fence while* JIMMY *holds the strands apart for him.*

Earlier that same summer.

JIMMY *and* YOUNG LYNN *stop before crossing the same fence. The man pauses to pull a green, fleshy bulb off of a weedy bush, opens it up with a penknife, and shows the boy how to eat out the doughy inside full of little black seeds, like a pomegranate but whiter when opened.*

The previous winter.

YOUNG LYNN *emerges through the fence again. The tree limbs are bare, the green leaves fallen off the post oaks and blackjacks. The only green to be seen is the occasional cedar; all else is brown and dormant.*

YOUNG LYNN

Everything's dead.

UNCLE JIMMY

Not everything. They's still a plant here and there if a body knows what he's looking for.

JIMMY helps YOUNG LYNN *down a steep gully.*

UNCLE JIMMY

Grab aholt of them tree roots.

He points to some black roots exposed by the wash out. The two of them come to the bank of the creek, and stone steps lead to a collar, fashioned out of a barrel, in the middle. YOUNG LYNN *stands still and watches the crappie hovering along the creek bottom.*

UNCLE JIMMY

I capped that spring just before you was borned. I used to keep bottles of beer cold in there and sneak off down here to drank a little bit. Nobody ever knowed the difference, and it didn't hurt 'em none either, far as I can tell. Here, I'll show you sump'n.

JIMMY rolls up his britches above his ankles and walks over the stones, bare-footed, toward the capped spring, YOUNG LYNN *in tow, both leaving their shoes on the bank.*

UNCLE JIMMY

You don't mind getting a little wet do you?

He has a hold on YOUNG LYNN's *free hand, and in the other hand* YOUNG LYNN *has his cane gig.*

UNCLE JIMMY

Set that down for a minute.

JIMMY faces the sun and dips his little finger into the shimmering surface of the water, framed by the collar, four times, each time touching his pinky to his tongue.

UNCLE JIMMY

Now, you touch water, boy.

YOUNG LYNN *looks inside the barrel. Unlike the rest of the creek, the water is crystal clear, and even in the dim fall light he can see the bottom of the stream, and the sand on the creek bottom bubbling up from the under-ground source beneath it. A water strider darts across the surface when* YOUNG LYNN *touches the rising and falling mirror as it changes shape and splashes over the sides of the collar. Even with the movement, so clear is the water that he can make out black pupae emerging on a rock at the bottom. He tastes the water four times, as instructed.*

UNCLE JIMMY

It's good to wash off in that.

YOUNG LYNN

But it's cold out.

UNCLE JIMMY

Good lord, you ain't gotta jump in clean up to your elbows.

JIMMY shows him, rinsing out his mouth, wetting his hair and slicking it back, splashing some on his face and arms. YOUNG LYNN follows suit. JIMMY points toward the sun, and YOUNG LYNN corrects himself, facing the right direction.

UNCLE JIMMY

That's enough for now, according to Gar's daddy. You can come back your-self whenever you take a notion. Down by the shoals is where we're headed. They pass a fast place on the creek where the water is clear, like back at the spring, but shallow and running over rocks.

I believe they is a sound in the water in that partic'lar spot where it splashes over the shoals that soothes your mind. It's like playing music, how it makes you feel better and eases up your loneliness a little.

YOUNG LYNN

Like when you play the dulcimer, Uncle?

UNCLE JIMMY

I reckon that's it, close as I can figure it. Over here is where we're aiming to go.

They wade down the middle of the creek. A heron lifts off downstream and rises into the sunlight still struggling to emerge out of a cloudy sky.

UNCLE JIMMY

That still pool, yonder.

JIMMY wades toward the spot, then stops and lets the mud settle. He bends over with his cane gig, peering into the water, the three-pronged metal tip just above the surface. He freezes, still as a statue, and the YOUNG LYNN tenses up like waiting for a fire cracker to explode. He looks up at the sun, and from the corner of his eye sees his uncle's sudden thrust. JIMMY sloshes over to YOUNG LYNN, *a wiggling red crawdad squirming on the end of his gig. He holds it out toward* YOUNG LYNN, *who looks down and squints at the crayfish.*

YOUNG LYNN

Don't amount to much, does it?

UNCLE JIMMY

JIMMY pulls off the tail of the crawdad, exposing the delicate white meat.

UNCLE JIMMY

I guarantee that if you put that tail meat on a hook, any self-respecting fish in these parts is gonna want to eat that.

He pops the morsel into his mouth.

UNCLE JIMMY

See, what I mean. I'm pretty fishy, and I done ate it. That's the closest either of us'll ever come to eating fancy Maine lobster in a restaurant.

YOUNG LYNN laughs, delighted.

YOUNG LYNN

I betcha I eat lobster in a fancy restaurant some day, Uncle.

UNCLE JIMMY

I hope you do, son. Save a bite for me.

They take a different path toward home, avoiding the steep gully. They pass through a cow pasture, dotted with persimmon trees, their orange globes weighing down limbs like the branches of over-decorated Christmas trees. The persimmons, on the trees and those fallen on the ground, fill the pasture with orange color, its grass yellowed and brittle. YOUNG LYNN picks up one of the fruits lying around and twirls it by the stem, and then, when it breaks off, picks it back up and practices tossing it one-handed in the air and batting it with a stick. He misses every time.

UNCLE JIMMY

Leave off batting my persimmons. Save it for the ball diamond.

YOUNG LYNN

But there's thousands of them. They'll just rot.

UNCLE JIMMY

That don't mean you need to go and beat the tar out of them with a stick. I oughta get you out here a-picking them up one by one and taking them to town to sell. That'd learn you not to knock the beejesus out of them.

> *The same field—the previous day.*
>
> YOUNG LYNN *and his cousins,* MATTIE *and* LEWIS, *are pulling persimmons off the trees and throwing them at each other, quickly dotting the ground with fallen fruit where there had been none before.* YOUNG LYNN *is losing and retreating, his cousins pummeling him with persimmons as he returns weak vollies, as he lacks their throwing strength and distance.* YOUNG LYNN *runs and hides in the woods for awhile, then makes his way over to a familiar blackberry bush that stretches halfway across the length of an entire fence line.*

YOUNG LYNN

(*To himself.*)
It's good I've scouted this field before. I've been through nearly every woods and briar patch in this country.

> *The blackberry bushes, where some vines have withered and died out, have a blighted center in the middle of the brambles.* YOUNG LYNN *knows just where to duck down and crawl toward the middle of the thicket, even though a clearing cannot be seen anywhere around the edge of the patch. He has done this before. His cousins come looking for him. He waits until* MATTIE *and* LEWIS *are standing directly in front of the tangled thorns, only a few feet away from where he has crouched down. He rises up from the center of the bush, and before his adversaries can gain their senses, bounces two fat, hard, green persimmons off the sides of each of their heads, and then ducks back down into the brambles.* MATTIE *and* LEWIS *madly run up and down the thicket, searching for a way in without getting torn to shreds. They pick up rocks and hurl them toward the center of the bushes, but by the time they fall through the tangled branches, the hurled stones have lost all their power.* YOUNG LYNN *laughs hysterically from the middle of his secret passage.*

> *Basement of the fraternity house.*
>
> LYNN *returns his allotment certificate to the portfolio and closes the trunk.*

LYNN RIGGS

I've got to go upstairs and finish KP.

> LEROY *follows him out of the small basement room and up the stairs into the kitchen.*

LEROY BOGGS

I've got more serious matters to talk to you about. Eileen and me had a date set for this Friday to go out for Cokes at the Varsity Club then head over to the Student Council Saturday night dance. I can't go. We have a golf tournament with the Megs after classes.

LYNN RIGGS

You'll be done before the dance, surely. You can't golf in the dark, can you?

LEROY BOGGS

I can't dance in the dark, either. All feet, forever tripping over myself. There's nothing that girl won't try to drag me off to and I'm running out of excuses. You're the man with all the fine words; what should I tell her?

LYNN RIGGS

You're not afraid of a suited-up Husker linebacker coming at you like a charging bull, but once around the dance floor with a ninety-pound sorority girl in an evening gown and a corsage has you sweating?

LEROY BOGGS

Yeah, those cornfed Swedish farm boys sure do outweigh and outsize us. We have to throw more forward passes against opponents that big.

LYNN RIGGS

You're a fullback, lean and light. You've got one up on them when it comes to running. A gazelle among elephants. You're a helluva punter, too. I remember when you booted the ball from deep in your own end zone, and the A&M crowd was chanting for a blocked kick. That punt exploded off your foot and spiraled overhead until I thought it had launched into the Milky Way. It traveled seventy-five yards on the fly.

LEROY BOGGS

I wish Coach Owens reserved such high praise for me. Say, poet, how come you don't go to the dance for me? Eileen likes you, and the sorority sisters nearly fight each other to get a dance with Gentleman Lynn. They say you're as pretty on your feet as a new-borned wobbly foal.

LEROY winks.

LYNN RIGGS

Hey, I don't coach your field moves, so don't razz my dance steps.

> *LYNN scoops up a handful of soapsuds and flings them at LEROY. They stick to the side of his face, and LEROY moves over toward LYNN and stands behind him, reaching around LYNN's waist and into the dishwater for a handful of suds to revenge himself. LYNN turns suddenly and faces LEROY, breathlessly.*

LYNN RIGGS

I could teach you.

LEROY BOGGS

Teach me what?

> *LEROY steps back, away from LYNN, and looks at him, puzzled. LYNN turns back around and starts washing dishes again, avoiding LEROY's stare.*

LYNN RIGGS

I could caddy for you.

LEROY BOGGS

Don't you want to go out with Eileen? You gotta help me out. It's either me or you with Eileen at the dance. I don't trust the brothers. She'll be safe with you, poet. The brothers are liable to put their dirty paws all over her. And if they ain't pawing her to death, some pretty boy who can glide all over the dance floor just might sweep her off her feet. And if some fine-dressed "gentleman" bringing her punch and talking her up don't steal her, then one of those Megs is just as likely to whisper all kinda dirty lies about me into her ear and scare her off of me and onto one of them. Some brothers, huh?

LYNN RIGGS

Well, she saw you step half-naked out of the shower the night of my arrival and that didn't frighten her off. Takes a pretty brave girl to see a skinny limb as sorry and scraggly and pale as all that and not run for cover. It sure scared me.

LEROY BOGGS

You've got a fine memory, poet. That bad, huh? C'mon, be a pal. If Gentleman Lynn, poet, scholar, high-steppin' ballroom dancer, and escort extraordinaire was to fill up her dance card all evening, then the brothers wouldn't take to swarming all over her.

> *Main Street Norman. Dance hall. Evening the following weekend.*
>
> *The entryway of a white stucco building is accented by a raised relief that simulates a gaudy painted pink shell. This fans out around the door in carefully cut stone. Those in line look like they are walking into a spiraling conch. It is a very strange addition to downtown Norman's single street of brick buildings—a grudging admission that if the twenties are not exactly roaring in Oklahoma, the university town has at least acknowledged their existence. The dance hall is a far cry from the handful of gothic stone university buildings that comprise the campus hidden away in a grove of elm trees and separated from the business district by University Boulevard,* LYNN's *magic passage.* EILEEN *and* LYNN *stand in line, waiting for the doors to open. A wood plaque with a shiny gold plate reads "University Members and Their Guests Only." Below this a picketed hand-painted sign stuck in the grass says, "No Coloreds Aloud."*

EILEEN YOST

Pleasant afterthought. Seems redundant since the university is segregated, too. Sometimes I wonder. Do you imagine that includes us? I know my granddad couldn't get in here, dark as he is. I grew up listening to white kids tell me I had a nigger grandpa. They never listened when I told them he was Indian.

> EILEEN *pulls herself closer to* LYNN.

LYNN RIGGS

Eileen, you know as well as I do that since territorial days, Indians have attended the university to play football. Look at Key Wolfe. He was squad captain back in'o8. He was Chickasaw and about twice as dark as you and me put together. That sign doesn't have anything to do with us. Blacks are a different matter. I never knew any colored that wanted to come here anyway. If Norman's high and mighty can't spell "allowed," likely as not they can't flush out a couple of white-looking Indians either. We both managed our way into our respective societies, didn't we?

EILEEN YOST

One of us seems to have managed his way into his respective everything. Correct me if I leave something out: the Men's Glee Club; the Honorary Drama Fraternity, Battle Ax; the honorary freshman society; and Blue Pencil, the honorary literary fraternity. I believe this covers all things honorary.

Let's see, I'm running out of fingers. Editor of the campus literary magazine; author of one fine farce entitled *Plumb Nuts,* scheduled to be performed homecoming week; teacher of freshman composition for the exorbitant sum of sixty-five dollars a month; and founder of an independent humor magazine called *Whirlwind.* And this is your first semester. Published poet before even arriving. Never in Oklahoma history has a single student taken the university by such a storm. By spring you'll be on the Board of Regents. What have I forgotten?

LYNN RIGGS

You overlooked the most important item in your little list.

EILEEN YOST

Which is?

LYNN RIGGS

I've never missed a dance or a football game.

EILEEN YOST

You seem to cheer especially loud for Leroy.

LYNN RIGGS

Us Chis have to stick together.

EILEEN YOST

Yes, you "guys" certainly do. Speaking of colored, you're nearly Br'er Rabbit to his Tar Baby. You sure have perked up since you got the teaching job and were able to move back upstairs with him.

LYNN RIGGS

Anybody gets a new outlook when he's no longer up to his elbows in greasy dishes every night. I've also staved off mortgaging my allotment for a month or two, at least until final tuition is due.

> TRUCKY *and* BUN *approach* LYNN *and* EILEEN *for "ups" in line. Those behind them complain.*

TRUCKY AND BUN

Hush up your griping; we just got a little invitation.

> TRUCKY *opens his coat, revealing a silver flask in the inside pocket.*

EILEEN YOST

Very discreet, Truck. There might have been a couple of birds just climbing out of their cars who didn't see you.

TRUCKY

Come have a snort with us. It's early yet.

EILEEN YOST

I'm sorry, but this gentleman here is solemnly sworn to protect my honor.

BUN

You're sorry he's sworn to protect your honor, or sorry you can't drink with us?

EILEEN YOST

I'm sorry the death penalty still applies for killing idiot men with more money than brains. You'd be a pitiful waste to swing for.

BUN

Then, swing *with* me, baby.

> BUN *opens his coat again and nods toward the car.*

EILEEN YOST

I'd rather swing from the trees with the apes.

> *The line begins to move inside the building.* TRUCKY *and* BUN *head back to the parking lot.*
>
> *Inside the club the string band finishes tuning up, and the violinist hits a double stop that kicks off a well-known fiddle breakdown. Young men in rolled up shirtsleeves cajole girls out onto the dance floor, and they move with the two-four beat, nothing fancy, not much more effort than walking.* LYNN *takes his and* EILEEN's *coats and puts them over the backs of two chairs against the wall. The inside of the club, with its giant concrete floor and plain whitewashed walls, marks a vivid contrast to the gay outside entry, which seems like a fake movie set front once the couples have entered.*

LYNN RIGGS

Rather like being on the bottom of a giant swimming pool.

EILEEN YOST

As you can see, Lynn, the excesses of our times have not quite hit Norman yet. No horns. No New Orleans brass. No flappers. No Charleston. We do have Prohibition, however. In fact, I think we may have invented it. These boys look like their farmer fathers, pushing a plow instead of a woman around the dance floor.

LYNN RIGGS

Perhaps that's because some of their dates rather look like plows. Otherwise, they might show a little more enthusiasm when their girls try to rouse them from their stupor.

EILEEN YOST

No, Lynn, that's a man for you. Won't let on that he might actually like something a woman wants.

LYNN RIGGS

Yes, Eileen, but they're playing "The Waltz You Saved for Me." And, unlike the men you describe, Lynn Riggs never sits out a waltz.

While most of the couples waltz Texas style, moving continuously forward in the same direction around the dance floor, LYNN *leads* EILEEN *through elaborate circles as if in a ballroom competition, wildly bisecting the room and impeding the uniform forward motion of the rest of the dancers. Many glare; some warn* LYNN *to watch out, but he is lost in the sheer joy of himself and the movement.* LYNN *and* EILEEN *return to their seats out of breath and laughing as if they are the only dancers in the hall.* LYNN *is aglow, more alive than* EILEEN *has ever seen him, something released in him on the dance floor like a dam that has burst.*

EILEEN YOST

I rather like a poet who can dance.

LYNN RIGGS

And much more. There are other things I can do you might appreciate. I'll go get us some punch. Drink up now because I plan to keep you on your feet all night.

EILEEN YOST

No, you don't. Not all night. I seem to remember a promise you made to tell me about Hollywood. We don't have any men around here who have been in the moving pictures.

LYNN RIGGS

I wouldn't exactly say I've been in the movies. I held a rope—normally the job of the horse who has his end dallied to the saddle. I was an equine fill-in, since the cow pony felt inclined to take a standing shit every time the camera rolled, and Will wasn't going for that kind of realism. The problem was auditory and olfactory, not visual. To use the language of the stage, it broke the actors' concentration. And the set was getting pretty "cluttered." On the other end of the rope, a balking steer spasmed and frothed while Will spoke sweet nothings in its ear before searing it with a red-hot branding iron. My hand was in the moving pictures, and that was the mistake of a rather incompetent cameraman. It seems there is room for only one Oklahoman in the movies at a time, the other famous son of Claremore—that is, unless you count the steer, who got a full body shot. But he might have been from La Brea, since he seemed more refined than a lot of Sooners. He got paid a lot more than I did; I know that much.

EILEEN YOST

Oh, Lynn, you tell it so pretty!

LYNN RIGGS

Given that Will's dad, Clem, and everybody else back home, has seen me ride, I thought I might get a part mounted on top of a horse rather than replacing one . . . as rope bearer. And in truth it took several of us to anchor our balking fellow actor. But only I managed to get my hand in the film, I'm proud to say.

> LYNN's *voice fades as he continues to tell the horse story.*

> *Exterior of the Cove, a private club on a public beach in*
> *La Jolla, Southern California—the previous year.*

> *The sign over a mosaic tile arch reads "The Cove," and, underneath,*
> *"Turkish Steam, Private Club, Men Only." The bath is on a side street two*
> *blocks off the La Jolla beach, and an overhead spigot hangs under a stone*
> *arch where another sign says, "Swimmers Please Shower Before Entering."*
> LYNN *hesitates, watching men go inside. A young man is pulling him by the*
> *arm, urging him on.* LYNN *finally acquiesces.*

LYNN RIGGS

All right, Brian, I hope this makes up for this bum film we're working on. I could subject you to one of my lousy puns and say it's been a real bum steer. I suppose all the sad and disillusioned extras come to this place to get discovered.

BRIAN

Well, not to brag, but I get discovered nearly every time I come in here. It was a real eye-opener for this Kansas boy, and I suspect the same will hold true for an Oklahoman.

LYNN balks again, but BRIAN pushes him up to the door.

BRIAN

Come on, Lynn, you know you want inside. You'll love it. It's something like a health club. Steam. Weights. Sauna. Massage. Pool. You can work out, then sit in the steam. You said yourself you're too scrawny to play an Indian.

LYNN RIGGS

That was before I knew most Indians were Italian. Verisimilitude doesn't seem to be the desired effect.

BRIAN

This will beef you up. You'll be a real Indian in no time. Some nights coming out of here even *I* feel like one. I've been known to give a war whoop or two inside on a good night.

LYNN RIGGS

I'm intrigued.

But LYNN balks again, and BRIAN steps in the dimly lit entry, pulling LYNN behind him. A TELLER sits behind a steel-barred window, taking money through a sliding drawer, as if at a bank.

TELLER

Members?

The TELLER winks, and BRIAN nods yes, though no membership list is produced or checked. A big metal door is opened from the inside, and a man in a towel closes it behind them with a loud clank, then bars it.

LYNN RIGGS

Like entering a prison.

BRIAN

Your eyes will get used to the dark in a minute.

BRIAN shows LYNN the way down a hall to a large Mediterranean-style cabinet, opens it, and hands him a towel. Steam pipes are everywhere along the walls, and the building clanks and groans. A man in a suit has a key on a long cord; he opens a locker, putting his coat inside. LYNN recognizes him as the producer who has occasionally been on the set he and BRIAN are working on. LYNN nods and smiles since he has spoken briefly to him once or twice, and the man grabs his coat out of the locker and walks off hurriedly without saying anything. LYNN looks at BRIAN, puzzled.

BRIAN just shakes his head, and LYNN does not know what he has done wrong. LYNN undresses slowly and shyly, grabbing an extra towel and throwing it over his shoulders.

LYNN RIGGS

I'm skinny as an old stick.

BRIAN puts his finger to his lips, indicating for LYNN to keep quiet. They leave the lockers and turn down another hallway, walking past open-doored cubicles, each furnished with a single cot and a sparse white sheet. A black man is lazing on one of them, his towel half-draped around his midsection. He is sitting up against the wall, one leg thrown over the edge of the cot, casually reading a newspaper. He puts it down and smiles at LYNN as he and BRIAN pass. LYNN starts, unaccustomed to integrated facilities, although he has been around blacks many times back home. They continue down the hallway. Some rooms are empty, their cots unoccupied; some doors are closed. There are other sounds besides the steam pipes. LYNN ties his towel tighter around his waist, and holds the other one around his neck like an old lady's shawl. BRIAN whispers directions to LYNN.

BRIAN

Slow night, I see. I'll get you started on the weights, then I'm going to take some steam.

LYNN RIGGS

Don't leave me by myself.

BRIAN

Everyone flies solo in here. You'll be all right.

They enter the weight room, which consists of a single bench and a barbell. LYNN is puzzled.

BRIAN

Are you sure you wanna do this? I can show you out if you'd rather.

LYNN RIGGS

This is what we're here for, isn't it?

LYNN sits on the weight bench.

BRIAN

You'll see.

BRIAN *feels* LYNN's *bicep, and he can nearly get his hand all the way around it.*

BRIAN

Maybe you better warm up with just the bar, Atlas.

LYNN *sticks his tongue out at* BRIAN.

LYNN RIGGS

Everybody's got to start somewhere.

BRIAN

You certainly got lots of room for improvement. I'll be in the steam room. If you get lost, just keep moving until you find me. It may be awhile. If you see someone you don't like, just keep walking. If you see someone you do, stop. Nature will take care of the rest.

LYNN RIGGS

Don't you want to lift weights or swim first? You'll be too spent from steam to work out.

BRIAN

That's what I'm hoping for.

BRIAN *leaves, and an old man enters the weight room and stands inside the door, staring down at* LYNN. *The fellow cocks his head, like a spaniel.* LYNN *starts to laugh but stifles himself when the man steps forward. He is skeletal, and the towel wrapped around him looks like a burial shroud.* LYNN *can count his ribs. He has white, wild hair, a mop atop a gaunt frame. He stands, one arm akimbo, staring into* LYNN's *face, but says nothing.* LYNN *jumps off the bench and hurries out of the room. The place is like a maze. He keeps making right-hand turns down hallways, as if headed toward the center of a labyrinth. He keeps running into the old guy who haunted him in the weight room, and the man seems to be following him.* LYNN *repeatedly passes places he has already been; the towel cabinet, the lockers, the hall of doors. Men, dark forms in the distance, come into focus as he passes them. They stand along the walls and look away when he gets closer. In one room, they sit in chairs, lined up in rows as if in a theater, but they are watching nothing, yet aware of all around them, as if something is happening in the stillness. One man stands at the door like he is keeping guard.* LYNN *sees something going on in the corner of the room: two men in the back row seated next to each other. He rushes past, in a panic. He comes to a dressing area, dimly lit, yet still a light in all this darkness, and two men are combing their hair in front of a mirror, fully dressed and about to leave.* LYNN *breathes a sigh of relief. He looks around for an exit. He sees a glass door. He walks up to it. Condensation has streaked the glass, and water is dripping down it in rivulets. He opens it and billows of steam escape into the dressing room. The mirror fogs up, but the men combing their hair have gone, and* LYNN *did not see where they exited. He pokes his head inside.*

LYNN RIGGS

Brian, I'm going to get my clothes and go.

There is no answer, just the clank and groan of the pipes. Enough steam has escaped so that he sees the movie producer sitting on a marble bench, yellowed and cracked from years of heat and moisture. LYNN *steps halfway inside, and in a moment the producer starts to fade away when the steam valve hisses back on. A disembodied voice growls, "Close the door and shut up."* LYNN *starts to back out, but he turns and sees the old man in the hallway, so he quickly steps back in and closes the door behind him.* LYNN *inches his way into the clouds, his hands held out in front of him like a little kid walking in the dark, stubbing his toe when he comes to the bench.*

LYNN RIGGS

Ouch!

LYNN *quickly sits down, grabbing his foot and massaging his toe. There is a rush of heat from the stirred-up inferno—someone passing by on his way out.*

LYNN RIGGS

Brian?

The door opens, a cloud billows, and a man's bare ass seems to float out the door, a white towel suspended in air beside it. LYNN *feels around him in the steam. There is another level, a platform above him. He climbs up. The steam valve has shut off for a while, and he sees the men below him beginning to reappear. He sees there is yet another, higher level, so he climbs to the top, escaping to safety from the men below. The steam valve comes to life again, and the heat rises up, unlike anything he has known. He rubs his face, breathing through his hands, trying to control himself, when everything inside him says he cannot take another minute of it. Some survival instinct kicks in, and he takes the towel off his shoulders and covers his head, holding the cloth over his mouth and nose and breathing slowly through it. He senses someone sliding toward him, the sound of sloshing water, wet skin moving across the marble. He peeks out of his towel, afraid to look. A leg rubs against his. It is black.* LYNN *is in the corner, the* BLACK MAN *is up against him, and there is no place to go.*

LYNN RIGGS

I can't breathe. The steam.

BLACK MAN

Hush, child. Those are clouds of joy.

Back at the dance.

As LYNN *finishes his horse story, he takes* EILEEN's *empty punch cup.*

LYNN RIGGS

And that, my fellow citizen of the Territory, is the strange but true story of what happens when you put one cow horse and a reluctant Oklahoma poet in a place where neither of them belongs.

EILEEN YOST

At the wrong end of a rope, you might say. Are you sure you didn't leave anything out of that rather vivid account?

LYNN RIGGS

On my honor, my lady. As we artists say, the truth is in the details.

LYNN solemnly crosses his heart, then goes all cross-eyed and goofy, pulling EILEEN *out onto the dance floor and breaking into a dignified foxtrot. She throws her head back and laughs with delight.*

EILEEN YOST

Lynn, when I'm with you I forget all about Leroy.

LYNN RIGGS

Well, don't forget too much. He's my best friend.

EILEEN YOST

That's not what I mean. What do you talk to a football player about?

LYNN RIGGS

That's easy. Football. They're just like actresses. You lavish them with what they want to hear. Only about their successes on the gridiron instead of in front of the camera.

EILEEN YOST

What about what I want to hear?

LYNN RIGGS

For that you go dancing with Lynn Riggs.

The dorm room—the following morning.

LYNN *and* LEROY *are sleeping in late after the dance. Outside the bedroom window an elm sways in the breeze, and shadows sweep back and forth across the room, brushing* LEROY, *then* LYNN, *over and over again, from one bed to the other.* LYNN *is in white boxers and a tee shirt.* LEROY *is shirtless in white briefs. Light blonde down, like that of an adolescent boy, covers* LEROY's *broad chest and can be seen when the shadows sweep away from him and cover* LYNN. LEROY's *red-knuckled hand rests on his stomach, rising and falling.*

A dream. LYNN *is tossing and groaning in bed.* LEROY *stirs, but does not wake up.*

LYNN *and his* FATHER *are walking down to the boat landing outside of Verdigris Switch. Their boat is tied up to a tree-lined bank.* LYNN's FATHER *climbs in the rowboat first, and he sits down on the plank bench, holding an overhead willow limb with one hand to keep them anchored.* LYNN *hands him their lunches, then the poles. His* FATHER *holds out his hand, and* LYNN *climbs on board and sits next to him. They each take an oar. His* FATHER *shows him how to push off shore, then reaches over and locks* LYNN's *oar into the guides. They both start rowing, but* LYNN *is slicing the water. His* FATHER *corrects him, showing him how to bear down on the oar, use his back and arms. It's windy, and* LYNN *points to his* FATHER's *white cattleman's Stetson. His* FATHER *ignores him, sets him back to rowing.* LYNN *watches the waves and forgets to row. The boat starts to go in circles.* LYNN *starts rowing again, yet his father's strokes still overpower his, and they keep veering off course.* LYNN's FATHER *complains, and calls him a sissy.* LYNN *stands up and dives into the lake, swimming and splashing for joy; his* FATHER *hollers for him to get back in the boat. Reluctantly, and after many threats,* LYNN *swims over and tries to climb back in, but he upsets the small craft and dumps his* FATHER *into the water. The boat has turned over, and* LYNN *sees their little lunches merrily riding the waves. The poles have sunk. His* FATHER's *Stetson has taken off in the wind and is flying back home toward Claremore.* LYNN *climbs on the bottom of the overturned boat and sits thoughtfully, his head cupped in his hand, comfortable and happy in the breeze. The hat takes a spin back toward the lake and lands between the lunch sacks.* LYNN *sits at the edge of the prow and kick-paddles with his feet, slowly moving toward the white Stetson. When the boat is alongside the hat, LYNN grabs it, but when he turns it over, he wakes up.*

Dorm room—immediately following LYNN's dream.

LYNN is staring at LEROY, who is still asleep. He watches the growing bulge in LEROY's briefs, transfixed. LEROY's hand is moving toward his white underwear. His hand slips under the cotton waistline. Just as he touches himself, LEROY awakens, and LYNN is staring right at him. LEROY turns away quickly and rolls over on his side. LYNN lies motionless on the other side of the room, barely breathing, pretending to still be asleep, but knowing LEROY has caught him looking. LYNN lies there, waiting for the explosion, the accusations. But there is silence, and LEROY's back remains turned.

Bonfire at a pep rally—the following weekend.

A hay wagon, led by horses, pulls up. Couples climb down from the hay and join the others seated around the fire built on the banks of the Canadian River. Laughing girls pull straw out of each others' hair. Three boys with megaphones in their hands, and dressed in sweaters that say "Ruf Necks Pep Squad," are standing by the fire, leading cheers. As couples walk down the pathway toward the river, the pine boxes they hoist as torches light up the night sky—a processional of dancing light, moving toward the water.

RUF NECKS
  It's hard to stop a Sooner lineman
    Harder than to rope a twister
    Texas girls are big and ugly
    Their men play football like my sister

LEROY, sitting next to EILEEN, their arms interlocked, grimaces.

LEROY BOGGS
  Let the poet try.

LYNN takes his guitar out of its case. He starts to hum the melody to "A-ridin' Old Paint." He works his way through the verse and the bridge, still humming wordlessly, as if he has all night to start the song. Everyone grins, waiting for him to begin his song and leave off with the teasing antics. EILEEN brandishes a smoking stick at him and hisses in jest for him to get on with it.

LYNN RIGGS

The Longhorns rode to Norman just to lose once again
  They went to a beer joint but couldn't get in
  Says the tavern keeper, Texans water in the draw
  Cause I'd sooner have a nigger than a Longhorn in my bar.
  Run around the little Longhorns, leave them cryin' on the field,
  For their defensive lineman is gonna get killed.

The Chis had a daughter, the Megs had a son
  They had to share a dorm room and keep their bed warm
  One woke up and rolled over, the other turned away in fright:
  But he keeps right on a-hoping night after night.
  Run around the little Longhorns, leave them cryin' on the field,
  For their defensive lineman is gonna get killed.

We'll make the Longhorns suffer until the last one falls
  We'll unsaddle all their girlfriends, put them back in their stalls
  We'll telegram the Texas governor to come bury all their dead
  Then pick a handsome Sooner, and cheer for Big Red.
  Run around the little Longhorns, leave them cryin' on the field,
  For their defensive lineman is gonna get killed.

Everyone cheers when LYNN finishes, and they respond with the school cry: "Hi Rickety! Whoop-te-do! Boomer! Sooner! Oklahoma U!"

RUF NECK CHEERLEADER

He sure sings pretty for the ladies.

The CHEERLEADER glances meaningfully over at EILEEN, then backs down when LEROY glares at him. LYNN says nothing. EILEEN gets up and walks away toward the hay wagon, lighting a cigarette.

LEROY BOGGS

Hey, don't climb up there with that smoke in your hand.

EILEEN YOST

Why not? Your guitar player is smoldering.

LYNN starts to get up and go to EILEEN.

LEROY BOGGS

Ah, leave her be, poet. She'll get over it. You don't have to fix everything.

LEROY pokes the fire with EILEEN's branch, then throws it in. LEROY begins nervously rubbing a wart between his index and middle finger.

LYNN RIGGS

You're gonna rub that thing raw. Let me see your hand.

LEROY BOGGS

What do you need my hand for?

EILEEN has walked back over, and watches with interest. She is standing away from the fire, in the shadows.

LYNN RIGGS

I witch warts. My Uncle Jimmy taught me how.

LEROY BOGGS

I don't need no doctoring. Not that kind.

EILEEN YOST

What are you afraid of, Leroy?

LEROY BOGGS

I don't believe in all that hillbilly mumbo jumbo. If I followed every home cure I grew up around, I'd be long dead.

LYNN RIGGS

If you're healthy as you claim, I can't hurt you any. Give me your hand.

EILEEN YOST

I still say he's chicken.

LEROY BOGGS

All right, for chrissakes!

LYNN walks around the fire and kneels in front of LEROY.

EILEEN YOST

Pathetic!

LYNN places LEROY's palm between both his hands. He looks into LEROY's eyes, searchingly.

LYNN RIGGS

Now, don't think about that wart any more.

LEROY BOGGS

That's it? If I don't think about the wart, what am I supposed to think of?

LEROY smirks and starts to pull his hand away, but LYNN holds onto his wrist. LEROY is surprised at LYNN's strength. LYNN has not lowered his eyes from LEROY's.

LYNN RIGGS

You'll know when the time comes.

> *LYNN stands up and, still holding LEROY's wrist, pulls him to his feet. Everyone is silent, even EILEEN, as shadows from the flames move across their faces and LYNN keeps LEROY prisoner of his gaze. LYNN lets go, finally, and walks over to where his guitar is leaning against the log; he picks it up and plays it as if nothing has happened. LEROY remains standing, transfixed, shaking his wrist as if his hand had gone to sleep. He looks at the wart.*

LEROY BOGGS

Just like I figured. Still there.

> *LYNN doesn't look up from strumming his guitar.*

Act II

> *Deep woods outside of Norman.*

LYNN RIGGS

Let's follow this fence line to the top of the hill. The walking is easier. See that cow trail? It's also a deer trail. It goes through that draw down to the river. I suggest you take that. I'll work my way along the outside edge of the woods near the top of the ridge. Whatever I kick up is likely to run in front of you across the trail. If you whistle, sometimes you can get a buck to stop and pause for just a second, long enough to squeeze a shot off. That's a lot better than a wild shot when they're running. Shoot behind the shoulder, at the heart. You'll bleed him that way. A running shot's liable to spoil a lot of meat. Aim toward the river, not back toward me. Generally speaking, it's best for two members of the same fraternity not to shoot each other—unless there's a woman involved. Otherwise, people might talk.

LEROY BOGGS

I thought you didn't know anything about hunting.

LYNN RIGGS

No, I know too much about hunting. I don't like killing things. I'm only doing this for you.

LEROY BOGGS

Don't you see the beauty of it, poet? Two brothers, a crisp November day, not a cloud in the sky. No classes, no homework, no football practice. And best of all, no women.

LYNN RIGGS

I don't know; I kind of like the ladies.

LEROY BOGGS

That's because you're not dating one. It's all art and refinement to you—
Leda and the swan, Lysander and Hermia, Helen and Troy.

LYNN RIGGS

Troy was a city, not a boyfriend.

LEROY BOGGS

Troy was besieged, and that's the state of most boyfriends.

LYNN RIGGS

Touché. That's what I like about you, Leroy. You have a life off the football
field. You sound like you were educated in the classics in one of our Territorial schools. We'll make an Indian out of you yet.

LEROY BOGGS

First, I think we need to make one out of you.

LYNN RIGGS

I'll be the judge of that, thank you. After all, I'm the superior deer hunter
here. Where do you start, Leroy, when you skin your deer?

LEROY BOGGS

You win. But you sure don't look like an Indian to me. Don't act like
one either.

> LYNN *gives up, seeing that the argument is useless.*

LEROY BOGGS

Are we sure we can find our way back to the car at Purcell?

LYNN RIGGS

Purcell is a city that straddles a river. Kind of hard to lose, wouldn't you say?
But you, my friend, are nonetheless lost. Totally at my mercy. Let's see, what
promises can I extract from you?

LEROY BOGGS

I offer Eileen as ransom. Did you know that someone carved yours and
Eileen's initials into one of the wooden tables at the Varsity Club? I know
I've seen you in there drinking Cokes. It wasn't you, was it?

LYNN RIGGS

The Varsity Club. Let me see. . . . Where is that? I don't exactly recollect its location. Across from the Engineering Building, is it? Thanks for the offer, as far as Eileen goes, but I think I already have her.

LEROY BOGGS

No, I mean you can have her.

LYNN RIGGS

Somehow, I don't imagine Eileen would appreciate being handed back and forth like a hot potato, nor being given away like a farmer's daughter. Did you feel that?

LEROY BOGGS

What?

LYNN RIGGS

A raindrop.

LEROY BOGGS

Mention the ladies, and it rains. It figures.

LYNN RIGGS

That's not all it's doing. Look over yonder, toward Lexington.

LEROY BOGGS

Um, which direction would that be?

> *LYNN points with his rifle at the same time a cloud-splitting crash is heard.*

LYNN RIGGS

Let's head back in.

LEROY BOGGS

No, poet, we just got here. We can stand a little water.

LYNN RIGGS

How about a little fire?

> *LYNN walks over to a blackened tree stump, split by lightning.*

LYNN RIGGS

No amount of rainwater is going to cool you off once you've been struck by that. You'll smolder forever. Look, there's water in the bottom of the stump. Water the color of roots and leaves. It has known both earth and heaven. Leroy—splash some of this on your face.

LEROY BOGGS

You first. I don't trust poetry.

LYNN RIGGS

It's poets you have to worry about, not poetry. Didn't I get rid of your wart? I'll go first.

> *LYNN sets his gun down next to the stump. He puts his hands in the water and washes his face off. LEROY steps up to the stump and hesitates.*

LYNN RIGGS

What are you waiting for? An invitation?

> *LEROY, not to be outdone, robustly plunges his arms in like a man standing over a washbasin and trying to splash himself awake in the morning. They continue on. When they separate at the top of the hill, LEROY taking the cow path and LYNN keeping to the edge of the woods, it has come a gentle rain. LYNN scours the ground for some signs; he looks for deer pellets, watches the trees for hair, anywhere there may be a rub or some other clue, but he sees nothing.*

LYNN RIGGS

Maybe if it was a first snow instead of this cold rain it would be better for deer chances. Of course, you can't tell that to a greenhorn. The only thing we'll get out here is damned cold.

> *It takes a mighty act of concentration for LYNN to keep his teeth from chattering. It starts to rain hard, and the land is dark. Lightning flashes touch down and illuminate everything, but in the downpour they only light up a gray refracted haze. The rain is coming down so hard that it is difficult to tell where the lightning is hitting, but it's definitely closer.*

LYNN RIGGS

Probably not as close as it seems, but I better go get Leroy.

> *Instead of returning all the way back to the fence line where they started, LYNN climbs down a bluff in a straight line toward the deer path.*

LYNN RIGGS

I hope he doesn't shoot me. How did I ever let him talk me into this?

> *LYNN makes his way through a stand of post oaks and comes upon the cow trail. He doesn't see LEROY in the heavy rain, but he knows he has to be in front of him.*

LYNN RIGGS

No use looking for tracks in this downpour.

LYNN keeps walking, knowing he has to run into LEROY at some point before he reaches the river. He gets to an embankment overlooking the Canadian, however, and he still hasn't seen him. He realizes that LEROY has wandered off the cow trail in the rain.

LYNN RIGGS

Wonderful.

LYNN watches the river go by, but he doesn't have to wait long before he hears LEROY bellowing in the woods, calling for him. LYNN heads back up the trail, and, at the same juncture where LYNN had just come out of the post oaks, LEROY stumbles back onto the path. He is disoriented, and he has no inkling which way to turn. He has been wandering in circles. LYNN walks up to him. LEROY is staring and speechless, wild-eyed, and he jumps at a tremendous thunderclap that sounds like the end of the world. He wants to bolt, but he has no idea which direction. LYNN takes LEROY's rifle, ejects the shells, and pockets them. LYNN does the same with his own smaller-bore thirty-thirty. He takes LEROY's gun from him.

LYNN RIGGS

Take it easy, for god's sake. I've got an idea. When the lightning got close, I came straight down a limestone bluff. There was a cave at the bottom. Maybe not much, but enough to get in out of the rain and wait for the lightning to quit.

LYNN grins.

LYNN RIGGS

The next step is . . . RUN!

LYNN leads the way out of the rain, carrying the rifles.

LYNN RIGGS

Over the river and through the woods, to grandmother's house we go!

They run toward the hill. LYNN stops and LEROY runs past the cave, unable to see it because of the way the opening blends into the dark hillside.

LYNN RIGGS

Back here. It's easy to miss. Step inside. Watch your head!

The two men stand hunched over inside the cave opening, watching the rain pour down, and the lightning flashes illuminating the dark forms of trees. LEROY, *in the safety of the cave, calms down.*

LEROY BOGGS

We better get out of these clothes. Well catch our death.

LEROY steps back into the shadows of the cave to undress.

LYNN RIGGS

Not too far. We don't want you lost again.

LEROY BOGGS

No worry. I can feel the back of the cave. I'm standing against it.

LEROY tosses a shoe, which falls at LYNN's *feet. Then another. Then his shirt. An undershirt. His pants. Underwear. Finally, his socks.* LYNN *picks them up, one by one, and arranges them on a rock, off the cave floor.*

LYNN RIGGS

Come into the light. I can't see your face.

LEROY BOGGS

No, you come back here.

LYNN steps toward the back of the cave.

LEROY BOGGS

Get out of those wet clothes first. I can see you, but you can't see me.

Instead LYNN *makes his way toward* LEROY's *voice and sits down next to him in the dark. He starts to pull off his hunting boots, then stops.*

LEROY BOGGS

It's OK, it's dark.

LEROY helps him with his boots, tugging on the heels. LYNN *finishes undressing. He sets his clothes in a neat pile in front of himself.*

LEROY BOGGS

They'll never dry out that way.

LYNN, too shy to get up and reveal himself, picks up the clothes, one by one, and tosses them toward the opening of the cave where LEROY's *already are.* LEROY *strides toward the mouth of the cave, picks up* LYNN's *clothes, and arranges them on the rock next to his own.*

LEROY BOGGS

Are your eyes used to the dark yet?

LYNN RIGGS

No.

LEROY BOGGS

Mine are.

> LYNN *squirms, no clothes in front of him, nothing to fuss over, so he pulls his legs up to his chest, and rests his head on his knees.* LEROY *is sitting cross-legged.*

LYNN RIGGS

I'm scrawny as a little old stick.

LEROY BOGGS

I'm tired of playing football.

LYNN RIGGS

But you're so good at it. It would be like me saying I'm tired of writing poetry.

LEROY BOGGS

It doesn't scare me anymore. I didn't know it until today, when I was lost in the woods. I haven't been that spooked in a long time. The first time I stepped on the field as a high school freshman I was scared clean senseless. First, there was the possibility of getting stoved up or crippled. I could go down and break a leg, bust a rib in a pileup, maybe fall someday and never rise up off the field. Not likely, but I knew it could happen. I could fuck up out there, and the home side would jeer me in the stands; my own team would hate me after the game; I'd face the look in my old man's eyes when I got home. You know what? I done busted my leg onced. I've limped around on bum knees for weeks after the close of a season. I've fucked up on the field so bad no one would speak to me in the locker room afterwards. And the only thing that ever happened was come next year I'd be out there playing again, all the pain forgotten. I survived. And it's boring. Winning isn't all that much better either. After a season streak of game after game where you skin them from here to yonder, it stops meaning anything.

LYNN RIGGS

Writing isn't like that. It's not what I do; it's who I am. The last time I shot a deer, he was sitting on top of a little knoll. It was a clean shot, and his legs buckled under. I saw him go down. When I walked over to the clearing, he had slid to the bottom of the hill. His front legs were out in front of him. He started struggling on all fours to make it back up to the top. He never gained his feet, and pulled himself with his front legs, inching his way along. I cut his throat halfway up the hill, and that's as close as he got to making it back to where he'd been standing before I shot him. No matter how well you do it; it's ugly business. I probably shouldn't have come today.

LEROY BOGGS

Then we wouldn't be sitting here next to each other.

LYNN RIGGS

You probably don't have anything to worry about. But I might have actually killed something. What about love?

LEROY BOGGS

Eileen and me aren't in love. We'd be fools to think we were. We're two tomcats slung over a clothesline, sharpening our claws on each other. Keeps us occupied. We never come to blows because we've found better ways to hurt each other, more lethal. Why don't *you* answer the question? Maybe you have to fall in love before you can have an opinion. Could be why I don't have one, either.

LYNN RIGGS

I have one. I was born lost, more lost than you've ever been. Stumbling in the darkness, looking for someone to hold onto who can see day approaching. If I see the flash of a lantern, I head toward it but get there and cannot speak. If I gather all my courage about me, the shadowy figure has retreated before the words come. The years have taught me not to cry out. You don't chase a dying light. It is better to say nothing.

Out in the dark unnamable things lurk, and that is the only place I belong, among the haunted. Every day is night. Every night is a night of storms, a mad dash, fleeing across the yard toward the cellar door. But when I descend the stairs, the cellar is full of snakes, fat bull snakes sitting coiled on the dirt floor, just beyond the last step.

The only chance is back up the stairs, out into the woods again which are fretful, alive. And every morning of this stretches unyielding into night. There is lightning outside, splitting the earth. We have a cave to hide in, a small opportunity for temporary comfort. There is verity in little else.

LEROY BOGGS

That's not love. That's high art. It has nothing to do with girl problems.

Like me and Eileen slugging it out for the heavyweight championship of the world.

LYNN RIGGS

You're not the only one who suffers. I've got my own troubles.

LEROY BOGGS

What are they?

LYNN RIGGS

Getting out of this cave, for instance.

LEROY BOGGS

Why won't you tell me?

> *LYNN gets up and walks toward the opening, into the light. He comes back with his pants. He reaches into his pocket and hands something to LEROY.*

LEROY BOGGS

What's this?

LYNN RIGGS

Lightning-struck wood. I pulled it off the stump. It's for you.

> *LYNN moves away and begins to dress.*

LYNN RIGGS

We can make it now.

LEROY BOGGS

Make it?

LYNN RIGGS

Back to the car.

LEROY BOGGS

Oh, the car. I thought you were still talking poetry.

> *Main Street Purcell, atop Depot Hill, front of the cast iron–railed Hotel Love, overlooking the Canadian River—two weeks later.*

Fraternity members are milling about under the balcony. The sorority sisters have rented rooms together and the brothers have been housed separately on the second floor, for propriety's sake, by Mr. and Mrs. Sand-

stone, the hotel owners. The students are there to watch the state high school football championships.

EILEEN YOST

So, Lynn, our hero turned tail and ran for his life.

LEROY BOGGS

You'd run, too, if you thought you were about to become a lightning rod. I didn't expect my best friend to tell everyone so soon. Or so gleefully.

EILEEN YOST

He didn't tell everyone. Only me.

LYNN RIGGS

Lightning does the strangest things. For those who've survived, it's been known to turn the most loquacious man into a mute. There is even a case back home of a boy who was struck twice—silenced the first time, his speech restored to its full capacity the second, his family astonished as he stood out on the porch, in the rain, admonishing them to let him in.

EILEEN YOST

And you two, recently come in from the storm. Have you returned muted or amplified? Or are you able to speak but simply unwilling? You know, that's a condition that cannot be blamed on lightning.

LYNN RIGGS

You ladies share your mysteries in a powder room, and we men . . .

EILEEN YOST

Share yours on hunting trips. It seems we ladies are much more highly evolved.

LYNN RIGGS

That, I must admit, is indisputable. Let's get over to the game. I don't want to sit too high up in the stands. They just built them last weekend, and, speaking of less highly evolved, I don't trust Chickasaw "architecture."

EILEEN YOST

A Choctaw girl's not going to argue with you there. We seem to have found something we agree on. But I'm going to beg off for the game. I'm heading back to Norman, catching a ride with Louisa. I have a geology exam in the morning. We're pulling an all-nighter. I'll leave you boys to your own devices.

LYNN RIGGS

C'mon, Eileen! It won't be the same without you. I'll dish out another Hollywood tall tale at halftime. I'll buy all your peanuts and Cokes. I'll let you wear my gloves and scarf. I'll hold your fingers in my hands to keep them warm. I'll make Leroy act like a gentleman, or something approximating one. How can you say no?

LEROY BOGGS

The girl'd rather study. No big.

EILEEN YOST

As much as I love it when you beg, Lynn, I must be going. I have a feeling, with a little effort, I could do rather well in geology.

> *Chalked-off grass field and temporarily constructed wooden stands.*
>
> *They are filling in on the Purcell side, but the Ada side—the visiting team's—is pretty scant.*

LEROY BOGGS

Let's go up on the Ada side. They're right behind the fifty-yard line.

LYNN RIGGS

We can't cheer for Ada!

LEROY BOGGS

Neither one of us is from Purcell or Ada. What difference does it make?

LYNN RIGGS

My granddaddy was jailed once by the Ada Lighthorse. My real mother would bust her spleen if she knew I sat over there, God rest her.

LEROY BOGGS

I've got an even better proposition for you. Let's skip the game entirely. I've had enough of football. You gotta remember, poet, I play the game every day. Let's go see the moving picture over at the Canadian Theater, right by the hotel.

LYNN RIGGS

I never miss a football game!

LEROY BOGGS

Your record is still intact for OU games. I now pronounce you our most loyal fan. That's done. Let's go to the movies.

LYNN RIGGS

Give me the quiz first.

LEROY groans.

LEROY BOGGS

I'm running out of questions. You know more about this stuff than I do.

LYNN won't move until LEROY gives in.

LEROY BOGGS

OK, for God's sake, as long as you'll go to the movie. Lemme see. . . . What rule changes did the National Football Committee make in 1912?

LYNN RIGGS

C'mon, give me a hard one.

LEROY starts to leave.

LYNN RIGGS

Alright, a touchdown scores six instead of five points; the field is shortened to one hundred yards, and the limitations on forward passing are repealed.

LEROY BOGGS

You're a real credit to your race.

LYNN RIGGS

Just one more.

LEROY BOGGS

This is the end of it. Then I'm going to the movies, with or without you. Who were the three brothers who played for the Sooners in 1912?

LYNN RIGGS

The "Terrible Hotts." Sabe Hott was one-eyed, and, of course, by that time, Coach Owens was one-armed, after having blown a limb off quail hunting down by the river bridge. There's the famous photo of him lobbing a football left-handed, his other shirtsleeve pinned up.

LEROY BOGGS

Lynn?

LYNN RIGGS

What?

LEROY BOGGS

You know damned well, what. Who were the other two brothers?

LYNN RIGGS

I told you already, the Terrible Hotts.

LEROY BOGGS

Their names, please. You're being evasive. Could it be you simply don't know?

LYNN RIGGS

Their names are irrelevant. Why resurrect ghosts?

LEROY BOGGS

Did you ever notice the way you skirt around the details? Not in regards to football; I'm frankly surprised you can't name the other two Terrible Hotts. Your life is another matter. Deep Dark Mystery Man. I'm surprised you don't join the club. Maybe you have, and you're not telling.

LYNN RIGGS

No, Leroy, if you'd been paying careful attention to events transpiring under your very nose, the Deep Dark Mystery Club was officially disbanded this year by order of the President and the Board of Regents after they got drunk after a game and looted the downtown drugstores for toilet water and lipsticks. Club members got drunk that is, not university officials. Norman merchants rallied together and presented a bill of $974.60 to the administration. You might have noticed, at least, that we had a class assessment of $2.00 apiece to pay for the escapade. You see, both the guilty and the innocent, in the end, must pay for the deep dark mysteries harbored by others. And I had nothing to do with it. Yet I paid.

LEROY BOGGS

Well, I might believe that you weren't rummaging the drugstores for toilet water. But, really, Lynn, I thought that someone of your refinement and taste would not have lowered himself to be one of the pallbearers for Mex, the team mascot. The papers said that it was the biggest funeral in the history of Oklahoma since statehood, and the obituary even recited Mex's "service" in the border war against Pancho Villa, when Mex supposedly stood bravely alongside U.S. soldiers in South Texas and New Mexico. Maybe history will prove me wrong, poet, but I'd say that kind of tribute is a sign of mass hysteria, not an appropriate response to the death of a white and tan rat terrier. Football around here is getting way out of line. Maybe with the campus radio station starting up, people can tune in and listen to phonograph records or something.

LYNN RIGGS

They're going to start announcing games. Remember when we used to have to stand in front of Barbour Drug downtown? The away game would be relayed by Western Union, and John Barbour would stand in the second-story office window over the drugstore and announce a play-by-play through a megaphone to the crowd on the streets. There were more wagons there than on ginning day.

LEROY BOGGS

No, I don't remember. I was playing. Whatever pummeling I was taking out on the field was reaching you delayed by the time it came over the wires, was shouted through the megaphone, and understood by the noisy crowd below. I could have died out there before you would have ever heard about it.

LYNN RIGGS

Now who's being dramatic?

LEROY BOGGS

Have you ever had your tooth driven through your lower lip, then been told that there's nothing wrong with you, slapped on the ass, and sent back on the field to face the same guy who inflicted the damage in the first place? That beats the tar out of drama. The damnedest thing is that you do it, and you don't give it a second thought. Not until after it's over, anyway.

> *Canadian Theater, on one of Purcell's main streets—two
> compact blocks of Victorian brickwork.*
>
> *The theater's Art Moderne sleekness contrasts with the rest of the buildings.
> The marquee reads, "Now Showing, The Palace of Silence." In the interior
> of the theater, red velvet drapes are pulled across the screen. The organ
> player is pumping away in a recessed pit—accompanying Mr. Sandstone,
> the hotel proprietor, who is onstage singing "Danny Boy."*

LEROY BOGGS

Not here. Let's sit in the balcony.

LYNN RIGGS

There's no one up there. It won't feel like the movies.

LEROY BOGGS

It's more like the movies. No crowd to remind you, when you look around, that it's not real.

LYNN RIGGS

I've been on movie sets, Leroy, and none of it's real. If the balcony's more real, how come all the spooners go up there to smooch the show away?

LEROY BOGGS

Because it's so real they can't keep their hands off of each other.

> *The balcony.*

> LEROY *sits enraptured in the front row, taking it all in, his arms dangling over the rail.* LYNN *is sitting back in his chair, waiting for the movie to start. A young man gets up from his seat in the main theater below, and a young woman stands up next to him. They stroll up the aisle to the foyer, hand in hand.* LYNN *recognizes the young man,* HODEL BYERS, *a geology major from the university. They are below him now, and as they pass under the balcony* LYNN *realizes that it is* EILEEN *accompanying* HODEL. LYNN *looks over at* LEROY, *but* LEROY *is hypnotized by the theater—every light, the beveled ceiling, the stage, and the projection booth behind them.*

LYNN RIGGS

I'm going to get some popcorn. Want anything?

LEROY BOGGS

Yeah, here's some money. I'll come with you.

LYNN RIGGS

No, you stay here. I'll get it. What do you want?

LEROY BOGGS

I don't know, surprise me.

> *The foyer of the theater.*

> HODEL *and* EILEEN *are standing in the concessions line. Without wasting any time,* LYNN *walks over to* EILEEN.

LYNN RIGGS

Eileen, Leroy is here!

EILEEN YOST

Can't you see I'm with somebody? What do you want to bring his name up for?

LYNN is rather speechless.

EILEEN YOST

Please, Lynn. You could have seen this one coming a mile away. Leroy is insufferable, and you're unavailable. I don't care anymore. Let him find out. He's got you to drown his sorrows in. Take him hunting. Go out and kill something. He'll get over it.

HODEL takes out a fat wad and pays for popcorn and Cokes, then turns to LYNN.

HODEL BYERS

Want anything, or you just here stirring up trouble?

EILEEN YOST

Hodel, could you go get my wrap? It's out in the Stutz.

HODEL goes out to the street in front of the theater.

EILEEN YOST

Nice car, a Stutz Speedster. Maybe you and Leroy can get one. Look, Lynn, I didn't mean that. I have to tell you something. For your own good. Leroy is going away. He's latched onto some crazy idea about working with the riggers on the oil boom. He's got an uncle who's drilling with a crew around Okmulgee who promises to get him on. He wanted me to come with him.

EILEEN laughs.

Can you see me taking care of Leroy every day when he comes in from the oil-fields, raising his kids in Okmulgee? When I was with you, Lynn, we had fun. But it was more than that. We listened to each others' ideas, shared dreams. I didn't have to play dumb to make some stupid frat boy feel like he owned me. But you have your eyes set on something else that I can never share. And you know what has become of Leroy; nothing brings him joy anymore, not even football, and certainly not drinking himself into a stupor with the brothers every Saturday night. So now he has taken up this notion of getting out into the real world, wallowing in experience, earning his own keep for a change. All your brother-to-brother chats, late into the night, stirred up something in Leroy, just like they did in me. And now he can't stay still.

HODEL comes back inside the theater and claps LYNN on the back.

HODEL BYERS

Maybe we'll see you after the picture, poet.

EILEEN YOST

Good evening, Lynn.

Theater balcony.

LYNN hands LEROY a Coke and a candy bar. He has nothing for himself. A newsreel is on, and war-bonneted Hollywood "Indians" come sweeping down the plains as the subtitles read, "Yesterday's War Party is Today's Americans. By Act of Congress, American Indians became citizens of the United States." The camera then focuses on the inside of a classroom, where Indian children in uniforms are sitting in rows of desks, and a friendly looking young white teacher, standing in front of a portrait of Abraham Lincoln, is giving a spelling lesson.

LEROY BOGGS

You mean I've been hanging out with a foreigner?

LYNN RIGGS

No, I think I have.

LEROY BOGGS

How does it feel to be a citizen?

LYNN RIGGS

I suffered that unhappy transition long ago. We Oklahoma Indians were made citizens when we were allotted land, and we became citizens of the new state. One of the many benefits of citizenship included dissolving our laws, constitution, and tribal government. Not to mention letting the likes of you people into the Territory. Sure, U.S. citizenship is a thrill a minute.

LEROY looks at LYNN, surprised.

LEROY BOGGS

Geez, poet, I suppose we could have stayed at the game if it meant that much to you.

LYNN RIGGS

You're not the only one tired of games. Shut up—the movie is starting.

Onscreen.

Camels are crossing the desert, their shadows elongating over the dunes. Scantily clad Egyptian men lead the caravan, bearing a litter on which reclines a mournful princess with sad eyes, fanning herself disconsolately. Off in the distance someone is approaching. The litter bearers shield their eyes and try to identify the new arrival. The princess does not look up; she is still burdened down with sadness. The boy comes trotting up to the caravan, out of breath. A turbaned man with a scimitar hoists him triumphantly to his shoulders. The boy is laughing with delight. The princess recognizes the boy's laugh and comes immediately to life, rising up on her litter, her arms outstretched, and tears of joy in her eyes. More children arrive to welcome the caravan. An oasis appears on the desert, a white palace, surrounded by palms and dates and water. The camels stretch their necks and begin to trot, headed for home.

Theater balcony.

LEROY *is still seated, watching the end credits roll by.* LYNN *is standing beside him, anxious to leave.* LEROY *stretches his legs but remains in the chair, his arms dangling over the balcony again; he is fascinated by the flickering screen.* LYNN *begins to cry.* LEROY *looks up.*

LEROY BOGGS

Good god, take it easy, poet. It's just a movie. Don't let it get to you.

LYNN RIGGS

Why didn't you tell me you were leaving?

LEROY BOGGS

I see you and Eileen must have had a heart to heart. Don't you tell your girl first when you're leaving town? I figured she might go with me. I was fixing to tell you. I wouldn't have headed out without saying goodbye. What's the big deal?

LYNN RIGGS

The big deal? We share a room. I'll have to make arrangements to get a new roommate and all. You know how broke I am. What if I can't find anyone before tuition is due?

LEROY BOGGS

C'mon, Lynn, you're being worse than a girl. Frat guys wanting to share expenses are a dime a dozen. I gotta get outta here. There's money to be made in the oilfields; a man can get enough of a start to go his own way. I admit I haven't figured out which way that is yet, but it beats staying around Norman.

LYNN RIGGS

I'm needing work too. You know how I'm trying to keep from mortgaging my allotment? Maybe I could get a job for awhile and kind of get caught up. I could go with you; we could share a place.

LEROY BOGGS

No, poet, it's too easy. It's like that cave you were talking about, a temporary comfort at best. Eventually you have to walk out into the storm. God a-mighty; now I'm starting to sound like you. Must be the movies talking. You've got too much going on here, things you love. I don't even know what I want, but I don't belong at the university. I'm going off alone. Cheer up, I'll keep in touch. It's not like I'm leaving for Egypt.

LYNN RIGGS

But what about love?

LEROY BOGGS

I tried to tell you when we went hunting. Eileen and me are quits. I think she might be seeing someone. And I don't even care.

> *Duck pond, just off campus.*
>
> *Couples—one of them being* LYNN *and* EILEEN—*are skating hand in hand. It is sunny and bright, and the skaters are full of a cheer resulting from the unusual weather, which has allowed them to frolic in the snow. Snowballs, thrown from the shore by jealous bystanders who could not rummage up a pair of ice skates, are zinging by the skaters.*

EILEEN YOST

It's been three years since the duck pond froze hard enough to skate on.

LYNN RIGGS

It's a cold year, even if late in coming. It began with a killing frost.

EILEEN YOST

Daddy says over home at Farris they're out on the stock ponds chopping holes with axes for the cattle to drink.

LYNN RIGGS

Only to freeze again, I'm sure.

EILEEN YOST

You're sure glum. If I wanted the company of a recalcitrant man, I could have spent the day with Hodel. Speaking of men, how do you like your new roommate?

LYNN RIGGS

Apart from oil, cattle, and wheat prices, he knows as little of the life of the mind as the next fraternity brother. He's as stimulating as a promenade through the corrals of the Oklahoma City Stockyards. I think he might be a cross between a spindly legged, wild-eyed brindled mongrel of a Mexican cow and a humped and horned Brahma bull. He charges into our dorm room at all hours in the middle of the night, and knocks things off the bedstand until he gets the lamp on—that is those nights he doesn't knock the lamp off first—then sits down drunk and bleary on the edge of his bed and parlays the details of the evening's conquests. I hide under the sheets, pretending to be asleep.

EILEEN YOST

Well, he's no "looker," that's for sure. Downright hard on the eyes. So, I take it you don't like him.

LYNN RIGGS

The thing of it is, Leroy never . . .

EILEEN YOST

Oh, I see. You must forget him, Lynn. I certainly did. Besides, you have me, your best friend. And never in the history of Norman has a poet quite taken the university by such a storm. You've got the Chautauqua singing tour coming up this summer. It will be here before you know it. Nothing like a road trip to forget the disappointments of home.

LYNN RIGGS

I know, Eileen; it's just that I'm not feeling so hot these days. A bug or something.

EILEEN YOST

You do look a bit pale. Perhaps ice skating wasn't the best idea. How does some warm brandy back at the house sound?

LYNN RIGGS

However do you manage such illegal boot?

EILEEN YOST

Dad's stock at Farris General Mercantile is a little more general than the county sheriff might suspect. And if he ever does take to suspecting, Dad might be disinclined to help get him re-elected. It's just such revenues that are putting me through the University of Oklahoma. Dad sees it as a contribution to civic improvement.

LYNN RIGGS

And no one deserves it more.

A snowball, thrown from the bank, hits LYNN *upside his head. Two culprits run out of the park, shouting "Pansy!" as they retreat.* LYNN *has lost his balance and goes sprawling backwards on the ice.* EILEEN, *who has been holding his hand, falls backwards as well, her legs out in front of her. She sits up, shakes her head, then turns toward* LYNN.

EILEEN YOST

Lynn, are you hurt? You look like you might faint.

LYNN RIGGS

It's not the fall. It's this sickness.

LYNN struggles to rise, but he's only on his elbows. EILEEN *pulls off a glove and feels his forehead.*

EILEEN YOST

My god, you're burning up. Let's get you home and in bed.

A small guestroom with a sunny window facing a hickory tree and some brick flowerbeds outside.

EILEEN YOST

Lynn, we've taken you over to Hodel's parents. We didn't want you staying alone at the frat house. Can you hear me? Doctor, should I send a wire to his folks in Claremore?

DOCTOR

How long has he been like this?

EILEEN YOST

Since last night.

DOCTOR

He has the symptoms of tuberculosis, the chills and fever, but that's not it. Has he suffered any nervous strain lately?

EILEEN YOST

None that I know of. He went through some inconveniences switching roommates recently. He has an artistic temperament.

DOCTOR

Sometimes in these sensitive boys minor traumas are more deeply felt than in the rest of us. I wouldn't alarm his parents, as long as he doesn't get any worse. They're probably used to such episodes. I'll check him for a few days. No cause for alarm.

LYNN tosses over on his side.

LYNN RIGGS
I can't swallow.

Dream sequence. LYNN is tossing in his bed.

LYNN is running out of the Claremore Theater. Its cupolaed roof casts a shadow over the streets of the town. The old men sitting in front of the barbershop stare as LYNN rushes past them. In front of the theater, workers are painting golden trim on the railing of the second-story theater terrace. Eddie Lyon, builder of Claremore's Orpheum Theater, instructs them, "Make it gay, but not gaudy, boys!" admonishing his workers, who are still putting on the finishing touches even as people walk out at the end of the Grand Opening show. The theater marquee reads, "One Show Only, Bosco the Snake-eater." Those coming out of the theater hold up their hands against the sun's midday glare. Couples move down the wooden sidewalk away from the entrance, at the intersection stepping down to a dirt street over which yellow dust hangs in the bright, blinding sunlight. The glare has not let up any, and still the theatergoers hold their hands against the light, though their eyes have long recovered from the darkness they came out of. They step around LYNN, who is seated on the bottom step, knees drawn up to his chest. LYNN rocks off his heels onto his toes, leans over himself and heaves, violently ill. His Stetson-hatted FATHER looms over the youngster, turning away in shame. His face is half-shaded by the white low-crowned cattleman's hat.

FATHER
Rollie Lynn Riggs, rise up from that sidewalk and leave off with your foolishness.

LYNN spits into the dirt, disgusted by the filthy taste in his mouth. He doesn't move.

FATHER
You just had to see Bosco the Snake-eater, didn't you? Well, I myself knew better, but I says let the boy have his fill if he thinks he can take it. I never heared the like, what with your whining night and day, weeks on end, until the theater opened. Now, here we are after a mule's age of your driving me plumb to distraction. Onced you got inside, cain't hardly wait for the show to start. The lights go up, and Bosco struts onto the stage, throws off his

purple cape, and spins and spins with that old python snake wrapped around his neck. Not enough to even scare a little girl out of her bloomers, but I thought you was fixing to crawl under your seat, hiding your eyes, then peeking out of your fingers like you waddn't half-growed up already. Turned white until I thought you'd quit breathing. He got that snake all unwrapped, and then you couldn't keep from looking any longer. That "python" waddn't no more than a swollen-up bull snake some poor widow woman caught down in her storm cellar amongst the fruit jars. Bosco, the Hungarian Snake-eater, my eye. Some drunk they found from over Oologah way, most likely will sober up sometime tomorrow! That snake swaying back and forth in front of Blotto's face and him breathing corn liquor all over it, pry clean stunned it into submission. Blotto closing his eyes, and the drunk python slithering into the closest thing he knowed as a snake hole, considering. And Bosco or Blotto or whoever opening up wider and wider, letting him unravel, the same way he lets whiskey course down his gullet. Until that snake's teeny tail was the only thing left poking out and waving a little bit and Blotto gone all cross-eyed. I liked to have laid a death grip on you, boy, just to keep you from running out of the theater. And after months of "Daddy, don't forget you promised to take me to see Bosco!" What a waste of a nickel!

> *Fraternity house.*
>
> LYNN *is still dreaming.* LEROY *looms over* LYNN, *as* LYNN *rocks back and forth on his heels, crying.* LEROY *sits down next to* LYNN *on the frat house steps and throws an arm around* LYNN'S *shoulder. They are both very drunk.*

LEROY BOGGS

You're the best pal I ever had. I don't deserve you. You're such a good buddy, and here I am leaving you. I'm a rat. A drowned rat.

> *The two men are looking into each other's eyes, tenderly.*

LYNN RIGGS

You're a soaked rat; that much is for sure. We nearly emptied that fifth.

LEROY BOGGS

And you're a hungry cat.

> LEROY *pulls away.*

> *Train depot, Norman.* LYNN *is still dreaming.*

LEROY BOGGS

Take care of Eileen. Maybe you can do better than I did. They're starting to board the train.

LYNN RIGGS

We could get a hotel room before you go. It's just across the street. Sleep off this drunk. You might change your mind.

LEROY BOGGS

If I don't go now, I'll stay here forever. That's what I'm afraid of.

The train whistle blows, and the porter yells, "All aboard!" LYNN *helps* LEROY *with his bags.*

LYNN RIGGS

We're climbing the scaffold.

LEROY BOGGS

At least I'm not leaving with that monstrous trunk you came to me with. Took up the whole dorm room.

LYNN RIGGS

No, you took up the whole room, every inch of it.

LEROY shakes LYNN's *hand and turns away, handing the porter the ticket, then disappearing into the train.* LYNN *staggers back to the Stutz Speedster and throws open the door.* EILEEN *and* HODEL *are making out in the back seat.* LYNN *slumps over the steering wheel, weeping bitterly.*

LYNN RIGGS

I'm drunk, and I can't drive. I hate driving alone.

University of Oklahoma. LYNN *is still dreaming.*

When LYNN *raises his head from the wheel, he is standing in front of Monnet Hall on the OU campus, looking up at the two owls that adorn the top of the building, each bird carved in stone and painted green.* LYNN *addresses the owls.*

LYNN RIGGS

Where I come from owls don't have much of a reputation, much less two green ones that won't ever go away.

Hospital recovery room—one week later.

> WITTER BYNNER, *an eccentric OU professor, has entered. He is dressed in a Chinese tunic and smoking a long onyx pipe with a bowl shaped like a frog, one of the many artifacts he has collected during his extensive travels in the Orient. He opens a window and waves the smoke away from* LYNN'S *face.*

WITTER BYNNER

Fresh air, that's what's needed here.

LYNN RIGGS

My Uncle Jimmy smokes a pipe. He had a clay one when I was growing up. Now he smokes a meerschaum I bought him for Christmas.

WITTER BYNNER

It's a tragedy how easily these ancient traditions are lost.

LYNN RIGGS

Uncle Jimmy is white, actually. And Indians have been smoking English pipes for three hundred years. They're better made than ours.

WITTER BYNNER

But you're not Indian, Lynn. Now take my house girl at Santa Fe. There's an Indian. I just adore her when she cooks posole, and does Indian things. But, of course, she's Catholic too. A shame. The Chinese, you know, are the only ancient culture still racially existent. I should have liked to have known your ancestors.

LYNN RIGGS

Most of them were bankers, like my dad. You'd have been deeply disappointed.

WITTER BYNNER

When you're up and around you should take me home with you. There is some great poetry among your people. I'd very much like to see how it compares to my Chinese translations.

LYNN RIGGS

You don't speak Cherokee. Neither do I. How could you translate Cherokee poetry?

WITTER BYNNER

From many years in Santa Fe, and my studies, I have a fair sense of the spirit of the Indian people and an assiduity in finding English equivalents for idioms, which literal translation fails to convey. The spirit, after all, is the essential thing, not the letter. And it's the spirit of this continent, embodied by the Indian people themselves, that may yet save us if we'll only listen. Your ancestors have much to teach us.

> LYNN *pulls himself out of bed and staggers over to the bathroom. He valiantly tries to keep his robe around him and preserve what little dignity he can.* WITTER *helps him settle to his knees, and* LYNN *throws up in the porcelain toilet bowl.* LYNN *rises and ties his robe again.* WITTER *helps him back to bed.*

LYNN RIGGS

You've been a great friend, Witter, a comrade in arms. We both suffer the same malady. But I'll never go home again. I'm too sick. Even when this is over, I'll still be sick.

WITTER BYNNER

But our sickness is a draught best drank deeply. Delicious for all its bitterness. Perhaps because of its bitterness.

LYNN RIGGS

I've had my fill. I want to leave forever.

WITTER BYNNER

No, Lynn. Accept the world exactly as you find it in all its terms. That's where you'll find solace. There is a value in loafing and inviting one's soul. I have something to talk to you about. Some friends in Santa Fe, artists, who could give you a place to rest while you recover, as well as support your plays and poems. They could introduce you to the right people, and I don't just mean the literati. Those like us. There are the like-minded in the colony who have learned a better way. They can teach you that the man who recognizes all men as members of his own body is a sound man to guard them. And they're young. And very wholesome. Indeed. And I know your interests, whatever you might, in the past, have pretended otherwise. A week with these boys, and you'll be on your feet again in no time. Mexican boys. Indian boys. Around all hours of the day. And night. We artists are a special breed. We do not couple with our own kind. We must return to the earth, and to those who come from the earth. The flesh, after all, houses the spirit.

> WITTER *winks.*

WITTER BYNNER

Here comes Eileen. We'll talk more later.

> *Two-storied brick train station in the stockyards area of Oklahoma City—two weeks later.*
>
> *A roofed wooden platform is in front of the main entrance. The parking lot is empty, except for a single car and some baggage carts. EILEEN and WITTER have LYNN in arm, helping him inside the building. The spring-loaded door slams behind them. LYNN settles onto a wainscoted park bench, and WITTER drapes a blanket over his shoulders. EILEEN opens a Thermos and pours LYNN a cup of hot broth.*

WITTER BYNNER

Now, nothing to fear, Lynn. All you need to do is rest on the way down. Mabel Dodge Luhan will meet you in Santa Fe and take you to the ranch. You will not be the first young man, weary of spirit, who she has rescued. She is a patron of the arts, and she insists on no authority but the authority of the heart. In this perfect freedom, surrounded by the hills of the Pecos wilderness, under the night stars and the clear light of day, these last few weeks will fade away like the uncertain memory of a bad dream. And then, young man, I want to see more of those poems of yours, touched by a new spirit.

EILEEN YOST

Lynn, you'll be back in the company of such famous people, Claremore's world traveler once again. It will be your Hollywood days all over.

LYNN RIGGS

Easy, Eileen. I was starting to feel better.

> *Four COWBOYS come in with their spurs still on. They have been loading cattle onto a stockcar and have gleefully ridden on top of it the short distance over from the stockyards. They approach the STATION MASTER, seated behind a barred window in a tiny office, and he writes them out a receipt. The door creaks, and in walks a Syrian PEDDLER, as if he has been trailing the COWBOYS.*

PEDDLER

My friends, what are you going to spend all that cattle money on?

COWBOY 1

Who asked you, peddler?

COWBOY 2

Curly here's got a sweet little missus over to Durant—prettier than a buttercup—who's got her hand in his pocket before he gets in the front door and lands a welcome-home kiss. Rest of us has got more options, being more of the footloose kind and all.

COWBOY 3

Clean hog-tied, Curly is.

COWBOY 4

Whupped as a tit-sucking puppy.

PEDDLER

You unattached gentlemen, the last keepers of the open range, might have need of some jewelry for those nights when the prairies get lonesome. Reminds you of the ladies, even when the ladies aren't around. Or, likely as not, when you are here in the wilds of downtown Oklahoma City, and you wander across the street from the stock pens to the boarding house and stand around goggle-eyed and speechless on the front porch, admiring the young womenfolk coming and going. I've got something that will stop them dead in their tracks, make them look twice, even at a stockyard employee whose life on the free range consists of opening and shutting cattle pens all day across from a smoking coke factory.

The PEDDLER *opens his overcoat and moves it back and forth in flourishes until the pinned jewelry dances to life.*

COWBOY 1

Watch it, peddler, you'll blind us with that snake dance.

The PEDDLER *continues to wave his coat, speaking all the while of his wares.*

PEDDLER

Let me direct your eye to a few of my finer pieces. Watch, young men, this gentleman's gold watch, watch it glitter; doesn't it shine with an everlasting light that makes you reach and reach and want to touch? Take it, my married friend, and you'll have all those things a wandering eye might take in when the missus is away; consider it carefully before you return to Durant and face another hijacking. A little gift for yourself, not to be shared. A man by the name of Curly could end up in jail someday, if his woman keeps robbing him. And you, in the red kerchief knotted around your throat. How about a lady's chatelaine watch, a down payment on your own inevitable hog-tying? And for you, long-weaned cur, knocking over trash cans in your frenzied independence and raiding the spoils, how about a little culture?

Might I suggest this pair of opera glasses, as naturally held to the eye as the pup pushes into his mama's belly?

> COWBOY 4 *bumps chests with the* PEDDLER, *and a locket in the shape of a horseshoe set with chipped "diamonds" skips across the floor at the same time as the* PEDDLER *goes sprawling onto the wood planks.*

COWBOY 4

You know that peddler's kinder pretty all laid down like he's ready for a little loving. All sissified and that cute little mouth curled up like it's afeard of being punched.

> COWBOY 4 *grabs the peddler's shirt and pulls him to his feet. The shirt rips, exposing the* PEDDLER'S *chest and shoulders.* COWBOY 4 *is in the* PEDDLER'S *face, snarling viciously.*

COWBOY 4

Or maybe afeard of being kissed. Curly here might lay a kiss on you since like as you was just telling he keeps getting robbed, but he ain't getting kissed, and likely as not you might be the kind to appreciate it. He's more the man for those opera glasses than me. He could look through them and spot a bull calf from a heifer and never get off his saddle pony.

> COWBOY 4 *grabs the* PEDDLER'S *crotch.*

COWBOY 4

Are you a bull calf or a heifer, peddler? You know what we do with bull calves? The branding iron is just the beginning.

> WITTER *stands up and approaches* COWBOY 4 *diplomatically.*

WITTER BYNNER

See here, young man, I'm sure the peddler didn't mean anything by his remarks. If you're not interested in his goods, then let him go his way. All of us would do well to learn a sense of inner accord that vibrates with the consciousness of the universe.

LYNN RIGGS

Shut up, Witter. You're fixing to get us killed. I grew up around guys like these.

> LYNN *pulls weakly on* WITTER'S *tunic, and he begrudgingly sits back down on the bench.*

COWBOY 4

I never seen the like. A white man coolie.

WITTER BYNNER

Let this be a lesson, Lynn, that the wise man goes about with the head of a man and the heart of a child.

LYNN RIGGS

The wise man is approaching with a log and fixing to brain these Neanderthals. And thank god, because you were just about to talk us into a thrashin'.

The STATION MASTER, *who has come inside from a trip to the wood bin on the station platform, throws a log into the stove in the middle of the room and casually approaches the* COWBOYS *with the other log brandished as a weapon. He chases them and the* PEDDLER *out the door, warning them about keeping away from decent folks. That job done, he approaches* LYNN *and his friends.*

STATION MASTER

Look, young man, I can see as how you're feeling poorly and all. But the Santa Fe train is the last one out tonight, and I'd just as soon get home as to sit around here waiting when you're sure to be the only passenger. It's been two days since I put anybody on the train to Santa Fe, and if they was any more a-coming they'd already have been here. Take this padlock to the front door, if you don't mind. Maybe your friends here can he'p you some. See that there handle on the vertical wire just outside my office? It operates a signal board on top of that pole alongside the tracks. The engineer of the Santa Fe line will stop for you when he sees you done pulled on that. After you signal the engineer, just padlock the front door when you come out on the platform. Can you do that for me?

LYNN shrugs.

STATION MASTER

Much obliged.

The STATION MASTER *shakes* LYNN's *hand and leaves.*

LYNN RIGGS

After the most recent away game, over 4,000 hysterical fans gathered at this very station to welcome home their triumphant Sooner football squad. Could this be the loneliest outpost on the continent right now? I'm a solitary passenger, waiting to flag down my own train, then lock up behind myself and board alone, speeding away from home.

WITTER BYNNER

Poets don't get the same sendoff as football players.

EILEEN YOST

But you have your friends here to see you off. And new friends meeting you when you arrive.

LYNN RIGGS

What about love?

> *The* COWBOYS *and the* PEDDLER *are still dawdling on the platform after* LYNN *boards the train and* EILEEN *and* WITTER *have driven off.*

PEDDLER

Did you see that full-grown boy break down? Crying like a baby.

COWBOY 1

All over leaving that girl he was with, I reckon. It sure sent him into a tailspin.

COWBOY 4

Well, mark my words. I'll never let myself get that torn up over a woman.

Baptists and Witches

Multiple Jurisdictions in a Muskogee Creek Story

Previous chapters have examined Lynn Riggs, delving into the way one man's art might have emerged as activism—and as more effective art—except for the fear that held it back, due to the homophobic time period Riggs wrote in, as well as his own limitations. His writings become an art of indirection, deflection, substitution. Melodrama most often stands in for his most compelling subject matter. In the imagined childhood tale, I concentrate on Riggs's artistic sensitivity, developed early on by becoming a reporter for Uncle Jimmy, who swears off the outside world—a metaphor for Riggs's own complicated positionality, since he must closely observe the details of his surroundings, like any artist, and then find ways to depict them that transcend the mundane. Instead of having a public audience for his observations, however, he is a "personal emissary" to one man, his uncle, with whom it is safe to share his inner world through a process that is as often mystic as it is articulated. Jimmy confers upon Riggs, nonetheless, the role of observer—the most important calling of any artist.

I further imagine Riggs becoming even more confounded at OU, which represents his last-ditch effort to connect to the social world of Oklahoma before banishing himself from the state. Oklahoma only corroborates what will become the major dilemma of his artistic life: the official story that obscures the real one, and the problem of creating art behind a façade. In *The*

See the online journal Southern Spaces *(www.southernspaces.org) for a live version of a talk based on this chapter, and, more importantly, three excellent sources: videotaped footage and discussion of Creek grave houses at the Fife family cemetery, published September 15, 2008; a reprint of the Durango Mendoza story "Summer Water and Shirley," published July 17, 2007; and a stellar reprinted article on the history and practices of Thewarle Indian Baptist Church, written by church member Sharon Fife, also published July 17, 2007. I reference these sources frequently in this chapter.*

Cream in the Well and *The Year of Pilár,* Riggs brings the subject of homosexuality into the open, but refracts it through so many weird angles (especially in the latter play), that the work becomes not so much a façade which
hides his truest subject matter—like his other melodramatic works—but itself
a kind of meltdown, something like Riggs's falling apart in Norman in 1923.
This play exposes the psychic contradictions represented by the fearful 1940
journal entry, in which Riggs reports the potential for the implosion to happen all over again.

If Jimmy's emissary, given the job of reporting back on the outside world, is
the mind behind *The Year of Pilár,* he is more like the reporter for Kurtz
(played by Dennis Hopper) in the film *Apocalypse Now,* who has gone mad
with his mentor in the jungles of Cambodia. *The Year of Pilár,* strongly influenced by Ramon Naya, necessarily involves all the overwhelming complications Lynn tried to negotiate with himself: Ramon, his art, and the outside
world. To my way of thinking it is by far Riggs's craziest, most fascinating, and
most brilliant failure. We find ourselves drawn in as voyeurs as we watch the
characters unravel, and sense on some kind of level the play's connection to its
creator coming unhinged with them. We get to watch a cast of characters go
nuts instead of them being hidden away—like Opal's mother, in the insane
asylum at Vinita. Unlike Roe Náld, who simply loses control of his film, *The
Year of Pilár* is about the artist losing control of himself. Although there
are strands of sanity in the play—such as Trino's increasing political involvement—they are placed in relation to all manner of other events that simply
cannot be fathomed, such as Pilár's "redemption by rape" and Trino's simulta-
neous accusation by Pilár and his own denial of gay incest. This is some crazy
shit, man.

On a more simplistic level, the OU breakdown, I believe, cuts off whatever fantasies Riggs might have harbored about becoming "Oklahoma's playwright." Oklahoma might imagine Riggs as such, but Riggs would never feel
comfortable in the role because he knew it demanded that he keep quiet—
about himself, about the state. He could always be Oklahoma's personal emissary—as long as he didn't tell anyone what he saw. Oklahoma's literary scene,
one more or less micromanaged by a mafia of Sunday school teachers, still
suffers the same fate today. Uncle Jimmy represents a fundamental paradox:
who might hear what Riggs has to say?

In turning to the fiction of Durango Mendoza, I want to further examine a
subject I have made the core of this book: the power of deviance in art. I have
posited that too often we have equated Native Studies with tradition. This
results in a lopsided formula. The real equation is not Native Studies = Indian

tradition. The equation should actually read Native Studies = Indian tradition + Deviance from Indian tradition. No artistic or intellectual, or any other kind of endeavor, can survive solely on conformity. If *The Year of Pilár* represents a kind of deviant extreme that ventures dangerously close to madness, I want to examine how another author, Durango Mendoza, demonstrates its creative potential.

A little-known short story entitled "Summer Water and Shirley," appeared in a relatively obscure anthology N. Scott Momaday's mother edited and published in 1972. While many recognize Natachee Momaday as a character in her son's memoir *The Names*, few know her as the author of the novel *The Owl in the Cedar Tree*, or as the editor of *American Indian Authors*, one of the first anthologies of Native literature that featured obscure writers at the time, such as James Welch and her son, the best known of the lot—who received the Pulitzer Prize several years earlier.

One of those little-known writers, Durango Mendoza, at the time a recent graduate of the School of the Art Institute of Chicago, would not go on to become as well known as his peers in Natachee's collection (I use her first name in order to distinguish her from her son). In fact, in spite of writing what might be one of the strongest short stories in American Indian fiction, and one of the strongest short stories in any literature whatsoever, Durango Mendoza would only author three other short stories.

On something of a detective trail myself in terms of trying to locate the man and figure out his reasons for quitting writing, I once asked Vince Mendoza—who, like Durango, has a Mexican father and an Oklahoma Creek mother, and has authored *Son of Two Bloods*, an autobiography—in what way he was related to Durango, figuring they had to be kin. To my surprise, Vince said he'd never heard of him. I didn't give up my sleuthing, however, and every fall, in my Muskogee literature class, I asked if any of my students were related to Durango Mendoza. Indian country being what it is, it was only a matter of time before Durango's niece, Melanie Frye, was a student in my class, and I found out that Durango was living in Illinois, employed as a social worker.

Then things happened fast. One day I found myself giving readings in Normal, Illinois, a town name I've always found intimidating, and Durango drove through a snowstorm to come hear me, since his niece in Oklahoma had clued him in that I was tracking him. Durango and his wife took me out to dinner, and the next day, Durango drove all the way back from Urbana, again through bad weather, to attend a presentation I made at the university. My story is anticlimactic. When I queried why he quit writing, he just shrugged and said, "Oh, I moved beyond that." Today, as a visual artist, he paints, photographs, and sculpts. His niece Melanie ended up taking more classes from me, and Durango has kept in touch.

I believe that "Summer Water and Shirley" deserves the kind of attention, let's say, that James Joyce's short story "Araby" has received around the world. Before delving into the Mendoza story, I want to give my recollections one more strange little twist. Apart from the fact that "Summer Water and Shirley" takes place very near my dad's birth town, Weleetka, Oklahoma— thus hitting close to home—I found the story pursuing me in ways that led me to seek out its author.

My friend Rosemary McCombs Maxey told me about an article published decades ago in *The Chronicles of Oklahoma* about one of the Creek Baptist churches. When she gave me a copy, I was amazed to discover that it was about Thewarle Indian Baptist Church, the very site where "Summer Water and Shirley" takes place. Authored by a church member, Sharon Fife, whose family roots go back to the congregation's founding in 1858, this article was published only a year before 1972's "Summer Water and Shirley."

It contains a treasure trove of information as diverse as sketches of the ritualized seating arrangements inside the church, maps of the location of the camp houses that surround the sanctuary on the perimeters of the grounds, the names of the families who occupy each camp house, and pictures of ritual items like the deacons' staffs and the cow horn that is blown to call people to services.

And that's just the illustrations. The narration covers the church's history since 1858, when Thewarle members first started meeting outdoors under the willow arbors. Fife recalls what she knows about the erection of the main church house in 1870. She compares the roles of male deacons and women class leaders. At one point she details the responsibilities of the Hoktuke Emarthla (or the Beloved Woman), who makes the communion bread after fasting in the woods. She tells how the church handles replacing pastors by describing the rituals involved in seeking spiritual signs in the woods. Fife explains the centrality of eighth Sunday meetings, which are bimonthly communion services. She lists the separate services for women and gives an account of what happens at them. In her recollections of the central ritual that gives Baptists their name, she highlights the attention paid to finding the right water in the nearby creek when a particular baptism is to take place. Fife reveals how Creek grave houses that go over cemetery plots are constructed— and a whole lot more that I am, by necessity, leaving out.

The pictures are drawn by Sharon's sister, and the main informants about church history are her parents. This essay has its own literary qualities, but it tells a very different story than the Mendoza short fiction does. It focuses on events inside the church house and Christian community, whereas the Mendoza story concentrates on the periphery of those same structures.

If we were sitting together I'd get into the spirit of my story with a hymn, maybe "Heleluyvn," one sung so often some people call it the Creek national anthem. In its popularity it's the Creek equivalent of "Amazing Grace," so familiar even a backslidden laggard like me can sing it. I am interested in its simplicity and its duplication of Christian theology, as well as its resistance. The verses essentially can be summarized this way: Christians are living there, and it's there they will sing alleluia, referring of course to the afterlife; each verse adds another group that will be there, too—such as preachers, older brothers, younger brothers, sisters, children, believers, and so on. All this is innocent enough until the last verse, which slyly works in the fact that our town relatives will be there singing alleluia—and this group of people constitutes our maternal relations, from which we inherit our traditional Creek town and clan affiliations under the old ceremonial system that some of us still adhere to today.

By the way, around Dustin, Oklahoma, where Durango grew up, he is known to his family as Turango. This is the kind of deep experiential knowledge that Indian critics have to offer the field of Native literary studies. That, of course, is a joke, and I usually find myself explaining all of mine. To continue the humor, however, Durango himself told me that his mom changed his name—though never legally—because she was afraid of schoolmates taunting her son by calling him "the Durango Kid." He said his family nicknamed him Tango, and they still refer to him as such.

Although the world of Thewarle Indian Baptist Church is something like a Creek version of Faulkner's own little postage stamp of Native soil, if Yoknapatawpha County is a stamp, Thewarle might be the net weight of the glue that holds it on the envelope. Nonetheless, it is one of many centers of the Creek universe that connects historic events that shape everyday realities where I'm from.

Before writing this I drove out to Thewarle. I was passing by on my way to a meeting in Dustin about a Creek Language immersion program I'm participating in. I visited with friends about Thewarle, and Tarango's short story.

One of them, the Reverend Rosemary McCombs Maxey, is an interesting story in and of herself. She is descended from a long line of Creek Baptist preachers. She felt the call early to take up her ancestors' vocation, but Creek Christians do not ordain women. When she expressed her calling to the ministry, the church leadership told her to marry a preacher. She did, in fact, marry one who today pastors Tuskegee Creek Church, but they still did not ordain her. Today she is a United Church of Christ pastor who has her own ministry, as does her Baptist husband. When recalling Thewarle, she expressed this idea of the little big church, if you will, thus:

> Thewarle is the birthplace of many a prominent Creek person: Chief Bill Fife—and his artist sisters who have made their ways to PhDs and the fronts of fashion magazines back in the day. Durango . . . also has his own prominence coming from a destitute family. The kid who could hardly raise his head to look around in the classroom is the pastor now and his sister is the women's leader. All, everything, is so very interesting, so interconnected. (Personal communication)

I might add here that Rosemary and Durango were in sixth grade together in Dustin.

The title of "Summer Water and Shirley" might first capture our attention since it contains no punctuation—as if the three nouns summer, water, and Shirley are somehow conflated into a single concept. The opening sentence of the story reads, "It was in the summer that had burned every stalk of corn and every blade of grass and dried up the creek until it only flowed in trickles across the ford below the house where in the pools the boy could scoop up fish in a dishpan" (96). These multiple images of drought occur in virtually every sentence of this tour-de-force articulation of a particularly oppressive summer.

When I teach the story in my Muskogee literature course I relate it to a host of Creek twin narratives that have to do with a wild twin and a tame twin, one deviant, the other obedient—the former always reinterpreting his father's, and others', instructions along the lines of "When dad said we shouldn't . . . what he really meant was. . . ." "Summer Water and Shirley" first leads us to believe that the eldest son is the most obedient. His name is not revealed until later, and he lives with his mother, his sister Shirley, and three younger children who seem marginal and appear infrequently. The boy's father is deceased.

The scene opens with a quintessential Creek reality. Whether at the ceremonial grounds or the Christian churches, there will always be Indian kids running amok without the supervision of adults, who are otherwise occupied. If I had authored the story I would have armed the children with munitions, since blowing things up seems to be a singular Creek childhood characteristic, and bottle rockets, cherry bombs, and firecrackers going off in the distance help to keep both adult Christians and ceremonialists from nodding off during manifestations of the sacred.

I didn't author the story, though, and there are no explosions. Still, the children must maneuver around the church deacon, a man by the name of

Hardy Eagle. The name sticks out like a sore thumb because it smacks of a pseudo-Indian name, not a very likely Creek family name. Mendoza is smarter than all that, however; while it is an unusual name for a Creek, it is the perfect name for a deacon whose eagle eye must spot any disruptive behavior before it becomes overly invasive in ways that could harm the ongoing ceremonies. The munitions must be kept at bay.

Shirley wants to run back and forth to the creek, and her elder brother—like his literary counterpart, the tame twin—warns her that their mom said to stick around the church grounds. Shirley reinterprets the rules and makes fun of her brother's wimpiness.

Before they get to the creek they see an old man coming out of the woods. Shirley hopes to sneak up on the old guy and scare the living daylights out of him. Shirley's brother, ever the obedient sibling, not only thinks this is a bad idea in principle, but even more so because he recognizes this particular stranger as Ansul Middlecreek. Much could be said about Ansul's name, which reinforces the boy's warnings to his sister about the rumors that surround Ansul. Creeks conceptualize the world in three different dimensions. The Upper World is the realm of sky, moon, sun, and stars, and thus represents order and periodicity. The Lower World is the underworld of caves, rivers, and lakes, and is associated with unpredictability, chaos, spontaneity, and creativity. This World, the habitation of mammals and people, always involves intricate balances between the other two dimensions.

Ansul's last name, *Middle*creek, places him in the realm of anomalies, straddling Creek spheres. The boy tells Shirley that Ansul is a *stiginee*. The word for witch and the word for great horned owls are the same in Creek. Witches often take the form of owls, a fascinating—and very frightening—tradition. The eyes of owls are striking. For all practical purposes owls seem to be birds, and thus creatures of the Upper World, but they have a frontal eye position that gives them eerie human characteristics, thus aligning them with This World. Like Ansul, they straddle two Creek boundaries—between the human realm, This World, and the bird world, the Upper World—at the same time. A seemingly human person like Ansul may sometimes be an owl or even a dog.

The normal behavior around such folks is simply avoidance. If you suspect somebody is a witch, you don't invite him over to your house for a barbecue. Ansul, it turns out, has seen Shirley pointing at him, which is a rather peculiar behavior for Creeks anyway, especially at someone suspicious whom you would usually go out of your way to avoid.

The siblings move back and forth between the creek, the woods, and the church house where the adults are inside worshipping. Churches and ceremonial grounds are located by creeks because of essential ceremonies that have to take place there. The church, while providing the central setting, somehow also remains notably absent in the story, in that none of the action takes place inside, even though we know services are going on while the children play.

As the adults worship, Shirley encounters Ansul a second time. Instead of just pointing, she charges him, and says cheerfully the simple greeting, "Henscay," then high tails it and runs. Obviously, and to her brother's mortification, she is giving Ansul a hard time, and he is a poor choice of someone to pick on.

Only two instances of overt comedy mark the short story. During the feed in one of the camp houses, Shirley tells her brother, "You better eat. . . . Next meetin's not til next month" (99). Both at the grounds and the churches, Creeks consume foods so gloriously greasy you can feel your arteries constrict as you swallow—things like salt pork, fried in more lard if it's done right, the culinary equivalent of the hazards of a double curve on a pitch-black country road. If the pork doesn't get you, the bacon grease it's fried in or the salt that permeates it will. In Creek country, Indians eat traditional and not-so-traditional foods like Sofkee, wild onions, abuske, salt pork, hominy, grape dumplings, and so on—mostly at special gatherings at the church or ceremonial grounds. Eating them all the time would have killed off the tribe a long time ago. Since Thewarle church meetings occur monthly, Shirley reminds her brother they will not eat this good again for a long time—a very Creek joke. There will only be one other joke, and it will occur at the end of the story.

In spite of the humor, things have already taken a serious turn, and Shirley complains her head hurts. The family begins walking home with their uncle, George Hulegy, "down the road that lay white and pale under the rising moon" (99). These services at Thewarle tend to let out around midnight, and in 1972 some church members would still be walking home through the countryside on foot; in my dad's generation some would still be going home on foot, in horse-drawn wagons, or—if they were affluent—in cars. Shirley falls behind, and her brother, who takes her hand to urge her on, is surprised to find it hot and limp.

When the family arrives home, things get a lot scarier. In a rising panic Shirley tells her brother she sees three little men over by the storehouse. Little people, the *stiloputchkogee,* are mostly benevolent presences, especially in relation to children—but not always. For the first time, the elder brother is named in the story, and named significantly in relation to his father's absence, since he is called "Sonny." Shirley says, "Look, Sonny! Over there by the storehouse" (100).

A more malevolent presence, an unusual yellow dog with brown spots, replaces the little people, and it jumps off the end of the porch. The narrator notes "the click of its heavy nails" (100). The mother puts Shirley to bed with a fever, and Sonny warns the adults of all that Shirley has seen.

The adults recognize the danger, and Shirley's mother sings a protective medicine song while George Hulegy goes to the creek to get some special pebbles he will place in the house to keep evil presences outside. The movement between the house and the woods might remind us of the symbolism of the boundaries in the story—the church house, the surrounding woods, those in the sanctuary, those outside of it, the supervision of the adults, and the freedom outside their purview. As George goes down to the creek to fetch the stones, let us remember that water is believed to be a generative force, especially water that ripples over rocks, an idea that we will return to later.

One of the story's central questions starts to emerge here. Why is it that the adults' medicine ends up failing? Why are the grownups so ineffectual? Another question of consequence has to do with cause and effect: is the witchery caused by fear, thus explainable in psychological terms, or are Ansul's powers to do harm actualities? Can these two possibilities be separated from one another?

I am convinced of the reality of witchery because of my own cultural backdrop, as well as my experiences with academics, but for now I will say that *fear* is also a predominant theme in the story. Sonny is called on to go get some wood outside, and time is of the essence since his mother hopes to intervene against the illness by making medicine. Needless to say, having witnessed his sister's panic at the apparitions by the storehouse, and having himself seen the big yellow dog leap off the porch, Sonny is scared shitless to go out into the dark. Yet he does go out:

> When he reached for the first piece of wood, the hysteria that was building inside him hardened into an aching bitter core. He squeezed the rough cool wood to his chest and felt the fibers press into his bare arms as he staggered toward the house and the two rectangles of light. The closer he came, the higher the tension inside him stretched, until he could scarcely breathe. Then he was inside again and he sat limply in the corner, light and drained of any support. (101)

While the passage might not call to mind any obvious heroism, Sonny gets out to the woodpile and back inside the house with a load of wood and his skin intact. What will become apparent from here on out is that Sonny's move-ment is increasingly pronounced, as is the adults' stasis as they quickly fall prey to hopelessness.

Briefly, I'll say something about the name of the uncle who lays down medicine in the house in order to protect Shirley from further evil. When I ran this by Rosemary McCombs Maxey, she commented, "I want to mention about George Hulegy—Hulegy sounds like vholoce [sounds like uholegie] which . . . means cloud. As an adjective folk use it to describe people who are like the cloud that hovers forecasting an omen—or some kind of change" (personal communication). In this story clouds—at first the lack of clouds, and then their restoration in the final paragraphs—provide a central image. George Hulegy, however, seems a rather ironic representation of change, since things seem to go from bad to worse in spite of his efforts to improve things.

In fact, in almost no time at all after George puts the medicine around the house, the adults give Shirley up for dead. Readers cannot help but wonder what happened to the medicine or why the adults even bothered, as quickly as they give up. Their resignation occurs after something evil invades the house that, this time, everyone witnesses, including the grownups. The evil crosses the senses; it is both heard and smelled: "[L]ike a great beating heart the sound rose steadily until they could smell the heat of a monstrous flesh, raw and hot. Stead-ily it grew to a gagging, stifling crescendo—then stopped. They heard the click of [a] dog's nails on the porch's wooden planks, and afterwards, nothing" (102).

The family brings in a non-Indian doctor who cannot discern anything wrong with Shirley: in fact, her fever will not register on his thermometer, and his prognosis is that she will be up and around in a few days. I have drawn on fact and fiction to show how fever pursued Lynn Riggs, a potent symbol that links desire and sickness. While Shirley's fever certainly has connections to transgression, Mendoza finds a much more balanced way to handle the sub-ject of deviance than Riggs does.

For the fatalistically minded adults in the Mendoza story, the "white" doc-tor's outlook only serves to seal Shirley's doom, and an old Creek woman, arguably speaking for the voice of Creek tradition, says that Shirley is a goner. The mother quarantines Shirley in a back room, and she is treated as if she is already a corpse. She has simply been overwhelmed, as far as the adults are concerned, by forces they can do nothing about:

> Everyone had accepted that Shirley was going to die, and they were all
> afraid to go near her. "There is evil around her," they said. They even
> convinced the mother to put her in the back room and close off all light

and only open it after three days. She would not die until the third day's night, nor would she live to see the fourth day's dawn. This they could know. A very old woman spoke these words to the mother, and she could not disbelieve. (102)

Of course, this is the oldest story in the world. When the prophet shows up and says you're going to kill your father, marry your mother, and not only is there nothing you can do about it, you won't even know you did it until it's too late, what are you to make of such a party pooper?

Well, it's all Creek to me, and in "Summer Water and Shirley" the adults agree with the Creek—and maybe even the Greek—seer. The heat images start to make sense because overwhelmingly oppressive heat parallels the adults' stasis, their immobility.

And here, Sonny—the ever-obedient son, the tame twin of the wild and tame narratives, the keeper of Creek tradition in all his warnings to his sister about treating Ansul cautiously—takes an uncharacteristically rebellious turn. He simply refuses to believe the adults, even the voice of Creek tradition, to whatever degree it is articulated by the old woman who proclaims Shirley already good as dead. (I believe the narrator's observation that the pronouncement cannot be disbelieved lends weight to the notion of connecting it with the social authority of conventional wisdom.)

Sonny, however, curses the flies that make "meaningless little rings, while the hot wind blew softly through the open window, stirring particles of dust from the torn screen" (102), thus challenging the stasis and decay represented by the flies, the heat, and the adults' lack of movement. Sonny reveals an even wilder streak when he refuses to accept a sealed-off tomb in his own house. He breaks through another barrier, just as earlier he had moved between house and woodpile in spite of his fear. Now he enters the room where the adults have left Shirley for dead.

Shirley's death chamber is certainly no less frightening than the woodpile, yet her brother decides traditions be damned, he'll do what he can to see her recover. Let me say something about Sonny's shift away from obedience and tradition. While it is a transgressive act that gets Shirley in trouble in the first place, it is also a transgression that will save her—through Sonny's intervention. In spite of the way Creek, and other oral stories, are often presented as morality or cautionary tales, clearly the treatment of cultural norms in them is equally balanced by social deviation.

This interests me because the party line in Native Studies has to do with respect for cultural traditions. In some ways this has always struck me as being at odds with art, which is all about deviance. To my way of thinking, if Sonny comes of age as anything in this story, it is as an artist in some sense. Whether or not he'll actually take up the tools of an artist, already he is beginning to draw outside the lines, to come up with his own picture instead of just coloring the generic sketch already provided for him.

In spite of the airlessness, the choking heat with the windows shut and blanketed, and the silence—a deadly quiet where even the droning flies are absent, Sonny perseveres inside the room. He touches his sister, who is barely breathing, and the heat of her skin frightens him. It is like being in the viewing line at a funeral, and Sonny observes how "the skin of the nose and forehead had become taut and dry and now gleamed pale and smooth like old ivory in the semi-darkness" (104). The absence of Shirley's name, reinforced by the detachment in the physical description of the body, certainly does not bode well for Shirley's recovery. The adults have already succumbed to Shirley as an "it," a non-being, and the fact that her physical features seem to confirm their resignation surely must daunt Sonny. He is further intimidated when evil returns, once again, in the form of heat: "A smell like that of hot wood filled the room, but underneath it the boy could smell the odor of something raw, something evil—something that was making Shirley die" (104).

This would be enough to scare anyone off, yet Sonny remains, removes a blanket from one of the windows, and lets the light in. Given the impossibility of the situation, wherein every indicator suggests Shirley's imminent death, Sonny is left with only one alternative, something the adults never thought of: simply to make up another story, one with a different ending, a more satisfactory conclusion than that provided by the old Creek woman speaking on behalf of tradition.

At this point the story begins to move me profoundly. As members of Tallahassee Wakokiye Creek ceremonial grounds, we say that Tallahassee is the place where we "touch medicine." In one way this means we are full members of the grounds rather than visitors, but the reference also has to do with the fact that this is where, literally, we touch medicine—we touch it four times with our little finger before drinking it during ceremonies. Sonny, the narrator tells us, "smelled the raw smell, and when it became too strong, he touched the smooth, round pebbles that had come from the creek where it still flowed, and the smell receded" (104).

If I may be anecdotal for a moment, I'm reminded of one hot summer afternoon when I was at the home of a Cherokee traditionalist who lives in a beautiful wooded area near Stillwell. We were down by the river where he had been gigging for crayfish. We came upon some shallows where you could hear water running over the rocks, and he told me that there was medicine in that sound AND that's what John Coltrane was thinking of when he recorded "A Love Supreme."

Inside the heat of Shirley's room, we further discover what touching medicine really means. In a crescendo of language, that seems to me, if I imagine it just right, to be the sound of water rippling over rocks, maybe even like a love supreme, the narrator says of Sonny,

> He began to force his thoughts to remember, to relive every living moment of his life and every part that Shirley had lived in it with him. And then he spoke softly, saying what they had done, and how they would do again what they had done, because he had not given up, for he was alive, and she was alive, and they had lived and would *still* live. And so he prayed to his will and forced his will out through his thoughts and spoke softly his words and was not afraid to look out through the window into the darkness through which came the coolness of the summer night. He smelled its scents and let them touch his flesh and come to rest around the "only sleeping" face of his sister. He stood, watching, listening, living. (104)

Note the difference between George Hulegy, who laid the medicine down inside the house, and Sonny, who takes the medicine up, who touches medicine in the fullest sense. The phrase "the 'only sleeping' face of his sister" references the "white" doctor's prognosis. As an artist, Sonny's act of the imagination is neither the doctor's denial of Shirley's illness or the adults' certainty of it, their fatalism. Like another Sonny, this Sonny's particular blues both embraces pain and transcends it, turns it into a work of art, invents a new story, risks an improvisation instead of just following the musical score.

There are few things "whiter" or more square than Julie Andrews singing "My Favorite Things." Some people can listen to her singing that without laughing, but these are very scary people. Yet, my god, what happens to that same song by the time Coltrane gets through with it, and returns it to the blues; our Creek Sonny also takes a square tune, a tragic tune, and gives it back its comic edges by making his own medicine, exquisitely, beautifully, imaginatively. In the Creek language this kind of love is called *anogetchka*, which isn't a concept but a participatory act: it calls things into being; it enacts relationships. Sonny improvises a new song, makes up a different story than the fatal rendition his elders have accepted.

Less poetically, it is my belief that many people do not succeed at touching medicine, so to speak, because it is simply a lot of hard work, and most people are unwilling. No one can possibly understand the labor that is involved in putting these ceremonies together at the grounds and churches unless they have actually witnessed it and worked alongside others doing it. Sonny's perseverance inside the room, and his mental catalog of all his experiences with his sister, require a good deal of effort. There are a lot more experts willing to hold forth on tradition and all it means then there are those who are willing to cook for hundreds of people in sweltering heat, mow grass on a summer day, or pick up trash at the churches or the grounds. And it is that kind of participation that teaches one about the ways in which deviance and obedience play off of each other in intricate balances. Many people have equated ceremonies with conformity to tradition because they have so little actual experience of them.

Like some significant writing during the seventies—Leslie Marmon Silko's "The Man to Send Rain Clouds," and, of course, the novel *Ceremony* come to mind—interior landscapes are also manifested in exterior ones. As clouds come, the temperature drops, and rain begins to fall in recognition of Sonny's labor of love. A dry season ends, and this is more than a matter of precipitation.

The story concludes with its second joke, a kind of Washington Irving jibe about conflated time. The room has cooled off so much that Sonny climbs into bed with his sister, and she wakes up. Shirley, like our imagined young Lynn Riggs who loses track of time during his fevers, does not realize she has been in a precarious sleep for days. Lynn is something like Dorothy in the field of poppies while the wicked witch—in Lynn's case his stepmother, working her crystal ball from afar—lures her into a murderous sleep. Shirley's mother seems more the embodiment of benign neglect, and her uncle is equally passive, making any witch comparison doubtful. Yet Shirley survives her family negligence with good humor: "You just now getting to bed? It's pretty late for that, ain't it?" (105).

The comedy suggests something has been restored. Sonny tells Shirley it will soon be morning, and we should remember that the elder had prophesied Shirley would not see her fourth dawn. The approaching sunrise is a very Creek reference since all Creek dancing is done from around midnight until an hour or two after the sun comes up, and it is that perseverance—the act of staying awake, remaining vigilant, keeping in motion all night without stopping—that is seen as an act of love of community at the ceremonial grounds. This, of course, is the opposite of the adults in the story, who barely move to swat the ominous flies.

The last words of the story have Sonny looking out the window, facing the very location where he and his sister first encountered the manifestations of evil: "Lying thus he could see in the darkness the even darker shapes of the trees and the storehouse his father had built" (105). Sonny has become his name, and he has stepped into the shoes of his father in a way the adults, who were supposed to be his and Shirley's caretakers, have not. Feminist interpretations of the story might center on Shirley's role as transgressor and Sonny's as potential father figure—whether or not gender is challenged as thoroughly as tradition.

I do not know if Sonny will grow up to be an artist in the same sense his creator did. A card Durango gave me is a photograph he took of an urban city square with a very stereotypical, familiar Plains warrior seated horseback and thrusting a lance up into the sky. Behind him is a city bus stopped at a red light. In front of the vague Sioux type is the incredibly unlikely life-size sculpture of a milk cow someone painted blue and touched up with white clouds that cover her from horn to hoof. Mendoza has titled the photograph "Partly Cloudy." Somehow it all fits, doesn't it? I would like to imagine that "Summer Water and Shirley" had some part in Mendoza's schooling in irreverence.

I want to conclude by taking "Summer Water and Shirley" in a slightly different direction, by considering the Fife article on Thewarle Indian Baptist Church. The Mendoza story never tells us what is going on inside the sanctuary. Yet one important fact that is stated is more than coincidental, I believe. It is eighth Sunday at the church. So let me tell you what would have been going on at Thewarle if Mendoza had chosen to render these details.

Eighth Sunday is communion Sunday. Church services would have begun Friday evening and people would have stayed overnight in their camp houses Friday and Saturday nights. Friday night's services would have lasted until around midnight. Saturday services would have taken place all day long. In between, people would have been visiting each other's camp houses and drinking coffee and eating. At the Saturday evening service would be an altar call, and the preacher would invite backsliders and unbelievers to repent. Christians who have backslidden, if they want to come back into fellowship, must voice their failings in front of the congregation. Church leaders discuss the case, pray, deliberate, and decide whether or not to let the person back in based on unanimous agreement among the leadership. Of these confessions Fife writes, "The Christians are not particularly interested in what a person has done, but *why* he has done it. If a person does not give his explanations, he does not take the wine. It will do him no good if he is unworthy" (460).

On Saturday night the women would have also gone off into the woods to sing and pray in patterns of four. The class leaders advise their female constituency and pray for the person who will make the communion bread the next morning, and the other women remain silent while the class leaders talk.

On Sunday morning, Hoktuke Emarthla, a term that means beloved woman, a special eldership role with complex roots in Creek ceremonial history, will be reverently working. Fife recalls,

> The most important job of Hoktuke Emathla is to make the communion bread. This is made before sunrise, before the birds sing or other creatures stir. All must be still while the bread is being made. While she is making bread, she must be praying. If she does not, the bread will tell on her. If the two preachers presiding over the Communion have not been good, the bread will tell on them. This is the miracle of Communion. (455)

After Sunday services, churches often have a big feed that includes many visitors showing up at camp houses to eat. I can certainly attest to the sweltering heat when you eat inside one of these houses where someone has been cooking on a wood stove on a brutal summer day with no air conditioning, captured in "Summer Water and Shirley." You wonder if you're the only one who might pass out, and yet nobody does.

So far we have communal confession, deliberation about sincerity, and the adequacy of explanations (whether they explain motives rather than merely failings). We have separate women's meetings and the importance of preparing communion bread properly, so it doesn't tell on you. Especially interesting is the apparent lack of interest in trans- or consubstantiation, the focus instead being on the possibility of the bread leaking information that you don't want told. I find this to be humorous and very Indian, the way this particular miracle also incorporates gossip.

Without trying to guess at Mendoza's intentions and the degree to which he incorporated church themes into the story, I could take a stab at the way in which "Summer Water and Shirley" examines motivations as much as failings—or maybe Shirley could even become the inversion of the Hoktuke Emathla, the elder woman appointed to make communion bread. Perhaps I could focus on the way the bread will reveal its makers' infractions against ceremonial rules. I could talk about the symbolism of "The Last Supper," or even Shirley's resurrection.

For me, however, a more interesting connection has to do with issues of jurisdiction. I mention these matters very briefly at the end of my chapter in

American Indian Literary Nationalism, which I co-authored with Jace Weaver and Robert Warrior. I believe the story contains three intersecting jurisdictions, some more pronounced than others, that are central to the events that unfold: the first is the activities of the Christians inside Thewarle Indian Baptist Church; the second is less obvious, and involves the traditions that have their central locus in the Creek square grounds; and the third is the dark practices of Ansul Middlecreek that take place in the woods surrounding the church.

We have to view the church woods carefully because the woods can also be an important sacred jurisdiction for both women and men church members, since church ceremonies take place there. We might observe, then, that jurisdiction is not the same thing as ownership, and it often involves shared spaces, in this case even between Baptists and witches.

In the jurisdictional spaces of the Christians in and around the church and camp houses, deacons are responsible for keeping order, and they are given their jurisdictional power by Creek pastors, other deacons, women class leaders, church members, and ultimately by God—*Hessaketemessee,* which means Maker of Breath in Creek, a different word than that used by ceremonialists, *Ofunka.* Fife writes of various deacon jurisdictions, for example, outside the church house as they blow the cow's horn that calls people from the camps and neighboring countryside to the services. One of the other signs of their jurisdictional authority is their staff, which church members believe has certain powers. Fife writes,

> A deacon uses his staff for many duties. It may be used as a pointer during usher duties. Also, it may be used during a baptism to assist a pastor. After one has been lowered into the water, the deacon may place the crook of his staff around the person's neck and assist the pastor in lifting him from the water. . . . A deacon may not touch a person with the tip of the staff. This could bring bodily harm, embarrassment, or could knock the breath out of the person it touches. If he does touch a person with his staff, he must do so by laying the side of his staff against the arm of the person he is touching. Nor can a deacon lay his staff flat on the ground. It must always be tilted with one end off the ground. When not in use a staff must always lean against something, even if it must be against the deacon's foot. (454)

Once again we see that deacons and church folks, in the case of baptism, have jurisdiction down by the creek and in the woods. This is not a Hawthorne story in which everybody who traipses off into the wilderness does so to get in touch with their inner demons.

Yet Ansul also has a certain jurisdiction of his own in the woods, rights that Shirley violates when she addresses him inappropriately on his own turf—down by the creek when it is not in use by church folks. Both Ansul's and the church's jurisdictions are deeply interrelated, central to the story and to its inevitable conflict. The jurisdiction of the Indian Baptist Church is not immune to the machinations of a Creek witch. Part of the problem occurs when Shirley removes herself from one space (the church house where adults could watch over and counsel her) and acts too freely in another geography. An equal problem is the adults in the story, who do not seem to have jurisdiction even inside their own home—where one might expect them to do more than simply give up when their own child takes ill.

In Shirley's case, she must, like all humans, enter other geographies away from home and church. So the idea here is not the stereotypical "stay home and listen to the elders"; it has more to do with the notion of how to act appropriately given the inevitability of various departures and returns, and knowing how the rules change on new turf. No one can stay home all the time, nor in church, nor in the woods. To put things in terms of the story's philosophy, no human can remain inside tradition all the time either, not even if he or she wanted to.

In Creek culture one can also observe individuals with granted jurisdictions at the ceremonial grounds: for example, the Dokpalas, the ceremonial equivalent of the church deacons, who keep order around the consecrated arbors that are set apart from other spaces at the grounds, are leaders who are given their authority from the Micco, the traditional chief, the grounds community, and, ultimately, *Ofunka,* the creator. At the churches, their counterparts, the deacons, get their authority from pastors, elders, the church community, and the Christian God, *Hessaketemmessee.* Varying jurisdictional responsibilities are evident in the roles of special leaders, men, women, and children—everyone who goes to the grounds or church.

Why is the church, then, to address a question raised earlier, an ever-present absence? "Summer Water and Shirley" is about the jurisdiction of children as much as that of the adult world represented by those inside the church. Although the story involves several jurisdictional realms, children are the focal point. In these regards I am reminded of Charles Laughton's directorial debut, *The Night of the Hunter,* which focuses on the jurisdiction of children as well, even though the film seems to be about an adult psychopath played by Robert Mitchum. The Laughton film also adds fascinating intersecting jurisdictions of its own, such as that of animals, when the camera pans on all the nonhumans who guide the children as they escape down river in a skiff.

In the Mendoza story it is one of the children, Sonny, who has a keener—and certainly a more artistic—sense of the responsibility within his own jurisdiction than the adults do, and the story is an inversion of the wizened elder who passes down knowledge to the next generation. Knowledge, it would appear, is omni- rather than unidirectional across generational lines. Within a child's, an adult's, a church member's, or even a witch's jurisdiction may exist significant knowledge, and people are expected to understand the different rules that apply as they cross various jurisdictional boundaries.

Sharon Fife recalls with humor that Creek preachers are liable to say funny things when they have to speak a foreign language. She writes, "When non-Creek speaking visitors are present, the sermon is sometimes given partly in English. This is usually difficult since many of the older preachers rarely speak English, if at all. And when a preacher is fervently speaking on a subject such as the destruction of Sodom, the least thing he is interested in is a well chosen word in English. Some people may think it odd to hear Lot's wife referred to as 'Old Lady Lot' " (458).

If one of the stories inside the church building has to do with breaking rules and turning into a pillar of salt, there are stories with much more artful conclusions outside of it. The power of such stories is their deviance—they will always sneak outside their own jurisdictions. Allowing art outside its usual boundaries and inside our politics, deviating from those things we have accepted as normative, as I have suggested in the chapter on Alexander Posey's freedmen stories, makes sense "because [we have not] given up, for [we are] alive, and . . . [we have] lived and [we will] *still* live" (Mendoza 104).

Works Cited

Fife, Sharon A. "Baptist Indian Church: Thlewarle Mekko Sapkv Coko." *Chronicles of Oklahoma* 48, no. 4 (Winter 1970–71): 450–66.

Mendoza, Durango. "Summer Water and Shirley." In *American Indian Authors,* edited by Natachee Scott Momaday, 96–105. Boston: Houghton Mifflin Company, 1972.

Maxey, Rosemary McCombs. Personal correspondence with author.

Resisting the Easy Connection

In my analysis of *The Year of Pilár*, I suggest that one of its powers is its refusal to give its secrets away easily. Its inscrutability has kept me obsessed with it for many years. I have explored the attraction of the artistic subject that resists our advances throughout the book, especially in the opening story that details Roe Náld's obsession with Justin. Lynn Riggs himself also held his secrets close to his chest, and it is not always the case that his life or his art flourished as a result. For all the times his mysteries are evocative, they can also simply be maddening.

In more recent Native literature an opposite extreme occasionally prevails, in which authors succumb to the temptation to connect all the dots for their readers. As happens in the case of what some critics have described as the homecoming stories, the oral tradition provides a kind of road map that guides the characters toward affirmational understandings that involve real-izations about the way stories inform their lives. Sometimes, however, the best road trips happen when you throw away the map and head out on the high-way, as the song would have it, looking for adventure.

I remember teaching a particular work of fiction in one of my classes at the University of Lethbridge, and a student asked if the tribe in question believed in reincarnation. I realized what I hadn't before—that the author had made the connections between her contemporary characters and ancient ones so perfectly that the former seemed like reincarnations of their mythical pre-decessors. The novel could have benefited greatly from some occasions where the modern characters deviated from those who came before them instead of fully embodying their ancestral relations. This, it seems to me, is one of the necessary adjustments when myth becomes fiction—that is, the fiction of short stories, plays, novels, and poems because, after all, myth and fiction are not the same thing. To collapse the two literatures into a single genre, I believe, does disservice to both of them. They do an edifying work on one another (a phrase I borrow from Phil Morgan's essay in *Reasoning Together*) not one of duplication. A Native novel that borrows from the oral tradition will suffer if it does not deviate just as skillfully from myth as it incorporates it.

"Summer Water and Shirley," like much of the literature that would come out of the 1970s, moves away from chaos toward a restorative and affirmational ending. Yet it does so in an unusual manner: its protagonist, Sonny, bucks the voice of Creek tradition in order to set healing forces in motion—restoration through transgression of tradition instead of its affirmation. I claimed I would have put some cherry bombs in the story, or at least some bottle rockets, and, while there aren't any explosions per se, the story builds to a crescendo of language when Sonny revives his sister by creating an artistic palette of imagined words and memories gorgeous enough to awaken a corpse. Some would simply argue that Sonny is more in tune with authentic Creek tradition than the adults, and that the old lady who foretells Shirley's death is out of touch with true Creek philosophy. To me a more interesting reading involves the necessity of recognizing when a thing, even tradition, becomes oppressive and should be resisted. No one could ever survive at the Creek grounds or churches without developing a capacity for understanding the balance between what must be accommodated and what resisted. You don't do what every single person tells you. The creator gave us a brain for a reason.

Durango Mendoza's only other stories, "The Passing," "The Woman in the Green House," and "A Short Return," are much more subtle than "Summer Water and Shirley," dealing with the daily grind of an abandoned mother and her children living as often as not in destitution as they do in miraculous awakenings.

The strongest of the three works, in relation to the superlative Thlewarle church imagining of "Summer Water and Shirley," "The Passing" makes its references to the Creek world fairly obviously, if less intensely than Sonny's coming-of-age story. There is Fish Creek, an actual stream around Dustin; the Indian church (although it is not named as Thlewarle, it is likely the same one by virtue of its location); the Indian graveyard; the Creek houses built over graves mentioned in the Fife article; Chilocco Indian School (a boarding school that many Creek students attended in north central Oklahoma, outside of Creek jurisdiction and close to the Kansas border), and actual Creek family names, like the surname Bear.

Mendoza's only first-person story is narrated by Sonny, whom we are already familiar with. All the Mendoza stories are concerned with seasons and close natural details: "The Passing" begins in later summer, and ends in late winter when snow is beginning to melt into a muddy mess, and it certainly captures many of the details of the plank houses, farm gates, rocky hillsides, bouldered creeks, thin post oaks, and pecan groves of this part of Hughes County. Not all tribal writers have been able to name land as well as they have described culture, though the stronger ones have; and Mendoza knows the place he hails from.

The story opens with Sonny's mother commenting on Joe Willow, who is passing down the road that runs in front of the house: a hard worker, she says. Throughout the story Joe is referenced as a young worker and his very bearing suggests labor—he carries a bucket, and moves "like someone who is used to walking, slowly, without spirit, but with the strength seen in a young workhorse" (61). The silence of Sonny's mother, and the way she shakes her head when she speaks of Joe's parents, indicate Joe's home life leaves a lot to be desired.

Like Hardy Eagle, the deacon in "Summer Water and Shirley," Joe's name is not a typical Creek one, and the reader is instead drawn to the flexibility of supple willow branches, their profusion next to water, the shade they provide Indian arbors as roof materials, and their centrality in Creek ceremony, especially Green Corn. I can hear willow-roofed arbors, turned from fresh green to brittle browns after their leaves have dried out, rattling in the wind. Fresh cut, they are full of the aching beauty of the creek beds they are found by; later into the season, outside the arbors, one hears them rattle in the distance, in mourning for water. After losing their green they are full of the blues. The Mendoza story is full of Sonny's aching longing for someone who understands his family situation, the way he has been severed from his father—more to the point, for anyone nearby who might understand him. He is a Lynn looking for an Uncle Jimmy, and it turns out that the need for friendship is mutual in the case of Sonny and Joe.

Sonny experiences some kind of attraction or interest in Joe, and he waits out by the farm gate each evening to see him pass, sometimes hiding, other times revealing himself, an action that gives the story its subtle title, suggesting how much can happen in the most minimal of encounters. W. H. Auden's poem "Musée des Beaux Arts" provides an ironic contrast, perhaps, to the Mendoza story. In a corner of the Brueghel painting the poem references, Icarus makes the tiniest of splashes as he falls into the ocean, while the rest of the world goes about its business. A young plowman on shore barely registers the sound, and a nearby ship at sea sails on, unaffected.

Not true of our young protagonist, Sonny, no matter how minimal his contact with Joe Willow. He is more like the narrator of "Araby," availing himself of every opportunity to sneak a peak at Mangan's unnamed sister. It is the adults in "The Passing" who are akin to all those in the Auden poem who miss "Something Amazing, a boy falling out of the sky" (1055), not Sonny, who waits daily for Joe to pass by, and he has felt Joe's falling profoundly. The title of the story not only references the two boys' eventual brief exchange at the farm gate, but Sonny's caretakers, who fail to note its impact and "pass" on its meaning. Like "Summer Water and Shirley," the intuition of certain children is contrasted with the lack of awareness in adults.

Joe Willow is full of mystery, and he becomes Sonny's obsession, like Justin to Roe Náld, Gar to Lynn, Lynn Riggs to me—the "object" of artistic desire.

The first time he encounters Joe, Sonny elicits a mere wave and smile from him when he says, "Hello, Joe Willow" (60). If Mangan's sister is associated with the promise of the Dublin bazaar, Joe is associated with the woods, an important jurisdictional space in Mendoza's writing: "In the stillness my voice carried, and he turned, his shadow pointing into the woods, and lifted his hand. He squinted into the sun and smiled. I waved, and he turned back up the road and soon faded against the shadow and trees" (60–61). Joe walks on the road, but his shadow reaches outside its boundaries, sneaks out of its jurisdiction, its limitations, and touches on the woods, which are full of creative—if sometimes dangerous—possibilities in Mendoza's fictional world. To whatever degree Joe is a young workhorse, a drudge for adults (often he is carrying a pail), part of him yearns for something else, and this desire—the way Joe represents escape from adult norms—attracts Sonny.

Like Shirley, Sonny dares to cross jurisdictional boundaries, calling more than once from his gate to Joe, outside on the road, whose shadow reaches all the way to the woods. Eventually Joe will set off down that road to faraway places, at least to Chilocco Indian School, a great cultural, if not geographical, distance; yet Joe will still not quite escape into freedom. Sonny begins the story by explaining he has already explored the countryside in his first years at the house, and he has stuck closer to home more recently, having already seen things far and wide and worn out his curiosity. Fittingly, for Mendoza, the woods do not provide a magical escape. Perhaps he is one of our great tribal realists.

Given his isolation and less-than-ideal home life, Sonny has long hoped someone like Joe might pass by, and pass by he does, the entire month of August, his lard bucket in hand, and he becomes the subject of Sonny's intense scrutiny: "He would come up from the hill, the sun to his back, and his skin, a very reddish brown, would be covered with a fine dust, making his brows appear lighter and thicker than they were. His hair was cut short, but it lacked the uniformity of a regular barber shop haircut, and he wore no hat" (61).

August is also the month, less happily, in which Sonny becomes aware that his mother is expecting a child from his stepfather, Miguel. We learn that Sonny's real father is dead in "Summer Water and Shirley," and his lot in life is not improved by a father's presence, or at least not by Miguel's, in "The Passing." "The Woman in the Green House" takes up the subject of pregnancy more fully, an experience that simply further alienates the children from their abusive stepfather and exacerbates their poverty and his absence. While the dreary rural grind of Dustin is not exactly the urban Irish streets of James Joyce's world, Joe Willow, nonetheless, is the light that brightens Sonny's darkness.

Sonny anxiously awaits his chance to say something to Joe. Unlike Joyce's first-person narrator, Sonny does not botch it. The occasion is momentous. The month has changed. Joe steps out of the new light: "It was early in September, and I was sitting on the gate watching the sun caught on the treetops, noticing how the leaves looked like embers across its face as it settled into them, when Joe Willow appeared like a moving post upon the road" ("The Passing" 62). Perhaps this sentence, as much as anything, explains why Mendoza became a painter.

The narrator's stepfather begins calling him into the house for supper, and Sonny ignores his calls. I'm reminded of the way Creek grounds and churches both begin with the ceremonial calls to dances and services that give you a particular number of times to get inside the sanctuary or under your dance arbor. Sonny resists the authority of his stepfather (who is possibly Mexican rather than Creek), instead waiting for Joe, who interests him a good deal more than another dreary dinner, to pass by. As in "Summer Water and Shirley" there is something to be said for ignoring the demands of adults.

This time Sonny initiates a conversation: "Howdy, Joe Willow. . . . You coming home from work?" (62).

Hardly a question a polite country Indian boy in eastern Oklahoma can ignore, and Joe stops, leans on the mailbox, and exchanges greetings, which, Indian enough, begin with family affiliations. Ironically, Joe starts the conversation with, "You're Miguel's boy, aren't you?" (62), a question that shows how Creek matrilineal reality is also mediated by rural Oklahoma patriarchy. Sonny, one suspects out of dislike for his stepfather as much as reverence for Creek tradition (though there may be some of that, too), says, "Huh-uh. I belong to Rosa" (62).

Joe, after getting to know his interlocutor a little better, shifts into this matrilinearity himself: "You know what? I'm the same way. Everybody calls me Jimmy Bear's boy, but I'm not. He's not my daddy" (62). The sun is sinking, and before it is time to move on, Joe says,

> "You see what happens when the sun goes down?" He pointed to the
> evening star and motioned toward the other stars that had appeared in

the east. "When the daddy goes to bed, all the little children come out." His teeth gleamed in the gathering darkness, and I smiled too.

We had watched the stars for only a moment when Miguel called again.

"You better get on home," Joe Willow said. "That's your daddy calling you." (62)

Let us return for a moment to the beginning of my musing about the powers of ambiguity, since here the story moves toward clarity rather than mystery. This is the kind of heightened occasion that marks the literature of the 1970s and other decades: the connection between the two boys, its relation to myth underscored by the star references, which could be analyzed in relation to Creek narratives about day, night, sun, moon, and stars—the meaning discovered by understanding one's life in relation to mythical patterns. The absence of Joe's and Sonny's biological fathers has a one-to-one correspondence to the oral stories.

But please observe the way in which Mendoza artistically colors his yin with a little yang as the story moves toward its conclusion.

September is also the month Joe goes off to school at Chilocco. Sonny hears no more news of Joe until early spring. His mother has come back from the hospital with his new brother, and Miguel comes into the kitchen stomping dirty snow off his overshoes, and nonchalantly announces that he heard Joe Willow got killed on the Santa Fe train tracks near school. Mysteries surround the death, which the reader might interpret as possible suicide, but it's hard to say. At the funeral the Bear family carries on in a way that they never did while Joe was alive, crying and fainting over his passing, and, of course, another meaning comes into the story's title, a sadder one.

Sonny experiences no such drama, and the story does not end in epiphany: "The dirt sounded on the wooden vault, and the little houses over the older graves looked gray and damp with the people standing among them. I went over to the pecan trees and kicked among the damp mulch looking for good nuts, but I couldn't find any" (63–64). There is no flash of insight, no healing in the woods.

The next line, from the perspective of making artistic choices, is really interesting to me. Sonny recalls, "That evening after supper I stepped out onto the back stoop to go to the bathroom, and the yellow lamplight behind me threw my shadow onto the patches of snow and earth, enclosing it in the rectangle that the doorway formed" (64).

Aha! It's sundown! We're going to get our Indian ending after all, thank god, after the disappointing funeral and its lack of revelation. We were just beginning to get worried. The earlier mythical reference worked into the story has prepared us for what happens when the sun goes down—the evil stepfather goes to bed, and the children come out to play. Life imitates myth.

Or maybe not.

Here's how Mendoza ends the story:

> I looked up. The spotty clouds looked like bits of melting snow pressed into the darkness, and the stars were out, sprinkled into the stillness beyond. The black trees swayed, and the cold wind was familiar.
>
> Behind me Mama moved around the kitchen, and I heard the chink and gentle clatter of the plates and pans as she put those things away. I shivered. And I knew that soon, as it did every spring, the clouds would come and it would begin to rain, a cold, heavy drizzle, and the land would turn to mud. (64)

The last word of the story is mud! And not the kind that people crawl out of in origin stories as they make their way into the light of a new world. Obviously, this is a different rain than the one that falls at the end of "Summer Water and Shirley," and, to my way of thinking, quite distinct from the good clean rain that falls after the aborted cow rescue in James Welch's *Winter in the Blood*, when the narrator finally confronts his repressed memories of his dead brother.

No, instead this is a tough fucking ending. There are little teases, with the stars and all, but we don't get the sundown, the evil stepfather out of the picture, and the children out to play—and authors who are artists, rather than writers, sometimes do not yield to their readers' wishes, even their Indian wishes. Sonny is going to go back to being awful damn lonely with an abusive stepfather and an ineffective mother. That's what really happens, sometimes, in Dustin and all other places in the world. And going to a stomp dance or listening to a story from the oral traditions might very well still leave you with this reality to deal with. Obviously, this doesn't mean don't go to stomp dances or give up on stories; it means life has never been particularly easy, and artists often have something to say about that.

"The Woman in the Green House," which actually takes up the subject of a mother's pregnancy and a stepfather (like Miguel in "The Passing"), ends with the children dispossessed in their own home, and the stepfather claiming they are not his kids. The family's future is bleak:

> The little boy began to whimper, and the fat woman took him on her knee. After a while he pressed against her, and she sat with him there. He looked at his sister and made a face. Suddenly she began to cry, and he jerked and became afraid. But the fat woman held him closer and called

him poor baby, and he felt better. The middle boy said nothing and held onto the woman's sleeve and watched his sister standing slumped near the door with her coat on. (58)

These are the very last words of the story. Given all the talent of the author, one wishes for a novel that reveals all these ups and downs of Sonny's, and being the eternal optimist I am (don't laugh), I still haven't given up hope that someday we might see one. If not, I'm grateful for the rich legacy we already have.

Framed by a dream, "A Short Return," Mendoza's only first-person story, contrasts Sonny's childhood in Dustin with a brief visit to his parents, still trapped in rural destitution, after Sonny has moved off to Kansas City with two of his siblings. Waking up after a dream that vividly takes him back to his childhood yearnings after a better life, Sonny realizes that his stepfather has lost some of his power over him, and, to some degree, is less abusive than the tyrant Sonny grew up with. While Shirley wakes up in the biggest sense, to a world of restored relations, Sonny's awakening here is harder. In this story the father is named Edmund. His decreasing machismo, even his kindness to Sonny in trying to arrange a ride back to Kansas City and bus fare, cannot make up for the past:

> I thought to shake his hand also, but instead I turned quickly and crossed the highway and did not look back until I had gone around the curve. When I glanced back they still stood together, looking after me. I lifted my arm, but a truck lumbered by and I dropped my arm and continued on out of their sight. (113)

Sonny had already shaken hands with his mother: "[A]s she always did when one of her children went away again, she shook my hand" (113). In the Creek world not shaking hands, especially at the time of a significant departure, means a good deal. One shakes hands with people, like immediate family, who would be hugged in the white world. Edmund has gotten some payback, comeuppance for how he treated his kids: "In the last few years I noticed that Edmund often sat in the kitchen alone, almost completely ignored by his three children. His two daughters seldom spoke to him other than to ask for money or permission to go somewhere" (112). They refer to Edmund by his first name, and this haunts Sonny. While Sonny sometimes feels compelled to tell the young women to be more respectful to their father, he never does, and one gets the sense that his concern is for his siblings' training in appropriate relations, not any great affection for his stepdad. Like "The Passing," the story does not end in reconciliation.

The editors of *Question and Form in Literature* included short statements from the authors after each story. (Mendoza appears in fine company, by the way. Fellow contributors include Doris Lessing, Anne Tyler, Flannery O'Connor, James Thurber, E. B. White, Kurt Vonnegut, Jr., Ursula K. Le Guin, Edna St. Vincent Millay, Alice Walker, D. H. Lawrence, and William Saroyan.) Mendoza's perspective on the story is a painterly one:

> As a young adult, my childhood was remembered as a series of emotional high and low spots.... These ... early years are all colored by the perspective of an introverted child. It seemed that the sightlines of my vision of the world slanted upward from me—things and people and events loomed over me ... the ground, the grass, and the details of floor-level life were closely sensed.
>
> The time came when I began to realize that my perspective grew less and less slanted as I grew, both physically and emotionally ... one day I crossed the plane between childhood and maturity and began to feel that I could comfortably look backward and forward . . . and, if not understand them, at least sense that life had different meaning for different people at different times.
>
> This is the state of mind I was exploring when I wrote "A Short Return." I did not analyze it then, but the process—taking a series of emotional vignettes and giving them a time, a setting, and characters— enabled me to express my feelings about the past and look to the future with my emotional accounts balanced.
>
> Is the story based on real-life situations? Yes if memory serves and has survived the child. (113)

Spatial and painting metaphors abound: color, perspectives, sightlines, slant, loom, details, floor level, plane, and so on. Reconsidered from a painterly angle of vision, the stellar "Summer Water and Shirley," seen from the floor level and the grass up, as a series of emotional vignettes looming over Sonny, reverses the pattern so that Sonny, by displaying the characteristics of a budding artist, eventually looms over his subject matter when he rejects the death tableau all the adults in the story have passively accepted, and imagines a more artistic rendering of the gritty destitution that surrounds him. Other times the bleakness itself, rather than it s transformation, is his artistic subject.

Works Cited

Auden, W. H. "Musée des Beaux Arts." In *The Norton Introduction to Literature*, edited by Alison Booth, J. Paul Hunter, and Kelly J. Mays, 1055. 9th ed. New York: Norton, 2005.

Mendoza, Durango. "The Passing." In *The Chicanos: Mexican American Voices,* edited by Ed Ludwig and James Santibanez, 59–64. Baltimore: Penguin, 1971.

——. "A Short Return." In *Question and Form in Literature,* edited by James E. Miller, Jr., Roseann Duenas Gonzalez, and Nancy C. Millet, 108–13. Glenview, Ill.: Scott, Foresman and Company, 1979.

——. "Summer Water and Shirley." In *American Indian Authors,* edited by Natachee Scott Momaday, 96–105. Boston: Houghton Mifflin Company, 1972.

——. "The Woman in the Green House." In *The Chicanos,* 53–58.

Morgan, Phillip Carroll. " 'Who Shall Gainsay Our Decision?': Choctaw Literary Criticism in 1830." In *Reasoning Together: The Native Critics Collective,* 126–46. Norman: University of Oklahoma Press, 2008.

Welch, James. *Winter in the Blood.* New York: Harper & Row, 1974.

Take Me Back to Turkey, Texas, I'm Too Young to Bury

The Riot Explained

In April of 2005, I drove from my home in Oklahoma City to Turkey, Texas, to attend the thirty-fourth annual reunion of Bob Wills and the Texas Play-boys. Well, Bob wasn't there, but this has something to do with the fact that he's been dead longer than the reunions have been held, and his demise, it would seem, never was much of a reason to cancel the party.

Bob Wills is part of my family's personal history. My granddad used to tell stories about chopping cotton all day, his only break at noon to come in for a bite to eat and a listen to radio station KVOO out of Tulsa, where Bob Wills held forth for a decade, offering up his infectious western swing music and cries of "Aha! Take it away, Leon, take it away," to his steel guitar player, the virtuoso Leon McAuliffe. This is a rich imagining for me, grandpa coming out of the cotton fields into one of those shacks he rented and fiddling with the radio to get it tuned in to Tulsa. I imagine the brief respite of lunch and music, then the sheer act of will it takes to force himself back out to the field where the hoe or the cotton sack or the mule waits for him. A good number of Indian and white Okies, at least the kind I hang out with, tell similar stories about listening to Wills on KVOO during his decade in Tulsa, throughout the 1930s and until the beginning of World War II, when many of the Wills boys, including Bob himself, either joined or were called up for service.

The influence of Oklahoma on the Wills band was tremendous; it was in Tulsa that they first started calling themselves the Texas Playboys, and Wills always wanted to live there, set up a kind of communal ranch for all the Playboys and their families to stay, and stick to regional rather than national touring. Wills's most important guitar player, Eldon Shamblin, was from Weatherford, Oklahoma, the man *Rolling Stone* magazine once claimed was the best rhythm guitar player in the world. The contemporary artist Edgar Heap of Birds tells me about his dad's love of the Wills band, a strong reality for Cheyenne jurisdiction in that part of western Oklahoma where Wills's music flourished. A great number of Wills's musicians were from that part of the world, and it's the epicenter of western swing whether or not it's on the Oklahoma or Texas side of the Panhandle.

In addition to the way in which Bob Wills is a part of my family's experience and stories, down through the years, by some strange coincidences, I've known some of the well-known western swing players, and even played music with them and their kids—informally, that is, around porches and kitchens.

So there I was in Turkey waiting for the Bob Wills concert. There's more to the story; my guitar teacher at the time, himself one of the Texas Playboys, was going to play there with them that day. After picnicking in the park next to a giant concrete statue of Bob in his Stetson and holding his characteristic big cigar, my partner and I headed down the street where a lot of preliminary bands were playing.

Turkey, only four hours southwest of Oklahoma City, is a different world. Cotton fields still abound on the west Texas plains there, and its citizens are white descendants of former cotton kings and black descendants of their slaves and other descendants of folks too poor to own slaves or land of their own, people not entirely unlike my own grandfather.

Today Turkey, Texas, like so many places in the rural American south, is becoming a ghost town. We passed by long-gone businesses people hadn't even bothered to board up; one brick storefront's door was ajar, and you could see where kids had been in there partying and doing the things young folks do in such places to keep from going nuts.

We stopped and listened to a western swing band, one of the side attractions before the big dance that night. Forget the Grand Ole Opry, whatever you might or might not know about country music, this ain't even close to that bullshit Garth Brooks/Alan Jackson/Toby Keith/Shania Whatever-her-name-is pop-schlop crap that's taken over the music business. This is the real thing, and in Turkey, Texas, it constitutes a musical and dance tradition that is passed on from generation to generation and has as much to do with what you hear on country music stations these days as Mozart has to do with Madonna.

In spite of its extinction on country music radio stations, western swing is still big in west Texas and western Oklahoma, and 15,000 people show up to see the Wills band reunited every year.

Well, the warm-up act wasn't bad. They were playing in the back lot out behind the only business I could tell was still open on the main street of town; the Texas Playboys would play later in the day at the high school football stadium. The sax player wasn't too hot, mostly played back the melody line rather than the kind of improvisation that the Wills boys referred to as hot solos, wild musical flights that took the melody to new stratospheres, but other people were cooking up on the bandstand and making him look better, and they served up some good stuff, from the slow West Texas waltzes to the fast swing numbers that sent the two-steppers all flocking out to an improvised dance area that they'd cordoned off (it looked to me like the former concrete floor of an old auto repair shop whose walls had somehow disappeared). There was a kind of Grecian feel to the town with all its decaying buildings, some partially standing but without roofs.

The bandleader, in a big straw Resistol hat and Nike tennis shoes, waved his *cataboga,* as my grandpa might say when he occasionally slipped into Creek, and announced he was going to do something that he said he always did to end every show: he called all the veterans in the crowd forward. It was a revealing sight as at least half of the men, of all ages, got up and gathered in front of the bandstand. That moment spoke volumes about what opportunities are like for young men in Turkey and its West Texas environs.

I was moved. I am used to honoring veterans. As for most Native people, it is part of the traditions of my home community. At my own Creek ceremonial grounds, Tallahassee Wakokiye grounds—where I touch medicine, as we say back home, and dance, and sing—we, too, recognize those who have served in the military.

What occurred next, however, was the bandleader gave a speech about how our freedom depended on the U.S. occupation of Iraq, thrown in with several ringing endorsements of George W. Bush, whom some people, even some Texans, still claimed at that time as the president of the United States. Then we were required to take our hats off as a salute to the war and its president.

This was a terrible moment for me. I don't have any problem whatsoever taking my hat off for a veteran. The level of sacrifice those men and women offered their country is something I'll probably never even be able to understand. I recognize their service; I am grateful for it; and I know that the life of a university professor is privileged in a lot of different ways, marked by opportunities that many of these men did not have when they went off to wage America's wars.

I do, however, have a problem, a big problem, with tipping my hat to the Iraq War; consequently, my OU ball cap remained on my head. I didn't feel good about leaving my cap on, and I certainly didn't feel good about taking it off as a show of support for the U.S. occupation of Iraq, which I have strongly opposed from the outset, and I was in protests against its "inevitability" even before it began. Arguably, one of the things we owe the men, and the women, who have served in the military is as vigorous a critical skepticism as we can muster in relation to the U.S. committing itself to war, so that they do not make these sacrifices unless absolutely necessary.

Things got a little scary in that West Texas back lot. People three feet away started saying things like "ungrateful bastards," and one woman commented that the veterans had given up everything to quote "save a lot of ungrateful butts." The hatred was palpable. Let me be clear: Bob Wills was popular in West Texas in the 1930s and 1940s. The median age of a typical Bob Wills fan, therefore, is somewhere around eighty-six. If we were going to get beaten up, most likely we would be bludgeoned to death by a lot of canes and nursing home walkers. With some luck, I began to ponder, we might could outrun them and make it back to our little blue Honda that was still parked by Bob's statue, his giant cigar poking at the cloudless west Texas sky. It now seemed to me that the cigar was pointing toward the quickest way out of town, and I contemplated the fact that Wills himself hadn't wasted any time getting out of Turkey as quick as he could, having left at a young age, and, as far as I know never returning to live there.

More seriously, my partner and I were standing very quietly and respectfully, trying our best to focus our attention on these men and honor them. I come from a tradition, as do many of you all, in which silence is a legitimate form of respect. I wondered which was more appropriate, I and my partner, standing quietly and seriously, or the people mouthing off about ungrateful bastards and drawing attention to themselves and away from the men who had come forward (I also wondered where the women were, since so many have served in America's wars).

The experience was harsh, to use my partner's word for it later, and it colored the rest of the day and the dance that night. I grew up seeing people two-step around concrete dance floors and have stepped around them often enough myself, but that Saturday it all seemed a good deal more sinister than it had before. It made me wonder about my own allegiance to western swing, so much a part of my identity as a musician. I cut my musical eyeteeth on those Bob Wills songs, learning to play them on my guitar in my teens. I wondered about the hatred that might form some of the backdrop for songs that I had only considered in light of their musical properties, which far exceeded much of the country music of their time.

I have thought a lot about that Saturday. I was reminded of events some few years before that spring of 2005. I was a keynote speaker at a conference at Mystic Lake, Minnesota. The night of my reading was the same night the bombs began to fall on Baghdad. The beginning of the U.S. bombing of Iraq cast a real damper on the conference. To my shame, I didn't say anything about it during my presentation. I read from my novel and played and sang some songs, old jazz standards that I sometimes incorporate into my fiction readings these days. This was new for me at the time, something I'd just started doing, the music and fiction together; maybe that's why my mind wasn't where it should have been since I was worried about coordinating the music and prose. At any rate, there wasn't, and isn't, any good excuse for my silence that evening.

The next night Simon Ortiz was the keynote speaker. Simon told a compelling story about his nephew recently approaching him with the news that he was volunteering for the army and the pain that this caused Simon, himself a veteran. Simon commented that he had not heard anyone at the conference mention the U.S. bombing of Iraq and went on to say that he felt that indigenous writers had not only the right, but the responsibility, to address such issues and made a case for the reason Native writers should have things to say about military occupations.

I felt guilty about my own performance the night before although I'm sure that that was not Simon's intention. Simon simply sets a higher standard.

Some years ago now, I read an editorial in the *New York Times* written by the Nobel Prize–winning novelist Günter Grass. Grass spoke of the pain of German history and the impossibility of any kind of pride in German nationalism in light of the Holocaust. Grass said that for the first time in his life recent events made it possible for him to be proud to be German, because Germany stood so very strongly against the U.S. in opposition to its invasion of Iraq.

Grass's statement about the impossibility of feeling a sense of pride about being German particularly struck me. Patriotism, in my view, is not an entirely bad thing. The loss of the ability to express pride in one's community is a tragedy. It is the loss of a piece of one's own self. In addition to the senseless loss of lives due to the Iraq War, one of the greatest things the United States has lost is its reputation, its goodwill, and, importantly, the right of its citizens to feel decent about themselves and their country.

Like most people, I look at U.S. involvement in the war based on my own personal and communal history. I believe, strongly, in constitutional law, in courts, and in parliamentary forms of government. I come from a tribe that has had a constitutional government since 1867 (when it was first put in practice, although Creek people had been preparing one for several decades before events like Indian Removal and the American Civil War interrupted the process). It's an understatement to say the Creek Nation hasn't always practiced constitutionality very effectively, yet I don't see the basis for these failings in the constitution itself but in the application of its principles—often, more aptly put, the lack of application of its principles. I oppose the Iraq War because I believe in constitutions, in courts, and in law. I have often wondered about the responsibility of minority writers in a political environment in which the United States still imagines itself as the protagonist in a John Wayne movie, this time extending its jurisdiction far beyond the Rio Brazos.

Given the stories I just told, and the fact that nationalism is the most frightening phenomenon of our time, maybe of any time, I might well wonder how I managed to create a body of work, acknowledged by others and myself, as a partisan forum for indigenous nationalism.

Recently, and sometimes for good reason, the larger public has come to doubt the integrity of tribal nationalism, given the immorality of recent decisions ranging from disenfranchising citizens because of African ancestry, passing hate legislation against gays and lesbians in the form of anti-marriage laws, proposing tourist bridges over sacred monuments, or using treaties as a justification for hunting endangered whales or clubbing seals to death.

My own work has been a response to what I see as two extremes that have proven ineffective in relation to these challenges. One is the position maintained by those who claim that whatever Indians do it is their sovereign right to do it, making sovereignty a matter of religious privilege rather than a legal and moral fact based in the U.S. Constitution, court cases, and the more universal right of peoples to determine their own destinies. The other extreme is to claim that sovereignty itself is inherently flawed rather than opposing abuses of sovereignty, and the justification for the critique of sovereignty often rests on a reductive claim that it is a European, not an indigenous, political institution, usually with little or no explanation as to why European political institutions are, by default, irrelevant to Native life.

I do not subscribe to either of these positions. I believe that sovereignty is an inherent, not a derivative, right of indigenous people that demands recognition, and I also believe that tribal sovereignty is subject to critique, the same as any of the world's sovereign powers who face criticism and even sanctions when they behave irresponsibly. As much as anything, this means taking sovereignty seriously by insisting that the tribal nation, like other sovereign nations, must face repercussions for injustices, and recognition for responsibly exercising their own powers in relation to the rights of their citizens and other governments at the national and global crossroads. Sovereignty has never meant that a nation can do whatever it wants. The issue is not whether sovereignty is relevant since any community has the right to self-determination. Instead, we must ask how sovereignty can serve human liberation and what is the responsibility of tribal peoples, and other peoples, when it does not.

I'm hoping that indigenous researchers and activists will author a particular kind of outrageous story—that is, stories about outrageous acts of compassion, about outrageously compassionate forms of nationalism and sovereignty. Creeks believe that physics is held together by, of all things, love—that compassion is the very force that keeps the orbitals in alignment. We need as much of this as we can get in our scholarship. I would like to see us attempt representations of sovereignty that do not even exist yet, dreams of nationhood that move toward inclusion and compassion, and a vision of community that involves an expansion of human rights rather than defining and limiting them.

In Oklahoma, I have taught freedmen students in Native literature courses. Those who have been disenfranchised are heartbroken about their tribes' decisions to disenroll them based on their African ancestry despite their community's legacy of loyal service, including a history of fighting side by side as allies of the southeastern nations in more than one war (their service on behalf of the Upper Towns in the Red Stick War of 1813–14 and on behalf of Loyalist Creeks who sided with the Union during the American Civil War comes immediately to mind). A nation must not treat its citizen allies with such contempt. I have often thought what might happen if one of those students comes along and turns into a powerful novelist? What if one of them has the capacity to see that she has the most dramatic story in the history of the world, as does anyone who wakes up to the power of her own vision? Dreaming of the chance, no matter how minute, that such a person might be a student in my classroom is part of my research and activist agenda.

Personally, I'd like to write a fantasy novel about a lesbian couple filing for a marriage license at the tribal complex in Tahlequah, Oklahoma, to which the tribe's leadership responds, "We'd *love* to be the first ones to have a chance to marry you!" I like my version better than what actually happened to Kathy Reynolds and Dawn McKinley. Maybe someone could write a novel that places the utopic story alongside real-life homophobia. Our stories are only limited by our willingness to engage our imaginations and to tell them in an ethical relationship to our communities. I will admit this is no easy chore, but still the fact that we've had so few such stories in my line of work, Native imaginative writing, says something not only about the literary marketplace but about the state of Native art and the tendency of even Indian writers to mold their work for the beads-and-feathers crowd. Apart from the work of some important writers that I discuss in the penultimate chapter, lesbians are virtually nonexistent in Native fictional worlds.

All of this is to say I hope for a different kind of national story. Many postcolonial writers have written of nationalism as a pathology with roots in xenophobia, triumphalism, oppositional discourse that pits an us against a them, and isolationism, but perhaps there is some other kind of nationalism they don't know about yet—one that tribal people can explore, one that may not even yet exist except in dreams waiting to become stories. Indian country seems to me a perfect location for exploring these questions, since it is a case study for what constitutes the modern nation. Consider tribes whose descendants now number only in the hundreds, whose primary language is English, who do not have a reservation base, whose citizenry is of mixed ancestry, or whose citizens look black rather than Indian, or who look white rather than Indian, or who have never had a treaty with the United States—can they constitute modern nation-states? In some cases the answer has been, and should have been, yes. How much is enough and what is the enough made of? Tribal nations should be the very locus of those studying what it means to be a modern nation in a global context.

Some of my writings of late have taken a defensive turn. Add this to the "You know you're a redneck when . . ." joke punchlines: "You know you're a redneck when you have to write a book to prove you're not." In *American Indian Literary Nationalism* I had to take a weird rhetorical stance, basically arguing, "I don't suck as bad as some people say I do." While perhaps the gauntlet had been sufficiently thrown down so I had no other choice but to take up the challenge, you start from the weaker position when you have to defend yourself against the claims of your failings. I have had so much more fun with *Art as Performance, Story as Criticism* because I returned to telling stories and talking about them, by far a stronger starting point.

I had the good fortune to participate in *Reasoning Together: The Native Critics Collective*, a work that deviates from the mode of the book I co-authored before it, where I set out to prove I was one of the good guys whose nationalist turns simply reflected inescapable legal and social realities, not the other kind of scary nationalist that some have come to assume is the only kind there is.

Reasoning Together returned me to what I love: analyzing imaginative writing, tracing out literary histories, and tackling the challenges of theory. I'm not sure where to begin to do justice to the creative, contentious, celebratory, and often compassionate, nature of this volume. First and foremost, it is not my book—which is why it turned out so good. It was co-authored with eleven other people. There are no contributors to *Reasoning Together;* there are twelve authors who share the responsibility for its communal composition. Some of those writers, I should note, were then—and some still are—graduate students, and I am proud to have participated alongside people who were likely to actually have something to say, rather than the usual suspects.

Reasoning Together puts twelve Indian co-authors in dialogue, since we assigned each of us this topic: "Describe an ethical Native literary criticism." The most unique aspect of the collection is that rather than submitting autonomous essays, each author's subject is also that of the other essayists in the book; thus, it is an interactive volume. We might even say we could accurately paraphrase our initial call as "Describe to *each other* an ethical Native literary criticism."

That *Reasoning Together* deviates from other literary anthologies is dramatized by the first inclusion after the introduction, in which Sean Teuton writes about working with Native prisoners in Auburn Prison in New York in his essay "The Callout: Writing American Indian Politics." One of the people who said we should visit prisoners was a theorist by the name of Jesus, and I'm reminded of one of the gospel parables. If you spend a lot of money on a party and the rich won't come, then invite the homeless. Rather than whining about all the ways the academy supposedly does not understand us, and failing to own up to the fact that some of us simply might not be understandable, we can also think about other logical audiences for our intellectual gifts who reside outside university walls. Prisons? Why not? If you teach as many undergraduates as I do, you may see a connection, anyway.

Seriously, the book, then, is about taking Native literary criticism in unusual directions, and even in search of an audience that might have new ears to hear, and especially beyond the kind of identity and ethnographic analysis that has dominated so much of Native literature for at least the last thirty years. Sean discusses the marked nonfictional and political bent of early writing, and what that implies for today's body of fiction. Sean's essay also suggests another deviation that comes up several times in the anthology when he argues that the term mixedblood, or even crossblood, should be dispensed with entirely and replaced with new imaginings regarding configuring citizenship. One author, Cheryl Suzack, who I'll discuss in a moment, puts it the most succinctly when she claims that the term mixedblood is a homogenizing one, whether employed by those who celebrate or denigrate it, and it tells us very little about a person's political and community commitments. Sean's essay tightly weaves a thread between prisoners who develop a political consciousness in order to understand the meaning of their incarceration, to the more overt politics of early Native writing, and the responsibility of contemporary critics to more closely examine celebrations of trickster identity and cross-blood literatures in relation to the politics that might ground these terminologies. Sean's opening example reminds us that the first Native writer to author work in English, Samson Occom, preached—and published the sermon he gave—at the execution of the prisoner Moses Paul, a fellow Mohegan.

Cheryl Suzack's essay is titled "Land Claims, Identity Claims: Mapping Indigenous Feminism in Literary Criticism and in Winona LaDuke's *Last Standing Woman.*" Cheryl also sends strong signals that something different is up in the world of Native literature. Her first sentences are not about Tayo, Abel, June, or some other tribal protagonist in a well-known Native novel; her opening comments have to do with the White Earth Land Settlement Act of 1986. Yet Suzack's essay, is, in fact, about a Native novel, Winona LaDuke's work of Anishinabe fiction which also takes place at White Earth, and Suzack explores powerful links between the fiction and the legislation. When is the last time you heard a Native literary specialist talk about the fiction of Winona LaDuke? The vast majority of Native novels have been ignored in the field of Native literature, and a Native novelist may have more of a chance of batting in next year's World Series than seeing critical attention given to his or her work in Native literary studies. In *Reasoning Together,* virtually every essay is about one of these lesser-known works of literature.

The famous novels have sometimes confined themselves to certain formulas, often in relation to the recovery of the tribal protagonist. Suzack, however, wants to talk about feminism and theory, especially in terms of challenging the claim that mainstream feminism is irrelevant to the tribal world. Thus, she cannot look to the modernist novels that have provided the bulwark of Native literary discussions. Suzack takes on Native critics who have written that Euro feminist ideals are incompatible with Native traditionalism by raising questions in relation to Native women who might want to form broader feminist alliances across tribal lines or even with mainstream feminists.

On a theoretical plane, the Suzack essay takes on the age-old dilemma that haunts human liberation: how to keep today's revolution from devolving into tomorrow's oppression. In other words, she deals with subordinate groups in Indian country who are marginalized by tribal power structures. She draws upon the novel *Last Standing Woman,* which dramatizes the struggle between a grassroots reservation group called Protect Our Land, which opposes the same clear-cutting of timber that the tribal government endorses. The challenge for these groups is to form dialogic relationships in a system of symmetrical power relations, rather than each new liberation front simply taking over the deposed party's dominance. Suzack looks to mainstream feminist theory in order to consider how hegemonic power centers can be challenged without duplicating their same authority structures. Heady stuff, and an essay that reads like a theoretical poem in the sense that each time I revisit it, I discover something I hadn't seen before. I think it represents some of the best of what might be called scholarly activism by examining real events, like the group of thirty-four appellants who challenged the WELSA legislation, in relation to theories that might help illuminate these actions so that people maximize the effectiveness of dissent.

Tol Foster was a graduate student at the University of Wisconsin when he joined the collective. We were at it so long he had a chance to graduate and get a job at Chapel Hill. His essay is titled "Of One Blood: An Argument for Relations and Regionality in Native American Literary Studies." Foster considers how tribally specific approaches to Native literature may need to be moderated by a consideration of the regional contexts that surround them. When we study history, for example, we know that an understanding of the Creeks, let's say, is incomplete if you don't know what was happening among other southeastern tribes in the same time period you are considering. Foster calls attention to certain figures who more easily fit a regional analysis than a tribally specific one, Will Rogers, to be exact, owing to his broad American appeal that reached far outside the tribal world. How has Native Studies somehow largely ignored the fact that one of the most well-known Americans in the 1920s, who may have had more access to American presidents and politicians than almost anyone outside public office, who achieved an audience of millions through radio and newspaper columns, and who was virtually the Tom Cruise of his day in terms of his popular appeal in film, was an Indian? No Native writer, no, not even Sherman Alexie, has been in the public eye in such a big way before or since. All of this should interest us.

Foster uses the Rogers example to talk about how certain kinds of cosmopolitanism—that is, an intense involvement in the larger world—energize Indian studies in ways that amplify its creativity without diminishing its Indianness. One further example of Foster's is John Joseph Mathews, and I always like to remind my students that not only did Mathews speculate about the meaning of Osage land in the 1930s in *Talking to the Moon,* but he came up with a theory about the global balance of powers between the two World Wars and how the United States was prepared only to understand its excess of power, not its inevitable decline—a potent lesson for us today. A certain portion of *Talking to the Moon* is focused on the larger world within and outside Osage country, and its Osage content, somehow, only becomes more Osage because of it. Foster provides a nuanced reading of cosmopolitanism that challenges the abstraction of hybridity that has failed to place the discussion in a specific historical context—that is, in reference to dates and places.

Rest easy, I won't tell you about all twelve authors, I'll let you check them out yourselves. Weren't we talking about, Texas, anyway?

History has come up a couple times, so I'll close on a historical note. Waylon Jennings used to challenge Nashville's claim as the home of country music in his lyrics, "When you cross that old Red River, hoss, / that just don't mean a thing. / Cause once you're down in Texas, / Bob Wills is still the king." When in 1832, the Choctaws, the first of the Southeastern tribes to arrive in Indian Territory, crossed that old Red River, the southern side of that sandy mess of briars and muddy water wasn't Texas at all but Mexico. The Choctaws' southern border was not the United States. The new illegal state, which calls itself Oklahoma, might have remembered this before just recently passing the most repressive anti-immigration legislation in the United States, only to discover that they had stood their own economy up against a firing wall and shot it in the head. Many businesses throughout the state have been adversely affected, and the satiric film *A Day Without A Mexican,* is everyday reality. Illegal states have a way of eventually doing themselves in, but they take a very long time going about it. Given that my genetic makeup is composed of so many of them, I'm not completely without knowledge when I say that nothing is as near to an Okie's heart as his wallet, so I'm not entirely surprised that some of the same rednecks who advocated the purge have now decided they want their Mexicans back.

When I'm down there, on the Territory side of the Red River, jigging for crappie and fighting off water snakes and chiggers, I stare across the river and dream of Mexico. I wonder if anyone stands on the Mexico side, just across from Ardmore, Oklahoma, and dreams of Indian Territory? At the global crossroads, coexistence with Mexico, and anywhere else for that matter, is a necessary survival strategy.

The Foster essay, with its focus on the larger regions that contextualize the tribal nation, reminds us of our relatives, the meaning of relationality, and the way that term always means a dynamic that moves inside and outside the tribal world, a subject that comes up constantly in *Reasoning Together.* In subtitling my first book, I might have at least explained how I had embraced a term like "separatism" instead of leaving readers to guess. In *Reasoning,* I see a more mature criticism emerging from my fellow authors than my own earlier efforts, and I wish I'd read the book ten years ago.

"Separatism" is a relevant term given the meaning of contact in our history. Perhaps, however, we are at a new historical juncture where tribal experience can be strengthened and challenged by contact rather than simply diminished by it. Maybe, even, instead of being on the receiving end of contact, we can imagine ourselves as the contactors rather than the contactees, in ways that emphasize sharing instead of displacing.

Works Cited

Foster, Tol. "Of One Blood: An Argument for Relations and Regionality in Native American Literary Studies." In *Reasoning Together: The Native Critics Collective,* edited by Craig S. Womack, Daniel Heath Justice, and Christopher B. Teuton, 265–302. Norman: University of Oklahoma Press, 2008.

Suzack, Cheryl. "Land Claims, Identity Claims: Mapping Indigenous Feminism in Literary Criticism and in Winona LaDuke's Last Standing Woman." In *Reasoning Together,* 169–92.

Teuton, Sean. "The Callout: Writing American Indian Politics." In *Reasoning Together,* 105–25.

Indian Decadence

I Want the Texas Playboys at My Private Party, and I Want to Sit In with the Band

Given the direction of this book in its examination of the relationship between visual and narrative art and the role of artists who create it, I might have chosen N. Scott Momaday's painter-protagonist Locke Setman, featured in his 1989 novel *The Ancient Child,* as an obvious subject of study. In focusing this work on deviance, however, I have tried to veer more toward unobvious choices, so I want to turn, instead, to another painter in fiction, John Grayeagle, who is especially interesting because of the way he interacts with novelistic and nonfiction treatments of painting in Osage literature.

Some days I feel like a higher power beamed me to earth for only one reason—to read Charles Red Corn's novel about Bob Wills and the Texas Playboys. Some readers, or maybe even the author himself, might not see Bob Wills as the central subject of the book, but I remain optimistic that, given time, they may come to a more mature understanding of the novel.

More seriously, *A Pipe for February,* Red Corn's impressive novelistic debut, is not the first Osage-authored book to contemplate the meaning of art and music. John Joseph Mathews's nonfiction classic, *Talking to the Moon,* a record of the ensuing years after he came home to take up permanent residence in the Blackjack ridges of his upbringing in Osage County, is organized along the lines of the twelve moons of the Osage calendar year. One might not associate it, at first glance, with art as a central subject matter, and the same might be said about Red Corn's novel.

While Mathews begins his account with disclaimers that he returned home without any preconceptions, which is to say he came back to the ridges to watch, listen, and participate rather than hypothesize, like most intellectuals he could not resist the powers of his own mind, and by the end of the book he proposes a full-blown political philosophy based on the "raw data" he observes in his natural surroundings.

Mathews most fully explores his ideas about art and philosophy in relation to "Single Moon by Himself," the month of January. Let me say that if I hadn't read Robert Warrior's *Tribal Secrets* in 1995 I probably would have never worked through these matters, since Mathews's philosophy is not easily accessible, and Warrior does an excellent job parsing complicated material.

During January, after having worked hard all summer to store food caches, and confined indoors because of weather, traditional Osages might find themselves freed from some of the daily work of summer and in possession of the idle time that Mathews feels is essential to the process of creating art. Having the necessary time available for reflection gives rise to thoughts focused on what Mathews calls "ornamentation" rather than mere daily survival.

To explain the concept of ornamentation we can begin by noting that we can understand certain physical characteristics of species in relation to their daily survival: colorings that aid camouflage, for example. Mathews points out, however, that other features resist easy scrutiny as to their survival benefits. The Painted Bunting, Mathews observes, has a coloration that draws attention to them and endangers them in the wild. The very title of Mathews's book has to do with the impossibility of explaining why coyotes sing in terms of how this might give them any advantages or protection in the food chain. Mathews relates ornamentation in nature to ornamental thought in man—to art, dreams of creativity, and forms of expression that go beyond meeting everyday physical needs:

> If the dim, uncertain, often flickering expressions of the coyote, the crow's bright trinkets, the squirrel's meat tin, the wood thrush and the mockingbird's spilling-over in ornamental song, as well as the emotionalism of birds in general, are expressions inspired by this Force, then such expressions might well be represented during the present stage of man's development by the most beautiful art, literature, architecture, music, philosophy, and the highest concepts of God. (216)

Mathews's "Force" is a somewhat mystical concept, particularly for an Oxford-trained scientist, but it seems closer to Dylan Thomas's "Force that through the Green Fuse Drives the Flower" than a particular belief in deity as far as I can tell.

Mathews's month of January, "Single Moon by Himself," serves as an example of how man must balance thinking with environmental realities. In light of the evolutionary scale, man is a relatively new species, and, as a thinker, he has even more limited experience. As the modern world, with its technological breakthroughs which lengthen periods of leisure, provides him more time for reflection, he needs to exercise caution because he comes to the thinking game only recently. (The "he" mantra here duplicates Mathews's own sexist language, marked by the 1945 publication date of the book, a time when few authors seemed to concern themselves with linguistic equity).

"Liberated" from a more physical interaction with his environment because of technological changes, man may forget the natural laws that not only govern physical survival but may also be relevant to his increasing social opportunities because of the increase of leisure. Osage religion, Mathews notes—one of the manifestations of ornamental thought that occurs when man has time to reflect instead of only to survive—though born of the contemplative opportunities idle time provides, still manages to maintain a connection to natural laws because its very symbols and practices remain earth related.

What will be the future of art, Mathews ponders, as man's physical realities evolve, and he becomes, increasingly, a creature of brain as much as one of brawn? Needless to say, this is a middle-class—well, in Mathews's case we might more accurately say an aristocratic—analysis, given that a great deal of the world then and now knows no such leisure.

Mathews concerns himself with the politics of the decades between the two World Wars (the book was published in 1945, at the end of World War II, but written in the thirties, during the rise of German National Socialism in Europe). After many years of intensely close observation—so close, for example, that he has passages about sitting and watching insect larvae hatch, and so close that he is able to take two decades of experience and extrapolate what goes on in the Blackjacks every month of the year in great detail—Mathews comes to the conclusion that there are four life stages: youth, virility, maturity, and senescence. The stages are constantly in flux. No one stays forever young, whatever the song might yearn for, and after senescence and death, some other whippersnapper will rise up to take your place, so cheer up.

Mathews relates this to the triumphalist assumptions behind U.S. political dominance during the 1930s. While lots of pretty (ornamental) speeches occur about peace (ironically, these are the decades after "the war to end all wars"), the peace speeches, in the end, have to do with maintaining U.S. global power at the cost of the natural growth of other nations. Emerging nations also have a natural inclination to move through stages of youth, virility, and maturity. The United States cannot realistically expect itself to be the only nation on earth that reaches the stage of virility, as well as the only one in history that stays forever locked in that category. Mathews argues that the United States' role as peacekeeper often involves forcing other nations to stay in the weaker categories (youth) instead of moving toward more powerful ones (virility). Mathews writes, "Forced peace, which is the only kind of peace man can conceive of now in his present stage of development, cannot last any longer than the powers that impose it" (226), and such a statement remains as potent in the year 2009 as it was when Mathews penned it.

Furthermore, the notion that the United States can stay eternally locked into the stage of virility because some god deemed it so forever and ever amen is simply an illusion, according to Mathews, that contradicts every indication of the way nature actually works. Faith in a permanent state of U.S. virility requires burying one's head in the sand with regard to the laws of nature, which teach us that everything eventually declines. The United States will also move through stages of senescence—either voluntarily, and as wisely as possible, or involuntarily—because such changes are inevitable in the natural order of things. Mathews contemplates what a new politics that recognizes and accommodates the need for younger nations also to increase their virility and older ones to accept their senescence might look like. Given the patriarchal leanings of Mathews, one might also wonder if he could have proposed a different model whose metaphors aren't rooted in masculinist terminology like "virility," a subject of much relevance in relation to the sexist depictions in his work at large.

Mathews considers art, philosophy, and politics to be interrelated parts of the same spectrum, and these philosophies, when functioning effectively, will take into consideration the physical limitations that order the natural world. Mathews's nonfiction and fiction are sometimes at odds: the idle time that gives birth to art, according to *Talking To The Moon*, is the same idleness that creates the restless malaise of the fictional characters of his novel *Sundown*— and I borrow from Robert Dale Parker's accomplished study *The Invention of Native American Literature* in describing them as restless, since he talks about a generation of restless young men.

After this brief introduction of Mathews's enthusiasm—and worries—about art, we can now begin our discussion of Charles Red Corn's *A Pipe for February,* since John Grayeagle finds himself in a competition between physical survival and his dreams of artistic expression. John, a guy with a lot of time on his hands, enjoys an idleness born of an appreciable affluence. When Charles makes public appearances, he points out that Osage County may have had more per-capita millionaires in the 1920s than any other place on earth. Like John Joseph Mathews's novel *Sundown,* the novel resembles an Osage *La dolce vita,* depicting Indians who have too much time and money. Flitting from party to party and enjoying the privileges wealth provides, they find themselves ever more frustrated in their efforts to find meaning in their lives. The Mathews novel is probably a bit more Felliniesque than Red Corn's in terms of swift movement from one ridiculous scene to another, as the restless young men become all the more debauched.

The affluence in these novels and other Native American works sometimes confuses students when they read *Talking to the Moon, Sundown,* or *A Pipe for February,* where they encounter traditional Osages with white or African American servants who drive their rich Indian employers around in the luxury cars of their day. Students often find their expectations reversed— or they simply ignore the wealth in the novels and pretend that the characters are impoverished in spite of all the evidence the books provide to the contrary.

I find this happens in relation to other Indian novels as well. My students, for example, have written about the grind of poverty in *Winter in the Blood*— which might be true in some general sense but not in relation to the protagonist of the novel, whose ranch family of ordinary means runs a rather typical cow-calf operation for northern Montana. Putting food on the table isn't their problem. Some students, who expect an Indian tragedy about poverty, miss much of the humor that abounds in the family's workaday life.

The out-and-out affluence of John Grayeagle and his friends, which far surpasses the wealth of any character in *Winter in the Blood,* is marked in particular ways: his cousin Molly keeps an apartment for socializing in Pawhuska even though she has inherited her family's house outside of town, and she orders new cars to match the color of her dresses. Another cousin, Ted Bearsky, builds a track and becomes a patron of Indian athletes running in the Olympics. Their friend Williard Watson, nicknamed "Roper," is a prosperous rancher who leases out Osage land other than his own 658 acres. Their time is mostly given to parties; drives around the countryside; jackpot ropings; and, especially, the local French espresso bar of its day, the Bon Bon Confectionary, a delightful recreation on Red Corn's part of an actual lively Pawhuska hangout. None of them have jobs, and Molly and John even try to imagine what it might be like to work every day.

The flapper age, remembered by most literary-minded Americans in the figure of Jay Gatsby, provides a subtle backdrop to the novel, recognizable by Red Corn's inclusions of jazz references, fashion trends, popular racehorses of the period, the Charleston, and the general social milieu of Prohibition, an era he depicts carefully by skillfully exploring its Osage particularities.

The tremendous affluence of the characters does not come easy. Parties, equal parts Charon and Dionysus, are invariably accompanied by someone showing up with the latest announcement of the "accidental" demise of a relative or a friend. In fact, John's own parents were killed in a car wreck years earlier due, supposedly, to faulty brakes. I won't repeat the history of the Osage oil murders given the amount of information on the subject in full-length books and articles.

John finds himself stalked by a shadowy figure that is eventually identified as Kenneth Carson. His malevolent tracker is somehow interested in John's financial affairs. By my count John has no less than seven Indian agents, lawyers, and business owners he has to maneuver around in order to find out anything whatsoever about his own finances: Alan S. Sanders; Walter Whitman; Mr. Bartholomew; W. W. Baskins; Ed Farrell; Mr. Hugel; and even John's girlfriend, Barbara Williams, daughter of one of the town lawyers, T. E. There are eighty-seven attorneys in Pawhuska, all told, and, of course, they are only one non-Indian faction with interests in the Osage tribal domain.

Wealth, then, also involves a loss of autonomy and the lack of opportunity to learn that normal lesson essential to growing up called minding one's own business—that is to say, tending to one's affairs and learning how to manage one's finances. John experiences arrested social development in a climate of social profusion. Though he has inadvertently financed some of the town's grandest structures, John has no recourse to information about these investments, which someone else made on his behalf. He finds himself surrounded by his handlers.

Of equal importance to the loss of individual Osages due to mysterious causes of death is the loss of Osage religion, though the word "loss" needs to be carefully qualified. The opening scene of *A Pipe for February* occasions the burial of one of the pipes central to the old religion of Wah-kon-tah. Mathews makes religious transition a central theme of *Talking to the Moon,* and he writes with some confusion, to my way of thinking, about the meaning of the new Peyote religion, which Mathews tends to over-associate with Christianity rather than Native religious continuity. Mathews also depicts the laying to rest of certain aspects of the old Wah-Kon-Tah religion but tends to associate it with an overall decline. To be sure, I have very limited expertise in these matters, if any at all, yet it seems to me Mathews views Osage religion in fairly pessimistic terms.

Red Corn's more balanced treatment, however, captures both the mutability and stability of Native religious tradition. Red Corn, of course, has the advantage, in that a little more than a century has passed since the introduction of Peyote to the Southern Plains, which was a newer development when Mathews was writing, and Red Corn has seen traditions like the I'n-lon-shka dances survive into the twenty-first century. Mathews probably viewed them from a more precarious vantage point.

Into the Red Corn novel's world of loss, change, and continuity enters the painter John Grayeagle. That a central concern of the book is art is borne out by the fact that before the first page of print it begins with Red Corn's hand-drawn sketch of the city of Pawhuska in 1924, complete with a numbered index that gives the name of each building. The novel serves as something of a model for Native writers depicting the details of their home country.

And what better way to convey the message that the novel is about art than starting with a sketch? It is a particular kind of art in relation to geographic realism, because the buildings of the Pawhuska of 1924 are also the buildings of the novel. Forget writing a fantasy about a tribe other than your own, a place you've never lived, or a community that can only be labeled with the stock cliché "the people." This guy knows his stuff. One of the art lessons in the Red Corn book has to do with having enough experience to narrate one's subject matter, and this parallels John's own journey of discovering his home country and how to paint it.

Such experience is not magic. Simply living someplace a long time (as if one becomes an artist by osmosis) or possessing certain "infallible" cultural traits—such as language speaker, ceremonialist, and so on—is no guarantee. Many traditionalists are not artists, fictionalists, poets, or literary critics, whatever their other considerable skills may be. Those who suggest that speaking a Native language, for example, necessarily guarantees literary authenticity are dreaming. Many Native language speakers could not author or critique novels. Native language skills, placed in the hands of someone who also has literary talent, could be an enormous boon, no doubt, but some have overly romanticized the role of language fluency as de facto competency.

Part of John's training includes study in Europe—some of it, significantly, in France. Given Osages' French-Catholic influences, and the novel's attention to the meaning of Catholicism in relation to Osage culture, John's concerns about how, for example, to sketch St. Francis's cathedral at Assisi in Italy (45) are perhaps central, rather than peripheral, to Osage artistic sensibilities.

John comes to realize the benefit of the artist who sees his or her home landscape in the light of a new sun: "When I was in the Tuscany region of Italy I thought the land looked so much like Osage country and I thought of that when we were riding across Roper's grandfather's land [in Oklahoma]" (42).

An artistic vision opens up landscape to the worlds that intersect it and has to do with the artist's ability to see Osage country in Italy and Tuscany in Osage country—a bi-directional vision. John goes on to say, "Tuscany made me feel artistic just as the Osage hills make me feel artistic and the land looked so much like Osage country that it eased a case of homesickness that had bothered me" (44). One might even imagine that Europe triggers memories, helping him recall which scenes from home might make appropriate artistic subject matter.

The artist, a cultural ambassador, embodies something different than a cultural hybrid since possibilities still remain in such roles for an intense and vibrant nationalism. In other words, a trip to Tuscany might only intensify the "Osageness" of John's vision. Admittedly, it takes John a good deal of time to reach such a conclusion—partially due to a decadent social environment at home that allows too much leisure, retards personal autonomy by virtue of the handlers that micromanage every aspect of his personal business, and proliferates violence due to large influxes of cash. Most artists struggle with poverty; John struggles with wealth. The novel, in its own kind of way, plays out Mathews's warnings regarding the inescapability of natural law even in worlds of prosperity.

Given John's lack of sense of urgency, quite frequently he aborts his paintings in progress:

> Sometimes watercolors are nice to work with and on that day I took the water paint and brushes and walked over the hill and waited in a stand of blackjack trees by a deer trail that leads down to water. I had seen a large buck with three does there. At sunset the buck and his herd appeared and I was surprised to see two fawns. My plan was to catch a glimpse of them then quickly paint the small herd, but it was getting dark and watching them make their way down the trail to the water was enough. I would paint them another day. (88)

If aborted paintings did not happen with some frequency, we could simply say the point of the passage might involve appreciating the experience itself rather than the need to reproduce it artistically. The affluence in the community, however, creates a false sense of immortality, and John treats his work as if there is no tomorrow.

Harrowing death announcements, however, prove otherwise, and they serve as a kind of muse. Under the best of circumstances, one only has so many days to engage his subject matter before the light changes, so to speak, and considering all the mysterious deaths, John would do well to paint post haste.

John lives in a world, though, where if he fails as a painter, it does not make that much difference as far as economics go. He can still hang out at the Bon Bon, drive whatever new disposable car he happens to have his hands on, and travel from friend to friend, making the scene. In such an environment it takes a tremendous personal motivation for anyone to convince himself of the exigency of painting. John's affluence has allowed him a college education and European travels, but it has not taught him how to make the most of such experiences or even why they are important. I believe that John Joseph Mathews himself faced such questions, not the least of which might have been what to do with his Oxford education. He didn't need a job to survive; that much we know. *Talking to the Moon* represents Mathews's own experience with ornamentation—the sometimes problematic liberty of being freed up from physical survival and given time to think and figure out how he might make the most of such a situation.

In *A Pipe for February* art becomes an important part of the novel's intrigue. Not all of John's handlers are crooks, and the novel has a kind of Osage County Sherlock Holmes by the name of Walter Whitman, whose literary name and English background are part of the wonderful funk of Red Corn's imagination. Walter becomes John's secret accomplice in trying to uncover the conspiracy that has wrapped John up in a moribund knot of legal entanglements and outside control of his life. Walter arranges a meeting at a particular location in the Osage hills:

> "You go up there and take your easel and brushes just a little before sundown and set up for painting," he said. "I will show up with my camera and we can both catch the sun setting. That should look innocent enough. Two artists catching the beauty of the setting sun. You know, John, people seldom take artists seriously. . . . We can see for miles around and we should be able to talk without being overheard."
> (169–70)

Whitman, much more than a sidekick, schools John in the art of craftiness, another dimension of John's burgeoning sense of the craft of art. John is a natural for being taken advantage of because he is such a sweet guy, one of the most likable characters one might hope to encounter in fiction. John, in fact, reminds me of Red Corn's own decency, a man marked by a humility and gentle compassion that can only be described as inspiring, something one might hope to emulate. John Grayeagle learns through a series of painful lessons, however, that he can not expect the same kindness from everyone else.

Craftiness gives way to craft, and John's art becomes a medium for personal ruse by providing a foil for anyone who might spy on him and Walter. Walther's machinations help bridge the gap between John's social circumstances, which involve personal danger, and his artistic depictions, which have to do with learning his subject matter. The question before John, and all artists, is how one accommodates the totality of one's life in the rather limited forum provided by one's art. Art and life, manifested in a plan to protect John from those out to harm him, merge here when Walter comes up with the scheme to foil stalkers.

Another of Walter's ruses sets up a hilarious cat-and-mouse game when he instructs John to retrieve his secret, coded messages, which create comic caricatures of Pawhuska's principal scoundrels, by retrieving the notes midway up the landing that ascends Agency Hill. Walter, in fact, makes spying itself an art form with his coded character portrayals in the form of the cryptic notes. Artful comedy is one of the few forms of resistance to evil in which the resistor can fight back without becoming evil her- or himself. John, an innocent who needs to face reality while holding on to the strength of his kindness, can learn much from Walter. A related issue involves finding ways for his art, mostly pastoral scenes, to accommodate the reality of the meanness in his world without losing the strength of its innocence.

The subject of painting portraits comes up throughout the novel and provides the final sentence in *A Pipe for February*: "Then, some day, when I know I am a capable artist, I will paint Grandpa" (269). A good portion of John Joseph Mathews's reflection on the "Yellow Flower Moon" (the month of August)—a chapter that he subtitles "For Posterity"—also takes up the subject of portraits. Mathews, aided by government WPA money, arranged the portraits of twelve Osage women and the same number of men.

Mathews explains the rationale for the portraits as cultural preservation, and he constantly tries to entice his sitters by telling them the paintings will matter one hundred years later. He further reminds them of the vitality of Osage community, and of individual community members, that will still need to be remembered after their passing as a culture. In spite of Mathews's conservative statements about the paintings in relation to culture, however, what ensues while the portraits are being made is anything but cultural "conservation."

Contrary to a conservationist mode for the sittings, his subjects, hardly dying species, resist tragic depictions. More to the point, they talk back to the painter and even the painting. In fact, the sub-chapter "For Posterity" is one of two great classics of Indian humor in *Talking to the Moon*, the other being the story of the Osage who "sure was a big man" (79–82), another passage about an Osage being dressed—but for dancing rather than having his portrait made.

For one thing, the subjects wreak havoc on the sitting schedule by not being at home or just getting up and leaving in the middle of portraits. In other cases, they demonstrate mind-boggling patience, sitting for several hours in 110 degree–plus heat for consecutive days during a record-breaking August.

A tribal council member and peyotist by the name of Abott is one of the strongest of the humorists. The painter comments on Abott's impressive house and premises and Abott responds, "Yeah, like white man, ain't it? Built fence to keep white man out, but it ain't no good; can't keep white man out. Can't keep myself in either, I guess" (129). Abott, it turns out, is a notorious debtor, and constantly faces creditors at his heels.

Abott taunts the young painter by constantly calling him "ole man." Keeping up with the Pittses, rather than the Joneses, seems a chief concern of Abott's, and if his friend Pitts dresses (an intricate ceremonial process, as Mathews carefully details) then Abott wants to dress in full traditional clothes as well. Otherwise, he'll let it slide if Pitts is doing casual wear. Interrogations of what Pitts might do are a constant topic of conversation.

Keeping Abott, and others, telling these kinds of stories is an essential part of the process, since the narratives convey the personality the painter hopes to capture. Mathews proves indispensable at getting the subjects to talk, even telling stories himself that elicit important responses the painter wants to depict. Mathews rises to the occasion by telling artfully comic stories of Abott that have to do with creditors chasing him. One creditor, a white lessee, simply wants to pay Abott rent. Another, a grasshopper, puts Abott in flight:

> [W]hen he was walking down the street of Hominy, a grasshopper happened to fly in from the country and lighted on his shoulder. You know the kind; the big yellow ones that plop against our windshield and flow? One of these lighted on his left shoulder. He increased his speed a little, and turned his head slightly as he said, "Pay you next week." (131)

Mathews's excellent stories help to make Abott an excellent subject for painting given the serious turn of the young artist, who often sees the people he paints in tragic terms: "[T]he artist was a very sensitive man, and he also put suffering in the face where I saw no suffering. As a child he had been in a pogrom in Russia and later had undoubtedly read Fenimore Cooper" (134). Mathews functions like Red Corn's Walter Whitman, encouraging the comic potential in his painter friend and subjects. Mathews's role as comic facilitator contradicts his own statement: "This was a real conservation, since these old men would soon pass away and with them the Osage as he was, the era and the type passing with the individuals" (126). In some cases, especially in relation to his pessimistic analysis of cultural continuity, Mathews himself tends to overemphasize tragedy rather than comedy.

Abott articulates an artistic vision rather than only allowing himself to be an artistic subject: "Ole man oughta paint Pitts with goggles, ain't it?" (130). When the artist asks why, Abott becomes painter and portrait, creating his own art: "Abott extended both arms and closed his hands as though he were driving a car. 'He's always goin' some place fast,' he said" (130). Such a statement about driving, and the way it symbolizes the fast life, represents much of the milieu of *A Pipe for February*, as well as the flapper age—given the Mathews passage's hell-bent-for-leather goggled driver, Pitts.

When Abott gets his first peek at the portrait, he responds as critic rather than subject, talking back to both the painting and its creator regarding its tragic origin: "Yeah—it's too what-cha-call it? It's like white man that lost his money. Maybe someday when I look at it, I shoot myself. White man got my money long time ago, but maybe when I see this face I remember it and hafta shoot myself" (131).

In relation to another of the Osage sitters, one of the "diehards" who had refused to accommodate the new Peyote religion, Mathews comments, "He was done in profile, and his portrait shows a classic American Indian contour that would not be out of place on a coin" (132).

Yet Nonceh Tonkah would not be coined. At one point during the sitting he tells his daughter, "Ask this white man if he wants my head when I pass away? . . . Ask him if he wants my head to put on wall like that of buffalo?" (132). At another juncture he ventures, "Tell this white man he must send his daughter to me. For this picture he must send his daughter—that is Osage way" (132). If Nonceh Tonkah's head will fit on a buffalo nickel, his repartee will not.

Most telling is the response of the traditional chief Claremore who endures four days of painting in intense heat only to find that the artist has painted him as a tragic figure, compromising his sense of dignity. Rather than getting angry, and thus belittling himself further, he drops this bombshell: "Come back tomolla; I paint you" (135), suggesting the possibility of revenging himself with an equally misplaced interpretation of subject.

Tellingly, Mathews almost leaves out the painting of the women entirely, but the third woman, who is unnamed (and this is also telling), refuses to wait to be invited to look at the portrait, breaking her pose and coming over to check out what the painter is saying about her on canvas: "She stood for some time, then turned quickly and fled back to her room and later appeared in her ordinary clothes" (135).

Mathews's refusal to take women seriously in these and almost all other matters, is inexcusable, but even this small detail speaks volumes about the way the woman overturns portraiture. While her husband is being painted, she "said to herself, 'O-skee-kah,' which means in Osage, among other things, liar and horse thief" (136).

Mathews closes the sub-chapter "For Posterity" with a reflection on the aesthetic challenges of capturing a particular moment, as well as the way in which art and life resist the frame that holds the painting. The portraits completed, the tribe celebrates the opening of the Pawhuska museum:

> If we cold have saved for posterity the picture of the descending sun shining through the strips of beef strung along the drying poles; the women busy around the kettles; and the dancers of the four clans coming together for the first time in many years to dance to the earth rhythm of the drums like befeathered and gorgeously painted gods, then posterity would need to ask few questions. If we could have saved the picture for them of the old men who, though dressed, were too old to dance but sat with closed eyes around the dance ground in dream-thought; or if we could have saved the picture of the dancers who, as they danced, saw nothing except that which was in their hearts, there would be little need to attempt to have their souls painted on canvas. (136)

Mathews's dream-thought, the vision of old men as they recount experience, proves important to Red Corn's John Grayeagle because the elders who are his subject matter seem to understand more about the reasons for his painting them than he does himself. The old men's dream-thoughts convey artistic messages John needs to consider:

> [Mon-tse-no-pi'n's] face is weathered and his eyes squinted just a little. His whole face smiled when he smiled and whenever he asked me a question his whole face asked the question. Mostly, his eyes were insightful and told me he understood my need for drawing his image. That was more than I understood about my need for the sketch." (206).

Mon-tse-no-pi'n's understanding reverses the artist/subject role Mathews's endorses when he explains to his sitters the justification for their portraits that will preserve them "for posterity." John's subject, on the other hand, knows more about the reasons for the paintings than he does, a fact he readily admits. Further, John discusses with Mon-tse-no-pi'n whether or not he should include his war club as part of the sketch, indicative of a more dialogic process than that of Mathews and his sitters, at least in reference to some of Mathews's micromanagement of the affair and his terminal creeds about the death of Osage culture. The war club provides one of the major themes of the novel—by the end John will have to learn to use it on his enemies in a way that conveys a strong "message" (it's quite a bit more physical than that), yet honors his peace clan roots as well.

John has to find a balance between the extreme of annihilating his enemies and its opposite—allowing his own annihilation by the same. Whether the war club should be in the "picture," so to speak, is an important question that once again interrupts the canvas with the imposition of John's life, and John's life with the imposition of the canvas—a further amplification of lessons also taught by Walter Whitman.

The portraiture seems a turning point for John. At stake are some small beginnings on John's part to improve on his track record of starting things and not finishing: "I thought of painting "Hu-ah-toin [Mon-tse-no-pi'n's wife] but I would wait until I was ready to start on the portrait before asking her" (206). John does not want to create an anticipation of the painting and then fail to follow through, a slightly less lax attitude than his earlier one of "there's always tomorrow." In this case he might let someone else down who is the subject of his work, a difference between portraiture and his earlier landscapes.

Before beginning some of his preparatory drawings of his Osage elders, John says, "I gathered the sketches of the cathedral and of the Rocky Mountains and leaned them against the wall in the corner of the room where they would be out of my way" (207). While John certainly does not discard these earlier influences—indeed, they seem formative—still, he needs to clear his path to begin his Osage work. He has explored these other models, but he also needs to ask the critical question, one I think I struggled with myself in my first book, about the way he might learn from primary sources in his own tribe. He says, "I would start and complete the painting sitting face-to-face with Mon-tse-no-pi'n but this would be a good preliminary piece and I would learn from it" (207).

John debates whether or not to study his grandfather's eagle-wing fan as a model for the one he'd like to include in Mon-tse-no-pi'n's portrait, then returns it to his granddad's trunk, deciding to use Mon-tse-no-pi'n's own. All the talking back to paintings and painters we saw in the Matthews passage is more centrally located inside John in the Red Corn novel, although surely his friends and artistic subjects are part of this process, too.

Why does John finally start to move forward with his painting? I could speculate that it represents a response to the increasing dangers that accompany more deaths in the community and the stepped-up threat of his stalker, Kenneth Carson, but I suspect it has more to do with John beginning to formulate a theory about his art that actually enables him to paint. I think the new urgency has to do with looking at his own process as an important source of knowledge: "It turned out I would wait a full day before adding more paint. The paint and the canvas and the brushes did control a great deal of what happened from that point on and as always I hoped that I was an equal with those materials. I suppose the final picture would determine that" (208). Here painting has more to do with imagining an Osage future than in Matthews's work, in which a major concern is the Osage past.

In Mathews we had subjects talking back to the painter; here we have paint talking back. One of the colors is ochre, which also, in other forms, is a ceremonial paint—face paint: "I mixed in some turpentine with the yellow ocher paint and added paint thinner to make it thin like before" (208). The ceremony of the materials instructs the artist. Yellow ochre is one of the teachers, and John waits to see what it will do. If, in some sense, we have face paint, the portrait of Mon-tse-no-pi'n also becomes a matter of John painting himself, or the latter painting him—since one's face is often painted by another in ceremonies. In short, John is subject as much as anyone.

Three powerful stories come to mind. I once heard Ovide Mercredi, former Grand Chief of the Assembly of First Nations in Canada, who, although a Cree speaker himself, grew up in a somewhat assimilated Cree family in terms of his early knowledge of ceremonial matters. As an adult he wanted to learn some traditional Cree songs, and an elder gave him a drum. When he took it back to the elder hoping to get some instruction, the elder's only response was, "Have you started singing yet?"

This is one of the most powerful stories about pedagogy I know. My interpretation is the elder was essentially saying, "Sure, I could teach you a bunch of songs, but don't you want some songs of your own?" One of the fundamental challenges of a teacher is getting students to recognize what they already know rather than what we can give them, the former an approach to instruction that places high demands on both students and those who try to teach them.

Another cogent story I heard from our academic elder, Blood tribal member, Leroy Little Bear, a founding father of Native Studies at the University of Lethbridge in Southern Alberta. Leroy recalled the reinstitution of a particular bundle that Blackfoot people had not opened for many years. Bundle openings require special knowledge of the songs and prayers that must accompany the opening. Evidently, in this case, that knowledge had been lost. "Do you know how we were able to get those songs back?" Professor Little Bear asked.

"We took it to the right *place*," he answered in response to his own question. The materials, in a sense—or perhaps we should say the origin site of the materials that gave rise to the bundle—contain the knowledge for its continu-ance and even the ability to pass it on to learners. Humans are not the only instructors. The materials, as John Grayeagle discovers, also teach.

One more. I remember Cheyenne artist Edgar Heap of Birds responding to a Native graduate student whose whining had become excessive. The whole world was against her. Professors were racist. The university was unsympa-thetic. So on and so forth. Edgar told her that ideas were spirits, full of their own energy. Once she discovered an idea that was sufficiently exciting, and claimed it as her focus, racist professors and unsympathetic university folks would become irrelevant in the face of the proliferation of that idea, a living being that would find a way to manifest itself whatever the odds might be against it.

There's a lot of medicine in these three stories. Much of it has to do with art. The point isn't some quixotic search for things that are purely Indian—rather, the point is not skipping over the obvious, the stuff in your own backyard, or even the stuff in your own head. Mikhail Bakhtin called this internally persua-sive discourse.

The first introduction of Bob Wills in *A Pipe for February* occurs when Ted invites Mavis Davis (what a name!) to a party: " 'It's at my place a few miles north and west of town. People will be dressed about any way you can imag-ine. Bob Wills is playing at the dance and we'll have lots of food and stuff to drink,' Ted said. 'Ever hear of Bob Wills?' " (32).

Ted intends the question as a joke, though it ends up that somehow Mavis has never heard of the Wills boys. As William W. Savage, Jr., writes in *Singing Cowboys and All That Jazz,*

> Bob Wills, the patriarch of western-swing music until his death in 1975, spent the best years of his musical career in Tulsa. Between 1934 and 1942, performing on radio station KVOO, Wills built a six man string band into an eighteen piece orchestra, the fabled Texas Playboys, known for its repertoire of dance music and its western "style." . . .
>
> Tulsa radio station KVOO provided a 50,000 watt forum for Bob Wills's musical ideas. Wills developed a noontime show that grew to be one of the most popular hours on radio in the Southwest. At different periods, he and the Texas Playboys aired their music early in the morn-ing, in the late afternoon, and late at night. There were live broadcasts from dances, and the Wills group played for many dances. . . .
>
> In April, 1942, Wills and the Playboys performed at dances in McAles-ter; Fort Smith (2); Ada; Oklahoma City (4); Coffeyville, Kansas; Fair-

view; Muskogee, Miami; Okemah; Seminole; Enid; and Pittsburg, Kansas. That adds up to sixteen dances. During the same month the band played ten dances at Cain's Academy in Tulsa. That adds up to twenty-six dance dates in a thirty-day period. All the dates were broadcast over KVOO. It was an average month.

Wills and the Texas Playboys evoked the image of the singing cowboy by dressing as cowboys, but whereas [Otto] Gray's [of the Oklahoma Cowboys] musicians had cowboy backgrounds, Wills's performers did not. Even in that, however, the Playboys were trend setters. They affixed the cowboy image to western swing, and inasmuch as their success encouraged a host of imitators, they rendered the clothing as acceptable as the music, even for people without appropriate antecedents. That the music had nothing whatsoever to do with cowboys is perhaps irrelevant. Postwar commercialism separated cowboy imagery in music from its historical roots anyway, and the Texas Playboys merely anticipated the process. (32; 38)

Charles Red Corn, in talks to my classes and in presentations he gives on the novel, recalls that his own parents hired the Playboy orchestra for private parties, though that would have been in the Tulsa Wills heyday from 1934 to 1942, rather than the previous decade, in which the novel is set. One of the Wills dance standards is "Osage Stomp," probably a testament to the Wills boys' experiences at just such parties (even though Wills learned the original melody from African Americans whom he grew up and worked with picking cotton, renaming the tune later).

Wills really was a man about Pawhuska to some degree. Infamously, Wills married a young woman from the town, and the end of that marriage, in 1940, got far more attention than its beginnings. The divorce proceedings inside the Osage County courthouse included claims that Wills's wife was not really pregnant when she was, Wills hollering at one of the lawyers and a recess called, the father of Wills's wife slugging someone in the Wills faction near the courthouse door, Wills and his wife emerging from the recess holding hands, smiling, and happily reconciled, the judge fining the slugger twenty-five dollars for contempt of court, and the whole melée reported all over the Southwest in major newspapers (Townsend 175–77). Wills, as his biographer documents, played many Pawhuska dances. Further, in one of the photos in the Townsend biography, Wills poses with Oklahoma Indian friends. The Wills faction is identified, but names are not provided for the Indians. Given song titles like "Osage Stomp," Wills's Pawhuska connections, Red Corn's own reminiscences of his parents' parties, and the photograph in the biography, it is virtually certain Wills had Indian friends.

The influence of Oklahoma on Wills and the Playboys can never be over-estimated. It was in Oklahoma, in fact, that the band first called itself the Texas Playboys. Their decade in Tulsa from the early thirties to just before World War II, which broke up the band, was the most important in their careers. During this decade Wills added the horns that make western swing highly distinct from country music. After Wills left Tulsa when he was inducted in the army, his brother Johnnie Lee continued there with his western swing band for decades. Wills's Tulsa days were the most personally satisfying of his career because he could both stay headquartered on a ranch he loved, with a large extended family of relatives and band members, and play dances in the region and still return home frequently.

Bob Wills is buried in Tulsa; he considered himself a Tulsan, and he has family there to this day. Western Oklahoma and West Texas is the epicenter of western swing, and the vast majority of Wills's musicians are from that area. Hardly anyone could have had more influence on the Wills band than his jazz guitarist from Weatherford, Oklahoma, Eldon Shamblin, a principal creator and arranger of the horn sound the band became famous for. The dance environment of West Texas and Oklahoma, which originated at home dances, and also in Dixieland jazz, was a major factor in the famous Wills two-four, two-step dance beat. The Texas Playboys, truly, are an Oklahoma and West Texas phenomenon, a southern plains indigeneity.

In *A Pipe for February,* the Wills party proves at first to be one of many distractions that keeps John from his art: "I drove the new Buick to Ted's place for the party, hoping the party would be a diversion from being un-able to paint and being concerned about Molly [whose cousin Martha has died in a suspicious accident]" (67). The party is much festive and a survey of decadence, Osage style: tuxedoed bartenders serving drinks, a bull rider re-enacting his eight seconds of fame, guests rumored to be Olympic athletes (and they are) milling about, a lady in a yellow evening dress posing with a cigarette holder, Molly appearing in a blue flapper dress that goes with the car she bought to match it, the ubiquitous Walter Whitman snooping around in his English tweeds.

It is at the party that features the Wills band, in fact, that John meets Walter for the first time. Though Walter ends up being one of the good guys, John cannot even go to a dance without one of the Pawhuska handlers wanting to have a word with him about his affairs.

On the bandstand, "Bob Wills was wearing a white hat and in the middle of the song he held his fiddle above his head and did a little dance and the crowd yelled and hooted" (71). This seemingly unimportant observation conveys much about art. Wills was the consummate showman, an entertainer. Contrary to the title of one of Merle Haggard's albums (*My Tribute to the Best Damn Fiddle Player in the Whole World*) Wills was not the consummate fiddler (which Haggard realizes full well). Wills's antics, like the little dance while playing the fiddle behind his head, sent the crowds into a celebratory frenzy. There's an old adage from the swing jazz days about showoffs who twirl their upright basses: "If you're spinning it, you're not playing it," a factual statement if you consider the physics of the thing. There's some bass-fiddle spinning (and in drag as I recall) in *Some Like It Hot,* if you don't know what I'm talking about here.

A marked difference existed between Wills's fabulous skills as an entertainer, his famous "Ahaa"s, "Take it away, Leon"s, and hilarious verbal repartee with his performers as they took hot jazz solos—as if Wills was as much teasing the improvised notes out of them as the Playboys themselves creating them—and the high level of the musicianship in the band. Wills excelled at playing traditional breakdowns, that is, melody oriented hoedown tunes. Growing up in West Texas, between two forks of the Red River (and not far from Oklahoma), Wills was one of the three best breakdown fiddlers of his time. The other two were his dad, John Wills, and Eck Robertson. Wills could win the contest fiddling if he wasn't competing against either of those two. Breakdown playing, however, with its emphasis on duplicating a melody, remains a far cry from improvisation—what Wills and the boys called "take-off fiddle."

The fiddle players Wills hired, however, improvised jazz solos, and had to be ready at any moment he might point at them with his bow or otherwise indicate to "take it away." (One of the things that fascinate me about such bands is the intuition and protocol about when it's your turn.)

Listen to the recordings—Wills does not take instrumental breaks, though he plays the melodies of any number of tunes. Although Wills added, perhaps ingeniously, a certain bluesy and jazzy quality with his slurs and other melodic devices, he stuck to the melody. With his hollers and ahas and hilarious verbal asides, Wills is the interpreter of other band members' genius—a cheerleader, calling them on to greater heights. Wills was not the equal, in terms of jazz improvisation, of any of the fiddle legends he hired—such as Jesse Ashlock, Louis Tierney, Johnny Gimble, Joe Holley, or Keith Coleman.

The Wills band, perhaps to a greater degree than almost any band in the history of country music, if you could even compare them to country players and singers, consisted of a group of serious musicians, and many of them would go on to make strong impressions in the jazz world. Wills hired some of them straight out of the leading swing jazz bands of the time. Even today, if you go to hear whatever is left of the Texas Playboys in West Texas, at least a third, maybe as much as half, of their repertoire will be instrumentals, not vocals. That's a very different kind of lineup than a country ensemble that always depends, almost exclusively, on vocal numbers.

A richly rewarding way of interpreting the party at Ted's in the Red Corn novel is to point out the subtle undercurrent of aesthetics every time Bob twirls his fiddle, so to speak, followed by one of the serious musicians taking one of the "hot" solos, a term Playboy members used to differentiate between the hoedown melodies and the spontaneous jazz improvisations that Wills couldn't, or didn't, play.

Its corollary in the novel is the European landscapes John has learned to paint, a scripted musical score compared to his growing understanding about how he might learn more organically from the materials, his own internal wealth of knowledge, and his immediate surroundings, an improvisation. Further, in terms of putting his time to good use, he can fool around and twirl the canvas, flit from party to party, engage in any other number of distractions—or he can sit down and put paint on the damn thing.

That these ideas are being gauged in the novel might be evident in the way John responds to the fiddle twirling, his initial thoughts still indicating his need for further artistic maturity: "I think the measure of whether or not music is good is how well people respond to it" (71).

Well, not exactly.

People respond well to fiddle twirling. This is like saying the measure of a good painting is how many people buy it, an argument that might make black velvet reproductions of Elvis portraits superior to Picassos. John's less-than-convincing conclusion comes early in the novel before John's more serious efforts when he takes up the portraits. The artist faces the dilemma that the vast majority of the public will always like fiddle twirling better than anything that challenges them. The artist's artistry, all too often, has to do with sneaking in enough of the challenging stuff to satisfy one's own taste for excellence while still giving them enough fiddle twirling to get people to come hear you. Miles Davis realized this sometime in the 1960s, as evidenced by fusion albums like *Bitches Brew*. He wanted to play jazz, but he also hoped for listeners during a tough decade for the music because of the prominence of rock and roll. Davis would both retain some of the swing, phrasing, and surprises of bebop (an infamously difficult style to play in its purest forms) and develop it into a much more accessible genre.

John seems on the eventual verge of such a discovery about aesthetics in relation to popularity when he follows the sentence with the statement, "I was thinking about that and realized no one there cared how or what I thought of the music" (71). No, they just want to dance, get liquored up, and laid, not necessarily in that order—and they're going to be like that at every gig. But that doesn't mean the Wills boys don't think about their playing, and John will later move toward a more cerebral relationship with his own art as far as the challenge of conceptualizing it in relation to the tremendous changes afoot in the Osage world of the 1920s.

Wills himself, although a melody player, had a tremendous respect for improvisation, and became the major inspiration for it in the Playboys, through the tremendous encouragement he offered on the bandstand and his verbal repartee when the improvisation grooved. Wills would fire anyone who couldn't improvise—a rule that, fortunately, he didn't apply to himself.

Interestingly, one of John's discussions of painting occurs in the context of gender tradition versus gender improvisation, and, at every turn, *A Pipe for February* takes women more seriously than Mathews's earlier work. Barbara complains that her father wants her to play croquet, tennis, sew, and cook all day rather than find meaningful work in town—to whatever degree it is available among the paper pushers and Indian handlers of Pawhuska. Barbara says, "I don't want an easy life. I want an interesting life" (73). John, at first, tells her to try painting, then amends his statement,

> "Come out some time. We can discuss art and painting."
> "Why do we have to discuss art? Can't we just paint?"
> "People do not just paint, they discuss painting. I thought everyone knew that." (73)

This is more than just a pickup line, as in "You wanna come up to my place and see my etchings?" John is starting to consider a future discussion of the conscious aspects of his work. The artistic dilemma, of course, is one can reflect on it rather than doing it, but too much thought never seems to be the real distraction for John. It is working through the various Catholic, Osage, European, and university legacies that inform the community that seems to be part of the puzzle he must put together in order to understand the nature of his subject matter, the topic of the last chapter of the novel. And there is also resisting the entropy that comes from the disturbing combination of wealth and murder.

After this conversation about art and gender, John reveals that he faces his own struggles with the meaning of tradition, since elder relatives have an arranged marriage in mind for him, yet he feels compelled to explore what it would mean to consider other alternatives. On the heels of all this, they run into Bob Wills himself.

Wills demonstrates a certain comfort level around Indians that may have been factual, and Red Corn, as mentioned earlier, actually saw Wills perform at his parents' parties. Wills says, "John, if you don't stop calling me Mr. Wills, I'm a-gonna start calling you Mr. Grayeagle" (74).

William W. Savage, Jr., writes,

> Bob Wills had learned black music while growing up in Texas. He lived and worked among blacks. He learned the music directly from black musicians, not from records or radio.
>
> Once, an inebriated Bob Wills hired a black trumpet player in Tulsa. The black Texas playboy survived for one performance. A sober Bob Wills decided that Oklahomans were unprepared to accept a black man playing black music in a white orchestra. (13–14)

Having known a few of the western swing players over the years myself, and having had one of The Texas Playboys, Joe Settlemires as my guitar teacher, it seems to me that Wills, and many of the Playboys, though hardly icons of progressivism in relation to race matters, had a far different attitude about African Americans, largely because of their great admiration for jazz, than some of the rednecks who came to Playboy dances.

Wills grew up working among African Americans, picking cotton with them, and learning music while they labored together. Wills's favorite singer was Bessie Smith, and Wills believed, correctly, that his own best singing was on blues numbers. On tour in Chicago, after their gigs, Playboys hurried nightly to the Down Beat Room to listen to their heroes, all prominent African American jazzmen. One photo in the Townsend biography shows Playboys Rip Ramsey, Joe Holley, and Teddy Adams with their arms around their heroes, J. C. Higginbotham, Red Allen, and Ben Webster. I don't want to overly romanticize this by claiming the Playboys to be racial progressives, yet research and my own experience suggest to me that they were different, say, than the average white West Texan or Oklahoman of the time. Wills, whose appreciation of black music may have somewhat moderated his experiences as a southerner in the cotton belt, might have also felt comfortable around Indians. It seems consistent with the little bit I know about the band and some very small degree of contact with the occasional member.

The novel concludes when John finally has no choice but to break out a serious can of whup-ass on his lawyers and handlers. John takes the war club out of retirement. He doesn't kill any of them, but they develop a deep respect for the strength of hickory. I am ambivalent as to how I feel about John becoming a kind of Indian superhero by embodying the warrior role, if only for long enough to run the yahoos out of town, toward the end. Personally, I don't find the drama (melodrama?) as interesting as the conversations the characters have drinking French espresso at the Bon Bon, but I realize this constitutes a matter of personal taste rather than a fault of the novel.

A war club might be the polar opposite of a brush, and the book concludes with brush not club—favoring peace clan relations, I should think, although these matters may be beyond me. The real point, I take it, is John's potential to manage his own affairs and shake off the Pawhuska handlers—fortunately, only a couple of them need braining.

And he takes control of his own art. The closing scene occurs at his grandfather's house, and John recalls,

> I am alone trying to conceive a way of painting a series of pictures that will explain the Osage experience.
>
>   The concept must include the clans, and the ancient philosophy, and the newfound wealth. That would include the many good things that have come from oil.
>
>   It is a difficult undertaking. An enormous, complex undertaking.
>
>   No doubt part of the Osage experience includes people like Sanders and Baskins. People who commit murder, or anything else, to get an interest in an Osage headright that allows them to share in the oil. (266)

Every artist, of any stripe, has to figure out how to accommodate the totality of one's life in the rather limited forum provided by one's art, as I have pointed out earlier. John has to further understand how to accommodate the totality of the tribe in the rather limited forum provided by his art, including those aspects that might be most painful or even seem the least Osage. It *is* an enormous undertaking, one that John Joseph Mathews certainly struggled with, given his tremendous vacillations over whether or not Osage culture would survive as well as philosophical questions that seem a bit muddled in terms of what constitutes culture.

As difficult as these questions are, one ends up choosing a focus and making a determination of what does and does not fit into the jurisdiction of one's particular study of tribal subject matter. I made that choice in *Red on Red,* and I certainly heard about it afterwards. As feeble as my theories may be, I cannot simply avoid intellectual choices, and I think some of my detractors, who have argued about too much separation in my work, have imagined a kind of utopia where people don't have to delineate one thing from another and decide which ones they want to study—a position that does not accommodate the real world very well. John says,

> There are others, like the people at the Agency, and lawyers, and busi-
> ness people, who may once have been good people, but their greed made
> them do evil things. I have no interest in painting them, or in painting
> experiences like theirs. I doubt that I will ever have that interest. (266)

I take it that John's statements are not contradictory. While he will study the impact of oil greed on the Osage, thus incorporating some of the unsavory aspects of Osage experience; he will not make non-Osages the center of his study, but Osages themselves. This has always seemed to me a perfectly legiti-mate artistic choice. John is more interested in painting his grandfather than the rip-off artist Alan S. Sanders, one of his non-Indian handlers. And why not?

Similarly, John Joseph Mathews has a host of non-Osage, and non-Indian, characters, and cosmopolitan inclusions in *Talking to the Moon*. Yet the center of his book is the Osage calendar, which provides the springboard for his political discussion about global affairs, as well as Osage people themselves. I believe there is a cohesive Osage center in Mathews's work and that such a center can be claimed without reverting to a naïve isolationism. Even Red Corn's flapper aesthetic and depictions of decadence on occasion (not all occasions, I should think) become significantly Osage. I have heard Red Corn comment on seeing elders chauffeured around in their fancy cars, the way John's grandfather is in his Pierce-Arrow; Red Corn recalls that in childhood he almost viewed these people as royalty, yet later, as an adult, he realized that they were not nearly as unapproachable as he had imagined. John's grand-father, chauffeured about town, is one cool dandy, and he has adapted the flapper age to his own style and individuality, befitting his years and bearing. John is learning to work through these issues of Osage essences and their counterparts in spontaneity, deviation, and difference. It's hard work:

> I have been searching to find that moment in time to start painting the
> Osage history. What will the subject of that first painting be? Will it be a
> life symbol, like the elk or an eagle or a star? Will it be a group picture
> like those photographs at an I'n-lon-shka dance, or could it be a portrait
> of a person I know, like Molly? (267)

Readers of these novels are tempted to interpret them by determining what is Osage and what is not, to come up with a formula that sifts the tribal from the nontribal. Such approaches have haunted Native literary criticism for many years. The formula can only work as a series of questions, something akin to the Socratic method. To the question "Is it Osage?" or "is it tribal?" Possible answers might include "I don't know, is it? Are you willing to claim it as such? What kind of work will you do to convince me it is? What negotiations might have to occur to convince others of its tribal legitimacy? How much home-work have you done already in terms of tracing its tribal roots? How much more are you willing to do?"

John hopes,

> Some day I will find a way to make my brushes and oil paints and canvas express what it was I saw in Mon-tse-no-pi'n's eyes on that day when I first sketched him and began work on painting his portrait. I plan to work to see if I cannot acquire for myself at least some of those qualities that allowed him to look so deeply into my soul. I do not know what those things are but I will try to find them. (268)

The artistic subject creates his painter. John wants to imagine, I think, how Mon-tse-no-pi'n' might paint *him,* a subject that also comes up repeatedly in the Mathews discussion of portraiture. This goes beyond mixing colors and brush strokes, obviously. How might John's subject talk back to the representation and, more radically, how might the subject create a representation of his or her own—and what might we learn about ourselves by allowing the Other to scru-tinize *us*? What might be the qualities worth emulating in such a process? How can we, as artists, facilitate these questions that break us out of the usual frames?

The novel concludes with John's artistic manifesto:

> It was the people, and the earth creatures, that created the clans that gave insight and courage and those other qualities to individuals like Mon-tse-no-pi'n. But, he was not the only one to have qualities like the ability to look through my eyes and into my soul and to know why I wanted to paint him. Many of them had those qualities.
>
> Qualities like that I suspect are not limited to a single group of people, such as Osages, nor are such traits limited to a race, such as Indians. Still, I must begin my search somewhere and I will begin with Osages. Those are good qualities that I want as a guide to live by, and I want to paint them so that others may use and enjoy them.
>
> That may be a lot to ask of some pencils and brushes and tubes of paint and linen canvas, but those things may very well be all I have to work with.
>
> Then, some day when I know I am a capable artist, I will paint Grandpa. (269)

What strikes me about Red Corn's ending is the way in which, in relation to visual art, this represents an older generation of Indian painters. In just a few years after the period in which the novel takes place, the Bacone School—strongly influenced by Creek-Pawnee artist Acee Blue Eagle, who taught at the Muskogee institution in the 1930s—would move away from portraiture into a much broader consideration of what constituted Native tradition and worthy material for the Native painter; Indian painting would become even more radically non-mimetic in the heyday of the IAIA painters of the late 1960s and early 1970s. Accuracy, literal translation of the sitting figure, is not the point of such painting; rather it is about altering the literal with one's own unique "angle of vision," to quote one well-known Kiowa painter-novelist. I see a fascinating link between John's innocence and the literal mold he still seems somewhat stuck in at the end of the novel with regard to portraiture. His earlier inability to see beyond the surface of his seeming benefactors—his Pawhuska handlers—and the lack of a more radical, less literal, vision, seems to connect his art and personality.

It may well be that these are not merely character flaws in John but indicative of an artistic milieu in the years before Indian art is ready to bust loose from some of its constraints. In terms of Indian-white relations, a parallel challenge surrounds John: his not-so-beneficent benefactors certainly do not encourage in him a spirit of free thinking and improvisation—"paint inside the dotted lines" is the order of the day, even in terms of managing one's financial affairs. I think this explains some of the artistic conservatism of the novel, and it is intriguing to think, then, that moving away from fiddle twirling and toward improvisation may be at the heart of it after all. I told you it was about Bob Wills.

Works Cited

Mathews, John Joseph. *Sundown.* London and New York: Longmans, Green and Co., 1934.

———. *Talking to the Moon.* Norman: University of Oklahoma Press, 1945. Reprint 1981.

Parker, Robert Dale. *The Invention of Native American Literature.* Ithaca, N.Y.: Cornell University Press, 2003.

Red Corn, Charles. *A Pipe for February: A Novel.* Norman: University of Oklahoma Press, 2002.

Savage, William W., Jr. *Singing Cowboys and All That Jazz: A Short History of Popular Music in Oklahoma.* Norman: University of Oklahoma Press, 1983.

Townsend, Charles. *San Antonio Rose: The Life and Music of Bob Wills.* Chicago: University of Illinois Press, 1986.

Warrior, Robert Allen. *Tribal Secrets: Recovering American Indian Intellectual Traditions*. Minneapolis: University of Minnesota Press, 1994.

Welch, James. *Winter in the Blood*. New York: Harper & Row: 1974.

Womack, Craig. *Red on Red: Native American Literary Separatism*. Minneapolis: University of Minnesota Press, 1999.

Beth Brant and the Aesthetics of Sex

In some ways we might have a hard time imagining two Mohawk writers as different from one another as E. Pauline Johnson (1861–1913), from the Six Nations Reserve, near Brantford, Ontario, and Beth Brant (1941) who grew up in Detroit and whose family is from Tyendinaga, also in Ontario. I wouldn't necessarily expect E. Pauline Johnson to have penned this passage about a woman, Mary, who finds sexual solace in her lover, Ellen, in the midst of the pain she feels over the loss of her daughter, Patricia, who was removed from their home when the state sanctioned the couple unfit as mothers because of their same-sex relationship:

> She comes to me full in flesh. My hands are taken with the curves and soft roundness of her. She covers me with the beating of her heart. The rhythm steadies me. Heat is centering me. I am grounded by the peace between us. I smile at her face gleaming above me, round like a moon, her long hair loose and touching my breasts. I take her breast in my hand, bring it to my mouth; suck her as a woman, in desire . . . in faith. Our bodies join. Our hair braids together on the pillow. Brown, black, silver; catching the last face of the sun. We kiss, touch, move to our place of power. Her mouth, moving over my body, stopping at curves and swells of skin, kissing, removing pain. Closer, close, together, woven, my legs are heat, the center of my soul is speaking to her, I am sliding into her, her mouth is medicine, her heart is the earth, we are dancing with flying arms, I shout, I sing, I weep salty liquid, sweet and warm, it coats her throat, this is my life. I love you Ellen, I love you Mary, I love, we love. (*A Gathering of Spirit* 104)

Since wild Indians don't even kiss according to "A Strong Race Opinion," Johnson would have had some explaining to do had she authored such a passage.

Yet similarities abound between the two writers in spite of the chasm of time that separates them. Both Johnson and Brant are Mohawk from their father's side of the family, a challenging lineage given Mohawk matrilinearity (though certainly not an impossible one, as both women's close community affiliations suggest). Brant frequently references Johnson in her books, and her opening reflection in *Writing as Witness: Essay and Talk* (1994) focuses an entire chapter on Johnson, titled "The Good Red Road." I would also point out that both authors make some of their most compelling claims in nonfiction writing, Johnson on individuality in fiction in "A Strong Race Opinion," Brant on the powers of same-sex desire, and sexuality more generally, in *Writing as Witness*.

Even similar philosophical contradictions mark the work of each. If Johnson hopes for individuality in depictions of Native women, she often settles for less in her own work and, instead, makes countless reductive claims for universalized characteristics rather than deviations. The phrase "like all her race," followed by some trait that marks all Indian women, has a corollary in Brant's work, with its own late 1980s twist, which applies the genericism to both Indians and whites—the former are mostly wholistic, and the latter generally oppressive. Brant makes frequent broad claims about Native and non-Native culture while offering little evidence whatsoever—oral, published, or archival—to support them. In this regard the work bears a very close affinity to Paula Gunn Allen's *The Sacred Hoop*, except Gunn Allen engages source material much more actively. In the introduction to *Reasoning Together: The Native Critics Collective*, I wrote about the strengths and weaknesses of the essentialized feminism of the late eighties, its relationship to the women of color writers during the time period, its location in a transitional phase between feminism and gender studies, and the debt we owe these foremothers for the space they pioneered in Native Studies, so I'll forgo that particular discussion.

I didn't come to damn Caesar, as they say, and I want to celebrate the tremendous integrity of Beth Brant's writing and the stance she takes as an out lesbian. If E. Pauline Johnson achieves her most effective voice through satire, I believe that Beth Brant excels at erotic writing—specifically, naming the creative possibilities of same-sex desire. As happens when Johnson takes on her wonderful smartass persona and specificity trumps generalizations, when Brant writes about same-sex couples their individual personalities emerge and challenge generic assumptions about entire races of people.

The above quotation ends with two names and three pronouns: Ellen, Mary, I, you, we. No one can mistake the fact that this passage presents us with two women in the act of lovemaking. One of the most important facets of Beth Brant's writing, a foundation that she builds the entire structure on, is that, beginning with her earliest book, one of the first words that appears in it is "lesbian." In the dedication of *A Gathering of Spirit* (1984), before the main text even begins, one remembrance reads,

Saralinda Grimes (Cherokee)
Born in 1957.
Lesbian, resister, organizer.
Died in Tilden Park, Berkeley, California, in 1976
From an overdose of morphine and codeine. She was a casualty of the war
Against women, against gays, against the Indian People.

In *A Gathering of Spirit,* the first anthology of Native women's writing, Brant includes letters from prisoners, thus challenging the notion of what constitutes the "literary," and in her replies to them Brant identifies herself as a Mohawk lesbian, just as she does in published autobiographical statements. As Brant herself recalls about the wonderful deviance of the anthology,

> Of the sixty women who had contributed to the book, ten of us declared our lesbianism. This was a new day in the history of Aboriginal writing. This time around, we were actively saying who we were—all parts of us—no coyness, or hiding, or pretending to be something we weren't. It was a great political and personally courageous act on the part of those nine women who stood with me. I will always be thankful to them and blessed in knowing them. (*Writing as Witness* 114)

Brant even lays down the rules, and identifies the ways in which she refuses to closet herself:

> I will not make a character heterosexual if she or he is not. In sending out my vitae I will not excise those anthologies or journals that have the words lesbian, gay, dyke or queer in them. I may as well excise those journals and anthologies that have the words native, Indian or woman in their titles. In my bio notes I usually say I am a Mohawk lesbian mother and grandmother. (80)

In all her books, Brant finds a prominent place for the gay and lesbian characters who frequently people her fiction and often serve as the protagonists of her stories.

I can hardly overemphasize how much Brant's willingness to name her lesbian identity constitutes a radical departure for Indian literature in 1984— as it still does today, when Native writers continue to reap the economic benefits and literary awards that come from remaining in the closet. As much as these writers might like to think otherwise, they still endorse the officially approved (as much by Indians as non-Indians) Indian princesses. I probably do not need to add that a proper Indian princess is never a lesbian.

None of the three most "out" Native women writers—Chrystos, Beth Brant, and Janice Gould—have had the kind of university appointments and literary awards that many of us do (I realize I benefit from these privileges, too, as a tenured professor and in other ways). Chrystos, for example, works as a maid. Gould has academic credentials and sometimes teaches in universities when she can. Although other factors contribute that have to do with personal choices, lack of degrees (except for Gould), and contingencies I cannot know since I do not want to speak on their behalf, I still would speculate that a significant reality for these working-class writers has to do with the fact that out Native lesbians do not receive approval from the Native literary mainstream, and this reality affects material circumstances such as employment.

Gender issues also apply. A little more space exists—not much, but a little—for depictions of Native gay men rather than lesbians, especially if heterosexuals author these depictions—particularly a writer as popular and skilled as Sherman Alexie. I like Alexie, and I like his writing, but I hate it when I hear people refer to him as a gay author or his work as gay writing. Alexie identifies as heterosexual, and if sovereignty means something, I think a person's sexual sovereignty—his claims about himself—ought to have some relevance. If Native literature means literature authored by Native people, how can Native gay or lesbian literature mean anything other than literature authored by Native gays and lesbians? The work of Native gay and lesbian writers gets scant enough attention without erasing them and replacing them with Sherman Alexie, who himself does not seek such a substitution. If an author is non-Indian—Tom Spanbauer comes to mind—opportunities abound for even larger success. The further removed the writing remains from the original community, the more likely the chances of broad, popular appeal.

Beth Brant, however, brooks no erasure, no matter the forces that might marginalize her. Unlike Native writers who have masked same-sex desire in their writings by a universalized second-person "you" that obscures the genders of the participants, Brant makes it clear she writes about sexual encounters between women: she clarifies the I, the you, and the we with the proper names Mary and Ellen, as we have just seen. Naming women participants in sexual encounters is central to Brant's project which has to do with, to quote the title of Chrystos's 1988 book, *Not Vanishing*.

It also has to do with an ethical responsibility: if we as gay and lesbian Native writers will not reveal ourselves to our own people, many of whom suffer in situations of extreme isolation and loneliness, then who in the hell will? Some of Audre Lorde's groundbreaking work emphasizes the ways in which sexuality, erotics, and physicality function as implements, rather than impediments, of knowledge—a fundamental challenge to the mind/body split the West has labored under for centuries. Lorde insists that honesty and naming, turning *toward* our intimate experiences, rather than denying them, constitute necessary components in such transformations.

Brant names women in sexual relations, I might guess, because it is important to give credit where credit is due in order to recognize the role of women in creating erotic knowledge together. The act of naming the sex of the participants, rather than obscuring it, is part of the very process that makes the knowledge possible.

Yes, it matters, and it matters profoundly, that the poet reveals to her readers that she is talking about women with other women rather than with men, as is possible with the fill in the blank "you" of the universalized second person when both poetic speaker and lover are thus labeled, giving heteros the right to fill in the "you" with an opposite-sex couple. To insist on women's encounters with other women means to take back one's poetry in the case of women writers.

If we add to all of this the problematic depictions of gay men in well-known Native novels such as Leslie Marmon Silko's *Almanac of the Dead* (1991), Tomson Highway's *Kiss of the Fur Queen* (1999), and James Welch's *The Heartsong of Charging Elk* (2001), as well as the complete absence of lesbians in almost all Native-authored works, the urgency of resistant Native gay and lesbian voices becomes all the more apparent.

The rest of the planet, it would seem, except for Native Studies, has come out. Given this whacky scenario, where Indian writers and critics seem akin to something like the Amish—determined to keep everyone down on the farm in a sexual horse and buggy culture for millennia after everyone else has tractors and cars—we should ask this question: What kind of aesthetic choices does Brant's writing reveal to confront this crazy scene?

We can begin with the quotation that opens this chapter, from Brant's short fiction "A Long Story" that links a contemporary lesbian couple's loss of a child in the late 1970s through the court system to an Iroquoian woman's loss of her two children when the Indian agent takes them against her will and sends them to boarding school in 1890. In virtually every letter from a Native woman prisoner that Brant publishes alongside this story in *A Gathering of Spirit*, the mothers mention the loss of, or separation from, their children as a primary concern regarding their incarceration. I believe that both the spirit, and the style, of these nonfiction letters make their way into Brant's fiction.

One mother, Share Ouart, writes,

I am sure I will never get my older son back and everything is at an alltime worst. So hopefully its up from here. I know that never a day will pass that I don't give thanks for my freedom and my 2 children I have. I think I might enjoy independence. I've been married literly ½ my life. When I get out I will be like you, single.

I don't have my health. This long battle has took its toll. I hope I am not back here for stealing my son again. That would be rough on my other 2. I fear I'll be back in here with a murder charge like my Sioux sister, Rita. I don't know why Oklahoma is so hard on sioux womens children. My mother always said whites would steal Indian babies. (74)

As does Brant, out of respect for the women's dignity, I leave the letters as written. The passage is marked by many declarative sentences that begin with the personal or possessive pronoun, I or my. The sentences vacillate between negation and possibility ("I will never get my older son back"; "hopefully its up from here"). The writer links her present incarceration to a historic narrative tradition, a warning in stories: "My mother always said whites would steal Indian babies."

Brant also structures "A Long Story" as two narratives that link past and present, since the two mothers from 1890 and 1978 seem to speak to each other across distance and time, even though they have no knowledge of each other's existence—only we readers do, through their first-person voices, which seem a lot like the prison correspondence. Brant herself, as correspondent and publisher, becomes a link between different narratives as she tells her story to Share and Share reciprocates—both women trying to reach across time, space, their own differences in circumstances, in order to communicate.

Another mother, Rita Silk-Nauni, writes, "I haven't seen my son for over a year now. Each second I'm away from him the lonely feelings I endure Becomes worse" (93). Rita writes in another letter, "Saw my lawyer yesterday. He says he'll bring Derrick (my Son) up to see me. But he's said that before, so I'll believe it when I see him. He says I have a real good chance of a reversal or a new trial" (95). In a longer section that details some of the history of Rita's separation from her children, she writes,

I was at my Moms one Summer. I was 14. I met a professional baseball player, much older than I. I became pregnant and was actually happy. When I start to show I couldn't hide it any longer so I talked to my Dad about it. He became angry and said there was no way he was going to allow me to keep my child. I was so hurt, but obeyed my Dad and went to a home for unwed mothers. My baby was put up for adoption against my will. A part of me died. That hurt me more than anything else could have. The Catholics Nuns at the home I went to told me I couldn't see my child at all. So I thought about running from there, but didn't know where to go or who to turn to. My Child was a girl. I caught a glimpse of her, she was so beautiful. My dream was to have a large family.

Then in 1968 when I gave birth to my Son, I was the happiest I've been. We were so close and I would never leave him, only to go to work. I tried having more after him and couldn't. I went to a specialist and he thought I had been fixed when I had my Son. He said I would have to have surgery in order to give birth again The surgery was so expensive but I thought I could make a way even if I had to work 24 hours a day.

Now that I'm here, I know I'll never have that chance. So now I think about adoption. And I think about my daughter, wonder where she is, if shes okay. And I know one day I'll look for her till I find her.

My precious Son is living with his Father and his Grand-Parents and most of his relations live close by. But I still worry about him, although I know they wouldn't let no one hurt him.

It's been over a year that I've seen him. Right now I'm trying to work out a way for him to come up to visit. (94)

This passage, like Share's letter, is dominated by declarative sentences that mark a fated trajectory—one event unfolds into another in a cycle of oppression, a dreary, inescapable sameness: I tried, I tried, I tried, and I tried, but I couldn't. Every once in a while a sentence wants to sneak in and break the first person declarative mode, to challenge the notion that life declares itself and the speaker cannot challenge its predetermined prognosis, yet such sentences are simply overwhelmed by their surroundings. Declarations outnumber possibilities, improvisations, deviations, new styles of sentence making. Dad told me, the nuns told me—most insidiously, I tell me, because I can't see my way out. "Then in 1968 when I gave birth to my son I was the happiest I've been" leaves the first-person declaration by beginning with a dependent clause. The sentence variation hopes to fly off and become a story about a new kind of I who escapes the declarations of others, as well as her own sense of limitations. But how? The 1968 story is simply drowned out by its competitors.

"A Long Story," Brant's short fiction, encapsulates the frustration of trying to break someone out of a tragic orientation within the confinement of prison correspondence, as evidenced by declarative sentences that brook little deviation of style. In the anthology Brant includes some of her letters back to the women's prisoners, telling her own life story, empathizing, trying to look for whatever hope she can convey. Yet Brant's own sentences often remain in the declarative mode. When she writes to Raven, who serves a life term in Maryland, Brant responds,

> I was so happy to get your letter. It made my day very beautiful. Please tell me more about yourself. I was very moved by your letter. It seems that so many of us have missed out on our own heritage. My family is Mohawk but education was the highest goal, and it was hard to not assimilate. I am not educated. I got married when I was 17. My three daughters are grown up now. I am 41, no longer married, am a feminist and a lesbian. I began writing about 2 years ago, and now feel like I can do my political work this way. (221)

Like her prison interlocutors, Brant's sentences constitute a list of short declarative statements, albeit a different kind of list since it begins with the factors that have made her life more hopeful rather than a string of inescapable problems. Brant understates the problems rather than allowing them to take over and dominate. "No longer married," for example, hints at difficulties while not expounding on them.

Yet something is missing, a feeling most anyone experiences who tries to reach out to prisoners from the outside, and I felt this acutely the day I tried to give the Chitto Harjo speech at Diamondback, as well as on many other visits. My most effective communications with the men, in all honesty, were the many occasions I simply played guitar with them in the prison band and said nothing (apart from singing). The most frustrating problem for a prisoner regarding intimate relations, whether sexual ones with lovers, familial ones with children, or even communication with a correspondent, is the distance created by incarceration and separation. For a writer on the outside, trying to convey hope, a different kind of distance presents a formidable barrier: how do I convince you that you are not entirely different from me, that we have a basis for talking, given that barbed wire creates very different realities for the two of us? More importantly, how can I get you to see beyond your own incarceration to the possibility of liberation—even if you remain inside prison walls? What kind of language can do that—overcome the declarative pronouncements about the inevitability of all the factors stacked up against you?

I would like to suggest that Brant employs the language of sexuality to break through these frustrating challenges, and she does this effectively in particular short stories that negotiate the limitations experienced in her prison correspondence. Writing to a female prisoner the kind of passage we have been studying from "A Long Story," like the one that opens this chapter, would be highly problematic—even setting aside issues of appropriateness, it might not make it past the prison censors. While Share, Rita, and Raven might not have ever received such an erotically charged letter from Brant, we can reasonably hope that Brant's correspondents read the short story—and since each contributed to the anthology, they must have received a copy of the book. Some might view these speculations on reception a tangential digression; I view the issue of who reads Native literature and what happens as a result of these readings as the heart and soul of the matter. Did any of these women make it out? How are they doing? Raven faced a death sentence. Is she still alive? Their health is the context for Mary and Ellen's recovery in Brant's fiction.

Brant transfers these dilemmas to "A Long Story" which conveys the spirit of Brant's correspondence concerning the frustrations of wanting to break someone out of overwhelming tragedy through the only means available when you're on one side of barbed wire and the person you write to on another—the gift of words rather than physical presence. Mary, the contemporary mother who has lost her daughter in the court system, recalls, "My lawyer says there is nothing more we can do. I must wait. As if we have done anything else. He has custody and calls the shots. We must wait and see how long it takes for him get tired of being mommy and daddy. So . . . I wait" (105). The Iroquoian mother who has lost two children to boarding school says, "The men sit. They talk among themselves. We are frightened by this sudden child-stealing. We signed papers, the agent said. This gave them rights to take our babies. It is good for them, the agent said. It will make them civilized, the agent said" (101). These fictional statements duplicate the declarative inevitabilities of both the prisoners' letters and even Brant's responses.

The fictional sexual passage, on the other hand, represents a linguistic breakthrough; the kind of language difficult to convey in a letter to a prisoner is more possible in the context of a short story, words that move beyond fated declarations, that bridge distances. The passage will take off and soar, reminding me of the old gospel song, "Like a bird from prison bars has flown, I'll fly away." While it starts out with a simple enough declaration, "She comes to me full in flesh," it is neither first person, bogged down in the speaker's own sense of events that have spun out of her control, nor third, where an authoritarian voice, often male, proclaims her inescapable fate. "Full in flesh," suggests ripe fruit, ready for harvest. It breaks the narrative of disintegration, things constantly getting worse, failed harvest cut off by infelicitous events—instead holding out hope for fulfillment, for sexual reaping. In the next sentence, the narrator's hands reach out to someone else, connect to another, so that the "my" becomes subsumed in the "her," decreasing the sense of being bogged down in one's own problems.

Brant still works within the style of direct statement, as in "She covers me with the beating of her heart," and the conjoined pulse is literal because of the physical fact of skin-to-skin contact. Yet the "covering" opens up poetic possibilities. Two grief-stricken hearts, by joining forces, hope to gather whatever strength they can. The union occurs inside the women's room, a sanctuary from outside authoritarian forces that would control their lives. Rhythm steadies, heat centers. Bodies, simply, are allowed the freedom to do what bodies are supposed to do, the polar opposite of a prison sentence where bodies are micro-managed on every level by keeping them apart—or, in another institutional setting, from the removal of children in which women find parts of their bodies excised, sent away.

When Ellen looms over Mary, unlike the forms of dominance that loom over women's lives against their wills, a merging occurs rather than an erasure, and this sentence contains the first poetic device, a simile, in "face . . . round like a moon." Ellen, gleaming like the moon, a female entity, becomes more herself, not less—a contrast to the experiences of the prison letter writers who find their identity stripped away by those who would control them, and even those of the fictional characters, until they break through oppressive structures by engaging in creative acts of sex. The phrase "suck her as a woman" evokes a wonderful sense of deviance since it implies a contrast with "suck her as a child," thus challenging narratives that would insist that female sexuality only relates to procreation and/or heterosexuality.

The passage keeps up its pace through active verb forms like "kiss," "touch," "move" rather than the passive verbs of the authoritarian discourse that diminish female agency by obscuring who acts in the sentences. Further, rather than an emphasis on unalterable circumstances, the active verb forms indicate the erotic encounter is heading somewhere, moving outside of passivity.

"Closer, close, together" notes a merging of spirits, so that the two become one flesh, to borrow a phrase, joining as close as is humanly and non-humanly possible, into a realm of mystery, the inexplicable. Who can explain desire? One can only reach toward possibility, and "my legs are heat," suggests a new internal fire that wasn't there before. Prison language has to do with definition—that's what a prison sentence is—rather than open-ended signification, which is what freedom, ideally, means. Desire resists definition, a problem any parent, or anyone else, who tries to explain sex to a youngster can relate to.

The phrase "We are dancing with flying arms" describes a disorderly dance, surely more raucous than stately, an important move toward rule-breaking, defiance of tradition, and even insanity. Craziness in Brant's work, as evidenced in her stories about mental institutions, can indicate forms of power and knowledge.

"It coats her throat," Mary's tears do, bathing Ellen's voice box, an organ of speech, a strong metaphor for sexualizing language, turning the one-dimensional tragedy of the declarative sentences into language that rocks and sways, makes the bedsprings squeak. And then the naming: the concrete insistence on both women's names, not just the pronouns—no way the narrator will let us assume that this is anything less than a sexual encounter between two women.

A story from *Mohawk Trail*, "The Fifth Floor, 1967," depicts a woman whose husband institutionalizes her for deviating from her "wifely" duties. While other authors have written on this theme—Charlotte Perkins Gilman's "The Yellow Wallpaper" comes to mind—I know of no one other than Brant who suggests that freedom from such a dilemma might be learned through sexual experimentation. The story contrasts sexual domination with sexual discovery. In the first case, the narrator recalls,

> At home this woman was a crybaby, but the tears never came out of her eyes. They spilled inside her skin, soaking her brain, trickling down the shelves of bones, coming out of her cunt and hands. She left trails of wet salt on her chair, in her bed.
>
> She would not allow her husband to fuck her. She told him his penis would shrivel and die from the wet salt. But he never listened. He climbed on her, shoving his cock against her face, coming in her mouth. She wiped the semen away, rinsing her head under the bathroom faucet.
>
> She dared not touch her daughters or their skin would stain. Their beautiful faces would scar from the wet salt. (72)

I am struck by how effectively the sounds of the words "salt," "cunt," "cock," and "fuck" amplify each other in this passage—all four letters, all involving a single vowel surrounded by hard consonants, creating a beautiful parallelism of fricative music. These sounds, like getting struck at the batter's plate by the pitcher's rapid-fire hardball four times in a row, make the more cautious "semen" and "penis" seem wimpy in comparison, like easy underhanded slow pitches thrown at leisure. Thus the language works by way of contrast, and this occurs on the level of theme as well. Internal and external, penetrated and protected, seeping in and leaking out, hiding and revealing, become the poetic link that undergirds the whole passage through these highly effective images.

Separated by her husband because of forced institutionalization, the un-named protagonist of the story does not succumb to the vapidity of drugs and regime but, instead, uses the newfound freedom from him to begin a series of experiments on ways she can choose to enter the internal and external spaces of her body, and her circumstances, on her own terms. How do I enter myself, how do I enter the world, and how do I do so by choice instead of someone else entering me against my will? These ideas strongly relate to the letters Brant received from prisoners and, not coincidentally, "The Fifth Floor, 1967" is about incarceration.

The narrator's experiment depends on artistic choices, and first she con-siders a narrative point of view, referencing herself in the third person:

> I explore the body of this woman. Hastily. Her breasts are flaccid and numb. I pinch her nipples, feel them rise. I place my hands at her waist, feel her ribs. Her rib cage is wide and round, like staves of a basket. Her thighs are cold and thin. I stroke the soft place of her inner thighs with both hands. Her skin becomes warmer. She trembles with each brush of my fingers. The hair of her cunt is straight and heavy and thick. I touch the slit, the opening of her cunt, the inside of her. She is wet and open. Her clitoris pulses under my finger. I touch her there. Try to find her. She is wet and open. I taste her juice off my finger. She is tart, like sweat and medicine. Both hands attempt to enter her, to go up inside her hole, to touch a place in her that will tell me who I am. I rub her clit. She spasms and comes on my hand, the syrup from her coating my fingers. I bring my hand to my mouth and suck myself to sleep. I have dreams about her. She looks in the mirror, and I see with her eyes. (72–73)

First of all, one can hardly help but notice the utter lack of place in the passage. No sights or sounds from the mental ward interrupt the sexual encounter, as if the surroundings are so unremarkable that they simply disappear as the woman turns toward more important matters—herself. Nothing marks a prison or state institution as radically as its mediocrity, a situation anyone who has been on the inside and dealt with the bureaucracy that dominates such places can attest to. By definition, a prison is a mediocre solution to a complex problem.

While the word "cunt" appears twice in the passage, it functions differently than it does in the narrator's recollections of oppressive sexuality. In the passage on sexual domination the word "cunt" is placed in a string of four-letter assaults. Here it is, instead, an opening—an opening to pleasure, experi-ence, and knowledge rather than a point of penetration. Instead, it functions as a place of emergence, a creation story. I love the word "pulses" in the passage, a real awakening since the recollection begins with its opposite, flaccidity. The sexual exploration challenges the physical realities of a body that is sometimes numb, flaccid, cold, and thin with poetic imaginings of restoration, "[h]er rib cage . . . like staves of a basket." The simile deals with the heart of the problem: how can you look at a prison and instead see possibility?

Let me see through her eyes, allow me to dream of her. Who can grant permission for such knowledge? Certainly not prison or mental institution personnel. Only oneself, of course—we are talking about a gift no one else can give us. We cannot say to someone, "please tell me what I like." Ironically, it is the mental institution where the narrator addresses these issues, not her home, dominated by her husband, where the latter insists on defining the narrator: "My husband tells me I am not myself" (69).

The unnamed protagonist hopes to bring the new woman back home with her upon her "release." In a sense Brant, I might guess, hopes for the same thing in her correspondence, to bring Share, Rita, and Raven "home" with her, to that place of recovery:

> I have not found me—yet—but the psychiatrist looked at my chart and my good behavior. Besides, my insurance will not pay beyond six weeks of treatment. And I do not have the resources to stay longer. Six weeks. Six weeks to make a crazy woman sane.
>
> I am taking the woman with me. I am smuggling her out. She will go with me as my secret. During these six weeks her face has begun to take on my features. My face has begun to take on lines, and my skin is toughening. Her hair has one thread of silver. My hair is getting darker and thinner. Her body is round, and when my fingers press her thighs, white marks appear which quickly fill with blood, leaving her skin soft, brown, and beautiful. My breasts feel everything. In my dreams, I remember my first-born suckling from me. I awake to wet spots on my nightgown. Inside me there is salt. At times it seeps from my eyes, dropping on my hands. Her body is not salted. Inside her is blood, muscle, electric pulses, and rage. Her fingers send currents through mine. Her fingers are long and rough and there are cracks in her nails. My hands are also rough and my palms are lined.
>
> I am taking the woman home with me. It is our secret. She keeps me alive. (75)

The protagonist of the story does not emerge with a name, a rare exception in Brant's fiction, and I do not believe this would be the case if the story was about an explicitly lesbian relationship; the stakes are too high to leave the characters anonymous. The protagonist simply has not found her name yet—

her escape from anonymity still relies on figuring out who the "other woman" is. She remains a secret. A central survival issue, surely, will be the challenge of introducing the "other woman" to husband, children, and acquaintances, who may be less than welcoming. While their bodies and spirits are contrasted throughout the passage, tenuous signs emerge that the two women can potentially merge into a single entity. Formerly flaccid, numb breasts now "feel everything." If a first-born can suckle, especially if he can suckle his transformed mother, some hope may exist for at least schooling the children in the woman's need for independence. The word "rage" provides a strong culmination in a list that moves from the physical—blood and muscle—to the increasingly emotional—electric pulses and anger. While these traits characterize the other woman, "[h]er fingers sends currents" through the narrator, another indication that she may integrate the newfound deviance rather than locate it outside herself in another.

Brant has a wide range of sexual or erotically charged depictions: marital rape, masturbation (women learning their own bodies in acts of recovery), gay men remembering important erotic encounters with former lovers, a girl child washing her mother's body to prepare her for burial, adolescent lesbian sex censored by parents, and many others. As my list reveals, not all are affirmative, some do not fit easily into a category of erotics or sex.

I want to turn next to an AIDS story that is less obviously sexual. "This Place," from Brant's collection *Food and Spirits,* features a Mohawk gay man who, in the advanced stages of AIDS, leaves the city and returns home to the reservation, where his mother arranges for Joseph, a medicine man, to treat him. In his treatment Joseph somehow invokes in David a recollection of a five-hundred-year history that contextualizes David's personal experiences with a broad communal backdrop—a visionary exchange between doctor and patient that surveys centuries of land theft, forced religious conversion, loss of language, introduced diseases, as well as David's own personal experiences in the city, where he'd moved to dip into the life.

For assistants the medicine man has two cats, named Tecumseh and the Prophet after the two Shawnee political leaders who would have changed the course of North American history if their pan-tribal alliance to halt further land encroachment had succeeded. (No book captures the spirit and hilarity of how close Tecumseh came than Don Birchfield's *How Choctaws Invented Civilization and Why Choctaws Will Conquer the World,* perhaps one of the most important books in Native Studies history because of the way it relates policy to history in a literary fashion.) The medicine man gives David four gifts to assist him in the difficult days to come, the most interesting of which is a Mohawk sovereignty document, a letter from Molly and Joseph Brant that reads,

We, as the original inhabitants of this country, and sovereigns of the soil, look upon ourselves as equally independent and free as any other nation or nations. This country was given to us by the Great Spirit above; we wish to enjoy it, and have our passage along the lake, within the line we have pointed out. The great exertions we have made, for this number of years, to accomplish a peace and have not been able to obtain it; our patience, as we have observed, is exhausted. We, therefore, throw ourselves under the protection of the Great Spirit above, who will order all things for the best. We have told you our patience is worn out, but that we wish for peace and whenever we hear that pleasing sound, we shall pay attention to it. Until then, you will pay attention to us. (57)

By linking a political accord to David's personal health, the Brant story extends sovereignty beyond the legal realm and includes issues of personal and sexual sovereignty; just as importantly, it extends David's issues beyond the personal and sexual realm and includes the larger treaties and accords that remain essential to Mohawk nationalism. The proclamation's insistence on the Mohawks' inherent right to pursue freedom could just as easily describe David's earlier life in the city and his gathering of strength in the final days of his homecoming, as it insists on Mohawk national integrity. This rather extraordinary story explores the relationship between the health of the nation and the health of its citizens.

Brant often deals with the problem of split or fractured identities. In some ways differently than queer theory, which celebrates destabilized identities, to my way of thinking Brant's writing focuses on healing such splits. In Brant's collection of nonfiction essays entitled *Writing as Witness,* she says, "In my thirty-third year of life I was a feminist, an activist, and largely occupied with discovering all things female. And one of those lovely discoveries was that I could love women sexually, emotionally, and spiritually—and all at once. This is why I choose to be a lesbian. It makes me more complete in myself, and a whole woman is of much better use to my communities than a split one" (56–57). Brant, unlike closeted writers, does not see anything particularly Indian about maintaining a gigantic gulf between her life and her art. If such a chasm somehow represents "Native tradition," then I think we need to broach the subject of which of our traditions might need challenging. An equally important consideration is an evaluation of the theories that have celebrated ambiguous sexual identities.

Janice Gould also echoes concerns about fractured identities when, in her essay "Disobedience in Language in Texts by Lesbian Native Americans," she writes, "Lesbian Indian writers merge the selves that language splits apart"

(39), a response to the way in which aspects of Native lesbian lives have been hidden from public purview. Brant is forever adamant about naming herself as a Mohawk lesbian, an impulse that seems to me a significant departure from the current trendy celebration of all things undefinable—as in I'm not gay, I'm not straight, I'm not Indian, I'm not white, I'm not male, I'm not female—I'm just me. I sometimes wonder if this juvenile philosophy even remotely resembles what Gloria Anzaldúa had in mind when she articulated the concept of the borderland. If this kind of shape shifting really characterizes tricksters, maybe we'd be better off without them.

The idea of the "naturalness" of gayness, some kind of coherent, rather than impossibly ambiguous, identity, also becomes relevant to our discussion here. Brant sees homophobia as a rejection of the natural world and the creator who made it. In a passage that recalls close observations of marsh birds followed by intimacy with her partner, Brant writes, "Those people who despise sex despise Heron and others like her" (61). Brant goes on to say,

> The denial of sexuality and of those who live according to their sexuality is almost unspeakable. It has been named homophobia, but that bland word does not tell of the blasphemous acts committed against us in the name of religion and state. I use the word blasphemy because that is what it is—a defilement of all that is sprit-filled and ceremonial. I also believe that the hatred and violence that is directed against us is a result of the hatred against their god. (63–64)

Yet in spite of Brant's insistence on the coherence of a lesbian identity, she does not advocate a monolithic one rooted in sameness, and she holds out hope for its nonconformity, the possibilities of deviance, and strategies against assimilation—the best senses of the word "queer." In a wonderful passage that suggests that gays and lesbians should be making radical proclamations of pride about being kicked out of the military, rather than seeking integration into it, she says, "Why would we want to be like them? Is our main concern that of serving in armies that routinely invade countries that have large populations of people of colour?" (65). In *I'll Sing 'til the Day I Die: Conversations with Tyendinaga Elders,* Brant interviews people from her home reserve, a number of them veterans, and they often express misgivings about serving in the military—another important reminder that the elders also have a sense of the necessity of deviance, not just conformity to tradition—in this case the tradition of military service in Native communities. Brant, then, mediates between a conservative gay identity based on integration and societal acceptance and a radically destabilized queer identity, impossible to define. She seeks a dynamic that balances normativity and a sense of natural gayness with deviance, infinite possibility, and resistance to integration.

"This Place" makes art performance, specifically singing, an important part of David's preparation to face death. The story is not in the strictest sense about recovery. When Joseph arrives at David's house, he pulls into the drive singing, "All My Exes Live in Texas," a George Strait song made famous by a Texas calf roper much influenced by Bob Wills and the Panhandle tradition of western swing. As Joseph presents David the sovereignty document authored by Joseph and Molly Brant, he sings, "Crazy," another Texas tune written by Willie Nelson and made famous by Patsy Cline, a song also inflected by the Texas swing tradition—in this case its slower, jazzy ballad vein. Joseph is also gay, and while explaining why he stayed on the Mohawk reserve instead of fleeing, he sings Hank Williams's "Your Cheatin' Heart," an Alabama deviation away from the Panhandle, I have to admit. During the preparation of the medicine that seems to facilitate David's journey through time to confront his personal and collective pain, Joseph sings the Patsy Cline standard "I Fall to Pieces." Cline, many readers will note, is also a favorite literary reference of Sherman Alexie's. David sings along. Music is the path through which participants enter ritual, and you've never heard Hank's version of "I'm So Lonesome I Could Cry" or Bill Evans and Miles Davis's "Blue in Green" if you think only Indian songs can get you there.

Joseph next sings a "more Mohawk song" (I want to draw attention to the problems of such a claim) with a turtle rattle, singing in vocables that seem to transition David from memories of the history of Christian missionization among the Mohawks to David's experiences with "the first man [he] ever loved" (63), and David's own recollections are encapsulated in song:

> [H]e fell into the sound of the rattle he was the rattle's sound the music the music he was dancing dancing with the first man he ever loved they were dancing holding holding the music the music the turtle's music was in them through them in them . . . *killed us* . . . he went home he went with the first man he ever loved the music was beating was beating their hearts the rattle the music they fell onto the bed the music the music touched them the turtle touched them the rattle touched them they touched they touched the touching of the turtle the first man he loved . . . *we fought back* . . . their bodies singing shaking joining joining everything was music was music so good so good good the first man he loved Thomas Thomas . . . *they kept killing us off* . . . Tommy Tommy singing sighing joining . . . *but we* . . . singing our bodies singing Tommy David Tommy Tommy . . . *survived.* (63)

Stream-of-consciousness passages are rare in Brant's fiction—this may be the only example. The vision-like state re-enacts David's memories with his lover at the same time as it incorporates Joseph's voice (represented by the italics) continuing the history of the effects of colonialism on the community. Attacks and fighting back weave in and out of the erotic passage, and the colonial threat, as well as resistance to it, parallels David's struggle with the ups and downs of the virus; its attacks, his resistance. A turtle rattle provides music in its elemental, stripped-down form, devoid of pitch. The voice, singing vocables, also tends toward lyrical minimalism. Like Miles Davis's radically minimal solos on *Kind of Blue,* where he plays far fewer notes than the boppers of his time, the complexity comes from the elements the rattle and the vocables interact with, just as Miles's stripped-down solos become luxuriant because of the beautiful chords Bill Evans plays underneath them. The interplay of the ensemble provides the complexity: the Texas songs that lead up to the Mohawk singing, the colonial history only recalled in interwoven snippets of phrase, David's remembered sexual encounter in actions like falling back on the bed, the couple's dancing, the importance of naming Tommy and David, the transcendence that makes bodies sings, the relationship between those who remain and those who have passed on—or will soon.

The music involves singing oneself back together, a metaphor I have discussed for years in relation to a particular Creek story about a turtle with a busted shell, and Joseph describes the process in similar terms: "They took parts of us and cut them up and threw them to the winds. They made lies we would believe. We look for the parts to put ourselves back together" (64). Disparate parts, separated by a process of fracturing lives, come back together in an artistic process that, although also disparate through a polyphony of songs and styles, moves toward a coherent center. "Lesbian Indian writers merge the selves that language splits apart," we might chant again, reminding us of Janice Gould's statement on identities that can be both deviant from the white and Indian mainstream and, at the same time, coherent in terms of psychic and spiritual health. Like the language of declarative sentences that Brant challenges through linguistic sexual variation, language patterns are thrown wide open to multiple possibilities, to deviation from a single uniform style. In fact, the very structure of the passage breaks up causality; it has an overlapping feel, and you can enter it at any number of different points because it will keep covering the ideas anyway as the lyrics are sung over and over, much like songs, often influenced by non-western traditions, that deviate from twelve-bar blues or thirty-two-bar popular music forms, and instead base themselves on patterns that keep repeating. "Blue in Green," in fact, has such a ten-bar structure. This is also true of Jim Pepper's "Witchi Tai Tai," which not only cycles but repeats the same note while the chords change underneath it.

These aesthetics, however, do not merely circle inward, always referencing themselves, as art for art's sake. Brant writes as if art entails responsibilities—because, of course, it does. Joseph tells David, "We make the truth about ourselves." The doctor is not talking about relativism but the sovereign right, and responsibility, to speak on one's own behalf, to narrate one's own history. Joseph and David, two important Old Testament names, represent both political and spiritual leadership in Jewish history.

Creating the truths about ourselves constitutes part of the aesthetics of courage, the persistent confrontation of fear and ignorance evident in Sonny's resistance to fatalism, which we discussed in an earlier chapter.

Cherokee citizens Kathy E. Reynolds and Dawn L. McKinley first realized they needed to be married when Reynolds was hospitalized for a back injury and McKinley could not even enter the room since the hospital only allowed family inside, and the mis-state of Oklahoma did not recognize her as family (Oklahoma is one of the states that passed hate legislation against its citizens that illegalizes gay marriage). According to the February 2006 edition of the *Cherokee Phoenix and Indian Advocate* the couple

> were married May 18, 2004, in a ceremony by a CN-sanctioned [Chero-kee Nation–sanctioned] religious official within the tribe's jurisdiction five days after receiving their marriage application from the CN District Court. When the couple obtained their marriage application, tribal law did not define marriage as a union between a man and a woman but as between a "provider" and "companion."
>
> "We had no problems getting the application. We were warned by the clerk that we might have trouble finding a minister, but we had no idea of the other trouble we would have," Reynolds said.
>
> In response to the issuance of the couple's marriage application, [General Counsel Julian] Fite filed a petition against issuing marriage applications to same-sex couples. Darrell Dowty, the JAT's [Judicial Appeals Tribunal's] chief justice at the time, initiated a moratorium on the issuance of all marriage applications.

When the women returned to file their application, they were turned away. The first suit filed against the couple was on June 16, 2004, by Todd Hembree, acting as a private Cherokee citizen. On the same day, the Cherokee Tribal Council unanimously passed a measure that prohibited same-sex couples from marrying.

On August 3, 2005, however, the Cherokee Court found that "Hembree lacked standing to bring suit challenging the validity of the marriage because he has failed to show that he will suffer individualized harm" according to the National Center for Lesbian Rights in a January 4, 2006, press release. The Cherokee Nation requires evidence of individual harm for a person to pursue litigation, one of the fascinating aspects of one of the nation's longstanding Indian democracies that may reflect an old southeastern indigenous notion that has been around quite some time—the legal principle of clan law along the lines of "if they ain't messing with me, I ain't messing with them," a richly conservative principle largely abandoned by today's conservatives of all stripes—to the great detriment of conservatism.

Two days after the failure of the Hembree suit, on August 5, 2005, according to the press release,

> Nine members of the Cherokee Nation Tribal Council filed a petition for declaratory judgment against the couple in the Judicial Appeals Tribunal of the Cherokee Nation. The nine members of the Tribal council, represented by Hembree, claimed to be filing the petition in their official capacity [not as individuals, as Hembree had on June 16, 2004]. The petition asked the court to declare that marriages between same-sex couples are not allowed under the Cherokee Nation Code marriage statute. Six members of the Tribal Council declined to participate in the lawsuit.

On December 22, 2005, however, the Judicial Appeals Tribunal dismissed the lawsuit because the council members, like Hembree earlier, could not "demonstrate a specific particularized harm." According to the tribal newspaper, the Cherokee Nation General Counsel—Diane Hammons at the time of this writing—maintains that the court could still refuse to file the couple's marriage application should they still choose to finalize it. The *Cherokee Phoenix* article quotes the courthouse clerk, Lisa Fields, on the matter: "They could come by and try to attempt to register it. At this point, we've been advised by our attorney not to make any comment on that because we haven't decided what we're going to do in the event they come."

At the time this book went to press, it was unclear whether the couple would follow through with the marriage, but the Cherokee Nation may have rendered the matter moot when the tribal council passed a same-sex marriage ban on July 14, 2004, by a unanimous fifteen-member vote.

Whatever the women may decide to do, I hope this discussion can be separated from all the flimflam about whether or not Cherokee tradition endorses same-sex marriage, a question that is impossible to resolve and philosophically untenable, and, instead, focus on the fact that constitutional democracies, the form of government Cherokees have enjoyed for almost two centuries, respect the rights of citizens—not the rights of white-looking Indians, heterosexuals, Baptists, Indian Ceremonialists, or some other privileged or not-so-privileged group over the rights of others. One constitutional democracy, the United States, has yet to realize this, but I have far greater hopes for the Cherokees, who have always prided themselves, occasionally for good reason, as the vanguards of civilization. The potential marriage, and others like it, rather than a liability, could provide the most exciting opportunity in recent Indian history to demonstrate that the tribes, not the state of Oklahoma, determine the laws by which they choose to govern themselves.

We make the truth about ourselves.

Works Cited

Allen, Paula Gunn. *The Sacred Hoop: Recovering the Feminine in American Indian Traditions*. Boston: Beacon Press, 1986.

Birchfield, D. L. *How Choctaws Invented Civilization and Why Choctaws Will Conquer the World*. Albuquerque: University of New Mexico Press, 2007.

Brant, Beth. "A Long Story." In *A Gathering of Spirit: A Collection by North American Indian Women*, edited by Beth Brant, 100–106. Ithaca, N.Y.: Firebrand Books, 1984.

——. *Food and Spirits*. Ithaca, N.Y.: Firebrand Books, 1991.

——. *I'll Sing 'til the Day I Die: Conversations with Tyendinaga Elders*. Toronto: McGilligan Books, 1995.

——. *Mohawk Trail*. Ithaca, N.Y.: Firebrand Books, 1985.

——. *Writing as Witness: Essay and Talk*. Toronto: Women's Press, 1994.

"Cherokee High Court Rules in Favor of NCLR and Same-Sex Couple." National Center for Lesbian Rights. January 4, 2006. www.nclrights.org.

Hicks, Lisa. "JAT Dismisses Same-Sex Marriage Injunction." *Cherokee Phoenix and Indian Advocate*. February 2006. www.cherokeephoenix.org.

Gould, Janice. "Disobedience in Language in Texts by Lesbian Native Americans." *Ariel* (January 1994): 32–44.

Johnson, E. Pauline. "A Strong Race Opinion: On the Indian Girl in Modern Fiction." In *E. Pauline Johnson, Tekahionwake: Collected Poems and Selected Prose*, edited by Carole Gerson and Veronica Strong-Boag, 177–83. Toronto: University of Toronto Press, 2002.

Nauni, Rita-Silk. "Excerpts of Letters from Rita Silk-Nauni." In *A Gathering of Spirit*, 93–96.

Ouart, Share. "Letter from Prison." In *A Gathering of Spirit*, 74.

Raven. "Letters between Raven and Beth." In *A Gathering of Spirit*, 221–25.

Womack, Craig S. "A Single Decade: Book-Length Native Literary Criticism between 1986 and 1997." In *Reasoning Together: The Native Critics Collective*, edited by edited by Craig S. Womack, Daniel Heath Justice, and Christopher B. Teuton, 3–104. Norman: University of Oklahoma Press, 2008.

Sappho's Round Dance

Springtime has arrived on the Isle of Lesbos. Crocuses poke their yellow heads above ground, and Sappho, known to Greeks as the tenth muse, throws the biggest bash since the Saturday night Ted Bearsky hired the Texas Playboys for his own private party. John Grayeagle, his easel set up on a grassy hillside, has been commissioned by Sappho to capture, for posterity, these festive events on the grounds of her finishing school for well-heeled young Greek ladies. The sun has set fire to the grassy hillside, metaphorically speaking, and John remembers the Oklahoma hills where he was born, way down yonder in the Indian Nation.

Far below John's fiery perch, Walter Whitman stands among unmoving white columns, examining one of them with a handheld magnifying glass, and—when Sappho turns away for a moment—defaces it with secret love notes scratched in yellow ochre crayon: cryptic messages he hopes a certain young lady at the school will intercept and decode.

"Elementary," his friend Beth Brant teases, feeling her oats from all the good food and spirits, and running among the party guests, searching out recruits for the round dance. "Just go up to her and tell her you dig her," she says to Walter, who reddens and quickly hides his crayon in his tweed pocket, feeling for his pipe to ease his panic.

Lynn Riggs, recovering in the shade of a Doric column, rises up off his cot and says, "It's too late for that, isn't it? I'm outside the light, and when I draw close to the fire, beasts lurk in the shadows."

"Drama queen," Brant laughs. "Rise up!"

Sappho—commanding in her flowing white robes and resplendent with her new crew cut and shiny Doc Martens boots spit-shined black—clears her throat at the podium and announces the arrival of some late guests, who enter the forum dressed like lawyers.

"We're the Anti Chiefs," the ringleader announces, "and we've flown all the way from Oklahoma." As he advances toward the podium, he adds, "We're here to discuss what we're against. We're anti-everything, including this Sapphic round dance."

One of the Anti Chiefs hangs back a little from the rest of the group, and he whispers, "What about casinos?" but the others quickly silence him.

Rosemary McCombs Maxey has a gigantic ring of keys, and she runs from class to class, trying to let students out early for the dance, except—out of Sappho's earshot—she has confessed to Roe Náld that she intends to liberate them permanently, and has in mind a proposal for alternative forms of schooling.

"The Auntie Chiefs?!" Rosemary exclaims delightedly. "A tribe run by aunties? I'm *for* it!"

"If there's to be a vote," one of the Antis insists, "I'm going to abstain. We're outside Oklahoma jurisdiction." The ringleader has traveled to Lesbos to try and drum up international support since his total loss of credibility after ramrodding a recent referendum through his legislature.

"Oklahoma?" Icarus queries, preening one of his wings nervously. "It's terribly hot there isn't it, close to the sun? And you let them have jurisdiction over you?"

"Let the dancing begin!" Sappho proclaims joyously, before the Antis can take to the podium, and in the rush toward the round dance, speeches are forgotten. Already couples clasp hands, join with others, fill in gaps, increase their circle. They have formed their more perfect union with Janice Gould at the center, cross-legged and seated at the foot of Aphrodite amidst the crocuses, snapping her fingers and counting off the beginning of an upbeat version of "Summertime." It kicks into gear with four-bar hammered dulcimer riffs, which Uncle Jimmy provides when he steps into the sunlight and solos on the hand-carved beauty already set up for him on a Greek cypress stump; and Bob Wills holds a parasol over Jimmy's head and rubs some high-octane sunscreen on Jimmy's sunburned back and shoulders, Wills's cigar puffing up a storm as he slathers on the lotion.

Man, does that ever get the Sapphic round dancers going, and they kick up their heels—as much as you can in a round dance, anyway, and still keep it traditional—pumping clasped hands to beat the band, except for Janice Gould, who needs both hands on her accordion.

"Take it away, Sappho, take it away," Bob hollers, and Sappho steps in on Jimmy's solo—she blows one mean lyre, that Sappho—sweet on the melody, filling in the gaps between the whole notes with sheets of sound that rain down music on the dancers from the gods grooving above them. Lynn Riggs, still on his cot, has picked up his guitar to play "I Ride on an Old Paint"—in another key—but the Sapphites just pump up the volume.

Sappho's lyre solo quickens the dead; Shirley wakes up and asks for a biscuit, and a statue of Athena comes to life, grows arms and a drumstick, pushes through the round dancers, and joins the quintet or sextet or septet or octet— depending on what night you catch them—using part of Jimmy's cedar stump for a drum like a 49er pounding on a car hood after the powwow. Bob Wills hollers, "Get it low, boys, you know what low means," and Athena crouches into a drum solo that makes even the Anti Chiefs—still gathered around the podium—dance in place, even if they're not ready to join the round dance just yet. Fact of the matter is they look a little like a military formation, but Rome wasn't built in a day.

One of the Anti Chiefs, the casino rabble rouser, keeps wandering off toward the round dancers, and the other Antis have to pull him back. He pushes his black-framed BIA prescription glasses—knocked down by his dancing— back on his nose with his thumb, and announces, "Lesbians are *hot!*"

The paparazzi have arrived from Athens to document the historic occasion, and Roe Náld, afraid of being photographed, hides behind Walter Whitman's graffitied column. Lynn Riggs pats the seat next to him on the cot, making room and looking as hopeful as Lynn is able. In the round dance line, Justin slows everybody down a little, since he can only take small, mincing steps in his tight evening gown, so Chrystos, dressed in her signature red cowboy boots, comes up behind him and rips a slit in his sparkling frock—to free the poor boy up, she says.

The dance line breathes a sigh of relief, and they're pumping it again, I mean just a-getting it. So very hard that Athena, who has joined the circle of dancers and left the drumming to the casino-loving Anti Chief, who has finally managed to defect and join the musicians, loses her arm again and has to seek out Icarus for repairs, temporarily excusing herself from the dancers but promising to return.

Euchee painter and poet Richard Ray Whitman, Indian hipster extraordinaire, has taken the podium from the Anti Chiefs, and swears them in so they can join the round dance. He has convinced them that if they take his oath they can dance unscathed. They have their right hands raised, left hands on the 1988 Indian Gaming Act. Richard adjusts his red headscarf and intones, "I solemnly swear . . . "

"I Solomonly swear," the Antis repeat.

"No, solemnly," Richard insists.

"No, solemnly," the Antis repeat, as if they'd learned their lines from watching *Blazing Saddles.*

"Never mind," Richard says in frustration.

"Never mind," the Antis chant, starting to really get into it.

Richard gives up solemn swearing. "I am not, nor have I ever been, a cowboy; neither do I have cowboy tendencies. I only did it for the money."

The chanting grinds to a halt. "I actually liked it," says one of the Antis, who bolts for the round dancers, and the other Antis seem glad to let him go, even though they are down two men now.

"You can't swear us in with one of your own poems," the chief Anti Chief protests.

"I changed the words some for the oath," Richard explains.

A class is going on in the forum, and E. Pauline Johnson tells the Antis to keep it down to a dull roar; a class is in session, for King George's sake. Dressed like a walking pow wow poster, Pauline stands and recites "Cry from an Indian Wife" to a small cluster of Greek finishing-school girls who pay her little mind; instead, they are giggling, picking wildflowers, and putting them in each others' hair.

Suddenly, from the direction of the Lesbian hills, a wild sow careens toward the party, heads straight for the dance line, knocks down Justin, and soils his costume gown. The sow spins on her heels for a moment, snorts, recovers her equilibrium, and charges toward the Antis, who line up in formation to fend her off. They part like the Dead Sea, however, when the two freedmen, Uncle Dick and Uncle Will, come running up behind the wayward pig.

Shirley, who had fallen asleep again—this time in Pauline's class—until the ruckus woke her up, leaves Pauline and her pupils, sneaks up behind the chief Anti Chief, and taps him on the shoulder. He jumps and turns around, and she clasps his hand and utters a heartfelt "Stonko?" but the Anti doesn't speak Indian. "The only stone I saw go anywhere," he says, "was that crippled statue."

"Handicapped," Richard Ray corrects.

Leaving his sister with the Antis and taking up with the musicians in the center, Sonny's blues reverberate through the columns of the finishing school and off into the hills, where John Grayeagle smiles and mixes in some blues with his yellow ochre.

"No, too dark," he says. "There's hope yet."

And hope there still was. And is.

Friends, you never seen a sunset like the one John pulled down from the falling light of that Greek hillside, swear to gods. He left the Antis standing around the podium and painted them into the dance circle without their permission.

"They can catch up later," he said, to no one in particular, and the round dancers below him started kicking up their heels like the Antis had already joined them. Sonny starts scat singing—so far from the melody he might not ever make it back. It's dangerous, I'm here to tell you. The dance line can barely keep hold of one another, like being on the outside ring of a fast stomp dance, trying to keep up. Shu doobie da bop a schlop doo wop a crawfish pie filé gumbo cause tonight suppertime I'm feelin' sad but it really gets bad round the water tower waiting for a train.

The dancers' spiral quickens; some can barely hold on to each other, others have to be pulled back to earth as their feet lift off the ground.

John is more interested in his canvas than the antics at the bottom of the hill, though. It demands his total concentration.

Dig it, man. That light on John's palette kisses treetops. His sun melts wings; gods fall. Those rays splash down on Indian cars abandoned on the Greek hillsides; junkers roar back to life, and one-eyed game wardens behind their steering wheels bounce joyously down ravines, past statues who break their fevers. Lynn Riggs borrows a pencil from Roe Náld and composes a telegraph to ask his agent to buy him a one-way ticket back home to Oklahoma, tells Roe Náld he finally has enough money and the right words and now a telegram as soon as he finds a Western Union.

John keeps right on painting.

The colors, when they hit the canvas, rise up singing, spread their wings, take to the sky.

It's a sight on earth.

Well, so Hotgun he say Secretary It's Cocked was trimmed the wick in his lantern and stuck a match to it, like old Diogenes, and was set out to see if he could find a man that didn't had his bread-hooks hung up under his coat tail for boodle.

Alexander Posey, *The Fus Fixico Letters*, 128

Index